How To Speak Effectively Anywhere

Real & Proven Ways To Develop Effective Communication Skills And Win Your Audience

Emma Floyd

©Copyright 2021 – Emma Floyd - All rights reserved

The content contained within this book may not be reproduced, duplicated, or transmitted without direct written permission from the author or the publisher.

Under no circumstances will any blame or legal responsibility be held against the publisher, or author, for any damages, reparation, or monetary loss due to the information contained within this book, either directly or indirectly.

Legal Notice

This book is copyright protected. This book is only for personal use. You cannot amend, distribute, sell, use, quote or paraphrase any part, or the content within this book, without the consent of the author-publisher.

Disclaimer Notice

Please note the information contained within this document is for educational and entertainment purposes only. All effort has been executed to present accurate, up to date, and reliable, complete information. No warranties of any kind are declared or implied. Readers acknowledge that the author is not engaging in the rendering of legal, financial, medical, or professional advice.

Table of Contents

INTRODUCTION 7

CHAPTER 1: WHY IMPROVE SPEAKING SKILLS? 9

CHAPTER 2: HOW TO IMPROVE YOUR SPEAKING SKILLS? 11

CHAPTER 3: WHAT IS COMMUNICATION? 17

CHAPTER 4: COMMUNICATION STYLES 26

CHAPTER 5: THE ART OF COMMUNICATION 36

CHAPTER 6: REASONS WHY YOU NEED TO MASTER THE ART OF COMMUNICATION 41

CHAPTER 7: WHY ARE COMMUNICATION SKILLS IMPORTANT? 45

CHAPTER 8: WHAT IS EFFECTIVE COMMUNICATION? 47

CHAPTER 9: WHAT DOES EFFECTIVE COMMUNICATION CONSISTS OF? 56

CHAPTER 10: EXAMPLES OF EFFECTIVE COMMUNICATION 63

CHAPTER 11: FIVE QUESTIONS OF EFFECTIVE COMMUNICATION 69

CHAPTER 12: BARRIERS TO EFFECTIVE COMMUNICATION 73

CHAPTER 13: THE IMPORTANCE OF COMMUNICATION SKILLS 77

CHAPTER 14: DEVELOPING YOUR COMMUNICATION SKILL 80

CHAPTER 15: WHY OUTSTANDING CONVERSATION SKILLS WILL CHANGE YOUR LIFE? 83

PART 1 BOOSTING YOUR ORAL COMMUNICATION SKILLS 91

CHAPTER 16: VERBAL COMMUNICATION 92

CHAPTER 17: VERBAL CUES – READING BETWEEN THE LINES 98

CHAPTER 18: HOW TO SPEAK FLUENT ENGLISH? 103

CHAPTER 19: EXPLORING YOUR VOICE 135

CHAPTER 20: USING SPEECH, TONE, AND PITCH TO YOUR ADVANTAGE 139

CHAPTER 21: TUNING UP – HOW TO MAKE YOUR VOICE SOUND PLEASANT? ...143

CHAPTER 22: TONE OF VOICE – THE OTHER NONVERBAL INDICATOR 150

CHAPTER 23: PRONUNCIATION STRATEGIES 152

CHAPTER 24: TRY GETTING RID OF FILLERS 157

CHAPTER 25: BODY LANGUAGE 162

CHAPTER 26: DECODING BODY LANGUAGE 193

CHAPTER 27: THE SECRET CODE OF BODY LANGUAGE 202

CHAPTER 28: MASTERING THE ART OF BODY LANGUAGE 209

CHAPTER 29: LOOK AND FEEL CONFIDENT 224

CHAPTER 30: DEVELOP SELF-CONFIDENCE TO COMMUNICATE EFFECTIVELY 233

CHAPTER 31: THE ART OF ACTIVE LISTENING 246

CHAPTER 32: WHY ACTIVE LISTEN? 259

CHAPTER 33: HOW TO ACTIVE LISTEN? 264

CHAPTER 34: THE BENEFITS OF BETTER CONVERSATION SKILLS 272

CHAPTER 35: UNDERSTANDING YOUR AUDIENCE 276

CHAPTER 36: BUILD A STRONG RELATIONSHIP WITH AN AUDIENCE 286

CHAPTER 37: FITTING ALL THE PIECES TOGETHER 297

PART 2: BEING A GOOD SPEAKER 299

CHAPTER 38: CHARACTERISTICS OF A GOOD PUBLIC SPEAKER 300

CHAPTER 39: BEING AN EFFECTIVE SPEAKER 303

CHAPTER 40: GET IN SOME PRACTICE 306

CHAPTER 41: USE NOTE CARDS TO AVOID RELYING ON MEMORY 309

CHAPTER 42: HOW TO USE VISUAL AIDS 313

CHAPTER 43: USING AUDIO AND VISUAL AIDS EFFECTIVELY 317

CHAPTER 44: BE ASSERTIVE 321

CHAPTER 45: BECOME A GOOD LISTENER 337

CHAPTER 46: HOW TO IMPROVE LISTENING SKILLS? 342

CHAPTER 47: THE IMPORTANCE OF LISTENING 350

CHAPTER 48: USING EMPATHY IN CONVERSATION 366

CHAPTER 49: OWNING YOUR CONTENT 382

CHAPTER 50: MANAGING YOUR STAGE 386

CHAPTER 51: WAYS TO CONNECT WITH A LARGE AUDIENCE 395

CHAPTER 52: PUBLIC SPEAKING 398

CHAPTER 53: THE ART OF PUBLIC SPEAKING 412

CHAPTER 54: THE GOLDEN RULES OF PUBLIC SPEAKING 420

CHAPTER 55: TIPS FOR PUBLIC SPEAKING 424

CHAPTER 56: ONE TECHNIQUE THAT IS SURE TO ENGAGE YOUR AUDIENCE 426

CHAPTER 57: HOW TO USE METAPHORS TO COMMUNICATE BETTER? 430

PART 3: ENRICHING YOUR VOCABULARY EFFECTIVELY 445

CHAPTER 58: VERBAL DEXTERITY 446

CHAPTER 59: STOP COUNTING VOCABULARY WORDS 453

CHAPTER 60: HOW TO MASTER GRAMMAR? 469

CHAPTER 61: HOW TO PRACTICE PRONUNCIATION? 473

CHAPTER 62: ACING THE LANGUAGE AND SPEECH GAME 479

CHAPTER 63: PHRASES TO PURGE FROM YOUR DICTIONARY 484

CHAPTER 64: EFFECTIVE COMMUNICATION IN PERSONAL RELATIONSHIPS 491

PART 4: BEING A GOOD THINKER AS A SPEAKER 501

CHAPTER 65: PREPARING YOUR VOICE, BODY, AND ENERGY LEVEL 502

CHAPTER 66: BE MENTALLY PREPARED 506

CHAPTER 67: AWARENESS OF SELF AND OTHERS 514

CHAPTER 68: KNOW YOUR AUDIENCE, UNDERSTAND THEIR NEEDS 520

CHAPTER 69: KNOWING WHAT'S AT STAKE FOR YOUR AUDIENCE 524

CHAPTER 70: PUTTING YOURSELF IN THE SHOES OF OTHERS 526

CHAPTER 71: BUILD YOUR SPEECH ON A SOLID FOUNDATION 529

CHAPTER 72: ORGANIZE YOUR THOUGHTS 533

CHAPTER 73: IDENTIFY YOUR PURPOSE 537

CHAPTER 74: UNDERSTAND PEOPLE'S EMOTIONS 541

CHAPTER 75: THE ART OF PERSUASION 549

CHAPTER 76: LOOK AT THINGS FROM A NEW ANGLE 563

CHAPTER 77: BROADEN YOUR HORIZONS 568

CHAPTER 78: PLAN THE LANDING 572

CHAPTER 79: DELIVER AND EVALUATE YOUR MESSAGE 585

CONCLUSION 600

Introduction

Have you ever felt that you were a terrible communicator? If that's the case, you'll want to get your hands on this book right now. It's chock-full of everything you'll need to communicate successfully. Keep in mind that communication may take various forms, both verbal and nonverbal. Before you attempt to communicate, you must first comprehend both forms. You'll be able to convey your message more effectively after you've mastered the methods in this book.

As we go through this book, you will learn many new concepts and be reminded of things you already know. You'll discover how to ask the appropriate questions to communicate effectively. Because self-confidence is essential to successful communication, I've included some suggestions to help you gain the confidence you'll need.

Communication is about much more than simply exchanging information. You must understand the emotions and intentions behind that information. You must convey your message so that it is fully received and understood exactly as you intended. However, you must also be able to listen and gain the whole meaning of the information being given to you so that other people feel heard and understood. Lack of these skills can become barriers between you and others that continue the cycle of misunderstandings, frustrations, and conflicts. You will learn more about these barriers to effective communication and how to overcome them.

Everyone has to communicate in a variety of situations. Therefore, this book explores how to communicate at networking events, including things you need to do before, during, and after those events. At some point, almost everyone must give a presentation. Yet many people are afraid of giving a presentation, so we provide you with essential tips that make giving those presentations easier. Not all communication is verbal, so I will help you to conquer the art of letter writing.

Unfortunately, not all messages are positive. At some point, you'll have to write someone a terrible letter. Following the techniques outlined in this book allows you to make sure that your message gets through.

Your body must deliver the same message as your words. Therefore, you need to conquer the art of gesturing, body language, eye contact, and personal appearance.

Effective communication will aid in the strengthening of your interpersonal connections. It will help you enhance your teamwork, decision-making, and problem-solving skills. You'll be able to convey all information, even negative or challenging ones, without causing conflict or losing trust if you have good communication skills. It's the substance that binds everything together.

Many individuals mistakenly think that just because they can talk, they can communicate successfully. Effective communication, on the other hand, is an acquired talent. Regardless, it is much more powerful when given spontaneously than by rote. If you make a speech from notes, for example, it will seldom have the same impact as if you gave it "off the cuff." Developing your abilities and becoming a good communicator requires time and effort. Your communication abilities will become more natural as you put in more effort and practice.

Chapter 1:
Why Improve Speaking Skills?

I magine a day when all of a sudden you can no longer speak. Imagine being in a situation wherein you want to say something, but people won't just pay attention. Imagine yourself being in a place where no one listens to you regardless of how important the things you are talking about are. Wouldn't that be one of the worst things ever?

If you talk firmly and with a professional voice, people will take you seriously and consider you a professional. So you must develop the skill in speaking about what you want to be (or perhaps, sound like).

Aside from the fact that when your voice speaks well for you, you create good communication and interaction with other people, here are some advantages of having good speaking skills.

1. **Being understood clearly.** When you speak well, people will be able to understand you better and clearly. When you speak very fast, then people will not understand a single word that you say. Also, if you speak well, people will better understand the message you want to impose. For example, if you mumble, people will feel that you may not want to be there. It may also appear that you do not want to talk to them, so you are just mumbling instead of speaking out clearly.

2. **Being a pleasure to listen to.** Isn't it good to know that people enjoy listening to the things that you are talking about? Keep in mind that effective communication also depends on whether the audience is listening to you or not. People will not listen to you if the experience of listening to you is unpleasant. If you sound nervous, people will most likely think that you are not prepared to talk. People will think that you are not good at speaking, thus taking you as boring. As a result, they will lose interest in what you are saying, and you will not communicate well with them.

3. **Being more confident.** Isn't it good to know that people enjoy listening to the things that you are talking about? Keep in mind that effective communication also depends on whether the audience is listening to you or not. People will not listen to you if the experience of listening to you is unpleasant. If you sound nervous, people will most likely think that you are not prepared to deliver your speech. People will think that you are not good at speaking, thus taking you as boring. As a result, they will lose interest in what you are saying, and you will not communicate well with them.
4. **Being able to convey authority.** When you speak with a steadier voice that implies authority, people will, in turn, take you seriously, thinking that you have authority over them.
5. **Being able to entertain people.** Speaking well can eventually entertain your audience and sustain their interest in your speech. Always keep in mind that entertaining your audience is one of your aims when speaking. It makes you think about your listeners and how you would keep them interested in what you are saying instead of focusing on how good or bad your performance will be.

Chapter 2:
How to Improve Your Speaking Skills?

Have you ever felt so nervous whenever you have to speak in front of people? Have you ever had your knees and hands shake whenever you are standing in front of your audience? Do not worry; it is not the end of the world for you!

There will always come a time in your life wherein you have to expand your boundaries. There will be a time wherein you have to move from speaking to just one particular person, let us say your friend or your parent, to addressing a large group of people, let us say your entire classmates in your lecture class or the people in your work team. The idea is that talking to the public audience is inevitable.

But in the first place, why are you afraid of talking in public?

It may be because you think that people could not care less about what you will talk about. You feel like once you start speaking, they will just be yawning and be waiting for you to end your speech so they can have their freedom. Perhaps you've had a terrible event in the past when you were humiliated while speaking in public.

However, these should not hinder you from speaking up. Now is the perfect time for you to know how to enhance your speaking skills and knock all your fears away.

Knock Your Fear Down

We know that your biggest enemy when it comes to speaking is fear. And when you fear, you hesitate.

You are hesitant to speak in front of an audience because you are unsure what you will say next. You may also start thinking that you are going to fail when you talk about a particular matter. You also feel like your audience does not care about what you are talking about.

Usually, you are hesitant or nervous, and you frequently say "um" or "er" or other fillers that are unnecessary to your speech. Also, your audience may find these fillers annoying, and they will no longer pay attention to you. You may also be tripping over your own words from time to time because you are rushing to express your ideas as your brain works faster than your lips. Most of the time, speaking faster implies that you are nervous.

For you to be able to knock your hesitations, consider the following steps:

- **Think more clearly.** Doing this will help you focus on the particular matter that you are talking about, which will, in turn, make you speak clearly and well.

- **Slow down and emphasize your points.** It is not good to speak fast and stumble upon your words; this will only make your speech hard to understand. It's also crucial to stress upon your main ideas so that your audience understands where you're going with your speech. This will also help you stay focused.

- **Breathe properly.** Proper breathing helps you stay relaxed. This will also help you speak properly so that your audience can understand you well.

When it comes to dealing with nervousness, consider the following suggestions:

- **Do not make your nerves hinder you.** Do not always focus on yourself. Know that other speakers get nervous too! But that is not the entire point. Just keep in mind that the people you are talking to are unaware of how nervous you are. There is a saying that goes like this: "It is fine to have butterflies—as long as they fly in formation."

- **Connect with your audience.** The success of every communication flow depends on the effects on it the intended audience. Therefore, as the speaker, you must know the people you will talk to and connect with. Make sure that you anticipate their mood as you speak. If they are bored, make sure that you are lively to sort of wake them up.

- **Have your objectives in your mind.** You must know why you are speaking. Giving speeches is not only about disseminating information; it is also about engaging your audience and giving them what they need. Always keep in mind your objectives or the reason why you are speaking. Do you want to entertain people? Do you want to inform or perhaps educate them?

- **Be positive.** Always think about succeeding. Imagine yourself speaking confidently and clearly. Paint a picture of yourself talking without any flaws or mistakes. Always focus your mind on your desired outcome—what you want to achieve.

- **Relax.** Again, you must stay relaxed while you are speaking. Remove all the tensions, hesitations, and anything fearful from your system as you speak. Tell yourself with a smile that you are good enough.

Speak up!

Here are ten ways you would be able to speak with authority and charisma:

When was the last time you heard someone talk with authority? With charisma? What were your thoughts while you listened? Did you feel like they were very credible?

Speaking properly is probably one of the most common things that we want to achieve. We want to sound authoritative so that people will take us as confident and credible speakers. This will also make your audience pay more attention to you and what you are talking about because they find you influential and powerful.

Here are some suggestions on how you would be able to improve your speaking skills:

1. **Stand with confidence.**

How you stand affects how you speak. If you stand confidently, then you will most likely be able to speak confidently as well. People will also perceive you as confident since they can see you standing with poise; thus, they will give you their attention. Standing properly will also help you produce a better sound or voice while speaking.

You can improve your posture as you speak by finding your balance. Is your weight properly distributed between your feet so that you don't trip? Stand tall as well and keep your chin lifted. Doing so also adds to your height without any effort.

2. **Speak clearly.**

If you speak clearly and audibly, you will sound as if you mean what you are saying. It will sound like what you are saying comes from your heart. This will also help you engage your audience to listen to you because they understand what you are saying.

Open your mouth well as you speak, even though you may not be that used to it. This may make you feel uneasy at first, but your audience may find it normal.

3. **Project properly.**

You must project your voice according to the message you want to impose on your audience because people will most likely take you seriously if your voice has an impact on them.

4. **Emphasize your key points.**

For you to be able to give your message to your audience clearly and effectively, you must emphasize your key points. This will let your audience know the important parts of your speech and give attention to you as you talk about these points. Also, there are times when other speakers give equal emphasis on every part of their speech, thus making it appear monotonous and boring. The sound is very flat, which in turn makes the listeners feel bored and sleepy. If you want to sound authoritative and charismatic, you have to emphasize your key points strongly.

5. Do not rush.

How fast or slow you talk can affect the impression you make on other people. If you speak very fast, it may appear as if you are excited about airing your thoughts on that particular subject matter. People may also think that you do not want to talk to them because you are rushing things. People may see you as dull if you talk slowly, and they will ultimately get weary of listening to you.

The point is that you have to monitor the speed of your speech. You neither have to talk fast or slow; you have to keep it in moderation. Your speed may also vary, depending on what you are saying and the message you want to give to your audience. Again, you have to emphasize important points, so you should not give equal weight and speed to every part of your talk.

6. Use your instruments.

We are gifted with different instruments. It just depends on how we are going to use them to be able to speak properly.

Make your tone rough or smooth, depending on what you want to say. You may also want to elongate your vowels and use them to express feelings. On the other hand, use consonants smoothly or sharply to make your speech clearer.

7. Practice, practice, and practice.

If you're having trouble pronouncing a word, rehearse it so you won't have any trouble the next time you have to speak it. Ensure that you also practice your modulation, articulation, and anything else that has something to do with speaking.

It is also important that you speak fluently. You have to think clearly and know what you are going to say next. Again, you just begin to hesitate while speaking because you happen to be unsure about what you will do and say next. If you have a big speech coming up about a particular subject matter, you must do your research to widen your knowledge about that topic. Then write your speech so that you know very well how it flows. Make sure you practice delivering that speech for as much time as necessary.

"Practice makes perfect," as the adage goes.

8. Just be positive all the time.

You are the only one who can help you. If you imagine yourself succeeding, then you will most likely act towards achieving success. Do not bombard your mind with the thoughts that you are going to fail because you are not. You will succeed if you are committed to succeeding!

Chapter 3:
What is Communication?

I'm defining communication because most people don't truly understand what it entails. Most people confuse "communication" with "talking." Talking is one form of communication, but it is by no means the only one. In addition, talking is the action of one person, while communication is an exchange between two or more people. You can talk to a wall, but that doesn't mean you're communicating with it.

In short, communication is the act of delivering a message from one person to another person or group of people. This message can take on many forms.

- Winking at someone across the room sends a message that you are interested in them.

- Walking away from someone when they ask you a question sends a message that you don't want to talk to them.

- Saying "no" tells a person of a boundary (we'll talk more about this soon) you have.

- Rolling your eyes sends a message that you think something is silly or annoying.

- Kicking someone sends a message that you are very angry at them and probably need therapy.

The sender must transmit, and the receiver must receive and understand for communication to be successful. If these things don't happen or happen poorly, then you have a communication breakdown, which we want to avoid as often as possible.

It starts with a sender, who (wait for it) sends a message. This message needs to be encoded, meaning that what the person wants to say needs to be put into words or some other form that the receiver can understand. The receiver needs to decode the message once they receive it. In other words, the receiver needs to try to understand what message the sender is trying to send. The receiver sends a reaction back to the sender, which is called feedback.

This cycle all happens very quickly. Here's an example to illustrate: Bob (sender) says, "hi" (message) to Jill (receiver). Jill says, "hi" back (feedback). This maybe takes a second or two, but every part of the communication cycle has happened here. Encoding, decoding, and the channel didn't come up in the example because they are often the invisible parts of communication we don't notice or can't see.

The channel or medium is just what the message is sent through. If you're talking face-to-face, the medium is the air and sound waves between you and the receiver. If you're talking on the phone, then the signal between phones is the medium. Depending on the medium, there can be different levels of noise or interference. For example, talking face-to-face with someone in a quiet room has far less noise than talking to someone on the phone with bad reception. Noise isn't always literal noise, however. It's anything that gets in the way of the message successfully making it to the receiver. If you're waving at someone with poor eyesight and they aren't wearing their glasses, their poor eyesight is considered noise and will interfere in their ability to decode your hand gesture.

The more noise, the more chances there are for a communication breakdown. Imagine trying to come up with family vacation plans in the middle of a rock concert or waving at someone on a foggy day. It usually makes for uncomfortable, awkward situations. If noise is bad enough, it can seriously interfere with how well the receiver decodes the information. The results of this miscommunication can range anywhere from mild confusion to a heated fight.

"So, why is it essential for us to know all these tedious technical aspects regarding communication?" you may wonder. That is an excellent question. Knowing about all the communication components can significantly improve your ability to understand how to communicate something successfully. For example, suppose you know you have to have a serious talk with your significant other. In that case, you're more likely to pay attention to things like noise, the receiver's ability to decode, and how you encode your message before having the discussion. When you consider these things, you'll have a better understanding of why trying to have the discussion with the TV on (noise) late at night when you're both tired (reduced ability to encode and decode correctly) is a bad idea.

For some of us, this is automatic. For many, however, we didn't learn how to communicate growing up and need to learn it later in life. It may seem daunting, but I believe it is possible! Practice is essential. Suppose you, for instance, practice spending a few minutes thinking about how you're going to encode a message before you communicate it. In that case, you will eventually get better and faster at encoding. You'll speak more eloquently, honestly, and clearly, which will improve all areas of your life.

When it comes to communication breakdowns, the most serious ones happen when poorly encoded or decoded messages (or both). For example, if a policeman pulls you over and says, "Do you have anything in the trunk?" You could interpret it as an allegation that you're a shady drug smuggler (wrong decoding) and get enraged with the policeman. You then respond defensively and say things you shouldn't (wrong encoding), and boom, you're in prison.

What are Boundaries?

A boundary is a rule or a limit that you have regarding how others treat you. Boundaries can be either physical, emotional, or both. A physical boundary, for example, might be that you don't like people getting too close to you when they talk, or perhaps you don't like being physically touched by anyone other than your partner. An emotional boundary may be that you don't let people call you names even if they are joking.

Having boundaries is one thing, but setting them is another thing entirely. There's no way anyone will know what your boundaries are if you don't tell them. While some boundaries are apparent (e.g., "Don't kick me"), some are very personal. If you have distinct boundaries that you need people to respect, you have no choice but to set them so that the other person can hear and respect them.

7Cs of Communication

There are 7 C's of efficient communication that applies to both written and oral communication. These are like the following:

1. Completeness

The interaction should be complete. All facts required by the audience should be conveyed. The message sender must take into account the mindset of the receiver and convey the message accordingly. A complete interaction has the following characteristics:

- Complete communication develops and improves an organization's reputation.
- In addition, they save costs because no essential information is missing, and if the communication is complete, no additional costs are incurred in conveying additional messages.
- Wherever necessary, complete communication always provides additional information. It leaves no questions in the receiver's mind.
- Complete communication helps the audience/readers/receivers of the message to make better decisions as they get all the desired and crucial information.
- It convinces the listeners.

2. Conciseness

Conciseness means wordiness— communicating in the least possible words what you want to convey without forgoing the other C's of communication. For effective communication, conciseness is a necessity. Concise communication offers the following characteristics:

- It is both time-saving and cost-effective.
- As it avoids the use of excessive and needless words, it underlines and highlights the main message.
- Concise communication provides the audience with short and essential messages in limited words.
- A concise message, for the audience, is more appealing and understandable.
- In essence, the concise message is non-repetitive.

3. Consideration

Consideration implies "to step into others' shoes." Effective communication must consider the audience, i.e., the audience's points of view, background, mindset, level of education, etc. Attempt to understand your audience, their needs, feelings, and issues. Make sure that the audience's self-respect is maintained and that you are not hurting their emotions. While completing your speech, modify your language to meet the requirements of the audience. The following are the characteristics of considerate communication:

- Emphasize the approach of 'you (i.e., the audience).'
- Empathize with the listener and show interest in the crowd. This will stimulate a positive audience reaction.
- Show your audience optimism. Concentrate on what is possible. Stress positive words like optimistic, dedicated, thank you, warm, healthy, help, etc.

4. Clarity

To retain its meaning, the message that the sender wants to convey must be simple, easy to understand, and systematically framed. Clarity is the key to communicating goals.

The aim is specified in terms of goals, actions, strategies, and values. Our purpose is exposed in business through communications, both deliberate and unintentional. In perception and reality, what we think is who we are

The communicator is empowered by simplicity. Simplicity, due to a lack of clarity, isolates the recipient from interpretation. Content and message sophistication strangles effective communication. Complexity often leaves your audience intentionally lost and making assumptions about the purpose and desired results. Higher quality outcomes are created by easy and transparent guidance.

The secret to encouraging others to take action is straightforward and precise messaging.

As a communicator, consider your audience and set your standards. Humans aren't eligible to be great listeners. Unfortunately, we all have hectic minds, countless distractions, and our attention spans are shorter than goldfish. Yeah, indeed, that is confirmed by research. In a 2015 review, Microsoft recorded that individuals now usually lose focus after eight seconds, while goldfish will concentrate for nine seconds. To be heard, no matter the content style, the message has to break through a lot of noise. Clarity makes a distinction.

Clarity means emphasizing a particular message or objective rather than trying to accomplish too much at a time. The following characteristics of clarity in communication are:

- It promotes comprehension.
- The full clarity of ideas and thoughts enhances the meaning of the message.
- A clear message makes use of words that are precise, appropriate, and concrete.

5. Concreteness

Instead of being fuzzy and general, concrete communication implies being specific and clear. Specificity reinforces trust. The following features have a concrete message:

- Specific facts and figures support it.
- This makes use of phrases that are clear and that create the right image.
- There is no misinterpretation of concrete messages.

6. Courtesy

Courtesy in the message implies that the message should both show the sender's expression and respect the recipient. The sender should be genuinely polite, diplomatic, reflective, and enthusiastic about the message. Courteous communications have the following characteristics:

- The courteous message is optimistic and audience-focused.
- It makes use of words that convey respect for the message recipient.
- It is not biased at all.

7. Correctness

In any sense, the information communicated must not be vague or false; it must be free of errors. There is more to the principle of correctness than proper grammar, punctuation, and spelling. A message can mechanically be flawless, meaning being grammatically perfect, but it still loses a customer and fails to achieve a goal.

Awareness of these 7 C's of interaction makes you a productive communicator.

The True Meaning of Communication

Communication may be seen from a variety of perspectives since it is such a broad topic. There is verbal communication, written communication, body language, and so on.

At its most basic definition, communication is believed to be the sharing of information or ideas in a way that there brings mutual understanding. This means that communication has not taken place until you say what you are supposed to say, and it has been understood in the right way. This means that the two people who are interacting or communicating are on the same page. Communication is considered to be effective when this occurs.

The true meaning of communication comes in how you, as a person, communicates and the results that you get from your communication. It is essential that you take full responsibility for your communication. You need to be accountable for your words and actions, reflecting a certain message. The way you communicate will strongly determine and influence how other people communicate with you.

How do you communicate?

Communication has four main pillars. These are reading, which you are doing at this very moment, writing, listening, and speaking. From these pillars, communication can occur in its entirety. Each of these pillars needs a different approach to be effective. In addition, if you are the initiator of the communication, you will behave differently than if you were the receiver of the message.

The rules that govern all your communication include the following:

- You need to be accountable for the way you speak and what you say, as these will affect how your message is carried across. Remember that if the message is misunderstood somehow, it is not the fault of the person receiving the message. It is your fault for not putting it across in the right way. This may seem a little harsh, but all that it means is that you should ascertain whether someone has understood you. If they have not, rephrase what you said and clarify the message for them.

- Are you expecting some result or response from your communication? If you are, please tell the recipient of the message so that they know. This is referred to as a "call to action."

When you are not clear about your expectations, you will have miscommunication, leading to frustration.

- Keep your opinions at bay when you have to listen to another person, no matter how much you want to jump up and air your point of view. When you have the full picture of what someone else has said and take time to digest the words, you are more likely to react constructively than with your emotions. Emotions can be quite unstable, so you should not consider them much when communicating.

- If there is a call to action due to the communication, you need to be accountable. This means that you must do what you said you would do so that people can trust in what you say. When you can accomplish this, then you will have reached proper communication.

The true meaning of communication is simple. You need to communicate clearly and be highly understandable. When you have a positive result, you will ensure that organizations can meet their goals.

Chapter 4:
Communication Styles

Have you taken account of your most practiced activity, one that you perform almost as often as breathing? It's "Communicating." Every moment, through different forms, channels, gestures, and expressions, we are constantly communicating, all as a natural reflection of ourselves. But while it is voluntary, it is not always conscious communication. Without our full knowledge, we often connect, leading to inaccurate or even contradictory phrases of our own.

And the secret to excellent communication lies in knowledge. We can align this to represent what we want to communicate if we can remain continuously aware of the subtle communication signals that we send out every moment. Our communications then seize being unintentional; they become incidental!

Types of Communication

Are you communicating at all times? How is it even possible? It's not like every minute you have your mouth open, asking something. But you see, not only verbally, but even non-verbally, and also informally, we communicate. Here the entire spectrum of the different kinds of communication networks and expressions we enjoy is illustrated.

There are six different forms of communication:

- Non-verbal,
- Verbal, oral, face-to-face,
- Verbal-oral-distance,
- Verbal-written,
- Formal, and
- Informal communication styles.

Add to this the limitless possibilities offered by the internet superhighway, and you have an absolute gold mine of possibilities for communication!

Formal communication

These forms of communication are also referred to as official communication and include various verbal expressions addressing a formal need. For example, many of your interactions within your profession include financial communication (from and to your bank, debtors, creditors, etc.) and legal expressions.

This formal communication consumes more time, as it follows a specific communication protocol. Even in cases of oral expression (meetings, seminars, etc.), written communication is often supported, which can provide documentary evidence of the conversation. This written communication could be as easy as a meeting minute, as complicated as a complete recording.

Informal Communication

Informal communication, also referred to as the (unofficial) grapevine, is shockingly common. This is through word-of-mouth records. It is this type of interaction that opens you up to unofficial but provocative data.

Informal interaction is spontaneous and free-flowing, without any structure or formal protocol. This sort of information is, therefore, less reliable— a communication medium that, as there are no structured rules to obey, spreads like wildfire, mostly verbal, with no proof of evidence. This is why many undermine the relevance of informal communication, calling it mere "gossip."

Informal communication is considered "user-friendly" despite its drawbacks and therefore offers huge advantages when used wisely.

Social networks from "unofficial" outlets (such as your own Facebook and Twitter accounts, LinkedIn, etc.) are strong informal communication sources in modern times. They are also used to influence public opinion.

It's unreasonable to try to stop all informal communication as social creatures-just the thought of working in an organization that would try to do that sounds quite depressing. But there are ways to control informal communication for the good of the company as executives, leaders, and HR professionals;

1. Over-communicating

Being transparent is one of the easiest ways to get ahead of rumors. This is accomplished in the workplace by communicating what is going on with more details. The establishment of formal communication channels as trusted sources helps reduce the need for informal channels that are unnecessary.

2. Encourage communication colleagues

Provide resources to explore, find support, and provide guidance instead of stifling communication among co-workers. Real-time chat, message boards, and online community features will simplify some without drawn-out structured processes to raise questions and suggestions.

3. Respond quickly

It's necessary to take action immediately when disruptive informal contact is detected. Gossip or rumors are often centered on what we see as "wrong," and the appropriate response is to concentrate on being solution-oriented and positive about what is "right." While we should improve areas where legitimate complaints are raised, disciplinary action should be taken against employees who repeatedly demonstrate a focus on the destructive conversation.

4. Build an environment for champions

A symptom of overlying inefficient business processes may be negative, informal contact. Although department heads should concentrate solely on their functional sector, a culture champion exudes and strengthens business principles in all areas in which they work. A real champion is not someone who simply enforces policies or reports criticism but instead recognizes and communicates when change is needed and provides an example of how to operate in the meantime. For a constructive engagement approach, recognizing and promoting such champions is important.

5. Feedback

To build a feedback community, you don't have to put the suggestion box out. Instead of toxic, secret complaints, 360-degree feedback platforms that allow for direct or anonymous feedback can help a move towards gathering constructive ideas for improvement.

6. Provide space

Consider opening up the sources and types of information you share, if necessary. Updates from teams and divisions can be helpful tools to explain what we are working on and remind everyone that we are working for the same target.

7. Open the door, open it.

One thing is to suggest that you have an open-door policy and expect workers to come to you with problems. It's another thing to display a completely open-door policy. Creating an atmosphere where everyone is secure with problems and complaints coming to their boss or HR will stop negative rumors before they start.

8. Consider the tone for the information

One field that may begin to generate rumors of opposition is when formal interactions are disrespectful or tone-deaf. Since we can craft and customize structured communication, it is necessary to understand how individuals, teams, and even outsiders may interpret the message. We leave less room for rumors and simple misunderstandings when we create an atmosphere of inclusivity.

9. To your advantage, use the grapevine

While sometimes it gets a bad rep, informal communication serves a purpose—connecting people across departments and hierarchy and filling in the gaps when it is too slow or ineffective for formal communication. It's less costly and can be more direct because it's not all at once targeted to a large audience. Using managers and leaders to spread pointy and relevant information as needed, you can tap into this.

There is no need to stifle the grapevine or view it as a purely negative source of data. The quick transmission of information can be taken advantage of, and criticism can even be used as an opportunity to identify aspects for improvement and growth as an organization.

Face-to-Face oral Communication

The most recognized type of communication is face-to-face oral communication. Here, what you express comes from what you say directly. Again, this can be formal or casual: in a formal meeting or seminar with your friends and family, work with your colleagues and boss, within your community, during professional presentations, etc.

Such forms of communication get better with practice. The more awareness you have, the more control you will have over your oral expressions. It is the most powerful type of communication and, with every expression, can work for or against you.

It engages the listener more than other forms of communication. With oral communication, the listener (or an audience) often expects to speak to you, enabling two-way communication more than any other channel.

For better communication face-to-face,

- Always meet your audience with trust, conviction, and openness.
- To perfect your tone and expressions, practice in front of a mirror so they suit the message you want to convey. Both aspects often convey more than your phrases do.
- Using role-play, rehearsal. This means that even though you rehearse in front of a mirror, candidly ask yourself, "Am I prepared with this tone and voice to receive this message?" If

you are not satisfied, neither will your audience be. So practice again until it's right for you.

- Become an active listener. An efficient oral communicator not only speaks but listens to his audience actively as well.

Distance Oral Communication.

Distance oral communication has made the world a more accessible and smaller place. All modern extensions of distance communication, taking its expression to the next subtle level, are mobile phones, VOIP, video-conferencing, 2-way webinars, etc. And your tone of voice and speed of delivery takes precedence over other expressions in this form of communication.

Communication in Written

Written communication depended on the trustful mailman a few decades ago, as we wrote to people who were far away. This also included a formal note or legal notice from the bank, landlord, business client, etc., on rare occasions. So it's no wonder that this mode of communication has now pervaded every area of our lives!

If you join the total written communication, you engage within a day: the text message you send over your mobile phone, Facebook and Twitter updates, professional and personal emails, heck, even the blogs you write—it would far exceed any other verbal communication you enjoy. Think about it. Correct? In this type of communication, it then makes sense to be an absolute pro. There are three rules listed below that can help you get there.

Follow a structure that is clear so that your communication is not all over the place. A brief introduction, message body, schedule, and conclusion can be included in this. In your communication mode (email, text message, a quick status update on social media, etc.), the cleverness and effectiveness of your communication lie in how you can capture this structure.

Clarify, where possible, the context of your communication. For a harmless text message, this might seem like overkill. But the amount of seemingly harmless (written) communication that reaches the wrong eyes and ears would amaze you. So make sure your context is reasonably clear, regardless of who the recipient is.

Always err on the cautionary right side. When written correspondence is strictly formal (addressed to professional peers and seniors or third parties) or strictly casual (addressed only to your immediate friend/family circle). Therefore, by adapting a semi-formal tone, keeping your communication clean (in speech and expression), and open (without offending any group), play safe. Your friends should think of you as a "stiff" communicator rather than as an "offensive" communicator for your boss!

Non-Verbal Communication

This form of interaction is more subtle yet much more powerful. It includes the whole range of physical postures and gestures, voice tone and pace, and the attitude with which you interact.

In the past few decades, experts in body language have revealed how your communication is affected by the posture you adopt, the hand gestures you support, and other facets of your physical personality. It is worth spending some hours on basic body language gestures, so you don't send mixed messages with your gestures and speech. You can also use this, making it more impactful, to support your message.

Expressions of face

Without a doubt, facial expressions are the most common and telling nonverbal means of communication. Human faces can create more than 10,000 different expressions, and each one easily articulates volumes of data. The best and most relatable gestures are smiling, frowning, blinking, and the favorite of any adolescent, eye-rolling, but even the slightest eyebrow twitch or nostril flare can be read with minimal effort. The safest way to connect with a stranger, customer, or even a long-time acquaintance: Smile! A smile is welcoming, warm, and sets you up as an individual with whom people want to spend time.

Movements of the body

Common practices, such as hand gestures or nodding, involve body movements or kinesics. Body gestures quite often express passion or excitement. We all know a person who "talks with his hands, for example." However, other aspects of kinesics include behaviors that we typically perceive with nervousness or anxiety, such as involuntary tremors, constant throat clearing, or a trembling leg. Standing your hands on a table or in a gentle clasp is safest during meetings. As these are always irritating, you want to stop "drumming" on your thigh or rubbing your face repeatedly.

Posture

In making a positive impact, posture is important. One of the essential aspects of how others view you is how you stand or sit. Someone who stands straight with their back and head held high exudes trust, assurance, and strength, while someone who is slouched or facing the floor shows uncertainty, indifference, or even weakness. Maintain an open posture to express friendliness and positivity. Stand apart with your hip-distance legs and keep your body exposed instead of your crossed arms, shielding it. Keep your head up and keep your facial expression relaxed. A closed pose creates the impression of boredom or aggression, especially crossed arms across the chest.

The contact of eye

Perhaps the nicest way to build rapport with an unknown person is by maintaining eye contact. Eyes can show attention, interest, and involvement, while failing to make eye contact may result in disinterest, inattentive, or rude. But, this doesn't mean you have to stare directly into the face of another person — quite the opposite. There is nothing more aggressive than staring intent.

The Paralanguage

The phrase "do not use that tone of voice with me" is familiar to any parent with small children. This is a perfect example of how paralanguage affects the message, the aspects of the voice that differ from the words. The most common example is sarcasm, in which the tone of what is said conveys the opposite of the message.

Proxemics

Thanks largely to Seinfeld, the concept of a "close speaker" has become part of our awareness. People are quite sensitive to their personal space, especially the area Mehrabian calls the "intimate space" (i.e., 6 to 18 inches). This is an area usually reserved for family, close friends, or romantic partners. You always want to be far enough when engaging in business conversations.

Changes in physiology

Nonverbal communication is intimately linked to emotion, and physiological responses are often connected with worry and pain. Sweating, blushing (or flushing), and watery eyes are all telltale signs that someone is not feeling well. When you recognize that an associate you're talking to has a bad case of nerves, you must make them feel comfortable.

You must have strong speaking skills to develop a successful relationship and a keen understanding of nonverbal signals accompanying conversation.

Nonverbal communication is mostly emotional; that is to say, it is spontaneous and cannot be faked. Having an awareness of the seven aspects of nonverbal communication will give you an advantage.

But, what these experts tell you will be moments when the body language you are supposed to adopt is in total contrast with how you feel (like when you feel challenged or intimidated internally using a "pleasant" posture). Therefore, when these three facets are consistent in your communication, non-verbal communication is most effective.

In your words, what you mean. What you and your postures and movements share can be learned to convey the correct message, however). What you feel within you, therefore, influences the subtle message you feel compelled to express.

(1) And (2) can be mastered with a little bit of practice, as you can see. But (3) needs to be designed deliberately to align yourself continuously with what you want to say.

For example:

It is because you like and care about people when you want your colleagues to think of you as a pleasant person. It's because you genuinely take responsibility for yourself and the team if you need your team to imagine you as a strong leader.

If you want your friends, seniors, and others to listen to you, it's because they're sure you're going to listen to them sincerely and affect their thoughts and opinions.

Communication is a strong practice that just as naturally comes to us as breathing. Our communication can be seamless with a little bit of understanding, so the other person not only gets our message but is also open to it. Communication with listening begins! To reflect on your listening the next time you find yourself in the middle of a challenging conversation.

This will assist you in determining what your audience need from you so that you can tailor your message to their requirements. You are interested in the best method of communication when you listen, and your audience listens too!

Chapter 5:
The Art of Communication

Indeed, communication is an art. In reality, it is an ability to reach out to all creatures of the world. It is a salient part of human life that is learned as soon as a child is born. As people grow, the importance of communication stretches to work, with the home life as its foundation.

Understanding, acquiring, and practicing good communication skills is an important efficiency tool. In most cases, it can make or break the future of a person. During childhood, inefficient communication skills can cause lots of problems for the parents and the whole family.

Children who learn to speak their first word at a later age can cause so much worry to the family. Often, this can create problems with sibling relationships. This can even be a cause of being bullied when the child reaches out to make friends with other children in the neighborhood.

If not remedied fast enough, this can cause more problems for the child and his family when schooling starts. Its derogatory effects can linger even after graduating from college when left unchecked. Inferior or deficient communication can often have devastating results:

- Lost moments;
- Being bullied in school;
- Hurt feelings;
- Development of inferiority complex;
- Failure at school;
- Futile meetings;
- Feelings of frustration;
- Ineffective teamwork;
- General lack of job advancement; and,
- Not achieving goals set.

Common Communication Blocks

Authentic communication requires both conversation partners to be in tune with each other. This means they must resonate on a mental and emotional level. A person who has gone through some serious problems will feel completely misunderstood if they decide to share the story with an emotionally unavailable individual. At the same time, an emotionally unavailable person might get frustrated if someone comes along, craving closure and attention.

Sometimes communication blocks can interfere in such an intense manner that the message received by the listener is entirely different from what the speaker was trying to convey. For example, a mother who's angry at her child for failing an exam will be "immune" to any explanations that come from him. Maybe she's so preoccupied with how her child's "failure" may reflect on her that she's completely indifferent to everything the child has to say in his defense. This example clearly shows how a person's beliefs and opinions may interfere with the act of proper communication. Remember that this is only a hypothetical scenario; communication barriers may come in various forms.

So what are the most common communication blocks that prevent us from creating healthy interactions with the people around us?

- **Stonewalling**

Stonewalling occurs when one person speaks while the other remains totally quiet or unresponsive, as the term suggests. The speaker feels like he's talking to a brick wall. He doesn't receive any kind of feedback or answer from the other person, nor does he feel emotionally connected. Since communication is like a tennis game, getting "stonewalled" by your conversation partner means that the entire "game" will soon come to an end.

Stonewalling is the most obvious communication block. You don't need to be an expert in communication and linguistics to tell if someone is not interested in talking and sharing ideas. For example, if your conversation partner says nothing but "Aha," "Yeah," "Sure," it probably means that they are not interested in what you have to say. In that case, you can either change the topic of the conversation or reflect his attitude (in other words, stop talking and wait for them to say something) to open a new topic of discussion.

- **Barking at the wrong tree**

Another common communication barrier is when a person tries to obtain information from the wrong source. Imagine that you're madly in love with another person who only sees you as a friend. They reject your offers no matter what you do or say since there is just no romantic desire on their part. If you don't catch this vibe and insist on "barking at the wrong tree, " that person will avoid you sooner or later. Moreover, this seemingly "naïve" mistake can often lead to serious arguments and conflicts.

Leaving aside romantic relationships, this communication block usually appears between clients and service providers. When, for instance, a client is desperate to obtain something but fails to address the right person, like people who get mad at the waiter because something on the restaurant's menu is unavailable.

Again, we see that different views can generate confusion and misunderstandings, thus creating the perfect terrain for arguments, hatred, and hard feelings.

To prevent making this error, always double-check that the individual in front of you is willing and able to give you the items or information you need. If not, try looking somewhere else.

- **Jumping to conclusions**

Often, a good conversation comes to a standstill because we are not patient or willing enough to listen. Moreover, if the message is not clear enough, we mistakenly jump to conclusions instead of asking additional questions. The result is that our conclusion may be completely different from the message that our conversation partner was trying to convey.

This communication block is mainly due to our brain's tendency to function as quickly and efficiently as possible. In other words, whenever our mind is confronted with a dilemma, it will almost instinctively choose the easiest option and since jumping to conclusions is easier than asking for more information, you can see why this mechanism can often drive a wedge between the speaker and the listener.

But just because our minds are "trained" to jump to conclusions doesn't mean we can't bypass this dysfunctional mechanism. As long as you manage to create an authentic connection with your conversation partner, this barrier and others will never interfere with the process of good communication. The art of creating authentic connections with other human beings is the essence of this book, so if you want to master it, be patient and read to the end.

- **Being somewhere else (mentally)**

This communication block is similar to stonewalling in the sense that the person who's doing it tends to ignore their conversation partner completely. Sometimes, our minds tend to drift off, and when this happens, we unwillingly forget that there's another person in front of us who needs our full attention.

There are many reasons why our minds tend to drift off during a conversation, but none of them can justify this behavior. Not paying attention to what your conversation partner has to say is usually perceived as a sign of rudeness and a total lack of respect.

If the topic of the conversation is too dull, try changing it, but in a gentle and non-aggressive manner. If you're busy with something else or simply too tired to stay focused, politely excuse yourself and reschedule the meeting. Anything is better than being completely absent from the conversation.

- **Being on different wavelengths**

This particular communication block is caused by the lack of empathy between two or more conversation partners. Just like two (or more) different wavelengths will never intersect, neither will the messages coming from two (or more) individuals who don't resonate with each other (emotionally).

For example, imagine a liberal and a republican trying to run a country at the same time. There's a small chance they might get along and forge a fruitful collaboration, but only if both of them are aware of their differences and strive to "coexist," despite their somewhat opposite views.

Overcoming this communication block requires tolerance and acceptance from both sides. If neither one is willing to switch wavelengths (even for a brief moment) and strive to resonate with the person in front of him, good communication and collaboration will cease to exist.

- **Sociocultural barriers**

There are times when communication blocks are neither the result of false interpretations nor the consequence of too little empathy but rather our cultural background. This can sometimes give rise to awkward situations between people.

Whenever you plan to meet with someone from a different culture, make sure you do some research in advance, especially if you're visiting other cultures.

To prevent culture from jeopardizing the quality of our social interactions, each one of us must strive to learn ways of interacting with people from different cultures. This means greeting, common courtesy, table manners, delicate topics, and anything else that might generate awkward situations.

You may slip a little at first, but remember that just attempting to understand the culture of others will be regarded as a show of respect.

Chapter 6:
Reasons Why You Need to Master the Art of Communication

Now that you have an idea about communication, its form, and its importance, you might be wondering why you need to master it when you are fine the way you are now. To understand better, here are some of the reasons why you need to know about the art of communication like the back of your hand.

Creates opportunities

One of the good things about mastering the art of communication is that more doors of opportunities are opened to you. Sometimes, when you have the right mindset and can converse freely, you do not need to go to job openings because jobs come to you. You never know when an opportunity might come your way, so it is good to have great skills to welcome opportunities with open hands.

For awkward situations

For situations that are awkward to which most people would react by getting their phones out of their pockets, like teenagers in situations that they do not want to belong to, the art of communication comes in very handy. Instead of pretending to text or call someone, trying actually to engage in a conversation with somebody in that situation will not only lighten up the mood but make everybody's life easier. While the conversation might not go anywhere and be productive, it helps you build a better character and mold you into a different person.

Everybody loves a story

If you are stuck in a traffic jam or riding the bus or the train home, it would be nice to try and strike up a conversation with that person sitting next to you. Sometimes, the stories worth re-telling comes from the random conversations you have with someone you have no idea about. Everyone loves a story anyway, and making a conversation with that person will help pass the time and makes you less bored on your trip.

Card collection

If ever you go to an event where there are many people, it would be nice to communicate with them and get as many business cards as you can get. If you are in the entrepreneur business or a sales agent, having these cards would help you in times of need. If you are on the other end of this, it would be nice to have calling cards and the power to convince people to get your calling card and persuade them to call you whenever they need you.

Something new

By communicating with other people, you can learn many different things that you did not know before. Sometimes, random conversations can even change your life. Talking to someone will give you a different point of view on the matter that you might be dealing with. If you're looking for some life-changing experiences, it's worth a try.

Confidence booster

When you know that you know the art of communication by heart, you will boost your confidence. Being proud of yourself is something that you should not lose no matter what has happened to you in the past.

Vocabulary expander

As of now, the Merriam-Webster dictionary has millions of words that you might not even have an idea about. That is why mastering the skill of communication is so important because it allows you to comprehend what people are saying about you, even if they use unfamiliar words.

Dating success

Being able to communicate well increases the chance of finding Mr. or Mrs. Right. This is because you are confident with yourself. Due to this, you can show confidence in your stand, and the better your communication with someone, the better your relationship will be.

Interpersonal skills

This is why communication skills are essential since they enhance interpersonal abilities. These skills are the ones that help you conduct yourself the way you do at home, at school, or at work. Honing these skills is important to communicate properly. No one is born an extrovert; these personalities develop as a person grows up, but having good communication skills helps you reach success.

Stabilizing friendships

If you master the art of communication, you will be credible, persuasive, understanding to others, and self-confident, and these are some of the traits of a likable person. In short, good communicators are likable people, and they are most likely to form friendships that last.

Business matters

Sometimes, knowing how to communicate well can even help you in your business. It helps you present yourself in front of other people and sell your product because you can convince them that you are selling something worth buying. You also know precisely how to contact people and make them listen to you first instead of just ignoring you outright. Your relationship with your employees or your boss also depends on your level of communication.

Finding happiness

The world today is full of misunderstandings, miscommunications, and misconceptions. By learning the art of communication and mastering it, you are preventing these things from happening. Without these things, you are going to be able to reach happiness at a faster rate. Effective communicators are most likely to achieve happiness than those who are not. This is because they have a good job, good relationships with people, and they feel fulfilled.

Finally, there are hundreds of reasons why you should master the art of communication, but the most compelling one is that you want to thrive in your chosen career and live a happy life.

Chapter 7:
Why Are Communication Skills Important?

Having solid communication abilities helps in all parts of life – from expert life to individual life and everything in between. All transactions, from a commercial standpoint, are the consequence of communication. Great communication abilities are basic to enable others and yourself to comprehend data all the more precisely and rapidly.

Conversely, poor communication aptitudes lead to continuous misconceptions and dissatisfaction. In a 2016 LinkedIn review directed in the United States, communication beat the rundown of the most looked-for after delicate abilities among bosses.

In past ages, instructed individuals created more grounded communication abilities that are generally utilized today as basic gifts for getting in reality as we know it, where all social and business associations were exceptionally close to home.

Letters took weeks and months to arrive, and newspapers and magazines sometimes covered events that were days or weeks behind what was going on in the world at the time. The significance of communication aptitudes was exceptionally prized and thought about as a wellspring of news, instruction, and stimulation.

In this day and age of moment communications, we frequently try not to inquire as to the reason communication is significant or with learning solid communication systems and substitute emojis, slang, shortened forms, short messages, and sound chomps as opposed to building up the aptitudes to express what we truly mean to the state. We can say we don't esteem the significance of communication aptitudes that much.

Profoundly viable individuals – in business, social and individual connections – inalienably comprehend the significance of communication abilities, which is why a few people appreciate achievement. In contrast, others consistently experience troubles conveying everything that needs to be conveyed and understanding others without creating strife, false impressions, and questions. The present advanced gadgets catch a lot of our consideration and prompt us to dupe individual discussions while stressing over our virtual connections.

Luckily, we would all be able to figure out how to improve communication abilities in our connections, social cooperation, and work environment exercises.

Chapter 8:
What is Effective Communication?

The practice of transmitting information from one person or group to another using mutually recognized words, symbols, and signs is known as communication. Communication is only valid when the message is successfully conveyed, received, and understood. This means that communication is only useful if both the message sender and the receiver can assign the same meanings from the message sent.

To communicate effectively, you need not dwell on the words you say; you must also take up several other skills such as expressing yourself assertively, body language, ability to convey emotions, understand those conveyed, and engage in listening. The result is that people deepen the relationships and connections they have with other people and improve various skills like decision-making, teamwork, and problem-solving since effective communication is a skill people learn. Individuals can get better at it if they put in extra effort and practice what they learn by engaging in more meaningful conversations.

Developing the Skills of Effective Communication

- **Become an Active Listener**

Whenever people think about communication, many turn their attention to the words from their mouths. We begin to worry about what we will say, how it will be received, and its effect on the receivers. However, the reality of effective communication is that it is more about listening than it is about talking. Listening is the ability to hear the words that the speaker is using and understand the speaker's emotions.

The definition above creates a significant separation between hearing and listening engagingly. Whenever you truly listen, you become engaged with what the other party is saying. You even begin to hear all the subtle intonations in the other party's voice, letting you know how the other party is feeling and the emotions the individual is trying to convey. Paying this close attention lets you in on what is going on inside the other party, and if you respond appropriately, the other party feels understood and heard. The connection between the parties will be deeper and stronger.

Once the communication is effective, your stress levels will begin to come down. Suppose the person you are listening to is calm; actively listening to him will calm you down because all your senses will be connected to his, and you will begin to catch his drift. In the same way, if the individual is angry, but you are calm, you can help restore calmness in him by listening to him attentively so that the person feels heard and understood.

To listen actively, you do not have to struggle or feign concern because once you make up your mind to connect with this person and understand all that he has to say, engaged listening comes naturally. Here are some of the few tips to help you become a better listener:

- Listen with your right ear: Funny as it sounds, listening with your right ear increases your reception and understanding. This is because the right ear is connected to the left side of your brain, and it is the side that processes emotions and promotes speech comprehension. Therefore, if you listen more with your right ear, you will catch all the emotional nuances of the speech, and you will understand better.

- Have an interest in what is being said: Maintain an open, inviting posture, nod at what you hear, and smile occasionally. Encourage the speaker with some 'uh-huh,' 'mmh,' and 'yes.'

- Give feedback: Right in the conversation, let the person know that you have so far understood what he is saying. If you haven't, ask for clarification. You do not have to repeat what the person said word-for-word; you could say, "What I hear you say is ..." You could also let the speaker know what the words he has spoken so far mean to you.

- Avoid interrupting the conversation or turning it around to yourself: Needless to say, it is selfish to turn back a conversation to yourself. Yes, you will have a chance to talk, but allow them to speak and express themselves without thinking about themselves.
- Ensure that your focus is only on the speaker: do not keep glancing on your phone, on hangings on the wall, or people passing by. Stay focused and pick up all the emotional nuances the person is expressing.

- **Take Note of All Nonverbal Cues**

Your facial expressions, movement, and general reaction to what they say tell loads, even more than your words can express. A person will watch for your eye contact, gestures, voice intonation, breathing, and muscle tension to see how you receive the information being given to you. Some of the expressions that will convey interest in what is being said include sitting at the edge of your seat, uncrossed arms, maintaining an open stance when you stand, patting your friend on the back, or pounding your fists.

In conversations, ensure that you use nonverbal signals that go with the words you are speaking, take in all signals, beware that people react differently, and ensure that you keep off negative body language. Use positive body language even when you are not feeling as such.

- **Be Assertive**

Assertive people speak clearly and directly. They express their feelings, thoughts, and needs honestly and openly, with respect for themselves and others, not allowing the truth to be swept down. They are not aggressive, demanding, or hostile, though. They only seek to express clearly what they feel and to understand other people well, without making an effort to win arguments or force their opinions on others.

To become a more assertive person, learn to value yourself and your opinions because they are as important as others you consider important. This means that you also ought to learn how to say 'no' to things beyond your limits, not taking other people to take advantage of you. Take any feedback given positively by accepting the lessons you get from failures and accepting compliments graciously. When you need help, do not hesitate to ask for it. Have a clear picture of what you need and want, and ensure that your needs do not infringe on the rights of others. Lastly, whenever you have negative thoughts about anything, positively express them, and be respectful.

- **Let Your Stress Levels Remain Low**

It is difficult to think of an amicable solution when temperatures are raging high and negative remarks are flying hither and hither. When parties are trying to pin each other to the ground, it is impossible to agree on anything. However, if you decide to keep the stress at bay and return to a calm state, you will not only save yourself from doing things that you might regret, you will also help to calm the other party. You'll be able to interpret the scenario well enough to determine if it necessitates a reaction or whether it's better to stay quiet.

To stay calm, use some stalling tactics so that you give yourself some time to think. For example, you could ask the other party to repeat his question or seek clarification of a statement before responding. During this time, try to collect your thoughts so that you are not rushing to respond. When you indeed respond, ensure that your words are spoken clearly, in an even tone, and maintaining eye contact. You should have an open and comfortable body language. Ensure that you include a statement that summarizes your response, and once this is done, stop talking. Even if the result is total silence, let it remain quiet rather than filling the air with angry words.

Advantage of Effective Communication Skills

Our survival needs to be able to communicate our thoughts, opinions, and wishes. Just imagine our great-grand-ancestors cave-dwelling not accurately conveying that they don't want to join that hunt because their leg hurts. Next thing they know, a tiger is running away, and not very successfully!

Even though most of us no longer need to run from tigers, the ability to communicate is more important than ever. People can now communicate with practically any person from any place on Earth thanks to our new technologies. Many people do just that regularly, particularly if they work for a large corporation. Indeed, communication itself is the primary objective for some people—successful talk show hosts and writers have mastered this ability to the degree that is simply communicating has become their primary job.

It is an incredibly significant skill to develop to know how to show ourselves in a good light and know the other party well enough to persuade them to help us accomplish something. Let us see a few of the advantages of effective communication.

- **Professional advantages**

Already mentioned the value of interacting in the workplace, let's first address the professional aspect of this ability. Some of the advantages of transparent workplace communication are:

- Fewer errors.
- A better atmosphere for workplaces.
- Good skills for persuasion

1. **Making fewer errors**

Have you ever been in a scenario when your boss or professor tries to explain something to you, but you don't get it? So maybe you say to yourself, "It's okay, I'll do it by myself," after asking them to describe it one more time and still not understanding it, and you end up making a mistake. Or perhaps you were too shy even to ask them in the first place to explain it to you!

The key cause of your error, either way, will be the fact that both sides failed to communicate effectively. Your boss/professor did not, to begin with, communicate their expectations in a way that you could understand. They probably speak from the point of view of someone who has been doing that job for quite some time, so it's simple for them to forget the errors they made at the beginning of the difficulties they encountered then. They think that now that they're more experienced, it must be as convenient for you to do as it is for them. In other words, they are only communicating from their perspective, without taking into account your perspective and your context.

Secondly, what might cause you to make a mistake is your fear of expressing your lack of understanding. Not asking for an answer is something that usually happens when you think your questions would offend and overwhelm the person you're talking to. But you could have asked them a clarifying question instead. For instance, saying, "Okay, so let me just see if I heard you right, so I'm 100 % sure I'll do it perfectly, and then repeating the task the way you heard it saves you from asking a million small questions. Instead, you're only asking for one, and if your manager finds a mistake in what you've stated, they're going to let you know.

Thus, assumptions about how much someone knows and how they feel about those items will lead to errors in both cases. Even though it's hard to get over the voice in your head, sometimes that says, "Stop worrying them, or they're going to think you're dumb and unable to do this!" If people want to be good communicators and prevent errors, it's something we all have to focus on.

2. Better environment at the workplace

Picture the next hypothetical scenario for you. This Friday, your colleague or classmate celebrates their birthday, and they bring muffins for everyone, including you. And what's up with it?! Naturally, you might think they don't like you and don't want to hang out with you without actually consulting with them on that hypothesis. So you could turn away and ignore them the next time they need support from you, causing them not to finish their assignment and to feel very bad.

But in reality, the reason you didn't get a muffin was that all the muffins your mom made for them were made with peanuts, and only after they started sharing them around did they remember your allergies? They were trying to defend you all this time, and here you thought that they hated you!

You both lacked adequate communication skills in that scenario. They must have apologized to you for forgetting all about your allergies on the one hand, while you should have asked them if the moment you noticed something wasn't adding up, there was something wrong in your relationship.

"If we look at this from their point of view, they should have said something like," I'm very sorry I didn't have a muffin for you, I forgot all about your allergies completely. How about we have a coffee together later so I can apologize properly? "You might also have helped solve this by simply asking them," Hey, I've noticed everybody has a muffin but me, and I feel left out. Could you tell me why I haven't received one? "A further misunderstanding would have prevented any of these two explanations.

Just imagine that it wouldn't be fun if a pilot and air traffic control communicated in such an inefficient and petty way.

3. Good skills in persuasion

It does not mean to teach you how to manipulate the people around you always to have your way of doing things. It mainly means selling abilities by "persuasion" and, well, if they also teach you how to persuade your friend to support you with your math, that's not so bad now.

What do you think these great businesses have in common? Yes, the most important thing is that many people want and can use what they all have. But it isn't enough in itself. If they didn't have a strong, compelling marketing team, they wouldn't even have been noticed by anyone. Having the opportunity to communicate with your product in a creative way is what will differentiate you and your work from the rest of the pack in this day and age, where new applications, innovations, and developments are made every day.

And not only that, but you need to know how to interact in the best way about your weaknesses and strength to sell yourself (not in an unethical way, more like-sell you are worth to a university you want to go to or sell your skills and character to your future employer).

- **Personal advantages**

You are probably already aware of the main benefit that good communication can provide you with better and more honest relationships in your personal life. There are thousands of online articles on the relationships between parents and teenagers and what can be done by both persons to make them better. But what if I told you that you could fix 90 percent of that relationship just by changing how you communicate with each other?

Parents have to be more open and honest about their fears and feelings instead of snooping around their teenager's room. It's a hundred times better for a relationship than looking for some kind of evidence for your hypothesis to simply say things like, "I feel sad that you don't spend as much time at home," or "I've noticed some changes in your behavior, and I'm very worried that something may bother you." If parents raise their kids this way, if they are not ashamed to tell them they are sad or hurt by something, they will be good role models for their kids to do the same once they start having issues.

Communication is much more than just what you say; it is how you behave as well. Non-verbal signs like facial expressions or body movements can sometimes tell us more than any words they might be saying about what someone feels. If your parents are nagging you about the C you received and you keep saying how sorry you feel about it, they probably won't be inclined to believe you all the while rolling your eyes with your arms crossed.

To get through your message, you communicate with your words, and your body language needs to be in sync. And not only this, you need to take your previous communication with someone into consideration. For instance, if you're prone to sarcasm, no matter how seriously you speak to them now, they might suspiciously nod their heads. It's a better idea to remember your last interactions and perhaps predict their reaction, rather than simply saying what you have to say and getting angry when they do not believe you. This is particularly important if something big is at stake — say, you want to ask your professor for extra credit, but after you've been late for 70 percent of their classes, they don't really think much of you. It's a great first step to start communicating better to take into account their perspectives and feelings.

You might begin by saying, "Look, I know I'm always sarcastic, but now I really need your help with this," or "Professor, I'm sorry I'm always late." It was irresponsible of me, but I will need some extra credit from your class to get into the university I want. Is there anything that I can do to help you achieve your goal? Communication is an astonishing skill.

Through words, hands, drawings, even eyes, we can communicate. And yet, we tend to repeat the same conduct so often. If a wife is mad at her husband, she will keep yelling at him, and he's going to keep withdrawing. Although they can both see it is not getting them anywhere, instead of changing it, it's easy to fall into their usual communication pattern. But if we dare to change that script, our lives will not only be easier but also more beautiful and fulfilled.

Start today, then! If you fight with someone recently, or if you continue to have fights about a similar thing, imagine which part of your communication is going to fall short. Take into account their point of view and try to change your style of communication. There are infinite ways of doing that, after all.

Chapter 9:
What Does Effective Communication Consists of?

What is communication? We regularly talk unendingly about our advantages and perspectives without thinking about what other individuals hear. If the individual indicates a lack of engagement, disarray, or dissatisfaction, it's an ideal opportunity to change our communications approach. This may include dealing with our worry to hear what other individuals are stating or defusing other individuals' psychological weight to cultivate increasingly viable communication.

Clear Expression Is Critical

When attempting to talk and listen adequately, it's essential to create compassion with every individual we participate in the discussion. If you're an architect, don't utilize specialized terms and language when conversing with somebody who doesn't comprehend the dialect. Rather than getting the message, this individual will probably block out or believe the speaker to be self-important or exhausting.

It's additionally essential to consider someone else's enthusiasm and mental state when conversing with that person. Somebody who's distracted at work won't value being told about the previous evening's social ventures yet may react well to efficient proposals. Somebody who simply got agitating news is probably not going to assimilate complex directions at work from a chief.

A superior method to pass on fundamental data sets aside some effort to empathize and request that the individual talk later or access is composed of guidelines to finish the work on schedule. This system will frequently help individuals who got awful news to recoup rapidly to concentrate on business-related basics.

- Stress and even exuberant feelings can bargain with our communication abilities by making us misrepresent issues or not give them due thought.
- Multitasking makes it difficult to listen effectively and react properly.
- Nonverbal signs can be confused as lack of engagement, propose what we're stating isn't valid, or suggest inferred endorsement of dismissing the message.
- Nonverbal prompts change what other individuals say to us, so it's essential to concentrate on them and not on staring off into space, forming instant messages, or thinking about different things while chatting.
- Using adverse signs, for example, tapping feet, crossing arms, maintaining a strategic distance from eye to eye connection, and shaking the head, causes other individuals to respond protectively.
- It's important to listen properly and set aside some time to consider the information given before expressing limitations, even if we don't agree and need to tell others.
- Clarifying Messages and Reflecting on Meaning

The significance of communication abilities influences all that we do, so, fundamentally, what we state and decipher doesn't become mixed up in interpretation. It's not the only language that affects how we perceive; it also affects our emotional states, our ability to concentrate, and our confidence in our ability to persuade people and communicate what has to be said. Successful listening is the initial step to expanding verbal communication aptitudes.

Inconspicuous sounds, nonverbal signals, and vocal tone can change the implications of words, which may be clear, mocking, or essentially befuddled. Abstain from interfering with others until they're done talking and have a go at rehashing information disclosed in various words to explain any confounding terms. Powerful methods for recapping somebody's words incorporate "Let me check whether I comprehend" or "I hear that…. "Don't rehash the words verbatim yet express the idea in various terms to explain the message.

- Ask open-finished inquiries to explain the data further.
- Encourage other individuals in gathering exchanges to express their conclusions.
- Ask follow-up inquiries to build understanding.
- Try to empower meeting sees when conceivable, for example, tolerating some portion of a proposition.
- Summarize what was talked about.
- Be mindful of conceivable social contrasts among individuals of various ages, ethnic foundations, sexual orientations, religions, and national starting points because these speakers regularly express unique nonverbal prompts to mirror their passionate states.

This methodology of explaining communications and responding to their significance can be utilized close to home, social and business circumstances with some minor tweaking in the language used and changing the procedures for formal and casual settings.

Traits of Effective Communication

It is not sufficient to just deliver a message; it must meet the sender's purpose. Keep this in mind; let us discuss the elements that make communication effective:

Effective communication characteristics.

- **Precise message:**

Facilitate a correct interpretation; the message sent must be concise.

- **Reliability:**

From his end, the sender must be sure that whatever he conveys is right to his knowledge.

- **Recipient consideration:**

The means of communication and other physical settings must be planned, considering the recipient's language, attitude, knowledge, level of education, and position.

- **Courtesy of the sender:**

The message drawn up must reflect the sender's courtesy, humbleness, and respect towards the receiver.

Key Pillars of Effective Communication

Communication is a skill and, especially between couples. You are more likely to have a better connection and fewer difficulties and bitter emotions towards your spouse if you know how to speak with your partner regularly. Most of the professionals whose work was researched and were asked the key aspects of a successful relationship said communication, communication, and communication. Tom Bilyeu also advises, "Communicate obsessively," when asked for relationship tips. Now, I know what you are thinking, that "I try to, but it just does not work the way I expect," or "what I want to say does not come out right, as it was intended."

To answer your question, let's begin by saying that there is a proper way to do it. It may work wonders for your relationship if done correctly. If your communication sounds more like an outburst and complaints, it will do more harm than good.

Let us discuss the three key aspects of communication that have been carefully thought about and chosen as the most essential qualities.

1. **Trust**

The number one thing that you need with your partner is trust. If you cannot trust your partner/spouse entirely, and if they cannot trust you, then there is no relationship. Trusting someone is a process; it takes time. They need to prove to be worthy of it, but your bond's very foundation is weak if you cannot develop it in your relationship. It cannot truly flourish without it. Trusting someone requires courage. As you fall for someone and commit to them, you decide to trust them and agree to get hurt in the process if things go downhill.

Our past negative experiences also tend to refrain us from trusting someone completely. We doubt them and their intentions more. However, you need to build credibility with your partner to know what you are saying is accurate and that you would not lie to them, and the same goes for your other half. They need to be trustworthy and reliable.

Now how to build trust, you ask? Trust comes with time; you need to do and say things that align with your beliefs. If your partner hears you saying one thing and doing another, they will not take you seriously. Still, if you "practice what you preach," as they say, they are going to respect you. You also need to build credibility. Suppose they see you, over time, keeping your promises, saying what you mean, and being reliable. In that case, they are much more inclined to take you seriously when you discuss an important matter, and they have no reason to doubt you and vice versa. Notice that if your partner is reliable, they will show up if they say they will do something. Once you have blind trust in each other, the other elements come naturally. Trust also includes an open and honest conversation with each other. Do not hide stuff, and do not lie to make each other feel better. As the saying by Erza Scarlet goes, " Hurt me with the truth, but never comfort me with a lie." When you communicate with your partner, be honest and be trusting, do not doubt the things they say unless you have a reason to.

2. Emotions

This includes a variety of things and is very vital. When conversing, you must keep your emotions under control. First of all, pick your time for discussing your issues wisely. Do not do so when your partner is busy, stressed out, or preoccupied with something else, or even when you are hungry or on the verge of crying. Always pick a suitable time when you both are in a good mood, well-fed and relaxed so that you are in your right mind and you do not get agitated or angry with each other. Also, when you do talk, make sure your tone is appropriate and delicate. Do not take up an accusing or a hostile manner, which takes the limelight away from the issue and forces your partner to get defensive.

Your tone has an immense impact on effective communication. If you adopt a soft tone, it will compel your partner to fix the issues instead of getting offended. Emotions also include the words that you use when you talk to your partner. Make sure that you do not use foul language or say things like, "this is all your fault," or "you never do anything for me." Instead, you can say, "let's discuss where this problem stems from," and "I would like you to do this." Make it very clear what you anticipate from them, so they know what to do. When you are communicating, do not bring up the past. Do not remind them of what they have done in the past, especially if they have apologized for it. Reminding them of the past will only make them think that you do not let go of things and that you never really accepted their apology. Discuss the issue at hand with empathy. Understand and listen to their side of the story; do not get angry in your words or tone, and allow them to make things right.

3. Reason

This is the third key aspect of communication. Use reasoning in your communication. Do not do it when you are hyper, do not only think of yourself, and expect that things should be perfect. When you communicate with your significant other, do not make it all about yourself. Listen carefully to them too, and any concerns that they might have to feel heard again. If you only think of yourself and don't let them talk, they will feel unimportant, and it will not be effective. Reason also includes handling problems immediately, when you are calm, rather than piling them up and blowing up at your partner when it has become too much. Also, you have to understand that they do not have to agree with everything you say.

You are two different individuals with different takes on life, so there should be ample space for healthy disagreement. Expecting them to agree with everything you say is not healthy. Relationships also evolve and change with time. You also need to know that both of you will change, so accept and embrace the changes, which might occur due to career demands, age, the good and bad times in life, or if you have experienced a close person passing away. Make room for changes and grow together in your relationship while being accepting of it. You cannot expect things between you to stay the same forever, but your love for each other should grow with changing circumstances. Also, some people tend to forget that your partner is not just your partner. They have friends, family, and a whole life outside of the relationship, too, as do you. So be accommodating of that rather than expecting them to spend every waking hour with you. Reasoning also means that you realize that every relationship is work, even the seemingly perfect ones. Every relationship has problems and quarrels. What you have to master is overcoming the bumps in the road without letting them affect your bond and your love.

These were the three key factors of effective communication between couples. If you adapt these, make them your habit, and work on them, you will be amazed by the results and how quickly your relationship will develop.

Communicating properly will give you peace of mind. You will overthink less and live in the moment and enjoy what you have in front of you more. Issues will be settled as soon as they arise. You and your significant other will have a great friendship if you know how to communicate right that you will be an unbreakable force together.

Chapter 10:
Examples of Effective Communication

Through various platforms, we are constantly communicating through various platforms, every moment of our lives, in multiple forms, expressions, channels, and gestures. We do it as a way to express ourselves. Unfortunately, however, while we may do it all the time, much of our communication is not conscious. Sometimes, we communicate without clear awareness, which leads to misleading or conflicting expressions of who we are. However, if you can learn to be aware of the signals you are sending out, you can correctly align your messages to reflect the emotions you intend to indicate.

Here are the different kinds of communication:

1. Formal Communication

This kind is also called official communication, and it covers all expressions and words that express formal issues and needs. It must follow a particular communication protocol and a pre-determined channel. Even when the communication is done orally, there often is documentation to act as evidence of the conversations. Formal communication is often perceived as reliable.

To excel in formal communication, take up the following tips:

- Start by clarifying the reason behind your conversation.

- Whether oral or written, ensure that you follow a well-defined structure that your audience will easily understand.

- Ensure that your tone is open, friendly, and professional.

- Re-iterate the agenda for the conversation either through a call-for-action or by clarifying your position on the issue.

- Always thank your audience for giving you their ear.

2. Informal Communication

Informal communication is unofficial yet provocative information. It is often given by word-of-mouth. It is free-flowing and lacks any formal structure or protocol, making it less accurate and less reliable. It does not have any accompanying documentation to serve as evidence and uses a channel that allows it to spread like wildfire. For this reason, many people term communication given this way as 'gossip.'

Despite being seen negatively, informal communication surprisingly plays a significant role in our society; it shapes public opinion.

3. Face-To-Face Oral Communication

This is the most common and most recognized communication type. In this arrangement, your words and how you say them directly express what you feel on the inside. Formal and casual spoken communication are both possible. It is the preferred communication when talking with friends and family and in various professional forums at the workplace.

Face-to-face communication is the most powerful communication type, and it can work either for or against you. It is a vibrantly alive communication method because despite the rehearsals you have made before you speak, everything you speak is what your brain is processing moment by moment. It is the reason you find that you had planned to say one thing, and in the middle of a conversation, something else slipped.

Oral communication has the advantage of engaging the audience better than other forms of communication. The listener speaks back to you and offers direct, unscripted feedback, enabling efficient two-way communication better than other communication channels.

Some people are afraid, and their minds go blank when they start talking, especially when talking to an authority figure. They begin to mumble and speak things that do not necessarily make sense. Fortunately, oral communication does get better with time.

How to improve face-to-face communication:

- Ensure that your eyes meet with those of your audience, ensuring that they ooze openness, conviction, and confidence.

- Practice perfecting your expressions and tone in front of a mirror, ensuring that they perfectly match the message you intend to convey. More often, your tone and expressions will express more than your words do.

- Engage the participation of your audience and avoid making your communication a monologue. Ask them questions, seek their opinion, and encourage them to build on the ideas you have expressed.

- Consider how your audience would interpret the message you're conveying via your facial expressions and if you'd be persuaded if you were one of them. If you wouldn't, practice some more.

- Become a more engaged listener. Oral communication is not just about the words you give; it is also about listening to others speak and giving feedback.

Example:

Suppose I need my wife to help me locate an item that is supposedly stored in the garage. I will begin by asking whether she has the time to help me with something or not. If she is available, right now or in a while, I will explain what I am looking for when I need it and why I presented the request to her. It could be that she arranged the garage last and would have a better knowledge of where the item is. Once we have resolved to proceed to the garage to look for the item, we should give a call of action such as, "Let's split and check inside the boxes. We might find it."

In your conversations, beware of the influence of the word 'but.' That word is a roadblock. It shuts down the conversation by creating an impression that one person's ideas are superior to the others'. On the other hand, 'yes' affirms and upraises.

If a colleague or an employee insists that he wants to work less and the company cannot handle that at the moment, do not say, "But you cannot; the company cannot handle it at the moment." Instead, say, "Yes, I hear that you want to work less, and I don't think the company can release its much-needed labor presently due to the heavy workload." When you respond in the affirmative, you affirm the individual and open up the conversation for discussion.

4. Distant Oral Communication

Distance oral communication has been made possible by technology expansions, making the world a more accessible and smaller space. People now communicate using mobile phones, video-conferencing, and others. For this communication type, your pace of delivery and tone take precedence over other expressions.

For effective oral distance communication, give precedence to the following:

- Make your speech slower than it would be in a face-to-face conversation. This will make you more aware of any subtle nuances in your tone and give the receiver enough time to receive and grasp what you are saying

- If the situation allows it, wear a friendly face, smile, and let your eyes twinkle. Ensure your tone conveys your receptivity and openness to the other party.

- Re-iterate what you hear when you listen to ensure that you do not miss any words and so that the other party can confirm their utterance.

- Prioritize listening over talking because when you all speak simultaneously, the entire conversation will be undermined.

- Where possible, back up your oral communication with writing. This will confirm what you're receiving out of the conversation and ensuring that everyone is on the same page with the discourse and call to action.

Distant oral communication also applies to when you address an audience or a meeting. Let's see an example:

Suppose your boss puts you in charge of informing your team that they will have to take up additional work, in addition to the tasks your team is handling; how would you break this news to them? The best way is to put a positive ring to it. Doing this will ensure that the team is receptive, the news is well received, and proper action follows.

One manager might say, "Sorry, folks! I have some terrible news for you! The boss says that from today henceforth, we may have to handle some extra tasks, and he says that he doesn't expect any grumbling from you." An announcement like that will be met with lots of grumbling and opposition, and, likely, the extra tasks will not be received warmly.

On the other hand, if the manager goes to the team and announces, "Good morning, colleagues! I have some good news from the management. You have done such a good job that our company now has the pleasure of handling some additional projects. The management is confident that only this team can carry the new responsibility and carry the project successfully. We are up for the challenge, aren't we?" Certainly, the team members will be pleased with the recognition and willing to take up the challenge and prove themselves again.

Whenever you talk to your employees or a team you are managing, avoid starting your statements with phrases like "I want," "I think we should," or "I need," because statements like these send the message that it is all you, and not about the team and their contributions or their perspectives. Instead, use inclusive pronouns like 'we' because they foster an environment of teamwork and provoking each other.

5. Written Communication

Written communication is now engrossed in our everyday communication, from text messages sent, emails, social media updates, blogs, and others. It has far surpassed verbal communication in all social spheres. To be excellent at it, do the following:

Have a clear communication structure so that your communication is not all over the place. The general structure includes an introduction, body, and conclusion.

Ensure that the context of your communication is clear to avoid people getting the wrong message.

Keep the communication clean, both in the formal and informal context.

6. Non-Verbal Communication Types

This is a subtle yet exceedingly powerful communication method. This method includes a wide array of physical signals, gestures, postures, speaking pace, attitude, and tone. We have mentioned how these non-verbal cues influence your communication, giving more information than the words convey. As a result, it's important to spend some time in front of a mirror practicing your fundamental body language motions so that your words and gestures don't convey conflicting signals. Turn them around so that they support the words you say and make your message more meaningful.

However, there will be times when your body language should imply the complete contrast of how you feel inside. For example, if you feel shaken and afraid when speaking in front of an audience, let your body language communicate confidence. For instance, during an interview, you might internally feel scared and threatened, but the trick is to maintain a friendly posture and to ensure that your facial expressions go along with that.

Even in this communication facet, ensure that you give precedence to listening more than speaking or gesturing.

Chapter 11:
Five Questions of Effective Communication

Rudyard Kipling, the famous English short-story writer, wrote, "I maintain six trustworthy servants (who taught me all I know); their names are What, Why, When, How, Where, and Who." The Elephant's Tale is a story about an elephant. While he wrote his poem in 1902, Kipling's principles still apply to effective communication today.

To have effective communication, ask yourself what information needs to be conveyed. This allows you to make sure that you are keeping your communication on track. In most cases, the person who is doing the talking tries to communicate way too much information at one time. This assures that your communication is staying on target and helps you organize your thoughts.

You will also want to consider just why you are communicating your message. Is it to suggest a change in the way things are done or a policy that needs to be changed to keep up with modern business practices? Perhaps you are requesting more information about a topic. No matter the reason for your communication, it should tie into the objective that you are trying to accomplish at that moment. If it does not, then the timing may not be suitable for that communication.

Effectively communicating why you are offering those suggestions or information helps the other person understand why they need to give you the time required to answer your communication. Take a step back and evaluate if you're asking the right person if you can't think of a particular reason why the other person should care.

If this is business communication, there is another reason that you need to communicate the why of the message. Security measures need to be very tight within companies. Therefore, before asking a person to reply to your message, make sure to tell the person why you need the information to meet the company's goals.

It is also important to answer when the right time to communicate the message is to capture the listener's attention.

For example, have you ever been guilty of communicating something at the last possible moment? Not because you did not know that there would be a problem, but because you put off communicating this information. In all cases, communicating the message earlier would have allowed the person to stop and think about a solution more rationally.

If you know that the person who will receive the message will be tied up thinking about other issues, it is not fair to the other individual to communicate the news at that time. Instead, wait until the person is ready to pay attention to your message.

It is essential to consider how you are going to communicate your message. Before you start to speak, take a second to make sure that you are clear about the message you want to communicate. Make sure to limit yourself to three or fewer main ideas in each communication. More importantly, make sure that you communicate all the information you have about the situation. Never expect the person you are trying to communicate with to read between the lines.

Before you start to communicate your message, try to put yourself in the other person's shoes. Organize your communication not only so that it not only delivers an organized message but does it as concisely as possible. If you are communicating in writing, then write a rough draft. Before sending your communication, ask if there are any filler words that you can eliminate. This assures that the person receiving the communication can deal with it quickly and shows that you care about the other person.

Regardless of how you are communicating, use words that your listener can understand. For example, if you are speaking with a professional in the same field, it may be very acceptable to communicate with acronyms; however, if you are communicating with people outside your profession, you will want to use abbreviations to a minimum. Choose which words you want to use very carefully to communicate your message clearly to your intended audience.

Being as concise as possible carries an inherent danger. Being straightforward means keeping your communication brief, but it also means sticking to the point. There is nothing an audience hates more than having to listen to a speaker ramble on and on after they've seemingly made their point. Likewise, no reader will want to struggle through a dozen sentences when fewer would do. Make sure there are no unnecessary sentences, which usually repeat your point in different words multiple ways. Besides sticking to the end and not rambling, you will also need to refrain from introducing entirely different topics. If it's a different topic, it deserves its email or conversation.

Make sure that your communication is complete and coherent. If you don't include complete information in the beginning, it slows down the communication process. Likewise, if your transmission isn't readable, you are likely to lose your audience's attention. A coherent message is logical; all of the points you are trying to make are connected and relevant to the main topic of conversation, while the tone and flow of the content are consistent. While being coherent, a complete message must contain all of the relevant information; think who, what, when, where, why, and how necessary depending on the type of message being conveyed. The most needful point of your letter should be the call to action. Tell your reader or listener precisely what you want them to do and why they need to do it.

Finally, make sure that you are courteous to the recipient. Not being considerate is a great way to ensure that you are treated rudely. This is the most common blunder individuals make, and it can rapidly turn communication into a bad experience.

Excellent communication should answer the five W's used by journalists when they write a story. It should include information about who, what, when, where, and why. While communicating, ensure that you are clear, concise, complete, coherent, and courteous.

Depending upon whom you are communicating, it will be essential to carefully choose how you communicate your message. If there's a possibility you'll need to discuss sensitive material, you'll want to limit who can hear it. Remember that people love to spread information that they do not need to know in the first place, so you need to take steps to control who knows the information in the first place. Remember that many companies have their privacy policies but that there are also laws in place, such as HIPAA, that can often take precedence over individual companies. These policies and laws are in place to protect the ones sending the messages and the ones about whom those messages are sent. Even in your communications, you will want to expose potentially sensitive information to public scrutiny. It can embarrass not only the subject of your discussion but yourself as well if the wrong people find out about it.

Chapter 12:
Barriers to Effective Communication

Many factors may obstruct good communication:

Linguistic Barriers

This is the most common type of communication barrier. Frequently, people speak different languages, or even if they speak the same language, their way of speaking might be different. For this reason, the chances are that the message doesn't reach the other person in the way that it is intended since the meaning isn't that clear. In addition to that, the use of jargon also over complicates the communication process.

If people use words that are not largely understood by the audiences, it can greatly affect communication and understanding. For effective communication to happen, it is best to use simple words and phrases to get across just as intended, and the other person can comprehend it much better.

Psychological Barriers

Many psychological obstacles may obstruct successful communication. A lot of people suffer from issues like different types of phobias, depression, speech disorders, etc. These issues are not very easy to manage and can cause great problems for a person when they are trying to understand what the other person is saying.

Say, for example, that your wife is suffering from depression. When you attempt to speak to her about anything, she may be in a different zone entirely, and she won't comprehend what you're saying. Not only is this a barrier to effective communication, but there's also a chance of accidentally saying the wrong thing and worsening the condition of the person you're trying to communicate with.

Emotional Barriers

A person's capacity to put their point forward or comprehend what the other person is attempting to say is influenced by their emotional state at any particular moment. A person who is feeling emotionally well will much better communicate effectively, whereas a person who lets their emotional state overrule their mind will face a lot of difficulties when trying to communicate effectively.

A lot of people have anger management issues. A lot of people cannot function properly when they're stressed, worried, or sad. All of this greatly affects how these people communicate with others in the workplace. People who don't have much control over their emotions may feel as if their emotions are clouding their judgment. What that eventually does is it hinders effective communication.

Physical Barriers

These are the most obvious barriers that exist and are also easily removable. These include background noise, the place where a person sits, closed doors, etc. You can understand this much better with the help of an example. If two employees whose work is pretty much related sit far apart, their communication can be greatly affected. This comes as part of a physical barrier because it is the physical distance between the two employees hindering effective communication. This barrier can easily be removed by simply changing their seats and making them sit much closer.

Let's look at another example. If your wife has traveled to another country for work purposes, you and her might face communication issues and might not understand each other's point of view in a way that you would have had she been with you at that point.

Cultural Barriers

These barriers mostly exist in the workplace. With increased globalization, there is a lot of diversity in the workplace. An office can have many people from several parts of the world, which can cause cultural differences. Culture does not solely include ways of speaking. It also includes non-verbal gestures, the way a person dresses, the way a person behaves, the way they eat, etc. All of this can also act as a major hindrance to communication. If a person comes from an entirely different culture from yours, especially if the language you speak isn't their first language, you might not understand clearly what they're trying to say. As a result, there can be problems understanding one another.

This can majorly act as a barrier to effective communication. Many multinational companies have seminars and coaching sessions about how it is extremely important to be tolerant of other cultures. But most companies don't, which is why cultural barriers are a major hindrance to effective communication.

Organizational Structure Barriers

The hierarchical structure of many organizations makes it so hard to approach higher management and talk to them about anything at all. Many organizations are also structured in such a way that there is a lack of transparency, and employees never get to know about a lot of the important things that are happening in the organization. These major barriers can hinder effective communication as employees might not know who to approach if they ever need to talk to someone.

Attitude Barriers

This barrier majorly relates to the personality and the attitude of a person. Some people are introverts, some are extroverts, and some think that no one is worth their time. All of these can be very problematic and can majorly affect effective communication. An introvert might not want to talk to you about most things even if the situation requires them to do so. In the same way, an extrovert might just try to talk excessively about things that needn't be talked about. People with ego issues also have a lot of trouble putting their egos aside and talking about things when the situation requires them to do so. Some attitude problems can easily be worked on. There are proper training sessions for anger management and shyness problems. However, an ego problem is something that only the person who has the ego can work on.

Perception Barriers

It's a fact that people perceive things differently. The way person X perceives something might be different from how person Y perceives the same thing. For this reason, it is extremely essential to keep perception issues in mind when talking about effective communication. Take this example: You make a statement to your wife as a joke. She doesn't understand that and takes your statement seriously and gets offended because her perception of what you were saying is extremely different from what you had in mind when saying it. This example was just in a casual, friendly setting. The damage that it can do in the workplace is even worse.

Physiological Barriers

These barriers mainly deal with certain diseases or disorders that can prevent effective communication between two parties. The shrillness of a person's voice, autism, and dyslexia are examples of these kinds of barriers.

Technological Barriers

Technology is evolving rapidly, so it is really hard to keep up with the new advancements that come up. For someone who is not very well versed with technology or is not very comfortable using it, this can act as a great barrier and hinder effective communication. Adding to this, it is also important to note that the cost of technology is high. Due to this, it's not always possible for new companies or small-scale businesses to get the latest communication software.

Socio-Religious Barriers

In many communities, there is very little tolerance for different types of religious groups in some companies. In the same way, women face a lot of issues when communicating in a patriarchal society. In most societies, transgender people prefer partners of the same sex, and others are marginalized and discriminated against in the workplace. These barriers only serve to hinder effective communication.

Chapter 13:
The Importance of Communication Skills

Strong communication skills contribute to every aspect of life – from professional life to personal life and everything in between. From a corporate point of view, all transactions result from communication. Good communication skills are essential if you and others want to understand information faster and more accurately.

How to Improve Your Communication Skills?

Here are certain tips for improving your ability to communicate effectively with others:

1. Listening

Being an effective communicator necessitates being a good listener. Active listening is important – pay attention to what others say and clarify ambiguities by rephrasing your questions for better understanding.

2. Conciseness

Transmit your message as quickly as possible. Avoid unnecessary words and go right to the point. Rambling will make the listener smooth or uncertain about what you say. Don't talk too much, and don't use words that can confuse the audience.

3. Body language

Good body language, eye contact, hand gestures, and watch the tone of voice when communicating with others are important. A relaxed body position with a friendly tone helps you look at others.

When communicating, make eye contact with the other person to indicate that the discussion is concentrated. But don't look at the person, as they might be uncomfortable.

4. Confidence

Be sure of what you say and your interactions with others. Confidence can be expressed through eye contact, a relaxed body stance, and concision talking. Avoid using angry or demeaning noises, and avoid making comments that seem like inquiries.

5. Open-mindedness

If you disagree with what another person has to say, whether it's an employer, a colleague, or a friend, it's important to sympathize with their views rather than simply trying to get your message across. Respect others' opinions and never degrade those who disagree with you.

6. Respect

Respecting what others have to say and accepting them is an essential part of communication. Being polite can be as easy as paying attention to what they have to say, using the person's name, and not getting disturbed. The other person would be respected by respecting others, which contributes to more truthful and fruitful conversations.

7. Using the correct medium

There are many means of communication – choosing the right one is crucial. For example, it is more important to speak in person about serious matters (relays, wage adjustments, etc.) than to send an email about the matter.

Good Communication Skills for a Great Career

To be successful in your job, you must have excellent communication skills. You must know what you want and how you can accomplish it. As an outstanding communicator, your career can be driven.

Strong communication skills can help you to get through an interview and the selection process. The ability to communicate well is a huge asset! To perform your work well, you must be able to solve problems, request information, communicate with people, and have excellent interpersonal contact - all of which need solid communication skills. They allow you to be well known and to understand your needs.

Bad Communication in the Workplace

Communication drives productivity in the workplace. While the downside of bad communication with others may not be evident in the short term, it has a detrimental impact on the workplace in the long term. Some signs of poor contact are here:

- Lack of specific communication
- Using the incorrect mediums to convey important messages
- Passive-aggressive communication
- Lack of follow-through and consideration
- Blaming and intimidating others
- Failing to listen

The layoff notices from RadioShack in 2006 are an indication of bad communication. The electronics chain has sent 400 workers by email notification. The business faced a major backlash after the move, with many people using email instead of face-to-face meetings.

Radioshack's poor communication arose from the incorrect means of communicating with its staff. The workers of the company felt dehumanized and later resented the company.

Chapter 14:
Developing Your Communication Skill

With clarity on what communication is actually about, it is possible to move forward and work on developing your communication skills. Once you do so, you will be able to perfect the way you communicate so that everything that you say is clearer and your message is much more effective. The more you practice your communication skills, the better it is that you will be able to communicate and connect with other people. This way, anyone you interact with will feel understood and believe that their voices have been heard.

Here are some fantastic pointers to help you improve your communication abilities.

Remember your Non-Verbal Communication

More than 75% of your communication is non-verbal, involving the tone of voice you are using, your facial expressions, how you move your body, your breathing, eye contact, and so much more. This is how another person will understand the message that you are trying to communicate. You need to control the way you use non-verbal communication and pay attention to how you translate this communication.

If you want to come off as a good communicator, you need to use open body language, including the way you stand, sit, or look at the person you are communicating with. This is what shall reaffirm the message you are sharing, and you need to be careful that your movements will complement rather than contradict the message.

When communicating non-verbally or in translating non-verbal messages, remember that there is culture involved. Culture affects the way messages are relayed and understood. It also affects communication in regards to a person's age, gender, and religion. With nonverbal communication, it is better to look at it in regards to how all the elements work together, rather than one signal at a time. This way, it becomes easier to have a cohesive message.

Be engaged as a Listener

When conversing, you're probably more concerned with what you're going to say than with what the other person is saying. This means that you are often poised to react rather than to contribute actively. Behavior of this nature is an indication that you are unprepared to be an active listener.

The first thing that you need to do to improve your communication is to be an active listener. This means that when someone is speaking, you are not just hearing what they have to say, you are listening to what they say. This is how you become engaged while listening to what another person has to say.

There are certain things you will begin to notice when you become more engaged in this way. To begin with, there are the intonations in the voices of the people you are speaking with. Listening to this will help you understand what another person is thinking or feeling when they are communicating. When you connect with a person in this way, it becomes easier for you to create a bond that is much deeper.

To become an engaged listener, you need to pay attention to the person who is speaking, note how they move their bodies, and any other non-verbal cues.

In addition, ensure that you allow the person to say what they want to from start to finish. When you interrupt them, you are not actively listening because what you are doing, in this case, is waiting so that you can have a chance to speak. In this instance, anything that is said will simply fly by you as your mind will be working towards forming what it is you want to say. The worst thing about this is that the person you are speaking to can usually tell what is happening simply by looking at your facial expressions.

Stay Away from Stressful Situations

Communication is negatively affected by stress. Therefore, you need to avoid stressful situations and ensure that your emotions are under control. You will inevitably experience situations that will lead to stress building up in some of your communication. This could also happen when you do not understand what other people are saying, or if you are sending messages that the other party finds confusing,

When you face stress-inducing pressure, you can try to stall the interaction with the other person so that you give yourself enough time to gather your thoughts and make a clear and informed response to their query. This means that you should pause before you speak, allowing for some silence that will enable you to regain your control. Furthermore, you do not need to try and give too much information at an interaction. You should focus on one point at a time to prevent placing yourself under too much pressure, which could hamper your concentration during communication.

Stay Confident

Confidence can break through any communication barrier, as it helps you better believe in what you need to say and make the right decisions. Being confident means that you are assertive, and this will be revealed in how you express your feelings, thoughts, and needs. In addition, you will find that when you believe in what you are talking about and communicating, you are honest, and others will note the respect you have for them.

To happen and help your communication skills, you need to have confidence in your opinions and what you think about yourself. This implies you should be clear about what you want from a situation and what you don't want. In addition, you need to have positive thoughts as this will help you respectfully express yourself.

You do not need to have innate communication skills. They can be developed over time. All that is needed is the right amount of patience and practice, and you will be able to communicate with ease.

Chapter 15:
Why Outstanding Conversation Skills Will Change Your Life?

Your communication abilities will determine your success no matter where you go, who you are, or what you want to do in life. The greatest communicators receive the best grades, the best jobs, and the most attractive relationships; it's the simple truth. They're the individuals who can brighten a room just by stepping in.

When you consider what you stand to earn, it's clear that you can't afford to allow any lack of communication skills to become your greatest disadvantage. There are many advantages available to you:

1. Enhanced Career Prospects

Consider the steps you'll need to take to get a job, excel at your daily duties, establish relationships with your coworkers, and climb the corporate ladder. Your social skills must be excellent at every step, from the first interview through your first speech as a board member.

You won't be able to contribute to projects if you can't communicate with your coworkers. You'll get a reputation as a bad communicator if you can't speak to your supervisor about any issues you're having at work. You get the picture - if you want to get that ideal job, you need to know how to conduct a conversation with anybody and everyone.

2. Better Business Relationships

One of the foundations of successful business partnerships is communication. You know how much of a barrier poor communication can be if you've ever had the misfortune of chatting with a drab person at a conference. You might be one of the greatest in your industry, but if you boring everyone you meet, you're unlikely to strike lucrative, mutually beneficial agreements and alliances.

3. Better Family Relationships

How many of us have spent hours attempting to explain ourselves to our parents and siblings? Contrary to popular belief, most family relationships aren't naturally simple, and many take a significant amount of effort.

You can only expect to create polite, loving family connections if you have learned the art of dispute resolution, know how to express your opinions without offending others, and know when to bite your tongue when required.

4. Better Romantic Relationships

This, along with my job issues, was one of the primary motivators for me to study communication skills. I had a few girlfriends in high school and college, but I was not very successful with women.

I couldn't figure out where I was going wrong for years. When I went on a date, I tried to be pleasant, humorous, and engaged. It took me a long time to understand that focusing on the other person is the key to having a good conversation. Even so, it's better to be late than never!

I'd like to believe I'm doing a lot better in terms of romance these days. When you enhance your communication skills, whether you're a man or a woman, whether you're in a casual or more serious relationship, you can expect fewer arguments and better moments together.

5. Improved Self-Esteem

What's the inevitable outcome when you enjoy success in your career, family life, and personal relationships? Better self-esteem, of course. There are few feelings more irritating in life than not living up to your full potential. Have you ever had the sense that if you had only said the right thing at the right moment, things would have turned out differently in your life?

You'll never have to worry about those "what-ifs" again after you've read this book. Your self-esteem will be boosted by the friendships and business connections you form. We are social creatures that flourish when surrounded by others who embrace us and make us happy. As a result, we can develop our social abilities even more.

The Myth of the Socially Awkward Genius

Some individuals are aware that they are inefficient at conversing and participating in social settings. Still, they comfort themselves by believing that there is a connection between a high IQ and an inability to conduct a good conversation.

Shows like The Big Bang Theory lead us to believe that very brilliant people are often socially awkward and that this is irrelevant since they are incredibly intelligent in other ways.

This line of argument has two faults. The first is that there is no scientific evidence linking brilliance to poor social functioning. There is also a slew of specific instances that refute this notion. Albert Einstein, widely considered one of the world's most brilliant minds, was courteous and socially successful. The second issue is that, even if there is a demonstrated negative connection between IQ and social ability, most of us are not geniuses.

This is a difficult reality for some of us to accept, given the fragile condition of the human ego. Fortunately, regardless matter whether you have a great intellect or not, you can learn to have successful social relationships with others.

Can Conversation and Social Skills Be Taught?

Suppose you've grown up with friends or family who have always done well in social situations. In that case, you may believe that social skills are something you're born with - you either can communicate with people in a variety of circumstances or don't. It's a sad idea, but the good news is that it's not true!

I know what it's like to be evaluated by others. Jason, my cousin, was always popular among his classmates, his instructors liked him, and almost every adult in our family adored him. If he hadn't been so courteous, I would have hated him. His mother always said that he was born with innate charm. Regrettably, her choice of words led me to think that charm and social ability were permanent characteristics.

Fortunately, I discovered that most individuals can improve if given the tools they need to assist themselves. Julian Treasure, Evan Carmichael, and Tony Robbins are just three examples I can think of off the top of my head of communication gurus who have helped a large number of people.

I believed I could improve my social skills after seeing how much of an effect they've had on so many people's lives. You have the option to alter your discussion, even if others have informed you that it is bland and useless. The greatest time to begin is right now!

Consider the treatments available to people with Asperger's Syndrome if you want further evidence that social skills can be taught (AS). Autism is a disease that affects a person's capacity to interact effectively with others. People with this diagnosis have a type of autism.

People with AS often talk incessantly about their hobbies, have trouble making eye contact, speak in a monotonous tone of voice, and show little interest in what others think or feel. Consequently, individuals often struggle to establish connections with others, which may lead to feelings of isolation and alienation from society.

The good news is that individuals with AS can be taught social skills, which may help them establish meaningful connections. Through role-play and training lead by trained therapists, they can learn how to "blend in" and function in most social settings.

What can we learn from this? The tale's lesson is clear: even if you have significant social skills deficiencies, you can learn how to connect with people if you are determined enough.

Finally, there's reason to think that you can learn to have excellent discussions, establish strong connections, and like being around other people at home and work. Even better, with practice, you'll become more accomplished.

It's important not to become too engrossed with the past. We've all been in uncomfortable situations and made social gaffes. That's perfectly typical! The most essential thing is to quit berating yourself for previous errors and prepare to alter how you interact with others.

Tips on How to Communicate Effectively

This will give you a few tips that can help you communicate in the best of ways. If you follow these suggestions, your communication skills will improve, and you will be able to have more enjoyable discussions with others around you.

Establish and Maintain Eye Contact

People often don't realize the importance of eye contact in communication. When you look at the other person while talking, you automatically build a great relationship that keeps the other person interested in the conversation. It tells the other person that you are into the conversation and makes an effort to get your point across to them in the best of ways. Imagine for a minute that you are in a classroom, and the teacher is talking to you. Would you be more interested in what she is saying if she looks at you and directs the conversation towards you? What if she turned her back on you and started writing on the blackboard while she was still speaking to you? That's your answer right there. When a person makes eye contact while talking, you can see the person's expressions, and you are much better able to understand what the other person is saying.

Eye contact also acts as a synchronizing signal most of the time. People look up after they finish a sentence to see what the other person thinks and see whether or not they give relevant feedback. At the end of grammatical breaks, too, people look up to get feedback and try to make their point in the best of ways. According to a source, a lack of eye contact can also signal that the other person is embarrassed or that there is no clarity in their thoughts. Research shows that people look at each other 75% of the time when they are talking and around 40% when they are listening. It also greatly depends on the personality traits of a person. People who are extroverts and are generally friendlier tend to look up more amidst a conversation and try to make eye contact.

The importance of eye contact in body language cannot be overstated. Research shows that to have the right kind of communication, appropriate body language is important. Frequently, our body language is known to speak more than our words and is the topmost factor that keeps the audience engaged. There is a famous saying that goes, "eyes are a reflection of your inner self." This saying is very apt in this context. Your eyes reveal a lot about you, and making eye contact allows you to communicate more effectively with the other person.

Send a Clear Message

When you simply try to say something, the message might not go to the other person as intended. When you make a conscious effort to say something with the right kind of intention, your message is understood well. When you are clear with your message, you can get your point across when you choose your words wisely. Keeping the communication objective in mind is the best thing to do. You must ask yourself what you are attempting to accomplish. When you know the answer to this, you need to make sure that you make the right choice of words to understand your point. If you choose words that might even have the slightest chance of distorting the message, you might not get the message across clearly, which can hamper effective communication. Just make sure that you understand the audience well and then choose the kind of words you should go for. Also, it is always beneficial to go for simpler words since that can ensure that your message is understood clearly. The use of jargon only hampers effective communication. For the other person to best understand what you're trying to say, you should choose words that are easy to understand. You need to be very clear with what you're saying so that there's no way for your message to be misinterpreted. The entire point of communicating with the other person is that they understand what you say to them and try to make sense of it in the context you want them to. That is ideally what your aim should be. To convey your message in the best way, it is essential to choose your words wisely.

Be Receptive

When you are on the listening end of a conversation, make sure that your gestures and body language are so that the other person also enjoys making conversation with you. When you are receptive, you give off a signal to the other person that tells them that you are interested, and that way, they will make more effort to get their point across to you. It all boils down to active listening. If the speaker is saying something that you don't understand, make sure to stop them there and then tell them that you don't understand what they are saying to adapt accordingly and engage in a productive conversation. There is no point in actually making conversation with another person when you and the speaker are not able to understand each other. While the other person is speaking, make sure you nod or smile to know that you are interested in what they are saying. Even if you think that you are not interpreting the information clearly or in the right way just like the speaker wants you to, make sure that you make a conscious effort to at least try to understand. The speaker will feel very satisfied when you do that, and that will increase the chances of you both being in a useful conversation.

Wait For The Other Person to Finish

Most people like to be on the speaking end and want the other person to listen. They don't even let the other person finish, and they interrupt them and start speaking out of turn. This doesn't give off a good message to the other person. When they see that you are not interested in the conversation, they also lose interest, and then there is no point in the conversation. You should always carefully listen to the other person when they are speaking. This also shows a lot of respect and shows the other person that you are interested in saying. Always remember that this is a matter of giving and taking. When you engage in active listening when the other person is talking, they will listen to what you are saying carefully. That way, it will be a respectful conversation, and both parties will understand each other, and the message will go out just as intended.

When both parties listen to each other, they care and are respectful towards each other. Most people who are self-obsessed are also known to keep talking about themselves to the other person. They genuinely feel that they are more interesting than the other person. Other people who have shy personalities are known to be overwhelmed by their feelings, and these people are not comfortable when talking about themselves. It is important to note here that monologues are never a good thing, and they send a really wrong message to the listener. This is why it is really important to engage in a two-way conversation. Two-way conversations get people closer and are much more likely to be successful conversations.

To feel included in a conversation, it's generally best to wait until the other person has finished speaking. Some people are generally impatient and cannot wait to get their points across. It is always recommended to inculcate this habit in yourself to wait it out and wait for the other person to finish speaking. Once the other person is done with putting forward his point to you, then you should put forward your point so that both parties can understand each other in the best of ways. The importance of effective communication should never be underestimated. Often, people in high management positions like doctors or politicians are great speakers, but they don't let others finish. Even to people like that, it is recommended that they first hear the other person out and then communicate their point of view.

If you keep these points of view in mind, you will much better engage in effective communication. Believe me; you will see the difference in no time. Simply keep these ideas or points in mind if you're attempting to strike up a conversation with someone.

Part 1
Boosting Your Oral Communication Skills

Chapter 16:
Verbal Communication

Communicating verbally is a way of orally communicating wherein the message is transmitted through the expressed words. Here, the sender offers words to his emotions, contemplations, thoughts, and sentiments and communicates them as discourses, dialogues, introductions, and discussions.

The speaker's tone, clarity of speech, loudness, pace, nonverbal communication, and the type of words used in the conversation all contribute to the viability of verbal communication.

The sender must keep his discourse tone high and unmistakably capable of being heard to all and must plan the topic remembering the intended interest group. The sender should constantly cross-check with the beneficiary to guarantee that the message is comprehended in a totally similar path as it was expected. Such correspondence is progressively inclined to mistakes as some of the time, the words are not adequate to express the sentiments and feelings of an individual.

The achievement of verbal communication depends not just on an individual's talking capacity yet also on the listening aptitudes. How successfully an individual tunes in to the topic chooses the viability of the correspondence. Verbal communication is appropriate in both the formal and casual sort of circumstances.

The Importance of the Content

Individuals invest a lot of energy consistently, stick to different screens looking on Facebook or watching motion pictures, in a nutshell, devouring content. As indicated by an examination made by Peak Media, the normal worldwide utilization of media in 2016 was 450 minutes, contrasted with the 415 minutes 7 years sooner. This implies somewhere in the range of 2010 and 2017, the media utilization has developed at a 1% rate. On the off chance that one thing is without a doubt is the way that later on individuals will, in any case, devour content.

Normally, this puts a great deal of weight on businesses and advertisers to make new bits of content.

All in all, how might you make new content?

The Methodology

Everything begins with assembling a content technique. I can't emphasize enough how significant this progression is. A content system will ensure that you're not strolling aimlessly in obscurity regarding speaking with your group of spectators. Additionally, the content procedure will furnish you with a structure, a spine to your computerized correspondence approach, just as sharp bits of knowledge in regards to the individuals with whom you need to speak with. When you've set up the correct channels for your image and recognized your crowd, we can discuss content creation.

The Content Columns and Small Scale Content

To connect naturally with your group of spectators, you need to convey pertinent data and submit general direction to their responses to improve your content. In a perfect world, you should set up some key columns to make the greater part of the content. For example, one of the most significant mainstays of our advanced correspondence system is our blog.

We can convey important data concerning Online life, Advanced advertising, from contextual investigations to forecasts and studies.

Another column in our correspondence is the disconnected segment, spoken to by occasions that we sort out or take an interest in concerning the advanced showcasing field. You may consider how disconnected exercises add to content creation. All things considered, disconnected occasions and exercises are an extraordinary wellspring of content. You can Livestream the occasion on Facebook or YouTube, make Gifs, compose live messages on Twitter, or make blog entries dependent on the occasion. For the most part, these are instances of smaller-scale content that were made from a disconnected action that can enormously advance your computerized content.

Notwithstanding, the information for small-scale content doesn't need to come exclusively from disconnected ventures and exercises. Online content can fill in also in giving information to miniaturized scale content pieces. For instance, a video meeting can be transformed into a composed meeting, an article, a Facebook post, etc. The key thing is to recognize the columns that can give you consistent bits of content, as they will speak to the main part of your computerized correspondence. When you've done this, you need to figure out which smaller-scale content piece you can make dependent on them, in this way augmenting the yield.

If you're just using the most basic pieces of information, you may discover that your computerized communication process lacks a certain fluidity (like a webcast or a blog entry). More or less, your once seven days blog entry, digital recording scene, and so on might be great and important for your group of spectators; however, on the off chance that you just communicate with it two times per week when you post them, your commitment will endure.

Content: Wrap-up

The fundamental columns are the fragile living creature and bones of your correspondence. At the same time, the miniaturized scale content is the blood that makes everything stream. You need everyone to be available and cooperate, all together, for your advanced correspondence to run flawlessly. Investigate your content procedure. What are your primary content columns? Is it fair to claim that you're making good use of small-scale content? These are questions you need to reply to on the off chance you need to improve your content.

Choose The Right Words and Right Content

Making sense out of picking the correct word is likely just the second most troublesome composition characteristic to ace (direct afterthoughts). Your assertion decision is a pivotal piece of your composition that legitimately corresponds with your perusers' responses to your content.

Indeed, you could have an astounding thought, yet without the fitting words, you're not going to strike your group of spectators. So, how would you go about cleaning up your assertion choices and improving the quality of your content? Clue: You're not going to require a thesaurus for this.

1. Recognize Powerless and Redundant Expressions

The absolute initial phase in the process is pinpointing which expressions you need to change, even though it's occasionally hard to limit the words that need a makeover. For straightforwardness, center around stamping words that you use time and again, that burden your sentence, or that simply feel cumbersome.

How might you distinguish these expressions?

1. Peruse your draft for all to hear. This causes you to hear the irregularities instead of simply observing them.

2. Search explicitly for frail expressions you speculate you're utilizing, for example, stuff, things, got, all of a sudden, it, and so on.

3. Use CTRL+F in your record to perceive how frequently you utilize explicit words, and think about featuring a couple for adjustment.

2. Conceptualize Choices

Conceptualizing new thoughts for more grounded and less dull expressions doesn't generally need to come down to flipping through the thesaurus. Rather, keep a scratch pad with you and record fascinating words when you go over them, for example, while perusing or in ordinary discussion. When you're prepared to alter your draft, you'll, as of now, have a few options arranged.

Another good thought for conceptualizing is to expel the word from your sentence, leaving a visual clear in your archive. Rehash the sentence without it; at that point, choose what may bode well to fill in the clear.

3. Go for a Passionate Reaction

Since you have a rundown of thoughts, it's a great opportunity to choose the most grounded option. Your spotlight here is to settle on the word or expression that will evoke the ideal enthusiastic reaction from your perusers. What are you truly attempting to state? Indeed, even a word that appears to be solid probably won't be the best decision inside your content.

For example:

I take a gander at him, unfit to tear my look from his face.

"Look" isn't the best word in this sentence. If I pick "glare," the perusers become more tuned in to the feeling of the piece, which establishes an irate pace for this situation. Maybe the man in this sentence has accomplished something incorrectly.

I frown at him, incapable of tearing my gaze from his face.

Obviously, on the off chance that I pick a positive option, for example, "gape," the feeling moves to one of astonishment. Maybe the man is attractive!

I stare at him, unfit to tear my look from his face.

Even though the words are altogether comparable, the whole tone of the work has been changed just because we concentrated on how our decisions will genuinely influence the peruser. Ensure you don't forfeit your message for more grounded words.

4. Get Explicit

One basic approach to clean your statement decision is to get down to the points of interest. For instance, if you wind up utilizing "pop" to an extreme, you can make a convenient solution by telling your peruser what sort of pop.

For example:

Anna tasted her pop.

Or then again

Anna tasted her Pepsi.

It's a slight change that can paint an unmistakable picture while staying away from reiteration.

5. Try not to Settle

I see how this goes. You wrack your mind until you don't accept there's an option, so you choose your underlying thought. Choosing an expression since you can't think of a superior one won't push your composition any further. Rather, mark the expression and return to it later. This allows you to look for motivation and clear your brain so you'll have a superior option once you return.

It is not necessarily the case that you ought to never utilize a thesaurus again, yet as much as essayists praise an extraordinary thesaurus, it's not generally the arrangement.

Chapter 17:
Verbal Cues – Reading Between the Lines

Whether you like it or not, the majority of communication today is done via words in ways it has never been before, whether written or spoken. With the advent of the internet, written communication through email or chat messaging has become the standard, implying that your ability to read people should not be restricted to face-to-face interactions.

Before we proceed any further, a word of caution: you should be aware that some individuals mean precisely what they say. Only when words are unclear or imprecise should you look for additional clues to figure out what someone is attempting to convey.

Let's look at some of the most effective methods for learning to read between the lines.

Being a Better Listener

Paying as much attention as possible is the first step in learning how to read between the lines. It's important to keep in mind that hearing and listening are not synonymous. The primary aim of listening should be to acquire new knowledge. Don't be one of those individuals who just pretend to listen to be nice to the one who is speaking. Many psychologists will state that there are two types of listening. There is listening to learn and listening to respond.

I'm sure you know people in your life who you feel never listen to you but are rather waiting for you to finish talking so they can share their thoughts and opinions, not conversing with you in a proper conversation. This is not a nice way to be and won't win you any friends.

Rather, try to learn something or get knowledge from them. You must be interested in what the other person is saying; else, you will not be able to absorb anything. Here's a test: if you didn't learn anything new from a discussion, you weren't paying attention.

How do you become a better listener? Here are some tips:

Ask More Questions

Asking questions shows that you're interested in what they're saying and that you're paying attention to what they're saying. More significantly, inquiries enable you to explain the issue, making it simpler to connect the dots between the information you've been provided. This allows you to simplify the picture in your mind, reach correct conclusions, and demonstrate empathy or compassion. In any event, asking questions enables others to expand and clarify their points of view. More significantly, it motivates individuals to be honest because they feel obligated to give you the whole truth in return for the time and attention you are providing them.

Practice Active Listening

This technique has been used for years and can help you understand and create a story in your head. According to the Center for Leadership at Northwestern University, active listening can be as simple as repeating back keywords of what the speaker just said. It's like a little verbal nod of acknowledgment that says you're on the same page. The fact is that there are lots of opportunities to misunderstand what someone is saying. Active listening or giving a recap of what the other person said tells them that you're on the same page. Or, if you aren't, it lets them correct any misconceptions you might have about the situation.

Wait Before Responding

Except when you need clarification, it is critical that you remain silent until the speaker has done speaking. It's a common guideline in discussions, meetings, and conversations, but you'd be shocked how frequently people don't follow it. People may be so impatient that they won't even listen to the whole of a proposal before choosing to express their views, opinions, arguments, or even agreements. Remember what we said about learning by listening and responding by listening.

This may be aggravating for the speaker, and it makes it difficult for you to absorb all of the information at the same time completely. Also, keep in mind that every interruption may distort the message that the person is attempting to communicate, making it more difficult for them to clarify their point of view.

Take Note of the Tone

A low voice adds a sense of authority, a high-pitched one conveys nervousness, stammering can indicate doubt, and fast-paced words can indicate anxiety. Also, paying attention to which words are given emphasis can change how the sentence is perceived. For example, they may be emphasizing the word maybe, or perhaps they stuttered the word yes as a reply. This could indicate that although they want to say no, they're put in a position where they feel as though they can't refuse.

Taking Action: Aligning Body Language with Verbal Cues

Let's say you're in a conversation with someone, and you're piecing together everything we've been learning about so far. You're reading their body language and picking up on physical cues, and you're listening to what they're saying properly and picking up on their verbal cues. How do you piece the two together to get an accurate image of what someone is saying, therefore providing you with the foundation of knowledge that allows you to communicate back most effectively?

First, start with the basics. Are the physical and verbal cues you're receiving in alignment? For a running example, we're going to say you're in a job interview for your dream job, and you're hoping to make a good impression.

You're talking to the recruiter. Their body language is open and positive. You feel welcomed, and things are going well. The verbal cues are also positive. The recruiter is saying positive things and saying you're doing well, and you'd make a great fit at the company. That's excellent. Keep doing what you're doing.

On the other hand, what if the cues aren't aligned? Let's say you're being told this is good. That's excellent. But what if the recruiter is closed off, there's a lack of eye contact, and you're not being paid much attention? You're reading the situation and reading that the recruiter is not on the same wavelength as you.

What do you do?

Well, you use what you've learned to turn the situation around. What body language do you read? If the recruiter is closed off and slumped, are they bored or having a bad day? If shoulders are raised and they are experiencing stress, this could be the case. Now you can decide whether to carry on or connect with the recruiter. You could say something like;

"Just out of curiosity, do you think it's incredibly stressful to work here? Should I be prepared for the worst?"

To which they reply:

"Well, you know how it is. There are good days and bad days. I'm just due for a day off."

"You know, if I did end up here, I'd be more than happy to advocate with you for more days off during the week. We could set up a picket fence and everything."

You're just joking, but what you've done is change the situation entirely. Instead of just being another candidate that sat in front of the recruiter who's having a bad day, you've made the situation personal. You've connected with the recruiter and lightened the situation. You're not just here for the job, but you're a people person who talks to other people like they are people, not just holding the image that you're dealing with a faceless business.

Guess who's going to stand out in the recruiter's mind now? I'm not saying you need to dive into the situation and give the recruiter a space to talk about all their problems. That's not professional. However, what you are doing is reading the situation, identifying the problems, and taking action to communicate as effectively as possible.

It all starts with reading and being aware of the situation. Then choose to react. If you're in a group interview with another candidate, you'll want to use your knowledge of body language to make yourself come across as confident and as though you're supposed to be where you are.

If you get onto a topic of conversation where the other candidate shrinks away and becomes quiet, you know this will be a topic that might be their downfall and can run off of this. On the other hand, if the recruiter is animated and shows a keen interest in a certain subject, you can bet that this is going to be a crucial area of business for the firm to investigate and that the segment you're about to enter will need more care and attention in your approach.

Of course, we could go into situations and examples until the cows come home. Still, the main takeaway I want you to think about is how you can actionably use the information you're learning in your day-to-day interactions. Through trial, error, and experience, you'll see dramatic results.

Chapter 18:
How to Speak Fluent English?

Useful Tips to Improve English Speaking

Here, I will give you very important, useful and easy tips to speak fluent English.

Read carefully and follow these tips.

First and foremost, I will discuss the four foundational abilities of English. The four fundamental abilities of language acquisition are reading, writing, speaking, and listening. It is difficult to build a home without a solid foundation. Similarly, if you don't build on the four pillars of language acquisition, you won't be able to speak a language effectively. These four skills listening, reading, writing, and speaking play very important roles in learning English and improve fluency and pronunciation.

- **Listening**

Listening to English is one of the different ways to practice your English skills. Listening is another way for children to acquire a new language. They do not speak the language when they first come into this world, but they learn through listening to their elders. They talk slowly at first, but eventually, they become extremely proficient.

In the same manner, listening may teach you a lot. You will learn more if you pay attention. Listening helps you become familiar with the rhythms and intonations of English. Once the sounds are familiar, try imitating them.

- Watch English films and pay attention to the conversations.

- Tune on to English news channels and pay close attention. It will help you more if you view the same news in your native language before watching it in English.

- Watch English-language television series

- Pay attention to other individuals who speak English around you. • Listen to English music.

- **Reading**

Reading is a necessary part of life in today's society. We learn to read as children, and we read to learn as adults. It is essential to read a lot if you want to acquire English fast. The more you read, the more your brain absorbs information about how language works. Reading in English may help you enhance your vocabulary, grammar, and writing abilities all at the same time. So start reading something in English every day.

- Read English advertisements, noticeboards, e-mails, and other materials.
- Read short tales or novels written in English.
- Read an English Newspaper—At first, you may pick a page in an English Newspaper that interests you. You may pick from sports, politics, economics, and other topics.
- Read English Magazines – You may choose any magazine that interests you.

For example, a culinary magazine, a cinema magazine, or a political magazine.

Remember to read aloud while you're reading. Reading aloud has a significant impact on your ability to speak English fluently, smoothly, and fluently.

You may improve your speaking skills by reading aloud.

Reading in English improves your vocabulary and sentence structure, which is beneficial when speaking. Reading English texts out loud will train your mouth and lips to pronounce English words more easily.

- **Writing**

Writing improves our communication and critical thinking abilities. Writing allows us to express who we are as individuals. It improves our communication skills also.

Practicing writing in English is also very important to learn English speaking. You can write a gist of what you read, or you can choose any page of your interest from your favorite storybook or magazine to write. You can write about your daily routine or how you spent your day in English. You can choose any topic of interest. Such kind of practice will help you register English words and sentences in your mind.

You should also practice writing your messages on social media in English.

- **Speaking**

Making vocal sounds is the act of speaking. Speaking may be defined as conversing or expressing one's ideas and emotions via spoken words. This skill gives you the ability to communicate effectively.

To learn to speak in English, you have to start speaking in English. Now you will think of how or what you can speak in English when you are here to learn English. But remember here I mean to insist only on speaking. You will not have to bother about your grammatical errors or others' opinions.

You can speak in English with your friend or a person whom you think knows better English. You can ask him to help you wherever needed. You will surely get support.

One more way to practice English speaking is that you can make a call to customer care which is absolutely free, and choose English to talk to that person. It is their duty to understand your problem and message. They will help you the best, and they will also talk to you in English.

- **Learn**

Learn a new word in English every day and try to use learned words in your conversation.

As I suggested, you practice reading so while reading, you can underline the words you don't know and learn their meaning. In this way, you will learn their use while reading then you can practice using those words in your conversation.

- **Think in English**

A human brain finds it difficult to quit thinking. To enhance your English fluency, you should begin thinking in English anytime you feel free since no one will stop you from doing so. Thinking anything that you want in English will help you speak the language.

What do you believe you should think now? You just need to do one thing: think in English about anything you're thinking. If you're thinking about anything for the following day or week, you should think about it in English, or you may think about how you spent your day today. Remember not to focus on your mistakes; instead, think naturally in English. This technique will show you a variety of ways to communicate effectively in English. While speaking in English, your brain will remember numerous phrases where you get stuck.

Importance of thinking in English

Have you ever considered the significance of thinking? What makes us think? Our minds are always buzzing with ideas. We intend to think. This, we think, is the most effective method to train our brains for a real-life situation. We consider how to deal with reality. We think to prepare ourselves to say what we're thinking.

Why should you think in English?

If you want to enhance your English speaking skills or become fluent in English, one of the most essential things to remember is to think in English. You are free to ponder anytime you have spare time. Take a pause from your daily activity to consider things in English.

It teaches your brain to speak English fluently if you start thinking in English. You learn to fix your errors and express your words properly while thinking in English. It's a kind of practice that allows you to fix and re-correct your errors. This kind of exercise prepares you to speak English more confidently and eloquently.

How to think in English?

You will have this question when you study English as a second language: "How do I think in English?"

I've included some helpful hints to help you think in English.

- **Using your vocabulary**

You should begin to think in English utilizing the terms you've picked up from your environment, whether via listening to people, reading in English, or any other means. It's essential to expand your vocabulary by learning new terms, but it's even more crucial to utilize those words in everyday speech. You should begin utilizing such terms while thinking in English if you want to use them in your speech. I'd like to point out that while you're thinking in English, it's not necessary to utilize new words or phrases in sentences. Still, knowing their meanings and using them properly in suitable situations is more essential.

For example, "not well," "ridiculous," "good going," "belated happy birthday," "take care," and so on.

- **Be Imaginative**

You'll need to be a little creative. Pick a subject and act as though you're talking to someone about it.

You consider the problem. For example, you may be conducting an interview or conversing with a buddy when you begin to consider potential discussion topics. As you must communicate alone, you must perform the roles of both a speaker and a listener.

This will allow you to envision and think about a discussion, giving you experience speaking effectively in that scenario.

- **Be a narrator**

Someone who narrates or reads the tale is known as a narrator. In novels, the narrator recounts the scene without using conversation or describing what is going on. Narrators are used in a lot of movies, especially documentaries, to explain specific sections. Now you may play the role of the storyteller in your own life.

It's simpler to narrate anything than to converse because you never know what the other person will say, while you always know what you have to convey when you're saying something. You may quickly think of anything to tell, such as your whole day or a specific incident, etc. This technique will undoubtedly assist you in improving your English speaking skills.

- **Be Creative:**

When learning English as a second language, you will often find yourself unable to communicate properly in certain circumstances. You can't seem to come up with the proper words to explain yourself or communicate exactly what you're trying to say. When you don't know the perfect phrase to describe yourself, you should consider alternative words to express yourself or convey your thoughts effectively.

There are always many ways to say anything. Even if you don't know a term, you may convey your message by utilizing your imagination and other words.

Consider the following scenario: When loud music is played, your baby falls asleep. You want to say, "Slow down the music or turn down the volume," but you don't know how. You may use different phrases to express your point in this scenario. as an example: "My baby is asleep, and the music is blasting from the speakers. So please bear with me."

If you don't know what a ventilator is, you may use other terms to describe it.

An aperture that enables fresh air to enter a closed area, for example.

- **Be Natural:**

Allow your brain to flow whenever you're thinking in English. Don't be hesitant. Don't waste time trying to fix your errors. Allow for errors to occur. Just keep thinking in a natural flow. Don't worry about grammar errors, punctuation, or anything else. You must keep in mind your fluency and the constant flow of your ideas. It will assist you in becoming more English-fluent.

- **Do not Translate**

When you're thinking in English, don't attempt to translate what you're thinking into your native language. If you translate in this manner, it will constantly hamper your English speaking and fluency.

Internalizing the language is also aided by thinking in English (without translating). You automatically adopt that language, which manifests when you speak English.

Consider the following scenario: When you employ these phrases in everyday speech, for example,

> Shut the door.
>
> Let's go.
>
> Excuse me.
>
> How are you?

You do not translate these sentences and speak them naturally. Similarly, you should think about new sentences, words, or phrases that you do not use in your everyday speech or that are unfamiliar to you without translating them in order to absorb the English language quickly.

This discussion focused on the significance of thinking in English and how to think in English.

- **Talk to yourself**

This is a crucial strategy for improving your English fluency. This technique will assist you in practicing your speech organs so that you may speak English effectively. It is a better method to enhance your English fluency if you stand in front of a mirror and speak to yourself. This technique will help you gain confidence in your ability to communicate effectively in English. Every day, you should practice for 5 to 10 minutes. You must pretend to be speaking to someone else in English while chatting to yourself. In some respects, practicing speaking is much simpler when you aren't concerned with other people's opinions and aren't afraid to speak to yourself. This practice will make you confident enough to stand in front of others and talk to them fluently.

- **Know the Correct way to use your organs of speech:**

You must acquire a speaking practice in English, just as your speech organs need practice. To retain fluency, you should naturally speak English. Lips, tongue, teeth, and jaws are all oral organs that play a critical part in human communication. You should learn to place proper emphasis on the words. You should not put a lot of emphasis on each word. Excessively widening your lips or mouth is not recommended. You will lose your fluency when speaking English if you do so. You may either listen to people talk in English or attempt to mimic a native speaker to learn how to utilize your vocal organs correctly when speaking in English. This will assist you in properly using your organs to speak English in a natural flow.

- **Tongue Twisters:**

Tongue twisters are difficult-to-pronounce words that make your tongue feel all twisted up. Many individuals use tongue twisters for entertainment or as a challenge, but they have a significant advantage. They may aid in the development of pronunciation abilities.

Tongue twisters are the most effective method to enhance your diction and speaking speed. They're a fantastic method to work on your pronunciation and fluency. To talk eloquently in English, you may practice twisting your tongue using tongue twisters.

> "The thirty-three robbers believed they had delighted the throne all day Thursday."

> "She sells seashells by the seashore."

> "In the kitchen, I noticed a cat eating chicken."

- **Describe the things around you**

If you want to enhance your fluency, it's essential to maintain speaking in English, and this advice is just meant to assist you. You should choose anything that you notice around you and explain it in your own words. Not attempt to construct complicated phrases. Simple sentences are preferred. It's essential to note that you won't be penalized for errors in grammar or vocabulary. All you have to do is say whatever comes to mind at the moment. You will immediately know which method and which term is more suitable to utilize when discussing that specific subject you have selected to talk about if you do so. Here you will have to be a little imaginative while choosing a thing around you to speak. I give one or two examples for your help. You can describe a scene outside your window or an autobiography of a fan which you see every day in your room.

- **Choose a Topic:**

If you wish to enhance your English fluency, you should attempt to choose a subject to discuss. It is completely up to you to choose a topic that interests you. It may be about friendship, a friend, a neighbor, a hobby, or anything else you like chatting about. If you choose a subject that interests you, you'll have plenty of opportunities to talk about it. Begin by making little sentences, connecting them, and then speaking. It will help you improve your English proficiency.

All of these suggestions will allow you to construct phrases in English, providing you experience in becoming proficient in the language. You will get an increasing number of ideas for framing English phrases and speaking them in a continuous manner.

- **Narration**

Choose a story that you know well and narrate it in English. You can narrate a story of your favorite film or latest film. This should be a simple job for you. I give you another easy option to choose from. You can narrate a conversation that you might have had with your friend, partner, or anyone during the day.

When narrating your tale, keep in mind to think in English. Instead of focusing on speaking properly, concentrate on communicating effectively. Make a mental note of each phrase and read it out to yourself.

Even if you don't have someone to speak English with, you may still gain confidence and achieve fluency on your own time.

- **Learn the most Common Sayings by you:**

Spend some time observing how you talk in your original tongue.

What are your most often used terms and phrases?

Learn how to speak the phrases and words you use the most in English. Knowing them in English will enable you to communicate in English fluently as you do in your original tongue.

- **Repeat what you hear.**

You can repeat dialogues while watching English plays or movies. You may improve your English fluency by singing along to your favorite English songs. This is a tried-and-true technique for learning a language.

- **Practice! Practice! Practice!**

As we know that Practice makes a man perfect. So you should practice English speaking following the above-mentioned steps. Use a speaking game to practice at home. 'Speak for one minute without pausing to consider...' Choose a subject, such as video games, and speak in English for one minute without pausing.

You should practice listening to others to improve your pronunciation. You should not practice only reading in English but also writing too. While listening to others speaking in English, observe how they pronounce English words, the places where they give stress, and the intonation they use. Then you try to pronounce English words and sentences with correct word stress and intonation. While practicing how to speak English, you should keep in your mind that you are correctly practicing everything.

- **Avoid**

Certain things should be avoided if you want to improve your English speaking skills.

Hesitation:

One should not hesitate while speaking English. He should speak with confidence. You just speak whether wrong or right, but speaking is a must.

Fear:

Do not be afraid of English speaking. Do not have any kind of fear in your mind like, "what will people think about me? How will they react? They will laugh at me."

Remove such kinds of thoughts from your mind if you want to speak in English.

Translation

Do not make it a habit to translate your mother tongue to English while talking to someone in English. Such kind of practice will hinder your continuity and confidence. You will take more time to reply, which will hinder the communication process, and there are more chances to make mistakes. Every language has its expression, so translation will not be a good idea at all.

Another issue with translating is that you will be attempting to integrate previously taught grammatical standards. It is improper and should be avoided to translate and think about grammar to produce English sentences.

These all are tips for those who want to learn to speak English fluently. Initially, you can face some problems, but little practice will help you speak better. Do not bother about your initial mistakes. Everybody makes mistakes while learning something new, so just make mistakes, and you will learn from your mistakes.

English Pronunciation

The way we pronounce words is referred to as "pronunciation." It is the pronunciation of a word or a language. Many words in English are not pronounced as they are written for a number of reasons, and several sounds may be represented by more than one letter combination.

Correct pronunciation is the basis for efficient communication in English. Bad pronunciation can fail to convey the message and can cause troubles in communication. You have only one chance to create good first impressions on others, and by having good English pronunciation, you can grab that chance easily.

Good pronunciation requires articulating the words properly. The other important things to consider are the volume and the pitch of your pronunciation.

To pronounce words, we force air from our lungs up through our necks, vocal cords, mouths, past our tongues, and out between our teeth and lips. (Occasionally, air passes via our nostrils.)

To alter the sound we make, we primarily regulate the shape of our mouth and the movement of air using the muscles of our mouth, tongue, and lips. Our speech is clearer, and others can hear us more readily if we can manage the contour of our mouth and the movement of air properly.

For pronunciation, speakers of various languages acquire distinct mouth muscles. Our muscles may not be properly formed for a new language, making pronunciation more challenging. Our muscles grow, and our pronunciation improves when we practice foreign language pronunciation.

To improve your pronunciation, keep the following points in your mind:

Learn to listen to others. You will be more successful if you listen more. Nowadays, there are many opportunities of hearing native English speech: songs, films, TV series, videos on YouTube and other sites, audiobooks, etc.

- Repeat the words which you find difficult to pronounce,
- Recite poems or sing songs, observing rhythm and intonation,
- Talk to your friends in English whose English is good or better than yours too – just for fun and practice.

It's not about getting rid of your accent when it comes to pronunciation. It's all about sounding clear and distinct in your English so that no one is confused about what you're saying.

Your English will become simpler to comprehend after you learn to speak the right sounds. You'll sound more natural, and you'll learn English faster.

It will improve your listening skills since you will learn to detect and recognize the noises of other individuals. Your self-assurance will skyrocket.

Important aspects of pronunciation include correct vowel and consonant sounds using the muscles of our mouth, tongue, and lips. A learner needs to know about English speech sounds and symbols, which help pronounce (transcribe) any word in English. Other important aspects of pronunciation include:

- **word stress** - putting emphasis on certain syllables in a word
- **sentence stress** - putting emphasis on specific words in a phrase
- **linking** - connecting words together

- **intonation** - how our voice rises and falls as we talk

Why Improve Your English Fluency?

Being understood clearly.

When you speak well, people will be able to understand you better and clearly. When you speak very fast, then people will not understand a single word that you say. Also, if you speak well, people will better understand the message you want to impose. For example, if you mumble, people will feel that you may not want to be there. It may also appear that you do not want to talk to them, so you are just mumbling instead of making them hear what you are saying. But when you speak clearly, people will listen to you and surely understand what you are talking about.

Being a pleasure to listen to.

Isn't it good to know that people enjoy listening to the things that you are talking about? Keep in mind that effective communication also depends on whether the audience is listening to you or not. People will not listen to you if the experience of listening to you is unpleasant. If you sound nervous, people will most likely think that you are not prepared to deliver your speech. People will think that you are not a good speaker, thus consider you boring. As a result, they will lose interest in what you are saying, and you will not communicate well with them.

Being more confident.

If you believe you are a good speaker, you will most likely gain confidence in your ability to talk in front of others. If you develop good speaking skills, then you will develop confidence as well. Speaking well guarantees that you will not fail because you are prepared to do so and know what you are doing. As a result, you'll feel more secure speaking out and persuade more people to listen to you.

It will be easy to communicate when you travel and meet new people.

One of the most interesting benefits of improving your English fluency is that you can travel around the world freely without worrying about communication issues. You have the chance to meet new people both when learning in a group and when traveling. People usually get more open and friendly when you speak their language.

Besides, when you learn a foreign language or even multiple foreign languages, your options for traveling destinations become greater. It is easier to visit a country and to enjoy your stay there if you know the language. The local people will appreciate that you can speak their mother tongue, and it will open up new opportunities for you to learn more about other people's lives and cultures.

And as you know, the world is full of interesting and extraordinary cultures that are so different from each other and sometimes so close to each other at the same time. Knowing foreign languages lets you discover more and see the world from a different perspective, from a fresh angle. Not everyone has the chance to see all of this, to enjoy and understand the lives of others, or know about their history, philosophy, and their way of living and loving. People who can travel the world have a greater appreciation for the finer things life has to offer.

Your brain energy is boosted.

Because a language is a whole new complex system that includes grammar, vocabulary, and different rules and structures, your brain has to retrain itself to think. It has to absorb and assimilate all of it. As a result, your brain starts working more intensively, and your cognitive thinking, critical thinking, and problem-solving skills begin to evolve.

When speaking English, one always has to choose appropriate wording and phrases to express themselves in a meaningful way. Different languages have different nuances, idiomatic expressions, and meanings. Hence the speaker has to choose words and structures from the variety that they may know and negotiate the meaning before using a word in a sentence or a phrase. This involves massive problem-solving processes and needs practice and more practice.

Your memory is enhanced.

Your brain will serve you better if you utilize it more. Improving your fluency doesn't just involve using different structures, rules, words, and sentences. It also involves remembering how to use all the things mentioned earlier. That is why people who master multiple languages usually recall names, directions, and places better than people who master only their native language.

One more thing to note regarding multilingual people is that different studies show that people who know more than one language have very sharp minds, i.e., they can notice things better than monolinguals.

Your mother language improves.

We hardly ever think before we utter a word or a phrase in our mother tongue. We use the grammatical structures and the vocabulary that we have built up over the years, and we do so automatically. However, when learning a foreign language, we start comparing it with the one we already know. As a result, we start paying more attention to the grammar, vocabulary, punctuation, and structure of our native language. This experience provides us with the opportunity to improve our mother tongue as well. As a result, we become better communicators, listeners, and editors. These skills surely help us in our everyday life.

You become good at other subjects too.

Learning a new language helps improve your performance in other subjects too. Different studies suggest that multilingual people get high scores on various standardized tests and listening and comprehension exercises, as compared to monolingual people.

You get better career opportunities.

Employers like employees who can communicate properly. For you, this means you will have a greater number of career opportunities. The majority of employers think that fluent employees add value to the workplace and that their skills are vital for an organization or a company.

Being able to convey authority.

When you speak with a steadier voice that implies authority, people will, in turn, take you seriously, thinking that you have authority over them. Moreover, when you are the leader in your school or your work, your people will then believe that you have authority over them because you speak authoritatively.

Being able to entertain people.

Speaking well can eventually entertain your audience and sustain their interest in your speech. Always keep in mind that entertaining your audience is one of your aims when speaking. It makes you think about your listeners and how you would keep them interested in what you are saying instead of just focusing on how good or bad your performance will be. Good speaking skills help give your speech a variety in terms of the subject matter, volume, pace, tone, and others. It also gives you spontaneity, humor, enjoyment, and stories or anecdotes as you deliver your speech.

Being able to build a rapport.

In communication, you must keep connected with your audience. Always keep in mind that it is important that you know your audience and you build a rapport with them. Good speaking skills will, in turn, engage your audience to listen to you. Through excellent communication, you will be able to form positive connections with them.

Ways to Improve Your English Fluency

Many speakers of other languages strive to improve their spoken English. Their shared goal is to become fluent in their speaking capabilities. There are a variety of reasons why individuals put such a high value on gaining spoken English proficiency. There are numerous ways that this goal can be achieved. The best way, of course, is through regular practice.

You have a word base, you know a thing or two about grammar, but the question is: Are you capable of expressing yourself in English?

Terms and notions are an asset only for those who can use them. Learning how to use the knowledge you've so carefully gathered will be the hardest thing, the ultimate milestone.

However, don't get intimidated right away. By now, you already have all that you need to conquer this last objective. Trust yourself. Your efforts will be rewarded.

I have established a shortlist of practical tips that learners of English can employ to improve their English fluency day by day:

Talk to yourself, or try vlogging

Sure, the ideal way would be to talk with someone else in English, but you can do it yourself with no problems since that may not be so easy to do. The important part is to say the words and hear them coming out of your mouth.

You are comfortable with hearing the language, with reading it, but when did you even verbally use it? Rarely since everyone around you speaks in the language specific to your area. Again, if you have a fluent English friend, do not hesitate to swap languages with them for your usual conversations.

But, supposing that you have to do this on your own, take the opportunity to talk to yourself in English when you are alone, preferably in your house. Remind yourself of things that need to be done or say aloud a recipe while cooking things like that.

If that does not work out, try vlogging. Everybody does it every day, so no one will think wrong of you if they see you walking around and talking to a camera. Of course, you can keep the vlogs private, just as a learning method. No one will force you to make them public. Just think of it as a spoken journal.

The vlog can even bring out some extra benefits because you can watch them again and focus on details. Is your speech forced or strained? Do you look stressed when not using your native language? Is your mouth moving in the proper ways? Those can be the indicator of incomplete assimilation of the language. And that is fine. You can always go back to past steps and repeat them until you become genuinely comfortable using them.

The idea is to be fully accustomed to the English language, and that's only going to happen if you: listen, read, and speak. Until you can manage all of those, you are not prepared to call yourself advanced in English.

Read books or newspapers in English.

For the books, it is highly recommended to try the volumes that you've read a couple of times before in your native language, so you know the sequence of action. At first, it will be a shock. It will seem like a completely different book. The information is the same, but the way it's delivered will confuse you a lot. That's because, in translations, many sentences and expressions need to be changed to better fit the meaning of the respective language. After a few pages, this feeling of disorientation will go away. At all times, do not forget to search every single unknown word until its meaning is thoroughly imbued in your memory. This aspect is crucial.

With articles, it's simple. You are used to searching for things on the Internet in your native language because it's simpler and quicker. Take some time to switch to English. You can search for a topic that you have some knowledge about or newspaper articles because they use a common vocabulary to make it easier to understand.

This is important as it enables you to practice saying English words and listening to your pronunciation, and self-correct any mistakes that you might make. You may also read aloud to a friend or family member who can listen to your pronunciation. Aim to choose broadsheet newspapers instead of tabloid newspapers as you will expose yourself to a higher level of vocabulary and the use of a wide range of sentence structures and expressions.

Pay attention to the stress

In English, words can be stressed in different ways. If you put the stress in the right place, you will sound more like a native speaker. Stress is shown to show that some sounds in a word and some words in a sentence are more important than others. The following are several rules on English stress that you should bear in mind:

Word stress is put on the vowels only

One word cannot have more than one main stress, but it can have a secondary stress.

Several two-syllable nouns and verbs have different stresses while written in the same way, e.g., PRESent (noun) vs. preSENT (verb).

In longer words, the second or the third syllable from the end is usually stressed, e.g., geoLOgic, teleVIsion, and serenDIpity.

Sentences in English are also stressed. As said above, some words turn out to be more important in a sentence than others. Sentence stress is logical; in other words, it depends on what you want to say and what you consider important in your speech. Reading aloud and listening to different dialogues will help you understand the principles of sentence stresses and use them accurately.

Listen to music

It is a song you've heard many times before; you particularly like, and you've probably tried to mimic the singer who was nowhere near the song's actual lyrics, but you still do it. This impulse stimulates your brain and starts the primary learning pattern of humans born with: reproducing what we hear and see. That's why you will automatically try to replicate what you hear as best as you can.

Sure, at this level, it's pretty senseless. Even if you search for different words and learn a few notions, you won't remember them as there is no base. But some that are excessively used will remain neatly stored in your memory. Music helps this a lot with its simple pattern.

But the most important thing gained here is a small degree of comfort with the language. It's starting to sound like something normal to you, not a whole bunch of nonsense. You can easily recognize it and even manage to sing along with your favorite singer, even if the process is mechanical.

There's a start for everything, and music is ready to present in your life, in one form or the other. Just find tunes that suit your taste. It dramatically improves the understanding and learning process.

Watch movies or TV series

Again, this is an activity that's both enjoyable and useful. Most movies and series are produced in English, but that has not stopped any non-speaker from watching them regularly with the help of the all-mighty subtitles. And no one tells you to give up on them, not now anyway.

However, you can start to pay attention to the language too. Start correlating words with their meaning and getting used to their pronunciation. For this process, it's advisable to go for comedies or even animation movies and sitcoms. They generally use simpler terms so that younger audiences can view and understand them. It's a shame to not profit from this situation.

You can do this at all times while also spending time with family and friends. By now, English is no longer something new. Not quite like your native language, that's for sure, but still, cozy. Those with a "good ear" may already be far along on the path of claiming victory and "adopting" the language. Choose one TV show every month and start watching it right initially, not to miss a thing. By following the storyline and the acting of the characters, you will be able to get the idea of the whole show even if you think you do not understand most of what is being told there. You will be able to identify which accents and speech patterns are most similar to native English and will be able to mimic them over time by listening to a range of accents and speech types.

Hopefully, you will find a TV show that you can get mad about. As soon as you find one, you will spend a lot of time watching it. As a result, your pronunciation will improve, and you will become a more confident English speaker.

Listen to BBC online

There are many interesting and topical debates to listen to and enjoy. Whilst listening, ensure that you note down any new or interesting expressions that you hear. Then check the meaning of each expression and aim to learn the meanings.

Listen to BBC news. Pay attention to the pronunciation of words and note any new vocabulary that you come across. Check the meanings of new vocabulary in a dictionary and try to memorize them. This is an important step that will aid you in your aim of widening your existing vocabulary.

In other words, if you want to speak better, you must learn to listen better first. Odd, yet true, right? As a result, in this part, I'll go over some more listening techniques and resources that will assist you in becoming a better listener and speaker. Here we go. These are fourteen tips to improve your listening skills easily and without frustration.

Audiobooks are awesome so turn them on!

If you like reading, you will likely enjoy this technique of practicing listening. You can find a free audiobook from the website, or you can buy one. There are also lots of mobile apps that provide free audiobooks. Make sure you listen to it everywhere: in a bus station, while driving back home, when having a bath, when eating your dinner etc.

Audiobooks are especially useful since they include a really wide range of vocabulary and sentence structures. Also, the intonation and the word and sentence stress used by the audiobook's reader are awesome from the correct pronunciation and punctuation.

Take an online English lesson

You do not necessarily have to pay for taking an English course since there are plenty of tutorials and video lessons on YouTube and other platforms. Watching these tutorials might be useful, especially for beginners. If you feel you have problems understanding what other people say, then maybe you should start with English language tutorials to pronounce, at least, the easiest words and phrases correctly and to the point.

Try to copy someone else's way of speaking

Choose someone who speaks English very well. This could be an actor, a friend, or a politician. As soon as you choose the person, you will "copy," listen to something they say (choose a speech that lasts for a few minutes), and try to copy what they say by repeating both their words and the intonation. Imitation is a great way to reach the desired tone of voice.

Right at the beginning, you might sound rather silly to yourself. However, as time passes, you will notice that your speaking has improved considerably due to these imitation games.

Try to listen to something with your peer

Find a friend who also wants to improve their English speaking skills and offer to practice together. Choose a short audio or a video and listen to it first. Then start asking each other questions about what you have listened to or watched. This exercise will allow you to verify one other's pronunciation and correct each other's mistakes if you make any.

Listen to automatically generated speech

When you read something, and there is no audio for it, and you want to listen to how the words and the sentences in that text are pronounced, you can use any "text to speech" program to help you turn the text into audio. The computer will pronounce the text for you. Though it may seem strange, listening to the pronunciation and word emphasis can be beneficial to you.

Listen to someone who has problems speaking in English

Remember, we were discussing that people sometimes do not hear their accent. That is, they do not imagine how oddly they pronounce words and sentences. To find out whether you are among these people, try to find someone who speaks really bad English and listen to them for a while. When people are unsure about their speech, they unconsciously use lots of fillers and sounds in their speech. It is important that you know these sounds for what they are and avoid using them when speaking.

Talk to yourself

I know, only insane people converse with themselves. Well, you're going to have to pretend to be crazy for a while. So long as you don't do it while waiting in line or on the subway, everything should be fine.

Get used to (in the privacy of your home, of course) talking your way through whatever you are doing, arguing with the TV and radio, or reading out loud.

And here is where that smartphone comes in again. Use it to record yourself for a while as you repeat lines from a TV show, read from your favorite book, or just talk to yourself throughout the day. Doing so will give you a chance to hear the sound of your voice and just how good your pronunciation is.

Repeating lines from a show will be good here as you can listen to the show clip and then your recording to compare. You shouldn't worry about sounding exactly like the show recording, but it will allow you to hear how far or close you might be.

Going through all of these different simple techniques will help you learn, improve and refine your English to the point where at least people will not be asking you to repeat yourself; if not, to stop people asking where you are originally from.

Talk to others

Just as an English-speaking group is useful for being able to hear the language spoken, it is also helpful for giving you the opportunity to practice speaking it. By engaging in conversation with other English speakers, you will observe their reactions to your speech and benefit when they correct things like pronunciation and word usage.

Again, these things will vary depending on what version of English you are trying to be most familiar with. For example, in America, the word "jaguar" is pronounced "jag-wire," while in Britain, it is pronounced "jag-u-er."

In addition to an English group, try to speak it any chance you get. If you already reside in an English-speaking nation, you'll have plenty of chances to practice your English.

If not, you may need to pay attention to shops with the signs written in English or where you notice English being spoken.

Whenever you find such a place, try to keep the conversation going in English for as long as possible.

It may be that you live in an area that does not have a large enough population of people who speak English as their first language to warrant English signs.

However, English is a widespread second language, and it is not difficult to find people who at least speak a little. Simply initiate the conversation in English, and you will quickly find out if the shop owner you are talking to speaks it or not.

Ted Talks

The idea here is that you can watch a variety of speeches by different researchers, experts, and entrepreneurs from all over the world. You can find talks with subtitles in over 100 languages. Ted Talks will allow you to learn new things and listen to English speech at the same time. Their blog also has a lot of fascinating information to read.

Breaking News English

This is a free and printable platform where you can find lots of useful and interesting stuff to read. You can choose the level of your English proficiency and start practicing going up and up from one level to the other.

Online TV and movies in English

- provides you with the opportunity to watch TV shows and movies in English. However, it is a paid service and may have different restrictions and limitations in different countries. At the same time, it is worthwhile to give it a go.

- It is another paid website that streams popular shows in the US. Again, depending on your region, you may need to use a Virtual Private Network to access the website. Hulu also has got a wide variety of movies in English.

- It is also a paid service that provides movies in different languages.

-

Quora

Quora is an alternative platform to help you learn English. People ask and answer questions here. It's engaging, entertaining, and simple to use.

Elllo.org

This is another website that will help you with your spoken English. You can take different English lessons or simply watch videos. The most important thing here is the so-called mixers which are interactive audios where several people try to answer the same question. By listening to such audios, you will improve your spoken English and gain the confidence to speak like other learners do.

Paraphrase. Try different words and expressions

As soon as you feel confident in pronouncing several sets of words and phrases, start paraphrasing whatever you will say. If you feel you will pronounce a word in the wrong way, just try to find some other word to substitute for it. Let us consider several examples:

Instead of saying, "The ideas are rather controversial, I do not know how to describe them more comprehensively," you can say, "The ideas differ from each other greatly, and it becomes hard for me to explain them."

Instead of saying, "This risk management software turned out to be surprisingly efficient," you can say, "I am surprised at how effective this software for risk management is."

Instead of saying, "The managers take pains to distribute the work between the employees and to make sure that each of them presents a substantive demonstration of their assignment," you can say, "The managers work hard to give work to every employee and to make them show the tasks they completed in a simple and meaningful way."

The British Council

The British Council provides a wide variety of useful articles, exercises, online games, and much more. You can even download PDF questions, exercises, and articles to improve your English further.

Urban Dictionary

This website is for you if you believe you know English but can't pronounce those slangy American terms and phrases. You can search words here, and you can also just scroll the page and see what new American colloquialisms you can learn for today.

Start using contractions, as they're awesome!

As you might have noticed, native English speakers love using contractions in writing and oral speech. This is done mainly because people find it easier to pronounce two words when they can pronounce just one. This will give you the chance to sound fluent and native-like. Hence, make sure you say "let's" instead of "let us" or "don't" instead of "do not," or "aren't" instead of "are not." You can search the web and find different lists of contractions that you can use in your everyday speech.

NPR

NPR is another website for those people who want to learn American English. Here you will find lots of news and interesting stuff that is only in American English. Most upper-intermediate and advanced learners can use this website.

Record yourself and listen to your speech

You should see what gestures and mimics you use when speaking. This will help you improve your pronunciation since English is about sounds and gestures and the expression of your face. You can use various online tools and programs to record yourself on a camera. As soon as you record yourself reading something or telling a story, start comparing the recording with something similar. See how you and other people pronounce the same words and expressions. Consider whether there are too many differences between your speech and the speech of a native speaker. If there are, work to correct them.

Also, you can try to record yourself when repeating a native speaker's words and sentences. After you finish the recording, again consider checking the similarities and the differences in pronunciation. Try again as often as needed to make it perfect and sound like the native speaker does. Also, you can ask someone to listen to your recording and the original version to see whether you sound like the original version or not.

Practice English in a variety of contexts

Do not stick only to books and formal language; try to find ways to listen to and speak in more colloquial English. The language that is being used in the street might differ largely from the one that can be used in a workplace, and even at home. So, you need to find ways to make yourself familiar with all the contexts. The contexts that you might consider for your language practice and exercises include:

- Formal and non-formal
- Fiction and the real world
- Lectures and small talk
- Academic and comedy

In order to master the language fully, you should read academic texts and research articles and listen to various types of songs or watch movies. Just feel free to make your learning experience more diverse and fun!

5 Minute English

This website shows how fun language learning can be. With its numerous grammar and vocabulary games and quizzes, it will help you improve your English speaking, writing, listening, and reading skills up to any level you desire.

Read out loud

What if you knew there was a simple practice that could completely change the way you spoke English? That if you participated in this routine every day for as little as ten minutes, you'd be building your English speaking ability, not unlike an athlete improves his skill through daily practice?

Read much, read often, and do it in a loud voice. Reading fast in English is one of the ways to help you become a more natural English speaker. You need to read aloud for some 15-20 minutes every day. When you are reading, try to be as straightforward to understand as possible. Additionally, set a goal to read faster and faster every time. After you repeat this exercise for several weeks, you will notice how fast you started to read. Your reading will undoubtedly affect your speaking too.

Imagine what it would be like to speak the English language like a native without even the need to venture into any conversation with another person. Think again if something seems too wonderful to be true. You're about to be introduced to a simple ten-minute daily method that will do just that.

Not only that, but this simple method can help you keep up with those conversations among native speakers who ordinarily speak so fast that most students get lost and even discouraged.

Read a book written in English out loud. Yes, that's all there is to it. But there are a few criteria that go along with this exercise. The first caveat is that you have to read the words as fast as possible while retaining proper pronunciation. At first, this may seem like you're reading at a snail's pace, but as you continue to practice, you'll find yourself getting faster and comprehending the words more quickly.

Part of the key to this is the careful and deliberate pronunciation of words. Keep in mind that pronunciation depends on you to open and move your mouth correctly. When you pay attention to the movement of your mouth, you'll be pleasantly surprised at the improvement in your pronunciation.

Many individuals try this suggestion but are, quite frankly, just a bit skeptical of it. They're not quite sure how reading a book aloud could increase their skill to no one in particular. So why does it work?

Try to invest at least ten minutes daily reading out loud five days a week. In fact, why not try it for a month. At the end of the month, see if you notice any changes in your fluency.

There's no way around it; reading a book or newspaper out loud must improve your fluency in English. Ideally, you'll want to take time out of your morning to read out loud. And yes, I do mention this for a reason. This short, simple exercise loosens your speech organs, getting them accustomed to making the sounds of English.

Not only that, doing it before class jogs your memory of the sounds necessary for the language. You'll soon discover that your fluency will be significantly enhanced on those days you take the time to do this exercise.

One of the best aspects of this activity is that you may choose a book that intrigues you. Choose a novel you've always wanted to read or one of your favorite authors. If you're a sports fan, for example, you could read an autobiography of your favorite athlete or merely read the newspaper's sports section daily.

Remember, though, that you'll gain the most from this exercise when you read actively or observantly. What do I mean by that? Be involved in what you're reading. Use your mind taking note of the material being presented and the structure of the sentences, and the order of the words in sentences. Ideally, you'll transfer these observations into your daily practices. And the next thing you know, you're speaking English like you were born into it.

Regular revision

Ensuring that you set aside time to review and revise topics learned regularly is key to helping you successfully achieve your learning goals. To make sure that you remain committed, create a study schedule to set aside some time each week to devote to your studies. New topics or concepts can, of course, seem overwhelming at first, so it is necessary to review them again at a later stage. It is useful to make notes around new topics or concepts using your wording. This will enable you to understand concepts better, and it will, in turn, help you to remember and master them.

Use PHRASAL VERBS in most of your conversations

Phrasal verbs dominate spoken English. If you speak with native English speakers regularly, at the very least, you will need to become very familiar with and use the most common ones. People in English-speaking countries use phrasal verbs constantly, and many do not even realize they are using them. Sounding more like a native English speaker means that you will need to utilize phrasal verbs in your daily speech, especially during casual conversation.

Here is a quick tutorial on English phrasal verbs: English has hundreds and hundreds of phrasal verbs, and this means that studying them can be frustrating. The fact that a phrasal verb may have two or more meanings adds to the complexity. Despite all of this, native English speakers still prefer to use one-word verbs when they write and phrasal verbs (if possible) when they speak. Why is this?

The reason why English speakers use phrasal verbs so often is that they are idioms. An idiom is a combination of specific words, often called an expression, which expresses a different meaning from the "literal" meaning of each word. Items in an idiom symbolize other things. So they do not mean what they "say." For example, "Catch you later!" is a common English idiom that people say instead of "goodbye." It does not mean that someone will "catch" you in the future. The word "catch" is a symbol for the word "meet." However, notice that the word "catch" is similar to "meet" because both verbs involve physical interaction between two or more people.

Native English speakers use idioms, including phrasal verbs, because their meanings are very cultural, so they are easy to remember and simple to say. Also, since an idiom's meaning can change and evolve over long periods, the meaning of a phrasal verb can change and evolve. This is why one phrasal verb can have more than one meaning, which makes them so adaptable and helpful.

Always use the correct PREPOSITION

Preposition using or misusing prepositions when speaking English is not very serious. Even native English speakers use the wrong preposition once in a while (especially if they are speaking quickly). However, the majority of English learners usually adopt too casual an attitude concerning their preposition usage. Hence, they too often use the wrong one, and their English never sounds as correct as possible. Because English students often use erroneous prepositions, their English instructors frequently fail to correct them, and they never really understand how and when to utilize each preposition. As a result, their English is never perfected. If you always use the correct preposition, your English will sound better than those who do not, and in this regard, you will sound more like a native English speaker.

Chapter 19:
Exploring Your Voice

The human voice is a big part of who we are and how we perform in society. You bring your voice wherever you go; you can't just leave it at home, unlike your phones or your wallets (which you should not leave at home as well, but that is already a different story). And before we even start learning how to develop good speaking skills, we must explore our voice first.

Our voice is a potent and essential instrument that we have, for it tells other people many things about us. It also affects the way people perceive and create impressions about you.

Experts consider the human voice as a person's "calling card." They say that the voice speaks for yourself more than your outfits or your physical appearance do. Once people hear your voice, they automatically create assumptions about you based on what they have just heard.

Most people also tend to judge you based on how you talk to them or basically on how you speak. Some think that a person is not authoritative enough because their voice appears soft, though the case may otherwise. There are also times when someone perceives someone as impolite or disrespectful just because of what they have just stated. So apparently, your voice and the way you talk tell other people a lot about yourself.

Poet Henry Longfellow once said that "the human voice is the organ of the soul." How you would inspire and motivate other people may depend on how you talk to others. You can also move them and affect their viewpoints in life just by how you talk to them and the things you say to them.

Judy Apps, an international voice specialist as well as an author of some books about speaking, suggested the following considerations on how the power of your voice can change the way people think about you, either by lifting them or putting them down:

- As a manager, you can either make the people at your work appreciate your support or intimidate them just by talking to them.
- As a caregiver, you can give the people you are taking care of peace of mind and make them feel better or add stress to them.
- As a group leader, you can either motivate and energize your people to work harder and follow you, or you can discourage them from going on.
- As a parent or a guardian, you can either inspire your children to strive harder to achieve their goals in life or demotivate them to reach all their potentials.
- As a teacher, you can either boost your student's confidence in themselves or take away all their self-respect and self-esteem.
- As a coach, you can either encourage other people to reflect on themselves and call them to action or make them think that you are being oppressive and take their confidence away.

"Voice is an integral part of the whole message," says Apps. Our voice is responsible for giving life and meaning to everything we say. If you speak with a professional and confident voice, then people will most likely take you as a professional and even take you seriously.

Let us admit, though, that not everybody is gifted with good speaking skills. There are times when you just can't speak the way you want to. Regardless of how many times you want to sound authoritative, you just can't because your voice is so soft and calm. You get the point.

Also, those who are confident enough to speak in public get more opportunities than those who are not that assured. Even former United States Secretary Colin Powell once admitted in his autobiography that speaking in public easily and early in his life made a huge impact on his success. He was even promoted in work because he has good speaking skills.

However, it does not necessarily mean that only those good at speaking get to succeed in life. After all, not all good speakers are good since they were born; some are honed through practice.

Vocal Variety, Opposite of Being Monotone

Remember all of those old wildlife documentaries your teachers made you watch when you were a kid?

Or the historical 'reenactments' drowned out by narrative?

If you were like most kids, these were hardly the most riveting movies you'd seen all year. The actors weren't going to win any Oscars, and the writers would win no Emmys. You likely watched the screen with a blank, glazed overexpression and failed to retain much – if anything – that the video intended to explain.

If you were a child with an active imagination, you might have stayed wide awake by escaping to your inner daydream world – but few would blame you if you began to nod off and drool on your desk.

It's also likely that, after you struggled or failed to show comprehension or retention following these kinds of videos, one can judge you as being a lesser learner, less attentive, or some troublemaker.

Well, let that all fall away from you now. Because the fact is, it was never your fault in the first place.

These kinds of documentaries are often delivered by the most uncharismatic, most monotone voices possible to be heard by the human ear. You've already taken a seat at your desk, and the lights have most likely been dimmed as well.

Studies have shown that the human brain activity scales back significantly after only fifteen minutes of sitting, and darkness in a room signals to your brain that it is nighttime... and, therefore, time to sleep.

As if that wasn't enough to distract you and dull your senses, the video narrative contains little or no vocal variety. You may have had a teacher like this as well, or a boss, or even a parent. Someone so relaxed and low-key that their voice stays on a perfect level – does not drop in volume or raise higher.

To be an effective communicator, you need your audience to listen.

But, listen as they may; if you do not supply their brain with enough vocal variety, they will either be sleeping or off in another world in their heads.

Your voice is like the action in a movie. The movies that force you to stay awake and pay close attention are the ones like rollercoasters that speed up and slow down, relax and burst forward, whisper and shout.

Your vocal tones act as highlighters on your words. A pack of three thousand words with no emphasis becomes just that – words. But, place the proper emphasis, and your audience knows what is essential. Motivational speakers know precisely how this is done.

Go to a motivational seminar, and you will never hear the speaker say, 'and now you may applaud.' You know when to applaud because the speaker highlights what is important and forces you to hear them. Just the same, an intelligent parent never shouts at their child.

Why? Because, eventually, all the shouting makes their message dull.

If two people are shouting, no one is listening. If someone shouts at you, do not act in kind. Lower your voice and speak deliberately – it forces them to do the same. It is challenging to keep up a shouting match when there is no competition.

Avoid monotone speech – highlight your words with vocal emphasis.

Chapter 20:
Using Speech, Tone, and Pitch to Your Advantage

Your message is important, but how you deliver is probably even more critical if you want to be an effective communicator. The way you use intonation, pitch, tone, inflection, and other elements add more meaning to your message. In turn, giving it more character and making it more interesting.

1. Emphasize on the Right Word

This may sound unbelievable, but merely emphasizing the wrong word can send an entirely different message to the other person. Let us take a sentence like, "Did you steal my footwear?" Now the meaning of the phrase will keep changing depending on which word you emphasize. Say, for instance, a person emphasizes 'you' while asking this question; it implies the person is unsure about or wants to know whether you did it or someone else did it.

Similarly, if they emphasize 'steal,' it may imply the person wants to know if you stole the book or borrowed it. Again, emphasizing 'my' implies whether it was the person's or someone else's footwear that was stolen. Then focusing or emphasizing on 'footwear' may imply whether you stole the person's footwear or something else. Do you get the drift? Emphasizing the right word can make all the difference in conveying the correct meaning without falling prey to any misunderstandings.

2. Use Inflection to Your Advantage

Use intonation to communicate the right emotions about how you are feeling or the emotions you are experiencing. That doesn't mean you should speak in a sing-song manner all the time. It just means you should vary your tone/pitch high and low if you don't want to sound dull or wish to communicate the right meaning of what you're trying to express. Intonation helps complement your words to know exactly how you are feeling.

It may also be used to show that you are confident in your statements. It communicates to the other person whether you are commanding, requesting, suggesting, or angry while speaking, eliminating any potential misunderstandings. Imagine how unfortunate it will be if a harmless or straightforward request comes across as a command. Or if a mere suggestion makes it seem like you are ordering the person to do something or coming across as condescending. This is precisely how misunderstandings in communication occur; when your intonation doesn't effectively communicate what you are trying to say.

Other than conveying the right meaning, intonation also makes your talk comes across as more interesting. It adds more color and character to your speech.

Again, there are three pitches while speaking. The high, middle, or regular, and low! And there's nothing like the perfect pitch while talking. Play around with different pitches while speaking. Use them to your advantage for putting across your point compellingly and effectively.

3. Rate of Speech

One of the golden rules if you want to convey your point more effectively and compellingly is to maintain a steady and medium-paced rate of speech (depending on your listener, of course). People may be unable to understand what you are saying if you talk too quickly. However, sputtering may make you come across as energetic, enthusiastic, and alive. Listeners will try to grab a few words here and there, but comprehension may seem tough beyond that.

Again, speaking slowly will make you sound serious, grim, and emphatic. Listeners may catch every word, but they are sure to be bored to death waiting for you to finish. A slow speech can be used when you are trying to communicate an important point or when you want the other person to reflect upon what you've spoken. This can be used in combination with pausing at the right moment to give the listener more time to absorb your message.

4. Use Proper Pronunciation and Articulation

It is easy to understand correctly pronounced and articulated words. Faulty pronunciation is not just annoying; it also has the scope to lead to plenty of misunderstandings. Get familiar with using phonetics to articulate words in the right manner. You'll produce the correct sound and representation. Always open your mouth and speak. You'll be loud and audible. Move your mouth, jaw, and tongue freely. Aspirate sounds are meant to be aspirated for greater clarity. A single letter can have more than one sound. Also, be mindful of short and long sounds.

For instance, beet and bit are pronounced in different ways by pulling and constricting the sound. Similarly, "fool" and "full" are pronounced differently. How words are pronounced changes their meaning. Different pronunciations can give words different meanings.

The "th" is pronounced as soft "th" in "thin" and a harder "th" in "they." Similarly, "tin" and "thin" are not pronounced in the same way. Also, "day" is not the same as "they." Know the difference between pronouncing hard and soft consonants. One of the best ways to get this right is by practicing tongue twisters and doing mouth exercises. Remember this, articulate the right sounds without exaggerating them to avoid sounding fake.

5. Practice and Use 'PAIR'

The idea is to put 'PAIR' into action. 'PAIR' is Pronunciation, Articulation, Inflection, and Rate. Start with the right articulation and volume.

Bring greater clarity to your speech, combine inflection and rate of speech to build a melody as one speaks. Practice enhancing your 'PAIR' to come across as smart, confident, and effective in your speech. Some of the most charismatic speakers use 'PAIR' to their advantage.

I share this tip with a lot of people. Record yourself while speaking to assess how you sound to others. Pay attention to your inflection, pronunciation, vocabulary, volume, and rate of speech. Another power-packed method is to practice in front of the mirror. Pay attention to your body language, mouth movements, gestures, and expressions while talking. It will give you a firm grasp of the nonverbal signals you utilize while communicating with others. Practice recording and speaking in front of the mirror to turn into an exceptional speaker or communicator.

6. Build a Powerful Vocabulary

One of the essential elements of being a powerful communicator is to enrich your vocabulary. You should possess an extensive vocabulary to convert concepts or ideas into words or compellingly articulate your thoughts. You can communicate what you want to express effortlessly if you have a rich vocabulary. A speaker also comes across as more exciting and confident when they use different words. Consider the difference between a black-and-white picture and a vibrant, colorful one.

Having an incredible vocabulary allows the listener to paint a colorful picture in their mind about what the speaker is saying. It also helps avoid redundant words and phrases. However, one of the traps to guard against while enhancing your vocabulary is using complicated or highfalutin words just to sound impressive. The idea is to articulate your thoughts and feelings using the most compelling and appropriate words. This makes the right impact. If you use unnecessarily complex words, people may not understand what you are trying to communicate.

Make it a daily aim to learn a new word. Keep a notebook to list down words, which can be highly effective. Remember the word by understanding its definition, stating it aloud, and writing it in a book. You can also use a ton of vocabulary applications available on your smartphone.

Chapter 21:
Tuning Up – How to Make Your Voice Sound Pleasant?

Your voice, like your face, is one of your most distinguishing features. People are reluctant to take you seriously if your voice doesn't match up. You may be a fascinating person in the room, dressed nicely, and have excellent listening skills, but if your voice doesn't line up, people are unlikely to take you seriously. It's unjust, but that's simply human nature.

We assess the quality of someone's voice in a few seconds. Fortunately, you can take advantage of this. Consider this: simply altering the way you talk, you might immediately improve your social standing.

It would be ideal if you worked hard to keep your voice heard, clear, and intelligible at all times. Even if you have a strange accent, voice training may help you communicate more effectively with others. The perfect voice represents the individuality of the speaker. It should, however, constantly convey that you are forceful and outspoken.

This does not imply that you should yell and attempt to take over the room. It implies you should be confident in both what you're saying and how you're expressing it. Let's have a look at some of the most effective exercises for improving your voice:

Loosen Your Lips

People with the most appealing voices effectively pronounce their words. Even if you don't agree with what they're saying or find their demeanor off-putting, listening to someone who pronounces their words correctly makes you more inclined to enjoy the discussion.

The key to excellent pronunciation is to maintain your tongue and lips relaxed, in addition to appropriate breathing. This technique may also help you conceal a lisp, which can boost your confidence if you have one. Start practicing if you slur your words or never sound them out correctly.

When you're alone, read aloud from a book or just practice repeating popular words. When you pronounce your words, pay attention to how your mouth, throat, and chest feel. You'll be able to determine how each word should sound with practice and adjust your voice accordingly.

Breathe From Your Diaphragm

The most powerful speakers breathe via their diaphragms rather than their throats. If you want a rich, full voice that doesn't quiver or crack, breathe deeply and steadily. If you breathe from your upper chest rather than your belly, your shoulders will rise and fall with each breath.

Silent laughter can help you learn how to regulate your abdominal muscles by engaging your diaphragm. Force yourself to laugh via your nose by closing your mouth. Reading aloud may also be beneficial.

Look for a paragraph in a book or article that has a variety of sentence lengths. Inhale deeply from your diaphragm as you begin each phrase and exhale as you near the finish. This will help you maintain a pleasant, even tone in your voice.

Hum and Sing

When we're alone (or even with people), we hum and sing, so why not utilize it to practice changing the pitch of our voices? Consider the range of your voice when you hum or sing your favorite tunes. Do you have a wide vocal range, or does it seem confined and limited?

Play around with the many noises you can create. Being forced to listen to someone who talks in a monotone is one of the most soul-destroying experiences one can have. You must learn to change your voice if you want other people to find you intriguing. It's as much about melody as it is about substance in a conversation. Many of us have developed the practice of speaking at a constant high tone, which does not inspire confidence or convey authority.

You shouldn't strive for a gravelly tone of voice, particularly if you're a woman, but deep and rich tones are preferred over high and thin tones in general. Don't attempt to alter your pitch in a single day dramatically. Your voice will be strained, and your friends and family will most likely inquire whether you have a cold.

Instead, concentrate on reducing it a little, then lowering it again in a few days. Experiment with different pitches while singing an "ah" sound. If you repeat this practice on a regular basis, you will acquire complete control of your pitch.

Watch Your Intonation

Varying your pitch doesn't just make your speech easier and more pleasant to listen to. It also changes how people interpret your message. This can have serious consequences if you get it wrong. For example, take the following question:

"Will you be home by midnight?"

On the face of it, this looks like a neutral request for information. But what happens if you vary the intonation? If you asked the question in a flat, almost disinterested voice, the person you are asking might infer that you don't care whether they make it home safely or not.

They aren't going to feel particularly loved or cared for, and this may lead to a fight. When certain words inside a phrase are highlighted, it creates a totally different impression. "Will you be home by midnight?" for example.

"Are you going to be home by midnight?"

Say each variation of this phrase aloud to see how different emphasis may make a difference. The speaker, in the first case, seems impatient or angry as if they had previously requested but not yet gotten the other person's schedule.

The speaker in the second case wants their discussion partner to come home, but they aren't sure it will happen - they need assurance. Examine your tone if you're talking to someone and they're not responding the way you'd anticipate. Are you unintentionally conveying a certain meaning? Is it possible that your discussion partner is offended as a result?

Move Your Voice Forward

Do you make noises at the front of your mouth or in your throat? Your words should ideally develop on your lips rather than in your throat. The key is to keep your jaw and throat muscles relaxed. You may accomplish this with a simple but powerful exercise.

Take deep breaths while lying on your back. Make use of your diaphragm. Exhale via your mouth rather than your nose at all times. Relax your jaw, mouth, and throat by making a deliberate effort to do so. Check to see whether each exhale is smooth. Say the sound "ah" as you exhale. Rep these actions a few times more, keeping your mouth open the whole time.

Should you ever feel as though your muscles are under any kind of strain? Then, with each exhale, count to five. Continue doing so until it feels natural and at ease. You should be able to pronounce each number without difficulty.

Keep in mind that the purpose of this exercise is to teach you how to relax your muscles so that your voice may flow freely. You are probably not calm if it gets tough. You may also sit down and stand up to continue this workout.

Vocal training is beneficial, but don't overdo it. You push your vocal cords and muscles to operate in new ways when you train your voice. It would be preferable if you did not harm them. The public speaking and leadership organization Toastmasters advises its members to keep training sessions brief (under five minutes) and spread out throughout the day.

Think About Rate and Timing

Would you mind taking a moment to consider the way someone you respect and admire sounds when they speak? Do they converse slowly or in a middle-of-the-road manner? A steady pace is seen by most people as a sign of confidence and authority.

However, there is no one "best" pace that should be used by everyone. If we all attempted to talk at the same pace, the world would be a pretty boring place. If you're naturally talkative, extroverted, or a rapid thinker, you'll probably speak quicker than someone who's introverted or prefers to think about everything before speaking. The average person speaks between 120 and 190 words per minute, which is quite a range.

To determine if you are a quick or slow speaker, do the following:

- Choose a paragraph from a book or article to read aloud.
- Keep track of your time.
- Do this exercise a few times more.
- Do the arithmetic to figure out which category you belong in. Because many of us aren't aware of how we sound, the findings may surprise you.

It's difficult to alter your natural speaking pace, but most people will comprehend what you're saying if you breathe properly and pronounce your words. You may opt to speed up or slow down during an important discussion with someone.

What if you don't have an engaging voice, and the activities above aren't working for you? You don't have to be concerned; you can employ a vocal coach. Few of us are born with great voices, but with a little assistance from others, you may develop one.

There's no reason to be self-conscious. Politicians and other prominent figures are constantly offered assistance! They understand that their public image is influenced in large part by how they sound, so if you think your voice is holding you back, search for singing coaches and instructors in your region. You may even take a few acting classes if you love the theater and performing.

When evaluating their students' development, most singing instructors record their pupils during sessions and subsequently play back the results. When you can hear your own voice, it becomes obvious – sometimes brutally so – where you need to improve.

This isn't very enjoyable at first. "Do I sound like that?" be prepared to exclaim. In the beginning, I found voice exercises to be a little distressing. I was shocked by how squeaky my voice sounded the first time I read through a speech and then played it back to myself.

I loved to imagine myself speaking in low tones. I was completely incorrect. Fortunately, I did some study and have gotten comments on my speaking voice! You can do it if I can.

If you realize that you might benefit from some outside input but don't have the funds or time to seek out and visit a vocal coach, enlist the assistance of your most eloquent friend or family. Even if they don't understand the mechanics of appealing speech, they'll be able to correct you.

Just be aware that you may get bad feedback. If you ask someone to be honest with you, be prepared to hear something that doesn't make you feel good! Don't get down on yourself. You will quickly notice a change if you perform voice exercises.

Sex Differences

Both men and women, on average, get more respect and attention when they talk in a warm, even tone with appropriate pitch and tone fluctuation. If you want to attract someone of the opposite sex, though, the picture alters significantly. Males, for example, like women who speak at a higher pitch than men, and women appear to know this instinctively — study indicates that when chatting to a guy they find attractive, they immediately raise their voices.

Women are attracted to guys who have a lower voice tone. Scientists are baffled as to why this is. It may come down to the qualities of an attractive partner. Men like young-looking women, and a breathy, high-pitched voice hints to a youthful, appealing appearance.

Women tend to choose dominant, masculine, and self-assured mates, and a smooth, rich voice implies that a man possesses these traits.

Both sexes may, however, sound equally dominating. Your voice, regardless of sex, may be used to convey confidence.

Size plays a role in the equation as well. A bigger physical size is linked with a deeper voice, while a smaller frame is associated with a higher pitch. Women prefer males who are bigger than the typical woman, while men prefer larger than the average man.

This implies that raising the tone of your voice will make you more appealing and feminine-sounding if you are a woman. If you want a lady to find you attractive, you should talk in a lower tone of voice.

Chapter 22:
Tone of Voice – The Other Nonverbal Indicator

In communication, nonverbal signals are far more compelling than mere words. One of these signals is body language. The other is your tone of voice. And like body language, tone of voice can heavily influence a person's meaning and can just as easily be misinterpreted, depending on pitch and volume. Pitch denotes highness or lowness, while volume concerns loudness or softness. And depending on the situation or environment (e.g., background noises) or even the person you are conversing with, you adjust your tone of voice accordingly. Your listener might be hard of hearing and will fail to catch what you're saying if your voice is too soft. If you end up shouting so, they can hear you, and it might backfire as they might think you're angry and yelling at them. Or you may think you have something interesting to say, but you can't figure out why your listener does not seem to share your enthusiasm. Perhaps you're so monotonous that the excitement of the subject is lost in the delivery. So how do you remedy such problems? It takes time and practice to create a clear and attractive voice, but it's definitely worth the effort.

But just what is the ideal tone of voice? Is it musical and lyrical?

Should it be deep and commanding like Darth Vader? Is it breathy, or should it be more cheerful, friendly, and high-pitched? Desirable as all these qualities are, the perfect tone of voice for you is the one that can adequately accentuate your message so that people understand you completely. Because you'll be more direct with the appropriate tone of voice, you'll be more enjoyable to listen to. Your listener won't have to work hard to get what you mean. For example, if you speak all the time and sound harshly as though you're barking, even if what you're saying is 'Hello' or 'Good morning,' no one's going to want to hear it.

To work on this, first, you must find out how your tone of voice sounds. As in body language, you could use a mirror to observe yourself as you speak. How do your mouth and tongue enunciate each vowel and consonant? Are your neck muscles tense or relaxed? Are you barely even breathing at all?

Then recording yourself would be ideal: you could read a piece from a book or an article from a newspaper, or you could record an actual discussion with someone. Make sure you speak and sound as natural as possible. Then play it back and listen carefully. How do you sound? Is your voice expressive, or is it flat and dull? Do you articulate clearly, or do you mumble? Is your tone too high or low pitched, or in a pleasant mid-range? Is your voice well-modulated, or twangy, metallic, or harsh?

If you are monotonous, one can fix this by adjusting your pitch to match essential points in your conversation. Explore your range, go up and down the scales, and exercise those vocal cords. Watch movies with speeches or monologues and observe how the actors deliver their lines and emphasize certain places. Try to emulate them and rehearse on your own.

Once you're satisfied, try reading the same passage and re-recording yourself. Are there any marked improvements in your tone of voice and inflection? Keep practicing till you acquire it for good.

Body language not only affects what you say but how you say it. Try to remain calm and relax your throat, shoulders, chest, and abdominal muscles so that you can sound more straightforward and more pleasant and in control. Lower your volume the closer you are to your listener. If you are some ways off from them, speaking loudly will work, but it would be even better if you approached them before talking so that you don't have to yell in the first place. It's common courtesy, too.

Chapter 23:
Pronunciation Strategies

Learning more about the language you want to speak is one of the first things you should do to enhance your pronunciation.

For example, if you want to learn how to speak the English language, you must understand the basic rules of English. If you don't follow those rules, you wouldn't be able to pronounce words smoothly.

Awareness

After learning the different rules of English, you should then try to pinpoint the common mistakes you usually make in your speech.

The ideal thing to do is keep a list that includes all the pronunciation errors that you often commit and those mistakes that people around you commonly criticize regarding the way you speak.

It will help if you can hire an English tutor who will help you improve your pronunciation.

However, if you don't have the budget to get a tutor, you can do it yourself by simply listening and repeating. There's an abundance of inexpensive audio books that teaches eager learners how to pronounce words correctly. Audio books are readily available online or at any local bookstore near you.

Continuously listening to yourself, taking note of how you say different English words, and comparing your pronunciations with experts will help you become aware of your pronunciation errors. Once you recognize these errors, it will be easier for you to correct them.

Monitoring

Monitoring simply means taking notes, both mental and physical, of all the corrections that you need to make to improve your pronunciation skills. This is critical since it allows you to keep track of the words you're having trouble pronouncing.

That is why it is also vital that each time you get corrected by somebody, you have to note down the correction given to you.

By monitoring and constantly updating your list, it will be easier for you to determine the words you usually pronounce incorrectly. Once you have determined what those words are, correcting them will not be hard.

Maintaining a list of the words you commonly say the wrong way will reveal that you repeatedly repeat pronunciation mistakes. Monitoring that pattern will surely help you correct your mistakes faster.

Practice

After pinpointing the words, you have a hard time saying that the next thing to do is to force yourself to practice saying the correct pronunciation repeatedly. The correct pronunciation will also include the proper syntax and how to use the words correctly in a sentence.

In almost every kind of endeavor, practicing regularly makes it easier for you to master things. As the saying goes, practice makes perfect. So if you want to achieve perfection in pronunciation, never get tired of practicing repeatedly.

The best way to practice is by saying the words out loud. Make it a habit to listen to the different sounds you make and compare them to those made by experts. Talking out loud to yourself will surely help you start thinking in English, rather than simply translating what you want to say. So, try to get accustomed to freely speaking in English without worrying too much that someone might hear you and possibly criticize you because you are not good with pronunciation.

It will also help if you practice in front of a mirror. This way, you can see how your mouth moves or where your tongue goes each time you utter a word. There are lots of exercises for the mouth that you can do to improve the way you syllabicate and sharpen your pronunciation skills as a whole.

There is no quick fix for bettering your pronunciation. Although practicing will not improve your English communication skills overnight, as though some magical wand has been waved, it will help you gain confidence in speaking a language other than your native tongue. It will be hard for you to pronounce some of the words at first, but with regular practice, both your mouth and tongue will get used to it – eventually making it easier for you to say things correctly.

Self-correction

With constant practice, you will surely develop the important habit of correcting yourself every time you mispronounce a word or two.

Self-correction is crucial in the improvement of your pronunciation. Acknowledging your mistakes and correcting them will make you a better speaker.

You should always be aware of how you talk in English to notice and hear the mistakes you make regarding pronunciation. Nevertheless, please take note that the capability to self-correct can only be done if you've understood the concept of awareness and monitoring.

Don't feel terrible about yourself if you believe you're correcting yourself much too often; in the end, being able to recognize your mistakes and doing all you can to fix them will make you a better speaker and person overall.

Write What You Say

Improving your pronunciation skills doesn't only involve saying words correctly. Another way of improving communication through pronunciation is by writing down things in English.

If you find it hard to say certain English words, what you can do is write these words down and ask someone who speaks the language fluently to tell you what the right pronunciations are.

Since pronunciation is part of communication, and communication can be both spoken and written, improving your pronunciation can be done through speaking and writing.

Increase Your Vocabulary

Another way of improving pronunciation is by increasing your vocabulary. Vocabulary means knowing the definition of a word so that you use them properly in communicating with people.

The best way of increasing your vocabulary is by constantly reading the dictionary. A dictionary is a book that contains a collection of alphabetically listed words and contains all sorts of information (such as the definition of a word, its origin or word etymology, proper syllabication, and right pronunciation).

Reading dictionaries to improve your vocabulary will have a positive effect on your pronunciation in the long run. After all, once you understand what different words in the English language mean, you will learn how to use these words correctly.

Think in English

People who wish to enhance their pronunciation often make the error of first thinking about what they want to say in their original language and then mentally translating it into English before speaking it.

This is a bad thing because there are lines of thoughts that can't be translated directly into English. English syntax and word order are two things that need to be taken into account when trying to translate anything.

If you want to say something in English, you have to be confident with what you want to say. Pronunciation needs to be done with confidence because you won't communicate effectively if you are unsure of what you are saying.

Another way to "think in English" is to try and imitate spoken English. In other words, you have to copy how someone speaks the English language. If you like how a person speaks English, why not try to copy some of that person's lines completely?

Have you ever tried to make fun of somebody who's from another part of your country by imitating that person's accent? To improve pronunciation, that is actually what you need to do.

Train Your Ears

If you want to improve your pronunciation, another thing that you can do is to train your ears. Train your ears in listening to how the English language is spoken as much as possible.

You may improve your hearing by doing a variety of activities. Try listening to radio programs and audiobooks. It'd also be advantageous to watch television shows (or movies) where English is the medium of communication. Also, you can listen to a free podcast on iTunes called "Elementary English".

One simple yet effective exercise that you can do to improve pronunciation through listening is closing your eyes while listening to an English song, show, or movie. Try to listen very carefully to what is being said, and then attempt to make the same sounds afterward. Hear the sound, not see the sound.

Chapter 24:
Try Getting Rid of Fillers

It's best if you wouldn't use fillers while talking. They just make you look nervous and would make the audience feel like they're listening to a person who doesn't know what he's talking about.

Fillers are any of the following:

1. Uhm, ah, hmm, ah, etc. (Filler Sounds)
2. Literally, actually (Filler Words)
3. You know, I think, I guess (Filler Phrases)

Fillers are signs of verbal static—which means that you have gotten suddenly nervous and you have no idea how to go forth with your speech anymore. They weaken your credibility.

So, practice! Here's something you could do to stop yourself from using those fillers.

Make an Assessment

For this, it would be best to seek the help of an audience member—or a friend. Try to make a speech (practice the speech you're planning to use for a presentation), and then ask your friend to keep track of the fillers you have used and their impact on the speech itself.

Make use of a digital recorder to playback your voice and hear what you have been saying. Or, you could also record yourself on video—so you could also check your gestures and facial expressions.

Then, answer the following questions:

1. How often do you use fillers?
2. Do those fillers distract you and the audience?
3. Does it taint your credibility?

Slow Down—and Embrace the Pause

One of the easiest ways to combat fillers is to make sure that you slow down a bit. No one's running after you, anyway. No one's coming towards you, and besides, not everyone would be able to understand you if you keep blabbing about without slowing down.

You don't have to be extremely slow, of course, but it would be nice to speak slowly so you could also enunciate the words clearly, instead of making people feel like they don't even know what you're talking about.

Now, when you're about to use fillers, choose to pause instead. Just make sure you won't let it go over 5 seconds or so. This way, you can also create momentum, and you can just ask the audience a question or make a joke. That's better than using fillers.

Be Prepared

Sometimes, you use fillers just because you are not prepared enough. In short, it would be best to:

1. Relax. Again, try to do some breathing exercises, and you'd be able to continue with your speech better.
2. Learn how to use variations of words. Try to brush up on your vocabulary a bit, and learn at least 5 to 10 variations of words (i.e., very = extremely, incredibly, awfully, exceptionally, etc.) so you'll have a lot of things to say, and you'll be able to express yourself better.

Monitor Your Progress

The next time you make a speech, record yourself again, and check the following:

1. What is the frequency of filler words in your speech now?
2. What is the correlation between preparedness and being filler-free?
3. Have you managed to slow down your pace?
4. Do you think the negative impact of fillers has already been reduced?
5. Are you pausing, or are you still using fillers?

Practice makes perfect. Sooner or later, you'll use fillers less—just make sure you have followed the tips given here.

Filler Phrases to Avoid Awkward Silence in a Conversation

Okay, so I'd want to inform you that speaking English is really very easy, yes! So, if I took away the phrases uh, well, you know, like I could have just stated, "English speaking is very simple," what did I just do? Why? Because filler words like the uh, like, you know, they make you seem insecure, but let me tell you, filler words, at least some of them, aren't all that terrible. Don't trust me when I say that a few filler words may really make you seem more assured. Okay, here's the truth: while I was learning English, a few filler words helped me keep my conversation going without any uncomfortable pauses or seeming insecure. So, if you're experiencing a similar problem, don't worry. I'm here to help you speak confidently by teaching you how to utilize filler phrases so that you don't seem like you don't know what to say or that there's nothing more you can say while you're talking, right? So let's look at some filler phrases that can help you talk fluently and confidently.

Basically

So, I've got two filler phrases for you, the first of which is a filler term called "essentially." Now, how can I use it in a discussion without seeming stupid since I don't know what to say? Well, let me tell you, it's essentially a filler term that you use when you need to think about your response or remark. For example, I might remark, "If I want to perform well, I need to study better essentially." Alternatively, "I essentially need a better study plan." So, rather than pausing to say, "I need a better study plan," you simply said, "I need a study plan," giving you time to think about what you were going to say next, right?" So, if you want to boost your confidence, don't be afraid to use that filler term.

Actually

"Really, I believe that a better study plan is very necessary," you may now say with 'or... actually.' Instead of waiting and pondering, utilize the filler word "actually I believe..." followed by your real point, which is that a better study plan is essential.

Something like that

Or... anything along those lines is a frequent filler phrase. So, what's the point of that? When you're not sure about the precise quantity, you express that in a sentence, so let's say I'm making a cake, right? How many of us like making cakes? So, I was making a cake so I could say, "This cake recipe calls for six eggs and maybe four sticks of butter or something along those lines." So, what am I doing in this place? Instead of providing the incorrect number and worrying about it, I'll say this cake needs six eggs and four sticks of butter or anything along those lines, or I might add, "Well, we'll take about ten minutes or something along those lines." Okay, so that's another filler phrase you may use if you're unsure what to say.

I mean

'I mean...' is the next filler phrase you may employ. Have you ever heard someone say that? Isn't it rather common? Why do they say that, exactly? They say that when they're trying to clarify or emphasize what they're going to say, so let's say I'm trying to hire a guy to work for me. I'm in an interview, and I think he's a great guy, but I don't think he's right for the job, so I can say something like, "I mean... you're a great guy, but I don't think you're right for this particular job," or "I mean Right? So, instead of being uncomfortable and saying, "Um, you're not qualified for this job," say, "Um, you're not qualified for this job." I'm just saying you're a wonderful person, but you're not cut out for this position. So this statement is intended to ensure that you rectify your errors when speaking. For example, if you make a mistake while speaking, you may remark, "I have 23, I mean 24 books on this subject." Alternatively, "I authored 25 articles, no-no, 27 articles on this topic."

So, how can you include filler words into your conversations? I feel it's a question of practice; when you're speaking, it's important to be conscious of how you can place things in the correct context, so I think it's fascinating to discover that native English speakers use filler phrases and filler words often. Still, you'll be able to learn from them.

Chapter 25:
Body Language
Body Language in Communication

Non-verbal form of contact is a tremendously difficult yet vital part of general communication abilities. Conversely, individuals are frequently unconscious of their non-verbal actions. Researchers connect big significance to the individuals' ability for verbal communication. However, people have a corresponding path of nonverbal contact, which might disclose more than our cautiously selected language. Most of the nonverbal gestures and understanding of pointers are involuntary and carried out beyond our awareness and power. On the other hand, we unsuspectingly convey plenty of messages regarding our physical and mental states using our nonverbal signals. The signs we bring out, the pose in which we embrace our hands, the expressions we put on our bodies, and the nonverbal persona of our talking contribute to how other people perceive us.

A fundamental responsiveness of nonverbal contact approaches, above what is stated, might assist in developing communication with other people. The familiarity of these secret languages might support individuals to speak about their worries and may result in a superior understanding, which is the function of interaction. When we speak regarding body language, we consider the delicate signals we give and get to from others nonverbally. Several individuals wish to understand how to interpret body language. Body language might be clustered into a few categories:

Facial expressions

Scholars revealed seven widespread micro-expressions or small facial signals every person portrays if they feel a powerful feeling. People are attracted to observing the face to know if somebody has concealed feelings. The small signals shown on our faces are a vital element of nonverbal communication.

Body Proxemics

This is an expression of how a human body shifts in air. We are continuously observing how somebody is making progress, making gestures, leaning, shifting forward or backward. Body activities notify people a lot regarding inclination and anxiety. Movements are involved in body language signals.

Ornaments

Outfit, necklaces, and hairstyles are all added to the nonverbal indicators. Specific paints and fashions send indicators to other people; how we interrelate with our ornaments is also important. Is somebody an adorer of their phone? Do they continuously touch their necklace? We must notice these vital body language signals.

Interpretation of body language

Reading body language might sound like a difficult task; however, mastering the art of interpreting them is vital. There are two methods of understanding body language in other people. Decoding is the capability of reading people's prompts. It entails how people read concealed feelings, information, and traits from an individual nonverbal signal. Encoding is the skill of sending signals to other persons. Encoding plays a key role in controlling your trademark. The first feeling you provide and how you make someone think when you meet them for the first time.

Significance of nonverbal cues in interactions

Emphasizing what is stated verbally.

For instance, individuals might nod energetically when meaning yes to emphasize that they concur with the other individual. A gesture of the shoulders and a gloomy face when stating, "I am okay, thank you" might mean that matters are not all right at all.

Convey information about their emotional state.

Someone's facial appearance, their pitch of tone, and their body language might notify somebody precisely what you are undergoing, even when they have barely uttered a sentence.

Strengthen the link between persons

When you have observed partners discussing, you might have detected that they tend to mirror one another's nonverbal signals. They place their arms in parallel poses, laugh uniformly, and frequently look at each other. These activities strengthen their affair; consequently, building on their relationship, and assist them to feel coupled.

Offer response to the other individual.

Laughing and nodding inform somebody that you are paying attention and concur with what they are putting across. Body shifting and hand signs might point out that you desire to talk. These slight signs provide information quietly but unmistakably.

Normalize the course of interaction

There are several signs that people use to inform others that they have completed or wish to talk. A resounding nod and strong closure of the lips show that someone has no intention of speaking anymore. Maintaining eye contact with the person in charge of a conference and nodding faintly shall show that you desire to talk.

Features of Body Language

There are many kinds of body language. This is because we are unable to group similar styles into a single category. It is possible to differentiate between several body languages. So, how can you tell the difference between various body language styles? Body language is usually split into two columns. This covers body components as well as the intention.

So, what sorts of people may be found in each class?

Let's start with the components of the body and the messages they send.

- The Head - The position of the head and its movement, including hair shake, back and forth, right to left, and side to side.

- Facial expressions are included in this category. It's worth noting that the face contains a number of muscles varying in size from 54 to 98, all of which function to move various parts of the face. The condition of your thoughts is depicted by the motions of your face.

- Eyebrows - The eyebrows may move up and down, as well as frown, to express themselves.

- Eyes - You can roll, move up and down, right and left, blink, and dilate your eyes.

- The Nose - The flaring of the nostrils and the development of wrinkles at the top of the nose show the expression of the nose.

- The Lips - The lips can be seen snarling, smiling, kissing, opened, closed, tight, and puckering.

- The Tongue - The tongue can roll in and out, go up and down, touch while kissing, and also lick the lips.

- Body Proximity - This is a measurement of how close your body is to other individuals.

- Shoulder Movements - Up and down, slumped and hanging

- Arm Movements - Up and down, straight and crossed

The legs and feet may express themselves in a variety of ways. They may be straight, crossed, legs crossed, feet facing the next person you're talking to, feet facing away from each other, feet hanging the shoes

When it comes to interpreting other people's body movements, the hand and fingers—or more specifically, the way your hands and fingers move—are very useful. Hands can move up and down, and they can communicate in a secret language that only members of the same group understand.

Although not considered a body component, how one responds to the handling and placement of items plays a role in interpreting body language. This may indicate rage, pleasure, and a variety of other emotions.

This involves making deliberate bodily motions, often known as gestures. These are the actions you plan to do, such as shaking hands, blinking your eyes, moving and shaking your body in a seductive manner, perhaps to entice someone, and so on. There are also involuntary motions, which are those that you are unable to control. Sweating, laughing, weeping, and a variety of other emotions are examples of this.

Facial Expression

The expression facial (also, facies, face), with the eyes, is one of the most important means to express emotions and moods.

Through knowledge and observation of facial expressions (that is, the moving face and not as a static object), we can better understand what others communicate to us.

We also judge people's personalities and other traits based on their facial expressions. For example, people with attractive features are often attributed certain qualities they may or may not possess.

The face and first impressions

In the first meeting between two people, the first five minutes are usually the most critical period. The impressions formed in this short space of time will persist in the future and even be reinforced by subsequent behavior, which is not usually interpreted objectively, but according to those first impressions.

Since the face is one of the first features we notice in a person, it can play a vital role in establishing relationships with others.

In these few minutes, we form opinions about your character, personality, intelligence, temperament, ability to work, habits, even about your usefulness as a friend or lover.

Talking to the face

Together with the eyes, the face is our best means to communicate without words. We use it (and the judgments of others will depend on the clues they get) to indicate how pleased we are, express our current state of mind, show the attention we pay to others, and so on. However, facial expressions can be used to reinforce the impact of verbal messages, such as when a mother scolds her child: the expression on her face will show if she is really angry if only a little...

The main function of the face in body language is the expression of emotions;. However, other parts of the body also contribute to the use we make of body language, so we should not believe that a message is clear and exclusively transmitted by a single part of the body.

The range of expressions is very wide, but there are a limited number of emotions that most of us can recognize with some reliability.

Paul Ekman and Wallace Friesen have discovered that there are 6 main facial expressions:

The smiles

The smiles can be light, normal, and large. They are usually used as a gesture of greeting to express varying degrees of pleasure, joy, joy, happiness. Even blind-born children smile when they like something. They are characterized by being beautiful and cheerful. Smiles can also be used to mask other emotions:

- Smile to hide the hardships.
- Smile as a submission response.
- Smile to make stressful situations more bearable.
- Smile to attract the smile of others.
- Smile to relax the tension.

- Smile to hide fear.
- Sadness, disappointment, and depression

They are distinguished by lack of expression and features such as the downward inclination of the corners of the mouth, low gaze, and general decay of the factions. Normally these emotions are accompanied by a low volume of the voice or a slower way of speaking.

Although in most cases they are not very well distinguished from each other, other bodily factors assure us of knowing which emotion is being carried out as:

- Sadness
- Eyebrows slightly tilted towards the ears, forming a semi-arch.
- Shoulders regularly decayed.
- Inclination of the commissures at 45% of their normal range.
- Hands together and face down.
- Disappointment
- Eyebrows not fully inclined.
- Looking back and down, usually to the left.
- Shoulders slightly down and with the hands at the sides of the body.
- Depression
- Normally inclined eyebrows.
- Tilt of the commissures slightly descending.
- Shoulders down.
- Legs and thighs parallel to each other.

But we must remember that each emotion is different according to each individual. Not everyone demonstrates the same factions.

Dislike / contempt

They express themselves with shrinkage of the eyes and puckering of the mouth. The nose is usually wrinkled, and the head is turned sideways to avoid having to look at the cause of such a reaction. It is the only facial expression that occurs in only part of the face, that is, in its middle. One end of the upper lip is lifted while the opposite side is in its original position.

Anger

The anger is often characterized by: gaze into the cause of the offense, closed mouth and teeth tightly clenched, eyes and eyebrows slightly inclined to express anger. Closed hands pressing and containing the feeling can also be seen in a situation of anger.

The fear

Fear is not a unique form of expression that reveals its presence. It can be revealed through very wide eyes, through the open mouth, or by a general tremor that affects the face and the rest of the body.

The interest

It is often detected by what is called "bird head," that is, the head tilts a certain angle towards the subject of interest. Other features are the eyes being more open than normal and the mouth being slightly open.

Another aspect to consider is the extent to which the complements in nonverbal messages are involved. Because the complements change our appearance, we must consider their effects on the perception that others have of us. From this, we can deduce that we do not always transmit the nonverbal messages we try to send. The more aware we are of these difficulties of body language, the better we can use it without words.

Other information about the face

Facial expressions and expressing emotions also serve as a means of expressing personality, attitudes towards others, sexual attraction and attractiveness, the desire to communicate or initiate an interaction, and the degree of expressiveness during communication.

The way men and women interact with facial expressions has been shown to be different. Women tend to laugh and smile more often than men, which does not have to be due to greater sociability or joy. It may be because they find the situation slightly uncomfortable.

The expression of the face is constantly changing during communication. Among the changes, we can mention the so-called "micro momentary" facial expressions, as its name indicates its duration is a fraction of a second and usually reflects a person's true feelings.

Posture

To develop the complete meaning being conveyed, posture and body orientation should be understood in the context of the overall body language. It is intended to express friendliness and begins with an open stance. The feet are spread wide, and the palms of the hands face outward in this open posture. Individuals who have an open posture are seen to be more convincing than those who have different stances. Standing or sitting upright with the head elevated and the belly and chest exposed creates an open posture. When you combine an open posture with a calm facial expression and excellent eye contact, you come off as accessible and composed. During a discussion, keep your body looking forward toward the other person.

Closed posture is when someone crosses their arms over their chest, crosses their legs away from someone, or sits in a slumped forward stance and displays the backs of their hands while clenching their fists. The closed stance conveys a sense of boredom, hostility, or disconnection. This stance conveys caution and the ability to defend oneself against any allegation or danger.

Adopting a confident posture helps to communicate that one is not anxious, frightened, or irritated. A confident posture is achieved by pulling oneself to full height, keeping the head high, and maintaining an eye-level look. Then, draw your shoulders back and relax your arms and legs by your sides. Speakers are more likely to adopt this stance in a formal setting, such as giving a presentation, during cross-examination, or presenting a project.

Postural echoing, which is employed as a flirting tactic by enticing someone in the guardian, is also essential. It is achieved by watching and imitating the person's movement style and speed. Replicate the leaning against the wall of the person. You're expressing that you're attempting to flirt with the person by changing your postures versus the others to get a match. Postural echoing may also be utilized as a joke on someone you know well and with whom you often converse.

Maintaining a straight stance conveys authority and confidence. Part of the confidence in this posture is that it optimizes blood flow while putting less strain on the muscles and joints, which improves an individual's calmness. The upright posture serves to elicit a positive attitude and feeling, making one feel energetic and attentive. In casual interactions, such as at meetings, presentations, or while delivering a speech, a straight posture is highly desired.

Being in a drooping position with a hunched back, on the other hand, is bad posture that makes one lethargic, unhappy, or impoverished. A slumped posture puts a burden on the body, making the person feel less attentive and uninterested in the current discussion. On the other hand, leaning forward and maintaining eye contact shows that one is paying attention. The audience is engaged in and responsive to the message if they lean forward in an upright posture during a speech.

Furthermore, when someone slants one of their shoulders during a discussion, it indicates that they are weary or ill. Standing or sitting with a sharp lean to one side suggests that you are tired or fed up with the discussion and anxiously anticipate the conclusion or a break. Consider how you or others responded when a lesson went on beyond the end of the period. Someone in the audience most likely shifted one of their shoulders to the left or right. In this condition, the individual's mind wanders away from what they will do next. If there is a tea break, pupils' minds will wander away from what they will do during or after the tea break.

Standing on one foot, on the other hand, implies that one is uneasy or weary. When a person stands on one foot, it indicates that they are attempting to deal with discomfort. The cause of your unease may be emotional or physiological. For example, you probably juggled your body from one foot to the other to alleviate the urge to take a quick call or pass the time. In most cases, one finds themselves standing on one foot when an uncomfortable issue is mentioned. It's a technique for disrupting prolonged focus, which may heighten the unsettling sensation.

If someone clutches their head or face with their hands and lays it on their legs, they are embarrassed or tired. When the speaker says anything that makes you feel uncomfortable, you'll probably cup your face or lay your head on your legs. It's a literal method of avoiding embarrassment. While standing, children are more prone to adopt this posture. When standing, this position may give the impression that the person is praying.

Furthermore, when someone stands with their arms akimbo, they express a negative attitude or rejection of the message. Standing up straight and facing the target person while gripping the waist with both hands creates the posture. The hands should grasp the flanks, around the kidneys, at the same time. A disapproving or sarcastic expression usually couples the arms-akimbo stance to convey attitude, contempt, or disapproval.

When a person extends both shoulders and arms and rests them on chairs on each side, they are weary and unconcerned. The position resembles a static flap of wings, with the shoulders and arms stretched out like wings and rested on each side's seats. It is one of the postures that indicate that you are bored, unconcerned about the repercussions of your actions, and unconcerned about the consequences of your actions. Other people's privacy and space are also invaded, and their focus may be disrupted due to the stance.

If one bends both knees, it indicates that the person is tired and less formal with the audience. It's also possible that the position indicates severe tiredness and the need to rest. Most soccer players, for example, bend without kneeling while gripping both knees, suggesting fatigue. Because one is looking down in this position, it may be improper in formal settings and make one seem gay.

When one rests their head on their cheeks with an open hand, it suggests that they are thinking deeply and are likely unhappy, mournful, or melancholy. When viewing anything with a high likelihood of bad results, such as a movie or a game, the stance is also employed. The position, which is similar to meditation, allows one to concentrate deeply on the problem.

Through this posture, an individual will avoid distractions and think deeper about what is being presented. If you watch European soccer, you'll notice that coaches adopt this stance while attempting to analyze a game, particularly when their side is losing. This stance, however, should not be employed in official settings since it implies rudeness. Peers should only adopt the stance.

Then there's the crossing of the legs when sitting in a chair, particularly a reclining chair, from the thigh to the knee. In this position, one is expressing that they are feeling less formal and comfortable. Most of the time, this posture is shown when one is alone at home watching a movie or at the workplace after hours. If this position is repeated in a formal setting, it denotes boredom or a lack of focus.

In an informal setting, such as at home, crossing one's legs from the ankle to the soles of one's feet indicates that one is attempting to concentrate. For example, if a wife or kid inquires about anything that the father has to consider, the person is likely to adopt this position. If this position is repeated in a formal setting, it denotes boredom or a lack of focus.

Eye Contact

Reading eye contact is important to understand the true status, even where verbal communication seeks to hide it. As advised, body language should be read as a group. We will focus on individual aspects of body language and make the reader understand how to read that particular type of body language.

Your pupils dilate when you are focused and interested in someone you are conversing with or the object you are looking at or using. The pupils will contract when one is transiting from one topic to another. We have no control over the working of pupils. When one is speaking about a less interesting topic, the pupils will contract.

Effective eye contact is critical when communicating with a person. Eye contact implies that one looks but does not stare. Persistent eye contact will make the recipient feel intimidated or judged. In Western cultures, regular eye contact is desired, but it should not be overly persistent. If one offers constant eye contact, it is seen as an attempt to intimidate or judge, making the recipient of the eye contact uncomfortable. Some studies suggest that most children fall victim to attacks by pet dogs if they make too much eye contact, as this causes them to feel threatened and react defensively and instinctually.

Winking

In Western culture, winking is considered a form of flirting that should be done to people we are good with. This varies, though, as Asian cultures frown on winking as a facial expression.

Blinking

In most cases, blinking is instinctive; our affection for the person we are speaking to causes us to blink faster subconsciously. If the average blinking rate is 6 to 10 times per minute, it can indicate that one is drawn to the person they are speaking to.

Eye Direction

The direction of the eyes tells us about how an individual is feeling. When someone is thinking, they tend to look to their left as they are recalling or reminiscing. An individual who thinks tends to look to their right when thinking creatively, but it can also be interpreted as a sign that one is lying. For left-handed people, the eye directions will be reversed.

Avoiding Eye Contact

When we do not make eye contact with someone we speak to for extended periods, we are most likely uncomfortable with the person or the conversation. We avoid looking someone in the eye if we feel ashamed to be communicating with them. When we feel dishonest about trying to deceive people, we avoid looking at them. While it is okay to blink or drop eye contact temporarily, people that consistently shun making eye contact are likely to be feeling uneasy with the message or the person they are communicating with. For emphasis, staring at someone will make them drop eye contact due to feeling intimidated. Evasive eye contact happens where one deliberately avoids making eye contact.

Crying

Human beings cry due to feeling uncontrollable pain or in an attempt to attract sympathy from others. Crying is considered an intense emotion associated with grief or sadness though it can also denote extreme happiness known as tears of joy. When an individual forces tears to manipulate a situation, this is referred to as "crocodile tears." Typically, though, if one cries, then the individual is likely experiencing intense negative emotion.

Additionally, when one is interested in what you are speaking, they will make eye contact often. This is not entirely eye contact, though. Rather, the eye contact on the other person's eyes is for 2-3 minutes, and then it switches to the lips or nose and then returns to the eyes. For a brief moment, the person initiating eye contact will look down then back up to the eyes. Looking up and to the right demonstrates dismissal and boredom. Dilation of the pupil may indicate that someone is interested or that the room is brighter.

In some instances, sustained eye contact may signal that you want to speak to the person or that you are interested in the person sexually. At one point, you have noticed a hard stare from a man towards a particular woman to the point the woman notices and asks the man what is all that for. In this case, eye contact is not used to intimidate but to single out the target person. You probably have seen a woman ask, "why is that man staring at me?" then she proceeds to mind her business, but on taking another look in the man's direction, she notices that he is still staring. In this manner, eye contact is used to single out an individual and make them aware that one has sexual feelings towards the person.

However, people are aware of the impact of body language and will seek to portray the expected body language. For instance, an individual that is lying is likely to make deliberate eye contact frequently to sound believable. At one point, you knew you were lying but went ahead to make eye contact. You probably have watched movies where one of the spouses is lying but makes believable eye contact with others. The reason for this faked body language is because the person is aware of the link between making eye contact and speaking the truth.

Like verbal language, body language and, in particular, eye contact can be highly contextual. For instance, an individual may wink to indicate that they agree with the product's quality being presented or agree with the plan. Eye contact in these settings can be used as a coded language for a group of people. At one point, one of your classmates may have used a wink to indicate that the teacher is coming or to indicate that the secret you have been guarding is now out.

The Language of the Eyes

Pay close attention to the eyes; they may reveal that there is more to the story than what you are being told. When a person avoids eye contact, there is a strong possibility that they are uncomfortable, disinterested, nervous, bored, or all the above. If their pupils are dilated, it is safe to say that they are comfortable or perhaps they like you. If they are blinking far too much (in an unnatural way), there is a strong possibility that they may not be entirely honest with you. If they often look to the left, they could be recalling a genuine memory. If they often look to the right, it could be a sign that they are trying to make something up. Body language can be fascinating, almost like you are a detective trying to unravel the different layers of the story and get to the bottom of the truth.

Eye Contact and Public Speaking

As you can undoubtedly see, your general posture, breathing, the way you hold yourself, the way you stand, and hand gestures all play a role in your performance as an effective public speaker. Another thing to master is eye contact. Maintaining intentional, deep eye contact with members of your audience is the single most effective way to improve your presentation and the influence you make as a speaker. Of course, it is impossible to do this with everyone, especially those seated all the way at the back of the room, too distant to see. However, for the audience members that you can connect with - the ones seated in the first few rows at the front - that is what you should be doing.

There was an interesting experiment that researchers at Cornell University carried out. In a study published in the Environment and Behavior journal, the researchers took the cartoon rabbit on the Trix™ cereal boxes and manipulated its gaze. As a result of that one manipulation of the rabbit's eyes, adults were more likely to choose Trix™ over other cereal brands if the rabbit looked directly at them instead of looking away. Eye contact, as the researchers of this experiment discovered, invoked powerful emotions and feelings within the customer, and that sense of connection was what made them more likely to buy this cereal. Even a cartoon rabbit's eye contact makes a difference!

You should stare into your audience's eyes as often as possible throughout your presentation if you want to connect with them. It's easier to do this when you are presenting in a meeting room full of colleagues at work; the room is likely smaller, with fewer listeners. In a larger venue, maintaining good eye contact with every audience member is a bit more challenging.

It's going to be to your advantage as a speaker, though, to lock eyes with your audience when you are addressing them, no matter the size of the crowd. Here's what good eye contact can do for you as a speaker:

- It allows you to appear more authoritative as a speaker, making you appear more believable in the eyes of your audience. Someone who understands what they're talking about won't hesitate to face people in the eyes and give them the truth.

- It helps you concentrate on who you are targeting. Allowing your eyes to wander aimlessly could lead to distractions as you take in the external images or stimuli that are happening around the room.

- When you look them in the eye, your listeners being to focus on you instead of being distracted by their thoughts. When someone is staring you in the eyes, it's difficult not to pay attention, and this is one technique to capture your audience's attention.

- When your audience focuses on returning your eye contact, there is a greater chance that they are listening to what you are telling them. You are increasing the odds of your message resonating with your listeners.

- It helps to transform your audience from passive to active participants. When you look them in the eye, you are creating a connection, and it makes them feel as though you are speaking directly to them. Suddenly, your speech is no longer a speech but a personal conversation which they are keen to participate in. They'll be able to stay up with your message if you make eye contact with them.

- It gives you the opportunity to spot when your audience might need more convincing. When you make eye contact with them, you are simultaneously reading their facial expressions. When you see skepticism in their face, it gives you the chance to step in and convince them before moving onto your next point. Acknowledging their concerns by saying, "I know it seems difficult to believe, but here's why it makes sense" will change the way that your speech is being received. Audiences will be intrigued when you appear to be able to answer their unspoken thoughts and convince them without them having to ask for more details. That's the power of good eye contact.

- It will force you to naturally slow down as you speak when you are looking someone in the eye anywhere from 3–5 seconds. Former President Barack Obama employed this tactic to help him become a more powerful orator.

- It allows you to be both empathetic and assertive at the same time. You can share your opinion with your listeners, and at the same time, observe their reaction, better understanding how they are responding to your message.

Good eye contact with your audience makes them feel like they matter. Despite being part of a large crowd, they get to feel involved in your presentation, almost like it was tailor-made for them. In turn, you appear more approachable, and a silent rapport is formed between you and the audience as you continue to engage them in your presentation with your eyes.

Strong Posture Makes a Difference

With the apparently endless list of things to prepare and remember for a successful presentation, it's easy to overlook the importance of maintaining excellent posture throughout. If you are going to try and breathe the right way and give as much power to your vocals as possible, you are going to need good posture to support you through that effort. Proper posture does not just give the appearance of being someone who is confident and assured—it is also necessary to ensure that you are not breathing through your chest throughout your speech.

Since the power of breath is so important, the subject is broached here once again, this time focusing on how it is linked to your posture. There's a lot of advice out there when it comes to public speaking, but the one piece to remember is: breathing through your chest is never going to be good for your posture when you are presenting.

Breathing through your chest is poor practice because:

- It facilitates a lot of tension in your upper body. When you are tense, it is going to negatively impact your posture, which eventually affects your public speaking capabilities.

- Chest breaths can't give you the same kind of sound quality that deep breathing can. When you are taking shorter breaths, you compromise the pitch, tone, volume, resonance, and overall sound quality of your voice. Only deep breathing promotes good posture.

- You're not fully utilizing your natural breathing mechanism when you breathe through your chest. By taking shorter breaths, you are not encouraging the use of your abdominal and diaphragm areas, which are also an essential part of your breathing process.

When you are nervous, taking shorter and sharper breathes only makes it more apparent! You will appear panicked when your breathing is visibly quick and rapid, heaving and panting. Also, it is impossible to maintain good posture when you are not engaging your abdominal region. As if your body were a pipe, consider it. What happens when the pipe has bends or curves instead of being straight? It produces blockages. Those bends and blockages affect the flow of air through those pipes. It's the same thing with your body. If you were presenting behind a podium or a desk, any kind of bend forward or slump is going to make it hard for you to breathe properly; the quality of your voice will be compromised. The advice to hold your head up and stand up tall is not just for the benefit of the audience, but for your breathing benefit, too.

You probably understand by now: maintaining good posture is essential if you want your presentation to be considered a success. Not only does it make you appear confident, but it also provides the following benefits:

- Taking deep breaths when your posture is correct helps you feel calmer and more in control of your emotions.

- When you look authoritative, audiences tend to pay more attention to you compared to a speaker who looks visibly nervous, hunched, or appears as though they wish the ground would swallow them up!

- Good posture makes it easier for you to talk clearly, so your words reverberate across the room.

- It helps to create a better first impression among your audience. When you walk onto that stage with a strong, tall posture, the immediate first impression given is resoundingly positive. Now, imagine you were in the audience, watching a speaker enter the stage shuffling their feet, looking awkward with their shoulders rolled forward almost as if they were trying to retreat into themselves. Which speaker would leave a better impression in your mind?

- A strong posture conveys enthusiasm, and when you are excited about what you should say, your audience will sense that. Listeners are affected by your emotions – they can't help but feel what you feel.

Tips on Improving Your Posture

Ideally, you'd want to practice maintaining good posture every day and throughout the day, but that is not always possible. It's easy to forget about posture as you get caught up in your daily tasks. When you do remember, though, it is easy enough to work on improving your posture and to do it so subtly that no one even realizes you are doing it.

To improve your posture, straighten your back, imagining that there is a string at the top of your head that is pulling and lengthening your entire body upwards. When you are straightened as tall as you can, roll your shoulders back, tilt your chin forward slightly and lift your head up high. If there are people around you, try to imagine yourself attempting to peer over the tops of everyone's head. You should do this quick little exercise on the go or at home whenever you remember to be mindful of your posture. You should especially do it before your presentation. The more you exercise, the simpler it will get to maintain excellent posture for extended periods of time until it becomes automatic.

To help you maintain good posture, stand like this when facing a crowd:

- Your weight should be mostly on the balls of your feet, not on your toes, and evenly distributed across both feet.

- In order to avoid unnaturally standing ramrod straight, keep your knees slightly bent as you continue to lengthen through your spine.

- Stand with your feet shoulder-width or slightly wider than shoulder-width apart.

- As you stand tall and roll your shoulders back, tuck your stomach in for better balance.

- Keep your head level at all times. A good reminder is to check if your earlobes and your shoulders are in line. Your head should not be too far forward or too far back. Keep it in a nice, even line with your shoulder.

Tips to Improve Your Eye Contact

Instead of seeing your audience as a large group, start to think of them as one listener. From the moment you walk on stage and greet the crowd, start scanning the room and look around for friendly, warm, and welcoming faces. That's your first step to building a connection with them, shifting your gaze from one audience member to another as you hold each gaze for three to five seconds at a time. Once you have established that initial connection, these are some other things you can do to improve that visual connection with your listeners:

- **Focus on Everyone** - This one is much easier to do when you present to a smaller crowd, such as in a meeting room at your workplace. In a larger crowd, aim to connect with as many members of the audience as you can. Divide your audience into various parts or groups, and then select a few people from each group to establish eye contact with.

- **Connect Just Long Enough to Make a Connection** - You do not have to hold their gaze for too long or make eye contact with only the same few audience members. That's going to be impractical, as you are only allocated a certain period of time for your speech. Instead, you should try to maintain eye contact for long enough to create some relationship with them. Each eye contact session throughout a presentation should last no more than five seconds, which is the average time it takes to complete a train of thought. This way, you do not risk losing track of what you are saying, and the five-second rule encourages you to slow down the rate of your speech.

- **Avert When Sensing Discomfort** - Bear in mind that not everyone in your audience is going to be comfortable with direct eye contact. Some participants are shy individuals, preferring to blend into the crowd instead of feeling like they've been singled out. You need to be able to scan their emotions quickly when you are making eye contact—and as soon as you sense them feeling uncomfortable (shifting their eyes or fidgeting slightly in their seats), avert your gaze and move onto the next audience member. This is an essential point to remember while giving a presentation or speaking in a foreign nation since certain cultures regard eye contact to be disrespectful.

- **Connect During the Critical Parts** - There will be some points you wish to drill into the minds of listeners; time these key points so they match with the eye contacts you make. When it is time to emphasize a point, make sure you are holding the gaze of an audience member and look right at them as you get the point across. Your ability to combine eye contact with emotion will make your presentation much stronger.

- **Meet Your Audience Beforehand** – Whenever possible, try to meet at least a few audience members before you take the stage. When you walk in, you already have a few friendly faces to engage with! It can be difficult to make an immediate connection with total strangers, so is it to introduce yourself to your audience beforehand, learning as few names as possible. Allowing listeners to get to know you personally prior to your presentation makes them feel engaged when you connect with them again on that stage.

- **Watch for the Nod** - During your speech, one important audience reaction to watch out for is "the nod." When your audience member feels like you have been talking to them and is feeling engaged and connected, they will subconsciously let you know by nodding along with what you are saying. When a person understands and processes what you have just said, they will nod to signal that, and you can take that as your cue that your message has been well received. It's also a great tip to pace yourself when you are speaking by waiting for your audience to nod and signal that they've understood before moving on to your next point.

- **Avoid the "Lighthouse" Connection** - The "lighthouse" connection here is when a speaker moves around the room so quickly that it is impossible to make any real contact long enough to leave an impression. Like the light shining from a lighthouse, moving and scanning the ocean so quickly and systematically that it is already made a loop around and come back again before you can count to five. If you are scanning the room in this rapid, systematic manner, you are failing to make any real connections with your audience.

- **Don't Linger with Long Sentences** - You need to know when to move on, even if you are in the middle of a long sentence when you do. If you try maintaining eye contact with one audience member per sentence (exceeding the five-second), you run the risk of making that person feel uncomfortable. Your audience wants to feel connected, not targeted. If you do need to make the shift during a long sentence, make it subtle and gradually shift your gaze to the person sitting next to a time. Make it natural, not abrupt.

Quick Bonus Tip

When you are giving a speech across cultures, it helps to do some research, taking note of your listener's cultural norms. Showing sensitivity and respect for another culture's beliefs and perspective shows your empathy as a speaker, and your audience will look upon you favorably for demonstrating that kind of consideration.

In some Asian cultures, it is considered disrespectful to make eye contact, especially if you happen to be a subordinate. Eye contact between members of the opposing sex is considered improper in Middle Eastern societies because it may indicate sexual intentions.

Gestures

Hand gestures, in general, are rather accidental. They are important in telling us a lot about another person who utilizes their hands when talking. Also, in the case of arm movement, there are guidelines for constructive body language.

Leave Your Arms in An Open Position

The first step is always to have an outstretched hand. Open hands imply transparency and approval. Open palms mean honesty and integrity as well. There's also a way to read the open palms, though. If the hands are open when speaking or facing down, the individual's attitude is somewhat dominant. This is particularly noticeable in the case of handshakes.

Nevertheless, it is a non-threatening indication if the palms are opened and facing upwards. This individual is accessible and can be perceived in essence as welcoming. The palms switch, therefore, totally alters the manner others view us.

Don't Cross the Arms

While talking, the arms ought not to be crossed, and the hands must not be caught. Fastened hands show the absence of responsibility and the absence of certainty. Crossed arms show a guarded or anxious position. It has likewise been seen that when an individual stands with his arms crossed, he gets little on of the discussion when contrasted with an individual with great affection with open arms. Additionally, protective non-verbal communication likewise prompts lower maintenance control.

It is in our normal nature to fold our arms to feel great. Regardless, studies have shown that such nonverbal communication is seen negatively by people. Besides, clenched hands are additionally a major no during discussions. The arms ought not to go underneath the midsection level and should consistently be raised over the abdomen while talking. The arms can at times go down; however, it ought not to be so all through the discussion.

Do Not Grip Your Arms

While addressing somebody, don't grasp your arms by intersecting them. It is an indication of being insecure. Continuously abstain from holding your arms together before your crotch region, as it shows frailty too. It is known as the Broken Zipper posture. This stance shows weakness and accommodation simultaneously and subsequently must be maintained at a strategic distance.

Try not to continue modifying your sleeve buttons in a public location as it again shows you are a lot of worried about your weaknesses of turning out in broad daylight. The women must note that they ought not to grasp their bags near themselves as they talk as it shows their cautious position and uncertain nature.

Zero Arm Blockage

When you are in an eatery, don't grip your espresso cup away from plain view. There ought to be no arm boundary when you conversing with someone else. Keep open non-verbal communication and hold the espresso cup aside.

Use the Parallel Over Perpendicular

In bunch talks, it is a command that when you need to point towards somebody, don't utilize the hand that will be opposite to them. Utilize the other arm that can point to them and can be parallel to your chest as well. Having the arm opposite to your chest to indicate out others is commonly an inconsiderate motion. Continuously attempt to have the arms parallel to the body.

Arms and hands must be utilized cautiously in discussions. The development of your arms and hands can make or blemish your exchange and change the results fundamentally.

Head Action

We use the head to communicate actively without using words as much as any other part of our body. A few basic head gestures you can learn to recognize and use to express different emotions and thoughts.

The most common one is nodding. Although it is frequently culturally constrained, it is usually an indication of agreement. For example, people in Bulgaria nod for "No," and you may get confused if you are meeting with a representative of this nation.

Nodding often prompts your counterpart to talk more because you are sending them signals of agreement. During a meeting, the more you nod, the better and more relaxed a person would feel because you express agreement with their statement and agree. You show support. However, don't overdo it because you risk looking funny.

On the other hand, head-shaking is considered a refusal, a literal "No". In business body language, shaking your head would mean you do not like the proposal being made. You may come up with a counter-proposal or refuse the deal altogether. If you see your counterpart shaking his head during your speech, change the direction of the conversation and try to understand their intentions, and meet halfway.

Leaning forward or tilting your head to the side can mean that you listen carefully and focus on what the other person is saying.

During meetings or in your personal life, you may see a person scratching their head. This may mean that they are trying to remember something or feel uncertain. It may even mean lying. However, you must always be careful to watch for other gestures to support your opinion because scratching can be purely physiological – the person may have dandruff or is just sweating.

More often than not, head gestures and positions are tied to gestures with hand or the body's position and facial expressions in the so-called clusters that map to interest or boredom, for example.

One of the gestures that most authors advise people to avoid is touching your face during meetings or dates. In most cases, this means that you are either lying or you feel insecure. Such gestures are often involuntary, but you can practice them at home and try not to use them. If you cover your mouth during a meeting, it will signal your partner that you are lying. The same applies if you touch your nose or rub your eyes.

Some simple rules to follow include the following:

Covering Your Mouth – you can cough, this way camouflaging the real gesture;

Touching Your Nose – if your hand or fingers involuntarily go towards your nose, you can either stop and put your hand under your chin and lean forward to show investment in the discussion or just run your fingers through your hair. It may show nervousness or confidence depending on your facial expression and the tone of your voice;

Rubbing Your Eyes – try instead to stop right before you have reached your eye and turn the gesture into one of interest – support your head with your palm rested on one of your cheeks and your index finger pointing up. This shows interest and assessment.

All of these are effective when you are listening. In case you are the speaker, try to avoid them altogether.

Not all gestures like touching your face or head are negative. As mentioned above, resting your palm on your cheek with your index finger pointing up means you are interested in the conversation and listening carefully while assessing the situation. However, the moment you start supporting your head with all your fingers, it signals boredom.

Women often use hair-flip or hair-toss unconsciously to show they are attracted to a man. In a business environment, the hair-toss gesture may mean that the woman feels confident about herself. In rare cases, when the hair-toss is preceded by touching or playing with her hair, it may mean nervousness or insecurity. Therefore, during business meetings, it is best to avoid touching your hair. A piece of advice – if you have noticed that you touch your hair often, go to the meeting with your hair tied to avoid unwanted body language signals that may ruin your position.

Another gesture is rubbing your chin. This usually means reflection and is used before you reach a decision. The same applies to rubbing your neck; although it may also mean that you cannot make a decision, you are still not convinced.

If you want to exude confidence or arrogance, you can put both your hands behind your head. This gesture, however, can only be used amongst equals or if people in lower positions than you surround you. Do not use it in front of your manager or people holding higher positions.

It Is Important to Understand Body Language

Most individuals rely on social networks and texts to connect in the modern digital age, which is a very reliable way to do so.

While digital communication enables people to speak at convenience and reduce stress on certain individuals, something can be lost. Because you are incapable of recognizing the person when you speak to them, you can miss key non-verbal signs in addition to verbal ones such as vocal inflections. Digital communication has become the main method for people worldwide, and to satisfy this, there is the likelihood that body language will proceed to develop. Most of the time, you may hear the negatives of body language. Maybe you are told not to twist in a certain way, sit this way, or that way. However, body language can influence your life positively. Let us look at what you should do to maximize body language.

Non-Verbal Communication

Body language refers to the nonverbal cues that are used for communication. Such nonverbal cues, as per scholars, constitute a major part of your daily interaction. The things we do not say can still express volumes of knowledge, from our facial expressions to our physical movements. It was proposed that facial expressions can speak for 60% to 65% of all interactions. It is important to recognize non-verbal communication, but it is also important to listen to other signals such as meaning. In many situations, instead of relying on a single event, you must look at signals as a band. You may be wondering what you should look at as you interpret non-verbal cues.

How to Use and Improve Body Language

After getting the tips, you may be asking yourself whether, indeed, body language influences your life positively. I am here to prove to you that, indeed, your life is bound to transform if you take your time to nurture your body language and its relevance in each and everything that you do. You should know what to use where to be organized and articulate. This book will focus on positive body language. That includes; good eye contact, effective engagement, targeted gestures that make your message more understandable and effective. In essence, body language has been found to create and enhance your confidence, influence, and all-around success. More studies have revealed that the people who know how to use their body language are more likable, persuasive, competent, and also possess a high level of emotional intelligence. That means that they can command presence, manipulate their way into various platforms, and win people's hearts. That also explains the success in negotiation, which we shall look at later in the book.

Let us go ahead and look at the ways that body language will transform your life.

Positive non-verbal communication changes your frame of mind. The research found that deliberately changing your non-verbal communication to make it increasingly positive improves your demeanor since it powerfully affects your hormones.

It leads to an increase in testosterone. At the point when you hear of testosterone, your mind can easily be swayed to focus on athletics, yet testosterone's significance covers substantially more than games. Regardless of whether you are a man or a lady, testosterone improves your certainty and makes other individuals consider you progressively dependable and positive. Research shows that positive non-verbal communication builds your testosterone levels by 20%.

Body language leads to a reduction of cortisol. Cortisol is a pressure hormone that blocks execution and makes negative wellbeing impacts over the long haul. Reduction of cortisol levels limits pressure and empowers you to think all the more plainly, especially in troublesome and testing circumstances. Research shows that positive non-verbal communication diminishes cortisol levels by 25%.

It makes a ground-breaking blend. While a reduction in cortisol and an increase in testosterone are incredible in their special ways, the two together are a ground-breaking blend normally observed among individuals in high positions. This blend makes the certainty and clearness of mind perfect for managing tight deadlines, intense choices, and huge amounts of work. Individuals who normally have high testosterone and low levels of cortisol are known to flourish under pressure. Indeed, you can utilize positive non-verbal communication to make yourself like this regardless of whether it doesn't occur normally.

It makes you progressively attractive and likable. During a study in a university, students watched soundless videos of doctors having an interaction with their patients. By watching the doctors' non-verbal communication, the students could conclude the doctors wound up getting sued by their patients. Non-verbal communication is an enormous factor in how you're seen and can be a higher priority than your manner of speaking or even what you state. Figuring out how to utilize constructive use of body language will make individuals have confidence in you, like you, and trust you more.

It shows capability. In an investigation, scientists found that a one-second video of candidates in a campaign could pinpoint the potential candidate that was voted for. All this is because of their body language. While this may not build your confidence in the democratic procedure, it shows that capability has a solid establishment in non-verbal communication.

Body language improves emotional intelligence. Your capacity to viably convey your feelings and thoughts is vital to your passionate knowledge. Individuals whose non-verbal communication is negative have a dangerous, infectious impact on everyone around them. Attempting to improve your non-verbal communication profoundly affects your emotional intelligence.

Chapter 26:
Decoding Body Language

Here, we're going to learn the art of successfully and nearly accurately decoding body language. A lot of factors like social, non-verbal, psychological, and physical factors go into it. You cannot just simply subscribe to a crash course and learn body language in two months. A great deal of patience and a greater deal of understanding of how a human body behaves is required to decode body language. Let's get started studying the fundamentals of body language decoding.

Why Read Body Language?

Before moving ahead, let's look at some of the benefits body language reading bestows upon you. When you're a successful body language reader, you naturally fine-tune your professional and personal lives. Verbal communication isn't all in social communication. Once you finally learn to read body language, you'll understand the emotions and feelings of others better. This will also help you broaden your abilities in communication. Body language will also help you prevent conflicts with others and yourself; you can detect and tone down hostility even before the verbal fireworks go off. Body language consists of more than half of human communication, and once mastered, the art of body language reading can reap a truckload of benefits for you. You can finally come to realize the hidden emotions and intentions no one speaks out loud.

And if you think that studying body language will perhaps make you any less significant because it involves a lot of observing from the sidelines, quite the contrary is true. The room for improving your presence substantially grows as your knowledge of body language goes up. How? Just the same way you evaluate others, you can evaluate yourself, and you can use that knowledge to control your emotions and feelings.

You'll also notice some things you've never known or heard before. You'll start to notice the small nuances of body language — how people interact with each other with few words or even none as if there was another world hidden in the deepest recesses of the current world. So, you see, there're tons of reasons why it's good to read body language.

Understanding the Complexity

Acknowledge that body language reading isn't a course. You cannot achieve a degree in body language reading. You just cannot hope to read a specified syllabus and expect to call yourself a successful body language reader. Kindly respect and recognize the complexity of body language reading.

The complexity of body language reading stems from the key fact that different people behave differently. For some, thumbs up may be a good sign of positivity, while others might be too formal for their taste. While it's considered a good thing to use index fingers just to point while giving directions in some parts of the world, even showing the index finger is called rude in other parts. Hence, the weird complexity related to body language reading is because of how diverse humanity is. This diversity could be of region, practices, culture, religion, customs, or even a set of beliefs.

To fully understand body language means understanding human nature fully—a scientific subject still debated today by scientists.

The Whole Picture

While trying to interpret a person's body language, you must also consider the bigger picture. An isolated body behavior is as good as a banana peel. You just cannot simply take into account a one-off display of body behavior and base your judgments on the same. You also need to take the following factors into considerations while making accurate interpretations of the body language:

Social

These could also range from the neighborhood the person currently lives in or the neighborhood he was raised in. The community he hails from adds its contribution to the mixture. The family background is also yet another great factor here. The upbringing can make one's body language. A child raised where negativity and violence may exhibit a different body language than a child raised with good child-rearing.

Personality

The person's personality, in general, may be in contrast with that single isolated body language inference you drew that one time. Always consider the personality of the person you've chosen as your subject.

Verbal

Some people's body language can also be successfully interpreted after considering their verbal behavior. You may not even need to delve into more complex interpretations once you've established a difference between their verbal and non-verbal behavioral patterns.

Body language reading is also relative in nature. Imagine watching your favorite television show. You don't watch one episode and form an opinion about who your favorite character will be, do you? Before being attached to a particular character on the program, you must watch at least one season of it. Body language reading is no different than simply watching your favorite television show. You've to consider the whole picture before concluding.

One Size doesn't Fit All

Don't go by the rulebook while trying to study a person's body language. There're no set rules or norms for studying body language. As mentioned earlier, people differ. When people differ, how they behave and act also sees a significant change and variation. The yardstick you used for James cannot be used for Katherine. Acknowledge the differences that are between two individuals. It's only after sufficiently acknowledging such differences that you'll start becoming a good body language reader.

Cultural Variations

A key factor while dealing with the study of body language is culture. Culture can be best described as the set of beliefs and practices predominantly prevalent in a particular community. A place's culture speaks about its heritage and roots. Culture also has a lot of societal and regional regulations attached to it. Culture varies from place to place.

While it's more than fine for someone to point the finger at another person in some cultures, in others, it's considered a rude gesture. It's considered offensive for a woman to leave her house without actually covering her head in certain Middle Eastern countries, while some western countries' tourism industries actually thrive on the income made from nude beaches. Cultures decide a great deal when it comes to judging or even drawing a conclusion regarding someone's body language.

In Finland, when a person establishes eye contact, it is supposed to signal approach or welcome. However, on the other hand, the same eye contact could lead to the inference of anger in the person establishing it. If you bow down in a New York street, you'll be called a freak or even a weirdo, while if you do the same in China, onlookers will observe that you're offering respect. In many Western countries, looking someone in the eyes is a show of confidence; yet, in many Eastern countries, doing so is considered impolite.

Therefore, we see that cultural differences also give rise to variations in the study of body language. When you attempt to read someone's real emotion through their display of body language, don't simply take one aspect of their physical activity into account and start assessing. Consider their background and their nationality as well. However, while doing so, don't discriminate in any way.

How to Read Power

Eye contact

Powerful eye contact when made gives rise to the impression of dominance or even anger. If your subject is trying to establish or has already established firm eye contact, they are either trying to assert their superiority over you or are pissed off about something. A struggle or effort to establish power can also be seen in the eyes. Do they look angry or perhaps just plain confused?

Smiles

Smiles are really good indicators of a person's state of mind. A smiling person is always assessed as positive while studying body language. If your subject is casually smiling, they are most probably genuinely happy without actually putting too much effort into it. However, those acquainted with body language techniques would know about this and artificially put a smile on their faces to try and please someone or impress somebody. A fake smile is easily detectable if you're looking at the face in general. A fake smile only moves the mouth, but not our whole face; a real one will reflect from the whole face and the actions the person makes.

Gestures

Gestures are usually hand motions, and when successfully employed, could convey really strong emotions. On the other hand, a rude hand gesture, usually made with the middle finger, displays annoyance and disgust. A firm handshake denotes full self-confidence, usually with the handshake's hand facing downward and the grip being made of iron. If others are trying to dominate you to benefit themselves, you should try to put your power equal to them. We'll look at some everyday gestures that you'll come across and how you can effectively interpret them. We'll also look at some baby gestures for you to understand and use.

Miscellaneous

Dominant individuals tend to walk ahead of a group and usually open the doors for a group of people to walk in. They can be seen as talking all the time, with their hands making all sorts of gestures, as if commanding an army against an enemy force. Such people tend to take up more space than normal and wouldn't hesitate to drown out your voice in a room full of people. They may have already established themselves as the supreme leader of the group, even without the people's consent in the group. Dominant males are generally loud in nature and talk with their arms open and voice firm. They usually try to be better than everyone to become well ahead of them and establishing themselves as a leader. People in a higher social position tend to touch more than those in a low social position against their position. This is because those with power feel more comfortable in their skin than those who are inferior to them in terms of having influence.

How to Read Attraction

Eye contact

Most women blink continuously when they're trying to show the other person they're attracted to them. On the contrary, most males tend to gaze deeply into the eyes of their female counterparts to show attraction or deep-felt love. You'll notice that their eyes are locked together, which's another indication of attraction. The length of time spent in eye contact also tells more if the person is attracted. The longer the eye contact is, the more gaze is spent, and the more that person is attracted. Side-glances coupled with that sparkle in the eyes (it's not a real sparkle, but you'll know it when you see it) is a great indication. The eyes will blink rapidly — a positive romantic sign. Though some eastern cultures frown upon it, winking is also a sure sign of displaying attraction.

Smiles and laughter

A person in love smiles, and it's not just any smile, but if they truly love each other, it's one of the truest of smiles ever seen (scientifically called the "zygomatic smile"). It doesn't matter when and where; a person in love generally smiles. The women usually are the ones who smile and laugh in courtship. It can even be used as a gauge and meter of how close the couple is. Making others laugh and smile is considered to be a dominant trait usually possessed by men. This person could also be seen smiling at the most random time of the day without any specific reason. When around the person they're drawn towards, they tend to smile even more than normal.

Gestures

People who're attracted to someone tend to come closer to them physically. You'll notice that if a person is romantically inclined towards someone else, they'll try to hover around them for this reason or that. They'll make every damned possible excuse on the face of the planet to bridge the distance between them. They'll keep their arms relaxed and uncrossed — they'll be open. There's also a tendency between the couple to mirror each other's actions, a natural tendency in us to bond with somebody. There'll also be a significant number of unusual gestures that could include head tilts, shoulder rolls, and shrugs. The head and shoulders are the most expressive of our bodies, so they can send the message to our loved ones when used in conjunction with each other.

Miscellaneous

A man attracted to a woman tends to lean towards her in general, whereas a woman attracted to a man would lean against him in his opposite direction. A man in love would try to catch the gaze of his lady while a lady would steal the line of eyesight away from the male she's attracted to. There would be a perceptible shift in the tone of the voice, which would be a good improvement. The voices become softer and higher-pitched.

How to Read Emotions

Straight signs

Crying in most parts of the world is considered a sign of grief and sadness. If a person is crying, safely assume that they've been or still are sad about something. However, crying can also be brought on by excessive humor leading to uncontrollable laughter. Hence, while assessing crying, you should look for other signs as well.

Anger

Anger is often times simply depicted by a person's narrowed-down eyebrows, turned-down mouth, and a crunched-up upper lip accompanied by an evident frown. The tone of voice can also give a person's anger away, even if the physical signs don't indicate whether the person is angry. When a person crosses his arms, sighs regularly, and is visibly not looking happy, it can be safely assumed that he's angry at something or somebody.

Anxiety

Anxious people display the most obvious of signs. They fumble while speaking, form their lips into a thin line and fidget with their hands. Anxiety can also be inferred from irregularly spoken words and jittery legs. There's also a tendency to fumble around with things without any particular reason. A few people have a habit of unconsciously tapping their feet while talking. One other sign of anxiety is drawing in a deep breath and releasing it slowly. It means that they're trying to relax and appear normal.

Embarrassment

When a person is embarrassed, they'll display shifty eyes, a thin mouth, and forced smiles. These individuals tend to constantly look down while talking and tend to curl up in their world. Sometimes, there would be a stuttering speech as if they're afraid to make another embarrassing mistake.

Why's Reading Emotion Tricky?

An emotion is something that stays locked inside your mind. Now, the mind is that part of the human body that no biologist has successfully deciphered. It is said to be the most perplexing portion of the human body. Something that gets manufactured in such a part of the human body is bound to baffle those trying to research and study it. Hence, it has been established long ago that even body language isn't an effective method to study emotions. However, the study of body language has, to some extent, proved emotions decipherable.

Chapter 27:
The Secret Code of Body Language

Carly Fiorina and Hillary Clinton were both case studies for body language during one of our past presidential elections. They were scrutinized as appearing too cold, stiff, and unlikeable. Their body language was attributed to losing the 2016 presidential election, which isn't far off base. Undergraduates at Harvard were shown tapes of unknown gubernatorial candidates and could predict the winner with incredible accuracy, just based on the candidates' body language alone. Here's another strange statistic about body language: We've all heard the disparities between men and women in the workplace. Women are paid less, given fewer promotions, and receive more criticism in performance reviews than men. But here's one rarely published bit of research, according to Carol Kinsey Goman: Women who can turn on and off their assertiveness at will are far more likely to get raises and promotions than both men and other women. Skillfully showing endearing body language at certain times and portraying dominance at other times can make women statistically more successful. Anyone can master the following skills, so don't worry.

Confidence 101

Let's begin with the large vertebral structure holding you upright. Outside of signaling whether you've fallen or fallen to sleep, your spine has lots to say. The goal is knowing how to say the right thing at the right time. It starts in your spine. When someone walks into a room confidently, they're easy to spot. Same with low-confidence people. Notice the spinal differences at your next networking event. It's all about the posture, baby.

There are two common body language tricks inside the public speaking circuit: (1) the superhero stance and (2) the winner's V. Both body language moves are designed to prepare you to be more confident when you need it. Do either in private right before you go on stage. Your stage can be a big negotiation, a difficult talk with your partner, or any event where a little added confidence is needed. These two tools are your body language hacks for winning. Both increase your body's confidence-boosting chemicals and help trick yourself and your audience into believing that you are a winner and a hero.

Creating Body Confidence

The winner's V was discovered by a team of researchers who studied people worldwide right after winning a big event. They found that winning has a universal sign language. Whether you are running an Olympic marathon or capturing your dinner in a remote jungle village, all winners from around the world display the same body language: they stand up tall and throw their arms up into a strong, high V shape.

Even more intriguing, studies discovered that you don't have to win at anything to get the advantages of winning. Standing tall and putting your hands up into this position tricks your body into believing that you have won. Serotonin and testosterone levels rise, and your body begins to carry itself more confidently right after.

Think of this as your espresso shot of confidence. When you need it, sneak off to a private place, hold your hands up high, stand tall, and count to 10 seconds. The longer, the better, but this is the minimum.

Imagine me standing in a bathroom stall before my executive strategy meetings doing this. It happens. Your body can't help but smile and walk itself with greater pride afterward, so pay no mind to the silly feelings you get during this exercise. I use this body hack when I need a shot of happy, confident chemicals to my brain right before standing in front of large audiences. Do it right before your event if you can.

How to Express Your Confidence

You should always be as confident as possible. Less confident people make far less money, ask for fewer raises and promotions, and get passed over all the time. This is as true in nightclubs as it is in the workplace. The body language you must stop projecting today is shoulders slumped, arms crossed. If you make yourself appear smaller, you will make yourself feel smaller. If you can't help but hunch over a computer all day, remember to take a moment to stop, spread your shoulders back, and make yourself feel larger in the room. The same rules apply to networking events. If you look around any networking event, the least social people will physically appear smallest: hunched over, arms tucked into themselves, legs crossed, or otherwise together. Pay attention to your body language with scrutiny. A large open stance will boost your morale over time and make you more comfortable in even the most awkward social settings.

Superhero Stance

Amy Cuddy's team of researchers found that when they forced college students to hold dominant poses, they behaved with significantly greater dominance, asserting themselves to a far greater extent than their peers. This dominance shot will improve your confidence and boost your ability to assert yourself. Do it right before you communicate, if you can.

Here's how it works: Stand up tall and imagine that you are Batman or Wonder Woman after a hard day's work of being rich while ethically fighting off evil villains all night. Assume the position: hands on hips, shoulders back, chest proud, and chin up.

Ignoring the fact that you are, again, doing strange things inside a bathroom stall, hold this pose for at least ten seconds. It is guaranteed to increase your testosterone levels and give you confidence in caffeine. Researchers have proven time and time again that our bodies respond positively.

Win People Over and Spot Fakes

Persuading others and identifying phonies is the hardest of all body language techniques and requires a fair amount of skill and practice.

Learn Your Face

We all know how and when to smile and to frown, but only trained professionals are clear on the third type of facial body language: no expression at all. This is an extremely effective approach to controlling whatever room you are in. There is nothing that tweaks a recipient faster than showing no facial expression whatsoever. Put on your poker face and avoid making any facial expressions if you want to make the other person uncomfortable. Give them no reaction whatsoever.

This is a common practice in hiring and recruiting. Good human resources professionals are trained to test how applicants react under pressure. It doesn't require any verbalization whatsoever. They simply sit, without reaction, and let you talk. Remember this next time you find yourself babbling. It's your body's response to seeking approval from your peer. Now that you understand this, rest easy with newfound self-control in knowing that this is simply a trick, and you're wise to it.

The Art of Becoming a Mime

If you want to win someone over fast, imitation is a fantastic technique that doesn't need you to talk. Clustered mimicry techniques amplify your pair-bonding with someone instantly. By clustered, I mean you must employ three or more techniques in a single interaction. A single expression may not get noticed, but research shows that three is the magic number for effectiveness.

You do this by adopting a similar facial expression to someone you want to develop a closer relationship with instantly. If that person speaks when they smile, well, so do you. If they speak with sternness, then do the same. Notice their hand gestures: Do they use large motions or none at all? Take this approach when it's your turn to talk. How is the person standing? Slightly alter your stance to match. Mimicry is all about similar body language and similar actions and reactions. You can create a kindred spirit in your recipient with a bit of practice without them even noticing.

Use Body Language to Spot Phonies

We might control our words, but most of us never take the time to control our body language. When a person you're communicating with is saying one thing, but their body language is sending a different message, this is your red flag that something is awry. When someone claims they are lovely, but their shoulders are drooping, for example, you know something isn't quite right. This is one of the reasons body language is so fundamental. It not only allows you to communicate better, but it can also make you more charismatic.

All people want to feel that they are known. The art of charisma is about making others feel that you know them and you want to know more. If you notice that their body language is arguing with their words, simply call them out.

In a simple setting, you see someone slumped over with unconfident language, but with words, they express that all is well. Simply ask them, "Everything okay?" And then truly listen. Talk through work, life, whatever is going on. So long as the person is willing to open up to you, you've just won over a friend. See the following sidebar for a master class to take this one step further and make someone change their body language.

There are more complex settings where bad body language happens, especially in business. Like when you are giving a big presentation to a room and someone's body language is sending you bad vibes. Calling them out works especially well here. Simply ask, "Dan, is everything okay?" This opens up the opportunity for meaningful dialogue that can get you to your desired goal. It's always better to be in the room when someone is talking about you. Think back to high school–gossip days. Position yourself to defend, not to be taken when you're missing from action.

Body Language Master Class

Once you practice and become comfortable with the basics, it is possible, if you desire, to control others' body language and your own. This requires a high proficiency in smooth body language techniques. Be sure to practice them to perfection, or you risk coming off a little crazy with these master steps. The secret to controlling the body language of others is to fill the room, take on mimicry, and then start moving your own body differently. If done well, the other person will move their body, too.

Example 1: You start a conversation. The other person's arms are folded. Now your arms are folded. You move through the conversation, nodding when they nod. When you can feel them catching on, break your body language. Unfold your arms and grab your drink. They will grab theirs. Now replace your body language with the open and dominant poses you've just learned. Your recipient is likely to play along. It shouldn't be perfect symmetry. That would be weird. But when you like, start the flow again of body mimicry and changing body language.

Example 2: The techniques in example 1 can work in group settings as well. If you're giving a presentation and everyone is seated, seat yourself. As you go through your presentation, connect with each individual through eye contact, a bit of body mimicry, and proceed like this randomly through the room. Then, when it's time for something important, break your body language and show deep interest. Lean in closely or even stand up. Embrace a dominant pose. You will own the room, and others can't help but take notice.

I strongly suggest you practice each of these techniques thoroughly, as good body language is crucial to becoming the skilled communicator you are meant to be.

Key Concepts

- Take on a winning stance to instantly boost your self-confidence
- Master facial expression control to win friends and trip up your enemies
- Clustered body language miming will win you new friends
- Pay attention to incongruences between words and actions to spot and win over phonies
- Employ mimicry and then change body language to control the room

Ask Yourself

I hope that you feel as confident as you can. Before your next meeting or presentation, step aside and ask yourself: "Am I feeling my most confident? Have I assumed a power pose?" Do not tread lightly, friends. A power pose can be the difference between success and failure. Assume yours.

Also, the next time you want to make a friend or win someone over, ask yourself: "What body gestures do they tend to show?" Assume those. To become a master, get into a flow with your audience. Ask yourself how that person moves and move like them. Become a mime, not overtly but with slight moves. Watch and learn what slight moves you can make. The less overt, the better.

Chapter 28:
Mastering the Art of Body Language

You've probably heard of the saying that 90% of all communication is non-verbal and body language, and while that urban myth is a little extreme, the actual number is around 58%. When you consider verbal communication around 38%, you still see how important body language is when communicating.

Okay, making that a bit more realistic, if you're trying to get a job at a new business and you've gone into the interview, how do you think you should present yourself? If you're slumped back in the chair with your arms folded while staring at the employer, it doesn't matter what answers you give or what experience you have; you're not going to get the job.

Body language is big business. The point is, your body language is sending out a message to everyone around you, and it works both ways. The body language of those around you is telling you messages about them if you know what to look for and how to read the signs.

Every facial expression, every movement of the body, and every position of your hands tell people what's going on. If you're sitting closed up and reserved and biting your nails while avoiding eye contact, you're giving away the impression you're nervous and on edge. If you walk into a room big and broad, making eye contact and smiling at everyone you pass, you give the impression you're completely at ease.

This extends into the tone and volume of your voice, the way you're standing, the amount of eye contact you give each person, and your overall posture. When you control your body language and read the body language of others, this puts you in a prime position to influence others effectively.

When it comes to body language, there's a vast library of information out there to explore. Still, when specifically focusing on persuading and influencing people, there's one key aspect you'll want to be thinking about known as embodied cognition.

Embodied cognition is all about defining the link between the mind and the body, exploring how the two are connected, and influencing others. It is how your mind controls the body, in all the ways you would expect, and how the body controls the mind in the opposite direction. Think about how leaning your elbow on a desk with your head in your hand acts as and signifies that you're bored. Even when you're not bored, doing this action can make you feel bored, thus triggering a mental and ultimately physical response.

This appears throughout our lives. Making a fist is associated with being violent, aggressive, and assertive. Writing down negative thoughts you have about yourself can solidify them in your mind if you write them down in your dominant hand, but it can oppositely affect you less if you write them with your non-dominant hand. This is the power of embodied cognition.

So, how to use this to influence?

In 1988, Strack, Martin, and Stepper conducted a study where they asked two groups of people to hold pens in their mouths. One group was instructed to bite on the pen while the other was instructed to keep it between their lips. Both groups then looked through cartoon sketches and rated how funny they were. The group who were asked to bite the pens, thus putting their mouths into a natural smiling position, found the cartoons most amusing.

This is an effect known as the Facial Feedback Hypothesis. Robert Zajonc researched this theory back in 1989 and found that the body language we make can physically trigger biological responses within our bodies. You know when you're feeling sad, and people say fake a smile because it will make you feel better—the fake it 'til you make it kind of an attitude? That's what he discovered.

Within his research, he asked German students to repeat vowel sounds (a, e, i, o, u) and found that when students said "e" and "ah," it made them make smiling expressions. Try it for yourself now. On a biological level, making these expressions cooled the blood in the students' arteries, lowering the brain temperature and making the students experience a more pleasant mood.

On the other hand, he found that making the "u" sound caused a frowning expression, which caused the opposite effects. The frown raised brain temperature and decreased blood flow, causing a more negative-slanting mood. This effect can work when you use body language on yourself and others.

Applying Body Language as a Persuasive Strategy

Imagine you're talking to me about a hobby you enjoy. It could be sports, food, travel, lifestyle, or anything you want. You're telling me the details of your passion and describing above-average detail. As you speak, I'm nodding my head. What do you feel? What is my body language communicating to you?

Since in the vast majority of cultures the act of "head-nodding" is a sign of agreement and open-mindedness, if I nod my head at what you're saying indicates that I'm on the same page as you. I'm listening. I understand. I'm following. I want you to carry on. My act of head nodding is a non-verbal cue that tells you all of this subconsciously without me saying a word.

Take control of this act to send a message. When you're speaking to someone, and you're going to ask someone to do something for a favor, or you're wanting to influence them with information, start bringing head nodding into your conversation. Since this has such a strong tie with the concept of agreement and understanding, you're encouraging a more agreeable statement of mind.

So, once you've made a request or shared information with someone, how can you make them agree? How can you bring the head-nodding action out of someone else? Simple. You use more body language.

When you're speaking to someone, there is naturally going to be a point in any conversation where someone will acknowledge what the other person is saying. Verbally, this will sound like someone saying "uh-huh" or "yes," showing their agreement. That's the verbal parallel to a head nod. However, to trigger these acknowledgment cues, you need to create these natural pauses.

Using body language, you can do this by physically pausing what you're saying for a minute, but not too long because you don't want to disrupt the flow and momentum of what you're saying. Alternatively, you can raise your eyebrows, another non-verbal cue that you're looking for acknowledgment. This happens in a fraction of a second and is done in such a way that no one will notice.

When you're in a conversation with someone, as you're building up to your request, start implementing these non-verbal cues into your body language to prime the person's mind into an agreement. Once they've agreed several times, you then share your request, and the person is far more likely to agree, which will be showcased as a visual head nod response.

Other Body Language Cues

In truth, every aspect of body language is saying something. Still, being aware of the core body language attributes, you can start to control them, thus controlling the message you're sending out to the world and the people around you. Remember what we said earlier about someone being defeated? What do you imagine? Someone bent or hunched over, the weight of the world on their back. This is the physical representation of someone being defeated.

Hand in hand with the persuasive head nodding and pausing cues above, let's take a moment to explore other body language cues that send a message. With awareness of these cues, you can control them how you wish, ultimately sending the message you want.

The Power of Posture

Posture is such a massive message sending form of body language. When someone walks into a room with their head held high, their body exposed, and their back straight, they ooze power and status wherever they go. People instantly respect people in this way because they expose themselves in a way that shows no fear. It shows confidence and authority. This person is meant to be here, and they feel comfortable doing it.

On the other hand, a slumped position, hunched over, or hiding certain parts of your body, such as your hands or chest, sends the impression you're anxious or nervous. Try it now, and you'll see the effect on yourself. Sit up straight, push your shoulders down, and hold your head high. Feels powerful, right?

Now slump your back, and hold your hands in your lap, hiding them between your legs. Look at the ground and never above the horizon. Feels weak and defeated, right? Even moving and positioning yourself in this way is affecting you and how you feel, and you're aware you're doing it, so now imagine what kind of subconscious messages you're sending out to those around you.

When applied to a conversation where you're trying to persuade someone, use your posture accordingly. If you're trying to convey authority to get somebody to listen to you, hold a high position that presents power and confidence. Likewise, when you strike this posture, you may see the other person physically backing down and slumping, which means they're feeling anxious and defeated in your presence.

When influencing someone, you don't want them to shut down completely, but instead respect what you're saying, so you don't want to go all the way. Just find the balance with each person you're speaking to on an individual level. On the other hand, you may want to empower and make someone feel good about themselves, in which case slumping back yourself may be the sign they need to feel powerful and believe in themselves.

It's all about finding what works in any given situation, depending on the outcome you want to achieve.

The Message Sent With the Eyes

We all know that eye contact is an important part of communication, and if you're speaking to someone looking everywhere else but at you, this sends the message that they're not there with you. Of course, depending on the circumstances of the individual situation, this can mean different things.

It could indicate boredom or distraction, or they may be shy or nervous about speaking with you. Aligned with this, where you're looking with your eyes as you converse will say a lot about you, but always on an unconscious level. Watch any street magician on YouTube, David Blaine being a prime example.

Watch how he always maintains eye contact with the people he's performing to. He directs such a powerful message and influences the people he's performing because he maintains such a strong connection with his eyes.

To cut a long story short, eye contact is direct and connecting and powerful for sending a message. Eye contact makes people listen, feel included, and feel a part of a conversation. A lack of eye contact creates the opposite effect. How can you apply this knowledge in your conversations? Well, think about the macro of your speech.

When you're thinking about what you're saying, chances are you tend to look away. Everybody does. When you're umming and ahhing, you'll look to the side or at your feet while trying to find the words to say. This breaking of eye contact detracts from your message, and it ultimately has much less impact and power.

If, however, you take a moment to think about what you're saying before you speak and then share your message while making full eye contact, then your message will retain its full power and impact. As the saying goes, always think before you speak. Eye contact also increases the perception of trust, whereas speaking without contact can seem suspicious and deceitful, so bear these in mind.

Exposure of Your Chest

This may seem like a strange point to consider because I'm not talking about undoing the buttons of your shirt and exposing your chest in the literal sense, but more in the sense that your chest and how open it is is a transparent body language sign that details how vulnerable someone is, and a whole lot more than that.

When I was a child, I used to play cops and robbers with my friends. I would always play the robber because my friend has a proper kids-play police outfit, and he would always run around the big tree in the back garden and shout, "Put your hands up!"

Of course, as anybody would and still do, people raise their hands and expose their chest even in real-time situations, but what message is this sending? Well, think of it oppositely. When you cross your hands in front of your chest or hold something up against it, what message are you sending now?

In most cultures and societies worldwide, crossed arms and covering your chest is a sign of self-defense. If I stand up and give a speech in a meeting and sit back down and cross my arms, I'm negating any chance for people to ask questions. When someone is sat with their arms crossed, they're defensive and protecting themselves from external harm.

Use this information wisely. If you need a favor from someone, when's the best time to ask? When they are open and free to do something or have something in their hands, their arms are crossed? The first option is best. If you can get your timing right, you'll see far more success with your persuasion efforts.

Cutting Off Your Message Before It's Over

Have you ever watched an advertisement, and it seems to glitch right at the end? Like it gets cut off abruptly, only by a second or so, but it feels blunt and unfinished?

If you head over to YouTube, hit the Music channel, and listen to any song for several seconds and then close the tab, you're going to remember that song for the rest of the day. Guaranteed. It's because you heard a snippet of information, and your brain is thinking, "Okay, well, now I want to know more. It feels unfinished," and the mind is eager to fill in the gaps, thus holding onto everything else that has been said before.

Oppositely, if someone is talking to you sentence after sentence, and they're just going on and on and repeating the same points, you're going to get bored, tune out, and forget everything.

Applying this tactic to your conversation, if you're detailing points to someone, share your first point and your second point, and then it looks like you're going to share a third point, but don't. See how it makes you...

Exactly. Stopping yourself in this way abruptly stops the flow, which engages the mind in such a way that it cements the information. Of course, I'm not saying be rude with what you're saying and just stop mid-sentence and walk off, but instead use body language cues, like opening your mouth, to fake continuing. This is a fantastic tactic when you want someone to remember what you're saying.

Gestures and Hand Movements

Hand gestures are known for being able to communicate so much in such small actions. If I wave, I'm saying hello or goodbye. A more energetic version of this movement would be to try and grab your attention. If I raise my hands horizontally, palms facing down, and pat the air, I'm telling you to be quiet and settle down.

This is all basic stuff, but it's still a very important form of body language, so we have to cover it. Let's go through this rapidly. As you read through, try mimicking the gestures to see how they make you feel, what they look like to do, and then imprinting them so you can see them in other people.

- **Touch**

While I don't recommend touching everyone you meet, touching in some ways is a very powerful way to connect with other people. Even just a touch on someone's arm or shoulder can connect you to them, and it displays signs of comfort, warmth, and connection.

Be careful with how you touch people, though. If you touch with just your fingertips, this can make people very uncomfortable, and it shows you're nervous but trying to hide it. When you agree with someone, placing a firm hand on their shoulder can amplify your acknowledgments.

When touching or being touched by someone, you can also tell their state of mind and be by their hands' temperature. Warm hands mean they are comfortable and positive, whereas cold hands may indicate tenseness and anxiety, but of course, the room temperature can play a big part in this.

- **Hand on Heart**

Placing your hand on your heart is an excellent technique to instill emotions of trust in another person. Hence the saying "hand on my heart," which means you can trust me or insinuates you are saying, "I promise." It means, "Believe what I'm saying or accept what I'm telling you."

- **Pointing**

Pointing can mean a lot of things. If I point at you during a conversation, it's a very imposing and authoritative gesture. Teachers and parents will point at their children when telling them off, almost as though it's directing the words of discipline they're saying directly at the children and their being.

This gesture amplifies your ability to talk down to someone and is often interpreted as angry, aggressive, and even violent. If you jab your finger, a more vigorous point, this is deemed very aggressive. As a whole, pointing is deemed impolite by most people and cultures.

However, depending on the circumstances, pointing with a wink or in a humorous manner may be a highly powerful gesture for the person being pointed towards. They can feel acknowledged and recognized, like saying, "You're the man!" when they've done a good job. It's all about the body language that accompanies the point and the context of the conversation.

- **Palms Up**

Just like exposing your chest, palms facing up is usually a very positive sign that means openness, readiness, and trustworthiness. Opening your entire arms up with upward-facing palms can be empowering and enlightening, but you can also say you don't know by shrugging your shoulders with your hands up.

However, this isn't a sign of weakness, but more a sign saying, "I don't know, but I'm comfortable enough, confident enough, and ready enough to admit that."

- **Palms Down**

With your palms facing down, you're saying you believe in what you're saying, and you're confident with your stand. This may be viewed with authority and trust, but it can also mean defiance, as though saying, "I'm not going to budge, and you can't change my mind."

- **Hands on Hips**

While there is a common idea that placing your hands on your hips can be a sign that you're unready to partake in something, or sometimes even frustration or irritation, it is much more commonly a sign that someone is ready to take action. That's why you'll see it all the time in athletes and work-lovers.

Sure, you will also see it in authority figures, such as police, military generals, and others in charge, to display assertiveness, but this still shows the individual is ready to take action.

- **Fists**

A very powerful gesture, a clenched fist, is all about resolution and determination. It can be seen as violent, depending on the context of a situation, but mainly showcases an unwillingness to back down. Think about when a sports team scores and the fans will raise their fists in triumph, not unlike when a business secures a big contract after fighting for it for a long time.

If someone has made a fist with their thumb hidden in their hands, this can be a sign of anxiousness, as though the person is hardening themselves for what is to come.

- **Hand Chops**

When someone chops their hands through the air, it's a power move saying, "This is what I'm saying. I've made up my mind. Nobody can change that." It's a very definitive and authoritative move. You'll see politicians and CEOs using this gesture a lot.

- **Hands Rubbing Together**

This is a gesture that represents excitement for the future, reward, and happy times ahead. When someone places a large bet on odds that are massively stacked in their favor, this is the hand gesture that comes to mind. It's all about channeling the stress and excitement that comes from an upcoming positive situation, as well as preparing themselves for it.

- **Hands in Pockets**

Hands in pockets is usually a powerful sign that there is a reluctance to do something or an unwillingness to proceed. If you're talking to someone and putting their hands in their pockets, this shows you've lost their interest, or their minds are elsewhere.

This can also signify that someone is hiding the truth since hand signals can give away the truth, and they're hiding the ability to show this.

- **Hands Behind Back**

We spoke about exposing your chest and keeping it open; placing your hands behind your back is a sign of confidence and comfort. Of course, it's always more trustworthy to show your hands in a situation, but if the level of trust is already there, perhaps if you're around colleagues, friends, and family members, then you may not need to do this.

Even if you're with strangers, having your hands behind your back can showcase signs of confidence and comfort. You're saying, "Here I am, and I am vulnerable," but in a controlled sense.

- **Steepling**

Steepling is the term given to the act of an individual placing their fingertips together without their palms touching. This is a massive display of power, which is why you see it with evil villains in movies, chess players contemplating moves, or lawyers. This move is all about confidence, especially self-confidence and assurance in the future.

If you saw someone doing this in a board meeting, you can read that they truly believe they know what you're doing, and they've got some powerful information related to what's being said.

- **Squeezing or Clasping Hands Together**

When someone squeezes their hands together, either their entire hand or their fingers, this is a sign that someone is uncomfortable, nervous, or anxious about the situation they're in. This move is all about self-settling and trying to ground themselves. It's like a comfort gesture people give to themselves to try and make themselves feel better.

Sometimes people will rub their wrists, and this is the same sign. When you spot this in someone or yourself, you may need to comfort that person, empower them, or there's an opportunity to find out what's going on.

Reading the Body Language of Others

While there are many advantages to managing your body language in every circumstance, keep in mind that it's not only about controlling your own language; it's also about interpreting the language of others. You're talking to a stranger and have just started a conversation, perhaps over the water cooler at the office.

The individual is talking and making a lot of eye contact, they're making wild hand gestures as they speak, and their chest is open, almost inviting you in. What is this body language communicating? It's saying, and I'm happy in this conversation. I'm engaged. I'm connected to you. This is a conversation I'm enjoying being a part of.

This shows you that the person is probably in a positive mood, having a good day, and is more likely to be agreeable and open with what you're saying. If you needed to ask a favor, this is an excellent person to engage with.

On the other hand, if someone is leaning against the water cooler and not looking at anyone, is blunt with their responses, and has their arms crossed, this says the complete opposite to the example above. Use this information wisely when choosing how to approach a situation and deal with certain people, finally allowing you to determine the best approach to influencing someone.

Mirroring Someone's Body Language

You may have already heard about mirroring the body language of others and the power that comes with that, but there's a fine line when it comes to using the art of mirroring correctly. If you mirror someone exactly, movement to movement, this is just obvious, and it's going to make the other person feel uncomfortable.

However, mirroring in the right way, with just the right amount of mirroring, you can connect far more profound than you usually would with even a stranger. This has been proven in ongoing studies, including Val Barren 2003, where waitresses made higher tips. In Gueguen, Martin, and Meineri in 2011, students convinced other students to write their essays for them.

Mirroring is a fantastic way to persuade someone and influence them to do something because it makes the other person feel way more at ease and connected. Because they're already doing the body movements and gestures, and now, you're doing them subconsciously. They believe that everything is acknowledged and accepted, providing complete comfort and a state of mind, which is much more agreeable.

If you want to mirror someone correctly, there are four basic procedures to follow.

Step One

Start by fronting the person you're speaking with, which means being with them and giving them your full attention. Put them in front of you and make them everything to you at that moment. Give them full eye contact and nod when they speak. Roughly, nod three times when agreeing to drive home your acknowledgment.

You can boost this further with a bit of imagination. For a moment while they're speaking, pretend they are the most important person in the world, even just for a second or two, and then stop pretending and return to giving them your full attention. Even in these few seconds, you'll send all the non-verbal cues that make them feel like, to you, nothing else but them matters.

Step Two

Start mirroring their actions. If they sit back in their chair and slump, wait a few seconds and do the same. If the other person starts speaking faster or louder, slower and quieter, then do the same. The two main things to remember here are matching their pace and their volume.

Step Three

Find their punctuator. A punctuator is the non-verbal cue or tell which the person will do every time they make a point and display the tell to clarify that point. A common one is tipping their head forwards and perhaps raising an eyebrow. Another common one is using a hand gesture, like the chopping or pointing we spoke about above.

Find the punctuator and start mirroring it!

Step Four

Okay, at this point, you and the person you're speaking to should already feel a strong connection, and they should already be in an agreeable state of mind, which makes this step optional, but if you want to see how strong the connection is, then test it for yourself.

The simplest method to accomplish this is to do something completely irrelevant to the discussion and then see how they respond. If you've gone out for a drink, you may take a sip or even just move your glass randomly to another nearby point on the table. If they mirror and do the same, you know your connection is strong!

One final point to remember is to ensure you're only mirroring the positive actions and cues the person is giving you. If someone picks up their phone, or is distracted and looks away, or sits with their arms folded with their chest closed off, don't mirror these actions. Instead, remain patient, keep mirroring the positives, and you'll see the connection forming.

When it comes to body language aligned with the art of persuasion, changing the way you act and stand isn't going to be the be-all and end-all strategy to influence people to do what you want while controlling their behavior.

However, when applied alongside the other strategies in this book, and when it comes to reading the situation and person and defining what approach you're going to take, the body language strategies you've learned here are invaluable.

Chapter 29:
Look and Feel Confident

I have a little story to share. You know Bruce Springsteen, don't you? He's one of the most popular musicians of all time and is also known to suffer from nerves—especially before performing. But, do his nerves stop him from performing and doing what he likes best? Of course not.

See, you can be nervous without it showing. In short, you have to fake your confidence, and eventually, you'll notice you're not faking anything anymore, and you're confident already!

Dress for the Occasion

One good way of feeling confident onstage is by looking the part.

You see, people tend to listen to those who look as if they know what they are talking about instead of those who look like they just passed by the event for nothing. You don't have to buy extremely expensive clothes, but it would help if you could invest in a few important pieces (slacks, a formal dress, some ties, leather shoes, etc.) so that once you get asked to talk in front of an audience, you'd get to show them that you are ready.

Try it. Dress up for a certain event you're invited to, and you'd feel like you belong there, instead of just feeling like you're just there to pass the time. If you want to belong, dress and act like it—and you will.

Focus on those who nod their heads

When speaking in front of a crowd, you'd be able to notice who is listening by checking out who is nodding their head and who is making sense of what you're talking about. Now, focus on those people so you'd also get responses and so the rest of the audience will feel compelled to butt—or blend—in and listen to you more intently.

Be mindful of Gestures and Body Language

Another way to make sure that you look and feel confident is by being mindful of body language. Here are some tips that you can keep in mind:

1. **Make use of space.** You can move around the stage. You don't have to dance, but you can walk from one end to the next to engage your audience. It would be so awkward if you'd just stay in place all the time, looking like a stiff tree. You can walk. You can help them understand your thoughts better by making your way to them, or at least helping them see you as a person and not a talking stick.

2. **Stop shifting focus.** When you look from one side of the audience to the other in such a quick manner, people will feel like you're rolling your eyes or that you are extremely nervous. Yes, it's okay to make use of space—but do not try to look from one person to another as if asking for approval. That's not the kind of message you'd want to impart to your audience.

3. **Be animated!** As Tyra Banks would say, "Smile! Smile with your eyes." When you do this, it shows that you're sincere with what you're doing instead of just looking bored and stiff and not knowing what to say. It makes you more alive and realistic—and that's the kind of speaker people want.

4. **Make use of open gestures.** Point your hands outwards, don't just point to your chest and think that people could understand what you're trying to say.

5. **Don't make it verbatim.** You don't have to prepare and type a long speech and read every word the way it was written. This would be so monotonous and would just make your audience bored. You can adlib—this is your speech, after all! The more natural it is, the better!

6. **Think about the gestures you use every day,** especially when you're at the dinner table or talking to people closest to

you—and use them for your speech. This way, you'd be way more natural!

7. **Avoid these mannerisms:**

> Touching your face.
>
> Playing with your fingers.
>
> Shifting your weight or swaying from side to side.
>
> Playing with your pens.
>
> Putting hands in your pockets.
>
> Touching your ears.
>
> Adjusting your hair.
>
> Pacing back and forth.
>
> Crossing the arms.
>
> Arranging clothes over and over again.

Make them Laugh

Laughter is not only the best medicine; it's also one of the easiest ways to get someone's attention and keep the atmosphere light and engaging. It's not about making slapstick jokes, but just about showing your wit and being able to make the conversation fun for everyone.

Just because you're making a speech doesn't mean it has to be overly serious, especially when you know that you can inject some humor into it. When laughter ensues in a room, people feel better, and they feel like they could reach you, instead of feeling like you're only talking about the things that matter to you. But of course, don't try to make jokes if it's a serious matter (i.e., death, grieving, etc.) Think of your audience.

Your speech should be about everyone—and not just about you!

Don't mind your Mistakes

Another cliché: Everyone makes mistakes. No one is perfect, and no one is immune to errors and the like—but will you let those mistakes get you down? No, of course not.

What you should do is just get back up. If you said the wrong word, don't make use of fillers. Try a few seconds of silence, and then make a joke, or just engage the audience.

When you recognize your mistakes, you'd easily be able to bounce back from them instead of just feeling like you are a failure. Even the most experienced public speakers make errors from time to time. Don't let those errors get you off track!

Are You Confident or Arrogant?

Okay, since everyone in today's world seems to be rushing towards one thing in common, what is it? Isn't it true that everyone aspires to be a leader, a boss, or a manager, especially young CEOs? They want to be recognized as a leader, and more crucially, as a successful leader, don't they? The term "success" is crucial in this situation.

There is one thing that you must have to be successful, and what is it? Confidence! There is a particular allure to confident individuals. When they're around you, their personalities make you joyful; they inspire and encourage you, don't you agree? Okay, we spoke about confidence because, do you agree with me, confidence is often misunderstood?

The difference

You should now see a fine line between the two, and it may make or destroy your career. It's done if you're confident, but it's done if you're arrogant.

We'll figure out what type of conduct you have and how to change it into a more confident version rather than an arrogant one.

Some individuals are now concerned that they may over the line and become arrogant if they gain confidence. On the other side, some individuals are concerned that others may mistake their confidence for arrogance. You may say to yourself, "Oh my God, what if people think I'm arrogant instead of confident?"

Now, let me tell you a short tale about a lady who had to choose between two guys, correct? Whether or whether she wants to marry. Now, the problem is, they were both doing very well in their professions, they both adored her, and they came from a highly-educated family. So she decided to ask them one common question and then determine and select based on their answers. 'Why should I pick you?' was the query. So the one replied, "Believe me, you will never be short of anything since I'm well established in my profession, well qualified, and I can buy you whatever you desire." Well, I picked you because you're honest and you want to be with someone who doesn't abuse this trait, and you should choose me because I recognize that quality in you, the other one replied. So, folks, what are your views on this? Which one was more certain, the first or the second? And who was the more arrogant, the first or the second? Isn't it a difficult decision? I'll tell you, the second response was confident rather than arrogant. The first one seemed to be an interview, which implies that this is what we need to know, right? Because of such and so, you should pick me. The thin line between the two was now the same as what you choose to respond to when and with what words.

Let us hear an interview example when asked, 'why should we choose you over other candidates?' One candidate said, "you should choose me because I have what others don't have, I have won every competition I have participated in at my college, and I am meant to lead." Now he thought that was confidence, on the other hand, the next one said, "it is only fair to talk about myself as I don't know other candidates, you should choose me because the company's goals and my interests and passion it's a perfect match." Now one is arrogant because arrogance only has big words and loud words, but it lacks basic information about anything, about other things. In contrast, the second candidate spoke only about himself where he spoke well about the company is wrong, so he balanced it out, right? Who would get the job, in this case, try to answer this one, and who sounds arrogant?

Signs of arrogance

What happens when individuals are arrogant is that they stop learning, right? And individuals who have self-confidence and humility are constantly learning, and success only comes to those who continue to learn because they are the ones who develop. Right, how do you know when you're being arrogant?

This is something we must comprehend and comprehend for ourselves. For starters, when you believe you are the brightest person on the planet. If you're in the office and someone gives you advice or tries to correct you, and you completely ignore it, your friends will think you're grammatically incorrect. They will try to tell you, but you'll ignore it because you don't like being questioned, and you'll be a fool to yourself and your team's growth. So, you're saying this halts my learning process? Of course, it does since you don't learn the correct information. That's it, my dear friends; this is a cycle. If you don't listen to others, you won't learn. If you don't learn, you won't succeed, right? What are your options for resolving this? Now, how can you overcome your arrogance and conduct and gain confidence? Take it a step further and request candid comments, right? Go ahead and ask your coworkers, speak to your friends, and ask them questions so they can provide you with additional information. Now, what you've done is developed a learning attitude, and this attitude will help you constantly grow, breaking the cycle. One last thing I want to mention is that learn to laugh at yourself, at your errors, because it's alright, we're all humans, we all make mistakes, so it's OK, right? So that others can tell you what is good or wrong, go ahead and do it.

Accept mistakes and take accountability

So, let's pretend I was meant to respond to an important email that I had forgotten about, okay? So, I was meant to perform this job, and I completely forgot about it. My colleague reminded me, and my supervisor received a complaint that I had failed to respond to several customers' emails simultaneously. Isn't it true that my employer questioned me? To be honest, I didn't give her the truth when I first told her, "I had responded." Then I told her, "I thought I responded, hmm," and proceeded to provide reasons after reasons. I know, I know, I should have admitted my error the first time around, right? So, the next time you see someone not acknowledging their errors and instead blaming others and making excuses, remind them that they should accept their mistakes and take responsibility for their actions. This is another method to learn when you are being arrogant and stubborn about things. "You guys, confidence leaders are modest. Use phrases like "you're correct, this was my fault." It is important to recognize that errors are not a sign of weakness and that you must learn from them. When you accept responsibility for your failure, I am certain that you will be allowed to make significant choices, and that, my friends, is what success is all about.

The I-me-and-mine person

Do you have friends that spend a lot of time talking about themselves? In college, we had this student who would constantly start recounting tales or incidents with 'I or me or mine, my mother and I,' do you remember that day when I went there... She tended to compliment herself. Now, some of her classmates, including many of our professors, thought of her as a confident young lady who spoke so much about herself and could speak so much about herself, but believe me, when she was asked to lead our class in a competition project, she never made decisions that were in the best interests of all of us. So that you know that we have a chance to win, these are arrogant individuals I refer to as self-centered. Now, I'm sure many people are aware of this, but they don't realize it's arrogant. To break this habit, start with small steps like remembering other people's names and basic information about them so that instead of just talking about yourself, you have someone else to talk about. As a confident leader, prioritize others you know by simply supporting, inspiring, and motivating them. Imagine a film in which the director, actor, producer, singer, music composer, and editor are the same. I'm afraid I can't. Guys, this individual just wants to boast about himself, speak about himself, show off his skill, and most importantly, not allow anybody else or others a chance. These are also the individuals who dislike being praised or appreciated by others. Someone who constantly praises oneself and is often seen as arrogant and untalented. Trust me, doing everything by yourself is not talent; it's simply arrogance, I believe. What can you do now to improve your chances of success? Guys, start with small things like patting someone on the back and saying "well done," right? What about shaking people's hands and congratulating them? Isn't this how you'll gradually show humility? And motivating others around you is a wonderful place to begin.

The verbal and non-verbal arrogance

Is there another way to tell whether you're arrogant and insecure? Are you curious as to what it is? This is also a very terrible habit to have. These are the individuals who don't give a damn about other people's feelings or emotions or who don't even respect them enough to care about them. Saying something like that's 'so stupid, oh how dumb,' makes one of the other errors giggle, such as oh my god, how foolish. Their arrogance may be evident in their verbal and nonverbal communication styles and abilities. Shaking hands exclusively with individuals in higher or better positions and not with juniors, for example, is a nonverbal indication of arrogance. When you're busy, anytime you're busy, whenever you're busy on your phone when others are chatting, right? It's verbal to raise voices when people are chatting to one another. Do you realize that people do not stay loyal to such people? They also lose respect from them as a result of this. For example, I will not glance at my phone while speaking to me, and vice versa. I will not use terms like "stupid," "I won't be able to do this," "you won't be able to do this," or "you won't be able to accomplish this," and I will strive to be more courteous in my behavior. The ultimate test of a gentleman or any human is his "respect for people who can be of no conceivable use to him," as they say. That is the last examination. So, gentlemen, make sure you shake hands with everyone and involve everyone the next time.

Okay, now you know a little bit more about the world and how you can treat yourself, others, and yourself far more gently, making fewer errors and learning from them. Remember how self-assured and successful individuals have faith in themselves? Pay attention to what others have to say and treat them with respect. I'm certain that after practice, you'll all be excellent individuals who have mastered each thing, okay?

Chapter 30: Develop Self-Confidence to Communicate Effectively

Dale Carnegie claims that a person's success in life is determined 85 percent by their ability to lead others and just 15% by what individuals know in his best-selling book *How to Win Friends and Influence People*. There is no place where this statement is more evident than when it comes to communication.

To lead others, you must have the courage to put yourself last while serving others. As a result, if you want to be a good communicator, you must learn to build self-confidence.

If you need to speak with someone but are nervous about doing so, there are several techniques you may take to seem more confident. The first of these strategies is to dress more formally. You don't have to have the most up-to-date clothing, but make sure they're well-maintained since it's a beautiful way to show people how much you care about your look.

Another trick is to change your stride. The way you walk may have an impact on how you are seen. People will notice if you move somewhat quicker or more uprightly than you already do. According to many studies, people who walk quickly are regarded as more significant than those who stroll. People who stroll along the street with their shoulders back and a longer stride are less likely to be accosted. As a result, just adding some enthusiasm in your stride may affect how your message is received. Of course, you are anxious to complete your goals because you are anxious to complete your life goals.

Practice excellent posture to give the impression of greater self-assurance. Maintain a strong posture with your shoulders back, and your head raised high. Make an effort to look the person you're speaking in the eyes. This boosts your self-confidence by making the other person more confident in your skills.

Try making a gratitude list when you're feeling incredibly timid. Take a piece of paper and write a list of all the things in the world for which you are thankful. Researchers have discovered that devoting a part of each week to writing in a thankfulness notebook has remarkable benefits.

Guard yourself against speaking negatively about yourself as well as other people. As your mother said, if you don't have anything kind to say about someone, don't say anything at all. When you speak hurtful things about others, you are undermining not just their self-worth but also your own. The Chinese leader and strategist said, "Know yourself, and you will win all wars." This includes the fights you'll have with yourself when you start to have those negative ideas. Imagine each wrong thought as an insect and then mentally stomp on it. Replace that negative idea with something good once you've crushed it out of existence. Be on the lookout for these nasty bugs; they'll sneak up on you when you least expect it.

If you've been putting off sending a message, now is the moment to do it. People respect you more when you take a position, even if they disagree with your point of view 90% of the time. Realizing this boosts your self-esteem significantly.

Regular exercisers are much more likely to feel better about themselves. When a person exercises, the body generates happy chemicals, which make them feel better. As a result, regardless matter how hectic your calendar is, make sure you arrange a time to exercise regularly.

Finally, it would be best to recognize that each individual contributes significantly to a project's overall success. You are included in this. As a result, ensure that you take pleasure in your contribution to any project.

Now that you feel confident about yourself, you are better positioned to communicate with others. Begin each conversation with praise and genuine gratitude. Everyone with whom you interact excels at something. First and foremost, figure out what you appreciate about that individual. If you have to send a wrong message, do it in the middle. Before you propose anything they've done that isn't precisely what you were looking for, soften the impact by praising them.

Never explicitly inform someone that they are committing a mistake. Instead, suggest that the person's effort be used for a different cause. The Dallas Cowboys, one of the best football teams in America, practices this effectively when they must get rid of a player. They call the player into the office without any other people around and tell the player that they are not suitable for their organization. They then tell the player that they hope to find a team where their skills will be helpful. Since they have not told the player that they do not have any skills, many players have gone home, worked on their skills, and come back to play for another team successfully.

When you issue commands, people's emotions are wounded. Instead of issuing instructions, ask questions to entice people to do the task at hand. Allowing oneself to become a drill sergeant in the army is not a good idea. Instead, find out how to persuade others to do what you want by asking questions.

Assume you're in charge of a team project and one of your workers isn't doing his tasks on schedule. Nonetheless, the employee approaches you, requesting a long weekend off. Rather than telling him no, try if you can come up with a solution that will satisfy both of you. Begin by inquiring about the status of the employee's job. Even if you already know the answer, this allows the employee to tell you the truth. Then inquire as to what it would take to finish the job.

In many cases, it doesn't matter when the job is completed; it is completed. This also ensures that the employee has the necessary resources to accomplish the task. You may create a win-win scenario by using questions to enable individuals to find their answers.

Good communication enables the other party to keep their dignity. There are flaws in everyone. It must sometimes address these issues. As a result, consider how you may do it so that the other person does not lose face. Many discussions devolve into disputes as a result of one person's desire to put another down. Avoid falling into this trap.

Consider a strategy that enables the other person to keep their dignity in every discussion, even if they are incorrect.

To do this, correctly time your discussion. A hurried discussion often makes the other person furious. Make your goals obvious by demonstrating that you care about the other person's well-being. While you may have strong feelings about a topic, remember to stick to the facts. Make sure that your views are not taken as truth. Allow yourself to consider the possibility that there are other things going on that you aren't aware of.

Check to see whether you're a good listener. Pay attention to what the person on the other end of the line has to say. Use good eye contact, and smile as often as possible. Watch to see if the person you are addressing starts to mirror your body language. If they mess with their phones or otherwise occupy themselves, assume that they are not actively listening.

There are also important clues that you can watch to make sure that your messages are being received positively. Often, these clues are much more subtle than the eye roll that a teenager gives his parents. Start by watching to make sure that the arms stay close to the body and that the listener's hands stay in a natural position. Most times, the person who crosses their arms in front of them does not hear your message or accept it. Angry people often have very minimal facial expressions, and the listener will not be looking at you. If the person subtly turns away from you, you can assume that the person is not listening.

It may seem like a person trying to help may make two steps forward and six steps back. Therefore, it is essential to praise even the slightest improvement and every improvement that you see after that. Find ways to praise the person they will appreciate, and you will soon find the other person is working even more challenging to make you happy.

If you must convey an inappropriate message, provide enough time for the recipient to process the information. After a day or two, check in with them to see if they have any more information or questions they'd want to address. Find a space in your heart to genuinely care for the other person while remaining loyal to your message.

When pointing your finger at someone else, remember that you have three fingers pointing back at yourself, as the old saying goes. As a result, be sure you're taking care of your own business before communicating. Everyone has flaws, so make efforts to recognize yourself and show people around you that you're trying to overcome them.

Developing Confidence While Speaking

To start with, you should overcome the fear of addressing an audience. Many people end up making mistakes while speaking to an audience owing to being nervous. Here are some tips to overcome it.

Expect nervousness

To start with, you should expect to be a little nervous. Do not try to mask your nervousness, thinking you do not intend to be nervous. Channelize it to boost your confidence and delivery.

Prepare yourself

Next up, you should know exactly what you are going to be speaking about. Knowing what to say dramatically cuts down on nervousness.

Breathe

Draw in a few deep breaths just before speaking, and then continue breathing deeply when you begin your speech. This will instantaneously cut down on nervousness and make you sound more confident.

Rehearse thoroughly

Think of this as an exam and prepare for it by rehearsing like mock tests. Practice everything out loud so that you can hear yourself speaking and know precisely how it will sound to others. Avoid remembering something verbatim, as it will not sound fluent.

Think about your audience

One of the most significant contributors to stage fright is thinking about yourself and over-focusing on yourself. Instead, put the focus on the audience and think about them. This can help you be less nervous and concentrate more on your speech. Address your audience and ask them questions to make it an interactive session. If you have enough time before the course begins, then you can consider speaking to a few members of the audience to get to know a few better.

Simplify everything

Do not try to do too many things in a short amount of time. Keep your speech short and simple and elaborate on a few fundamental concepts. The primary aim should be to convey the basic idea, and so, it would be best to avoid making the speech too long or confusing.

Visualization

Visualization is a meditation technique that is quite popular and can help you do your best in delivering speeches. According to this method, you must find a quiet place, lie down, visualize yourself on the podium, and deliver the speech confidently. You must also visualize your audience accepting and applauding you. This will make you less nervous.

Poker face

One of the best things to do when you cannot calm your nerves is put on a poker face. Even if your knees are shaking or your palms are sweaty, adjust your face to look calm and peaceful. Your audience will perceive you as a confident person and, as and when the speech goes on, you will start feeling less and less nervous. Once you overcome your nervousness, you can successfully start addressing the audience. Here are some suggestions for preparing for a speech.

Practice every day

The basic idea is to sound confident and fluent in speaking, and the best way of doing this is by practicing every day. Put yourself and your mindset in a place where you have behaved confidently. For example, imagine that you are asking your boss for a raise and are approaching him very confidently. Think of the audience as your boss and address them positively. You can make use of the old trick of standing in front of the mirror and reciting the speech as that can make you less nervous and help you speak more fluently. You can record your speech if you like and listen back to check how you are sounding.

Tone

Pay attention to the tone that you are using while speaking. Some people raise their tone at the end of a sentence in a bid to sound more assertive. However, doing so will make it look like you are asking a question and or seeking approval from the audience. Both these will make you appear vulnerable and stab your confidence. If you wish to ask questions, keep them simple such as "Isn't it?" or "Do you agree with me?" maintain an even tone throughout and make sure you have your audience respond to your questions.

Talking speed

According to experts, it is best to limit your speech to around 190 words per minute while addressing the public. This will make it easier for your audience to understand what you are saying and be able to respond in a better way. If you speak too slowly, you run the risk of boring your audience, and if you go too fast, you will appear nervous to them. So it would be best to maintain a consistent speed that is not too fast or slow and focus on your diction and fluency.

Use movement

I'm sure you have heard this one before—use your body and move around as much as you can while speaking to an audience. This is an essential consideration since it allows you to connect with your audience more effectively. They will respond to your body language and display enthusiasm and interest. But make sure you are using the right type of movement, such as moving your hands while explaining something and walking up and down the stage to cover the entire audience. It also showcases your confidence levels and your knowledge on the topic. Avoid confusing signals such as touching your hair and adjusting your clothing, as they can distract your audience and make you appear nervous.

No fluff

Avoid fluff at all costs while speaking to your audience. Do not make the mistake of throwing in caveats and empty fillers just to keep your speech going. Avoid saying, "This is my opinion," "What I mean to say is," etc. These will make you appear nervous and unable to speak fluently. If you are using these phrases, then practice in advance and make sure you do not use these phrases while giving your speech.

Remain hydrated

Since you will be using your vocal cords quite a bit during the speech, it will be essential to remain hydrated to prevent dryness and keep your throat moisturized. Instead of having a large glass of water just before the speech, drink water throughout the day. You may drink any beverage you like to calm your voice and get ready to speak. Maintain a glass of water in front of you to sip if your throat gets dry.

Say thank you more often

It does not matter whether you are speaking to individuals or a broad audience; you must express gratitude if you wish to remain confident. As per experts, gratitude helps cut down on people's nervousness and makes them more open to addressing an audience. Thank your audience for patiently listening to you, being a part of the show, directing questions towards you, etc. These will make you less nervous and allow your audience to accept you better.

Make sure you smile

Smile more during your speech and keep the atmosphere light. This will help you cut down on your nervousness and make your audience listen to what you must say. Smiling also helps in making your voice sound more pleasant and makes you seem more approachable. You will appear composed and sorted to your audience.

Making use of silence

One of the biggest fears that people have when addressing an audience is silence. People tend to worry about forgetting their speech or losing their train of thought when they pause momentarily. However, most of such fears are unfounded, as silence will not affect your thought process unless you take a long pause. You can always take advantage of quiet. Take a few strategic pauses during your speech to help you gain composure and move on to the next topic a little more fluently.

Body language

Make sure you enter the room or the stage confidently with your head held high and your shoulders rolled back. Maintain a straight back and ensure your focus is on getting to the designated spot on stage. Draw in deep breaths and project a confident persona on stage. Avoid putting your hands in your pocket, crouching down, looking at the floor, looking at the roof, etc.

It's All About Your Confidence

There are several ways to build your confidence, and one of the most important ways is to stop self-depreciation. You are enough. The more you self-depreciate yourself, the more you kill your confidence.

It's one thing to be modest about your skills. It is another to self-depreciate yourself and the skills you have. Self-depreciation hinders you from communicating effectively, hinders your chances of success in life and at work, and kills your happiness.

To stop self-depreciation, it is important to note the reason we fall into the self-depreciation mode. Why do we fall into self-depreciation mode? Is it because we tend to dismiss our achievements to avoid coming off arrogant? Let's find out.

- **We don't want to come off as proud and arrogant** – Unfortunately, this also has a way of presenting us as inadequate to others. Be proud of what you have achieved and be proud of those that you haven't achieved just yet as you steadily work towards it. When you start complaining about things that you can't do when there are other things that you can do, you come off sounding like someone who is self-centered and has an unhealthy sense of entitlement. Subjecting others to a pity party for your sake will just push them off while wasting their precious time and positive energy. Don't understate your accomplishments for anyone and any reason; learn to live in the glow of the aftermath and bloom in it.

- **We are scared of failing** – Well, who isn't? But the moment you let the thought of failure trap you into not doing things that you might actually excel at is pure suicide. We may not be good at everything, but the moment you give in to failure, even before you start, you've failed. We tell people how unskilled we are so that they don't get disappointed when we eventually fail. It makes sense to us, but unfortunately, it limits our heights and chances of succeeding.

- **Low self-esteem** – Negative thoughts can make you have low self-esteem and make you self-depreciate yourself, and reduce your level of confidence, don't buy into it.

What are the consequences of this action?

- **You feel much worse than before** – Let's face it, playing a bad record repeatedly doesn't and will not give you a good vibe; it worsens over time. You can't tell yourself that you are inadequate every day and expect to come off excellent when you need it. The brain is so powerful that it picks up what you tell yourself. It grows and works according to the affirmations that you say to yourself. Positive affirmations make you positive and negative affirmations will only create negativity all around you.

- **It repels opportunities** – Your friends would know how accurate your self-assessments are, unlike your colleagues or acquaintances. The new ones may not necessarily know how competent you are if you are currently constantly putting yourself down. The opportunities that would have been given to you are now given to others because of your self-deprecating attitude. You've given them a wrong impression of yourself and your abilities. They become hesitant to build a relationship with you because you are always telling them how incompetent you are and how you can't do this or that. No one will give a job to one that isn't particularly competent, and numerous such opportunities will pass you by. Modesty is one thing, self-depreciation is another.

- **It repels people** – If you can badmouth yourself, then it definitely means that you can badmouth others. If you can judge yourself so badly without giving yourself enough credit, then it's safe to say that you will judge others without giving them the credit they deserve. It may not be the way you think of it or how you think it will be received, but that's the impression that you are giving off every step of the way. People don't trust a prejudiced judge, especially one that only sees the faults and flaws and never the good or strengths that abounds in one.

Here are ways to break out of the habit of self-depreciation. It is not going to be that simple. It may take you days, weeks, months, or years to break out of this habit, but constantly and steadily doing it one day after the other will ensure that your confidence grows and that your confidence grows self-deprecating habit decreases. It only matters if you are ready to make that conscious effort to stop your self-depreciation attitude.

Here are two steps that will help you consciously develop an answer to combat the self-depreciation habit.

- **Step one – Be conscious of every word that comes out of your mouth before you say them.** This is one of the hardest steps ever and one of the most difficult as it means you have to stop and think about every word before you say them. It will be a real struggle, especially for quick to point out their inefficiencies and inadequacies to others. It is hard, I know that. But if you want to break out of this habit, it has to be done consciously. Leave nothing to chance and be mindful of every word that you utter. Before you complain to someone about what you can't do and what you are not good at, learn to do it and say it in a way that doesn't belittle your abilities and strengths. We understand that there are a lot of things you need to learn, but there are also a lot of things you already know and are excellent at. Cherish those ones and be patient with yourself.

- **Step two – Change your mindset or your mentality.** This simply means that you should change the way you think. Get to the root of the problem. Why are you self-depreciating yourself? What is the reason? Get to the bottom of the issue and solve it. Find out why and when you do, take active measures in tackling it. Write out a list of the things you dislike about yourself and steadily tackle them one by one. Change the way you do them or change the way you approach those things. If you believe you have an unhealthy ego, work on it, change it, and find positive ways to do them instead of belittling yourself in a bid to contain it. Another way to change your mindset is to accept yourself for who you are. No one in the world can claim to be perfect or claim to be flawless, we all have one flaw and fault, but instead of letting it hinder us, we have learned to accept it and work on it every step of the world way. Expectations lead to disappointments. The moment you expect yourself to be flawless and successful in all areas of your life is the moment you start getting all things wrong, get disappointed, and become a total self-deprecating fellow.

What to Avoid When Communicating with Confidence

I have to say this again, the biggest way to show you are confident is by relaxing and being authentic. This will get you very far in many situations where you need to be an effective communicator. As you communicate with different people, remember that they get dressed the same way you do every day. Avoid putting anyone up on a pedestal, and this is a sure way to wreck your confidence. Show the person respect and expect respect in return.

Here are a few things to avoid as a communicator:

- Looking at the floor
- Fidgeting
- Interrupting others speaking
- Ending sentences with a question
- Overthink

Here are a few things to do as a communicator:

- Be honest
- Show Respect
- Stay Calm
- Empathize
- Breathe
- Be authentic

Chapter 31:
The Art of Active Listening

Surprisingly, one of the most important tools you need to develop in your communication skills is not your mouth. It is those two things that lie on either side of your head.

The concept of listening sounds rather straightforward. All you have to do is receive the sound waves coming from a person's mouth and have your brain interpret what those waves are carrying. And so, as long as you have a perfectly healthy (and clean) set of ears, you are bound to be a rather decent listener.

But to truly be listening in the sense that you get the essence of what the other person is saying to you is often hard to pull off. Conversations are tricky, after all, as they are fraught with nuances, innuendos, non-verbal cues, and other hidden messages. And there are topics out there that are hard to interpret if you do not give them your undivided attention.

At these moments, you have to learn how to understand a person, even if they are not sure of what they are trying to say to you. This is where you will apply what is called active listening.

What Exactly is Active Listening?

The most basic definition of active listening is that it is a kind of listening that requires the entire attention of the listener. This kind of listening aims to comprehend the person who is giving the message.

By understanding, it means delving deeper into their message and find out what exactly they are trying to say. This not only includes the words they use but also the emotions and body language that accompanies such.

Using this type of listening, you are expected to form the most appropriate response to what had just been said to you. At the same time, you have a better chance of recalling fully what you just listened to.

The premise of active listening is that it paves the way for a clear exchange of thoughts and feelings. This, in turn, would increase the chances of you coming to an understanding of every person involved in a single conversation.

One key element necessary to make active listening possible is empathy. This is the ability to see things from other people's perspectives, even if you do not agree with them in principle.

With this quality, active listening is made possible, especially in three critical areas.

1. Empathetic Understanding

The most basic aspect of active understanding simply involves listening while also trying to perceive things similarly to how others perceive them. In essence, you subtly tell the person that you understand what they are saying and understand what they mean and are feeling right now.

2. Listening Without Agreeing

If you understand where that person comes from, does it mean that you agree with them? No. It simply means that you now understand their perspective and can formulate a response that counters that without disrespecting the person on a personal level.

In essence, you can now tactfully share your viewpoints while respecting the differences that other viewpoints have with them.

3. Willingness to Listen

This aspect covers your readiness to listen to what a person is saying with no distractions at all. This is the more challenging part, as many distractions could prevent you from listening to that person fully. This includes your busy schedule and the devices that you surround yourself with.

This also includes fighting all urges to pretend to listen. This is not only rude but runs contrary to the basic concept of actively listening to another person. If done all too frequently, you run the risk of damaging relationships, personal or otherwise.

The Steps towards Active Listening

Active listening is a skill that means that you have to develop it over time. Here are some suggestions to help you become a more engaged and successful listener.

1. Eye Contact

When you talk to a person, and you try your best to avoid meeting their eyes, this is a telltale sign that you are not giving the conversation your full attention. This includes constantly checking your watch or phone, scanning the room, or looking out the window.

Most Western countries value eye contact as a basic foundation for active communication. This is quite important as certain conversations can take a while to get finished. If you are not comfortable locking eyes with the other person, you invite all urges to get up and move.

As such, when a person is speaking to you, put everything unnecessary down. If you are typing something at your computer, stop it. If you are writing something down, stop it. If you are eating, for the sake of the conversation and prevent yourself from choking on your food, stop it.

"But what if the person does not want to make eye contact?" There are some cultures out there where eye contact is either discouraged or subtly not recommended. This includes some parts of Asia and the Middle East.

If the other person finds it hard to make eye contact, let them be. Stay focused on your gaze to lock in your attention to the conversation at hand.

2. Relax

There is a distinction to be made between establishing eye contact and staring someone down. You can always look away and maintain a mindful awareness of your surroundings since this is a basic human instinct.

Being "attentive" can mean a lot of things. This includes being present at the moment and giving most, if not all, of your attention to the object in front of you.

The goal here is to actively maintain focus while tuning out all distractions, like noise and activity, in the background. Lastly, do not let yourself be distracted by your feelings, biases, and other inner trains of thought. Your mind must be open enough to let the information come through from the conversation so that you can respond appropriately.

And speaking of your mental state...

3. An Open Mind

When someone is speaking to you, it is common for you to take mental notes on their unique characteristics and behaviors. For instance, if they say something incredulous, your mind immediately makes a mental note along the lines of well, that was a stupid thing to say, followed by an instinctive raising of the eyebrows.

Or what if the person has a visible distraction on their face, like a mole on their cheek or a piece of lettuce in their teeth? Your eyes would immediately travel there, and your focus is now on the "fault" and not on the messenger.

Either way, indulging in mental criticisms in the middle of a conversation will impede your ability to listen to the other person effectively. As such, you must listen without making any hasty conclusions.

Despite their mistakes, the person always remembers that they are doing their best to relay what they are thinking and feeling. If you don't listen, you will never get to what they truly want to say to you.

Also, it is at this point that you must correct your tendency to hasten the person in finishing their narration. You may be the type of person who wants to speed conversations up or is just bothered by people beating around the bush. Whatever the case, do not force a person to get to the point at your pace.

4. Visualize

The best way to retain and process information in your brain is to convert that information into a "mental image" of sorts. This could be a sequence of abstract things forming a narrative or even an actual mental picture, but the image helps you focus on what the person is saying.

This is rather important, especially if the person relays a narrative of events leading to an incident. That narration could go on for several sentences and paragraphs, which takes a while to get condensed in your brain without some mental aid.

Your mental picture can be a sequence of mental images, or abstract things, or even keywords. The point is that it will help you formulate what to say next.

But here is the kicker: while you are listening, you must not spend even a fraction of your time planning what to say next. The mind is not designed to listen while also rehearsing your response internally at the same time. While listening, your only focus should be what the other person is saying, even if they happen to be rather boring.

5. Avoid Interjections

When we were young, we were most likely taught that it's a rather rude thing to interrupt people talking. Despite what modern media is telling you (i.e., that in-your-face, aggressive behavior is good), being rude and obnoxious during conversations will always lead to an aggressive put-down, verbal or otherwise.

When you interrupt a person, you can convey many messages, including "My story is more important than yours" or "I do not have time for you." It's important to realize that individuals think and feel at various speeds.

This means that the burden of adjusting to the speaker's pace is, well, on you.

And even if you do not wish ill, you can be an interrupter if you tend to provide a solution when not solicited. Think of it this way: if they seek your advice, they would gladly ask for it once their narration is over.

If not, then refrain from giving unsolicited advice. More often than not, people just want a person to listen and not a solution. But if you do have a brilliant idea, always ask the speaker if they want to hear it. But only do this once that person has said their piece.

6. Wait for the Stop

How would you know that a person has stopped their narration? It is easy to say that this is when their jaws stopped flapping, but there is an actual "pause" that you have to look for, the intangible "stop" that signifies that a sentence or paragraph has ended.

The stop happens when a person does not add anything else after a second or so of not talking. You could even tell in certain people that they are not about to add anything else because they do not visibly catch their breath as if winding up for another narration paragraph.

Once the stop has occurred, you can then present your response. Or, better yet, you can ask the person to go back on some details, especially the ones that you were the most confused with.

This makes for a perfect segue with the next step, which is...

7. Maintain Course

Picture this scenario: Your friend has just been talking to you in the last few minutes about a wonderful experience he had at the last Superbowl season. You, in all of your meticulousness, zeroed in on the part of the story where he was sitting next to an acquaintance of yours that you hadn't heard from since 2010.

Then you asked, "Oh, you were sitting next to Bobby from way back in high school? How is he? I heard he's going through a rough divorce. It must suck for the kids."

Question: Was what you just said relevant to his Superbowl experience, or did you just unconsciously veer the conversation into somebody else's personal life?

If you answered the latter, you at least know that you unconsciously committed one of the biggest mistakes in communication: changing the topic. The things that we say right after a person is done talking have, more often than not, nothing to do with what they just said. It takes a while to get back on topic, but it is easy to derail an entire conversation this way.

If you know that you have an annoying tendency to do this, you have to learn how to veer back to the primary topic. After the person is done answering what you just asked, say something like, "Oh, that's hard to hear coming from Bobby. But tell me more about your Superbowl experience. It was great, right?"

In just a few sentences, you just shifted the focus back to the speaker's topic, with them none the wiser for it.

8. Step in their Shoes

As the person speaks, you might notice that their emotions would start to surface. This is good as emotions are rarely hidden, especially if the person is talking about something personal.

What you have to do here is synchronize your emotions with that of the speaker. If they are joyful, show joy. If they are fearful as they describe what is troubling them, show concern.

A key element here is to make your reactions visible through the words you say and the expressions you show. And this is where empathy can help you as it allows you to see things from that person's point of view. It takes concentration and time to master, but it will eventually help you become an effective listener and communicator.

9. Give Feedback

It is not enough to see things from that person's perspective or understand what they are feeling. You also have to confirm to the speaker that you are listening.

There are multiple ways to do this. The easiest one is to vocalize your reactions with phrases like "Wow, that's wonderful!" or "I'm sad to hear about that," or "That sucks. I can see why you're frustrated!"

But what if the person's message or feelings are unclear or you don't know how to react out of fear of being misunderstood as indifferent? You can easily confirm that you are paying attention by nodding or using filler words like "mm-hmm" or "uh-huh."

The goal here is to assure the speaker that they have your undivided attention and that you are following their narrative. This is important in situations where the person is telling a story and giving you instructions for performing certain things.

10. Pay Attention to What Isn't Said

Email notwithstanding, most of the direct forms of communication you will regularly encounter are non-verbal. There are a lot of things that a person can tell you without opening their mouth. It is up to you, then, to know how to pick up on these non-verbal cues.

Here's a good example: When somebody talks to you over the phone, you might wonder how to tell if they are happy or not. Listen for the tone they use whenever they start the conversation. If it is a happy one, you can be 75% sure that the rest of the conversation will be a lighthearted one. If you detect a sense of seriousness in their tone, you could be certain that what they are about to tell you is urgent. And so on.

These non-verbal cues are even more pronounced in face-to-face conversations. If you are that astute, you can even detect things like boredom, irritation, and even sarcasm coming from the other person and obvious facial expressions. These are things that any person could not ignore, which is why you should consider them when responding to what the person has just said.

Some Exercises to Improve on Your Listening Skills

Active listening is something that you would not develop overnight. It takes time and practice to master to be an effective listener. To do that, here are some exercises that you could implement in your daily interactions.

1. Paraphrasing

Most of the time, it is hard to process a lot of information in one passing. There's a high possibility you won't understand all the individual says, which means your answer will be inadequate.

So, how could you make them repeat what you just said without giving the impression that you were not paying attention? You paraphrase.

How this is done is easy: you only have to repeat what they just said or what you understood about the situation and ask for a clarification at the end.

A paraphrase should sound like this: "So, you (the speaker) just had (insert situation here), and you would like to (insert their question or proposition here). Is that right?"

More often than not, the speaker would indulge you by clarifying certain details of their story without going through everything again.

Paraphrasing is also good for summarizing all their key points, which keeps the conversation going. If a person is angry at something you did, you can zero in on that point of their narrative and say something like, "Would you like to hear the reasons why I did that?"

Or what if a person made an observation? You could follow it with a question like, "Are you referring to (information A) or is it (information B)?"

Paraphrasing works not only to clarify any detail in the speaker's story, but it also helps the person collect themselves and reorganize their thoughts. In either case, you and the other person have a better chance of reaching an understanding.

2. Words to Avoid

Reacting to what has just been saying is important. However, we often make mistakes when responding to a message. All of this can be traced back to our instinct to solve the problem instead of listening to the person.

Here are some of the responses that you should try your best to avoid saying when a person is speaking:

- Telling a story: "That happened to you, too? That reminds me of that time when...."
- Pitying the person: "You poor thing...."
- Correcting them: "Uh, I don't think that's how it went...."
- Comforting them: "I know it's hard, and none of this is your fault...."
- One-upping the person: "You think that's bad? What happened to me was worse!"
- Cutting them short: "Uh, I'd love to listen more. Can we do it later?"

What you normally say when in a conversation might be different from the ones above. Either way, you should identify your response gaffes so you would know which ones to avoid when talking with other people.

3. Your Non-Verbal Cues

Listening to what isn't said works just as much on yourself as it does on the speaker. What are your usual ticks when listening to a person while he's talking? List them down and find out whether or not they help the conversation or harm it.

For instance, crossing your arms while a person is talking can be perceived as uncomfortable with either the message or the speaker. The same is true when you constantly tap or shuffle your feet or make a loud clicking noise when a person is talking. It signifies that you would rather be somewhere else.

As such, you have to identify which of your non-verbal messages are hostile or could be potentially perceived as hostile and find ways to minimize doing them when in front of people. Doing so could make the conversation that follows easier for you and the other person.

What Makes Active Listening Hard?

The truth is that active listening is not the easiest thing to perform at all times. If it were, then a lot of miscommunication would be avoided, which is far from the truth as far as your personal experiences can be gleaned upon.

As such, you have to identify where you could also make a mistake in trying to be an active listener. Here are three areas to consider:

1. The "No Solution" Stance

The biggest issue with active listening is that people, by default, are problem solvers.   Some fields and disciplines have this mentality so hardwired that it becomes hard for people in those areas to become effective listeners.

How hard is it, you ask? Here's a classic example: Let us say that a friend of yours tells you that one of their families is sick with something serious like cancer. As they are narrating their story, you are already coming up with suggestions like where to get treatment, dealing with the complications, and managing the stress.

What you are not doing, on the other hand, is listening to the narrative. You fail to get the story's context or even understand the person's intention to relay this information to you. In your haste to provide them with solutions, you fail to reach an understanding with the person.

Arguably, it is your eagerness to solve problems that should be dealt with the most in learning how to listen actively. That is not to say that providing advice is not good (it is), but you should get the story's context first before you start doling out advice.

2. Dealing with Tough Emotions

If the subject is rather personal, emotions are expected to run high. Like the example above, you can expect the person telling you their story to start tearing or choking up. This signifies that their emotion for the story is still raw, and they are visibly hurting from even relaying it to you.

However, the first impulse with people is to find a way to make the person stop crying. Perhaps you might say something like, "It's okay. Don't cry!" or try to change the topic. The reason for this is rather simple: it is rather uncomfortable to see a person display strong emotions. In some cultures, being emotionally expressive is even seen as a sign of weakness. Either way, many people are not designed to cope with the emotions of others, let alone their own.

The biggest challenge you would face here is embracing the emotions being directed at you, no matter how hard it is. It is essential to let those feelings be seen and heard for you to respond appropriately.

3. Dealing with the Silence

Being silent is often uncomfortable in a conversation. While you are refining your skills, you might even allow entire seconds of silence to go by before the conversation resumes. In most cases, those periods of silence can be awkward for you.

However, dealing with those periods of silence is but part of the process of becoming an active listener. What matters more is that you visually confirm what has been relayed to you by your own emotions and the expressions you make.

You can cut through the silence with the clarification or paraphrase to help the other person relax. This could also give the impression that you were trying to understand them and pay attention to their story, thus validating themselves before your eyes.

The key here is timing. You have to hone the ability to detect pauses and stops in the person's narration of events. Once you identify when these occur, you can add to the conversation without coming off as rude or impatient.

To Conclude

If we were to summarize the active listening process, it would look something like this:

Sounds straightforward, right? That's because it is.

The only thing that you have to remember to be an active listener is to invest yourself in the conversation fully. Allow nothing else to distract you from receiving the message and its context so that you can mold the best possible response.

Of course, it takes time to develop this skill, which means you must constantly engage in conversation to improve as an active listener. Sure, you will make mistakes down the road, but you will eventually learn how to listen first before acting or responding.

Chapter 32:
Why Active Listen?

Undivided attention upgrades your capacity to retain and pass on the information and data given during the trade. Building up your aptitudes and procedures to effectively listen to your communications will offer your audience members more outstanding clarity and sympathy.

A fundamental part of undivided attention is your capacity to shut out any diversions available where you are conveying. By giving 100 percent to your discussion, you will hear and understand the genuine substance of the message, just as having the option to get all the oblivious signs showed.

On the off chance that your regular inclination is to race into a reaction, work on slowly inhaling before you talk with the goal that the other individual has the chance to complete what they are stating. If they don't do this and remove the individual's reaction before clarifying their entire perspective, you won't have a total picture. Be careful with this and the numerous boundaries you should keep away from to pick up the advantages of undivided attention.

Without the entire image of the discourse, you are bound to misjudge the trade. To maintain your emphasis on what is being said to you, offer the speaker hints that they have your complete consideration by moving your head or eyes. You may likewise need to ask others in the circumstance to be calm so the speaker can communicate.

By carrying on these lines, you will most likely assemble progressively convincing answers and accomplish your communication objective. It additionally represents your comprehension of the speaker's perspective and how this identifies with your convictions.

By focusing on the other individual's reactions, you will most likely precisely judge their subject learning and change your communication style suitably. You likewise have the chance to criticize the person that you have fathomed what they are stating to you.

This makes them feel esteemed and willing to contribute further and guarantees that trade is a two-way process. This can be accomplished by just after you sum what they have said with so many statements as:

- Does that sound good to you?
- What do you think?
- Would you concur?
- What's your view on this?

Furthermore, you can urge someone else to commit to your trade by utilizing a respite or staying quiet. This offers both of you favorable circumstances. First, it gives the audience time to pull their musings together, and individuals want to fill a void, so they start to talk.

The two-way communication undivided attention empowers likewise furnishes you with the chances to give contemplated, legitimate input, just as enabling you to pick up explanations of what you accept has been said to you.

This is one of the procedures that empower you to limit the diversions during a trade or discourse. Having the option to hold the focal point of the communication on your goal is fundamental for progress. A significant symptom of such conduct is that others will pursue your lead when directing their communications.

By building up your capacities to utilize every one of the three segments of undivided attention - listening direction, intelligent strategy, and addressing abilities - you will almost certainly amplify the adequacy and profitability of the people in your group.

Undivided attention is an expertise that can be obtained and created with training. Be that as it may, undivided attention can be hard to ace and will, in this manner, require significant investment and persistence. Appropriately utilized, undivided attention may give three extremely positive outcomes:

Initially, the audience picks up data since undivided attention urges the speaker to discuss a more significant number of things in more prominent profundity than the individual in question would probably do in essentially reacting to order questions or recommendations. Such profundity of discourse frequently uncovered hidden issues, including ones the speaker had not perceived already.

Besides, the components of listening direction (sympathy, acknowledgment, compatibility, and solidness) are probably going to increment as the intelligent listening procedure proceeds. These are the fixings your requirement needs for an open, confiding in association with your colleagues.

At long last, undivided attention invigorates and channels persuasive vitality. As the audience, you acknowledge and empower the speaker. However, you leave the activity in their grasp. Therefore, your colleagues will perceive new roads for activity and start making arrangements to seek after them, making themselves increasingly powerful and beneficial.

Some more reasons why you have to listen incorporate the accompanying effectively:

Distraction Is Impolite

We've all been there: you're talking in a gathering, and somebody at the table is noting messages on their cell phone.

How could you feel? In case you're similar to me, you felt affronted. Regardless of whether they intended to do as such, the individual who was messaging during the gathering was imparting the message, "You – and anything you desire to state – are not significant enough to the direction of my complete consideration."

Distraction Is Crushing

Or on the other hand, what about this one: you're imparting an issue to somebody in their office, and you can observe their PC screen ...

where you can check five visit windows open, and watch the other individual reacting to all of them while you are talking!

Do you have certainty that that individual can add to the arrangement of the issue? No chance! How right? They haven't been focusing.

So, what do we need to do?

Get in the privileged mental spot to tune ineffectively.

Undivided attention begins before we ever enter a discussion. It starts with an individual pledge to be completely present at whatever assignment we are participating in. We can choose at the start of every day that we will do one thing at once: i.e., react to messages or partake in Google Visit or converse with somebody. "Or then again" – not "and."

Separate from Gadgets to Interface in a Discussion.

So now it's a great opportunity to chat with somebody. Regardless of whether you are on the telephone or face to face, we urge you to quit everything else, so far as you are capable. Mood killer your email; close down from Google Talk or Facebook; enable your telephone to go to a phone message. Even if we don't react to a message when it comes up, as long as we know that a message has shown up, we will, in general, get diverted. We regularly think, "Who just messaged me? Consider the possibility that it's a significant message. Should I pause for a minute to react to that IM?" This occupies us from truly captivating in the current discussion.

Reflect and Rework to Confirm Understanding.

Here's the last advance in undivided attention: we must practice (and it takes work on!) reflecting and rewording back to the next individual what we hear them state. Reflecting and summarizing back to the next individual does numerous things:

- It encourages us to center around the discussion, pose keen inquiries, and keep diversions under control.

- It communicates our regard for the other individual.

- It guarantees that we have genuinely comprehended the current issue so we can contribute adequately to the arrangement.

Presently, reflecting and summarizing isn't contributing to the periodic, "Um-hm," "Gotcha!" or "Right." It implies re-expressing what we have heard and verifying with the other individual that is the thing that they planned to communicate.

The Test to Effectively Tune In

Undivided attention is an extreme test. It means modifying our outlook and disengaging from our devices. It means focusing our consideration as opposed to parting it. It means believing that we can complete everything – and improved – if we go about assignments consecutively instead of all the while.

At whatever point the test gets somewhat harsh, and you're enticed to sneak a look at your cell phone or PC screen, pose yourself one inquiry:

Don't you need to be effectively heard?

Chapter 33:
How to Active Listen?

Here are the means of being an attentive person. This rundown may appear to be somewhat broad, and honestly, it is somewhat long.

Try not to consider it a schedule that you need to separate each point as you achieve it. Or maybe, see it as a general rule.

On the off chance that you can achieve the vast majority of these insignificant discussions, you are en route to turning into an attentive person!

1. Keep in Touch

You don't need to be laser-centered around somebody's eyes with your own. You do, be that as it may, need to keep in touch with them. This is extremely more for you than for them.

When you keep in touch, you are compelled to focus on that individual. It's less simple to get diverted.

It additionally passes on to the next individual that you care enough about what's being said that you are taking a gander at them while they talk.

2. Try Not to Squirm Excessively

See, re-orchestrating and getting settled now and again is fine. What's not fine is always playing with a pen or grabbing your telephone, or looking everywhere.

Being uneasy gives the feeling that you aren't keen on what the other individual is stating.

3. No Hindering

Presently this is anything but a rigid principle. If you have to get an explanation on a specific guide, it's alright to ask considerately.

What you would prefer not to do is intruding on somebody each other sentence to make your very own point. Or, on the other hand, to include your shading into the discussion.

What you should do is tune into their talking.

4. Watch the Non-Verbal Signs

A lot of correspondence occurs in a non-verbal way. That implies you can get a ton of what an individual imparts to you through their non-verbal communication and not the genuine words leaving their mouths.

Watch the nonverbal signs that the other individual is emitting while at the same time talking. On the off chance that they are awkward, they may squirm. If they're worried, they may not be able to look at you without flinching. These sorts of nonverbal information can enable you to focus on how the other individual is feeling.

5. Rehash and Explain

At times when somebody is addressing us, it's not as clear as we'd like. Whenever required, rehash what the other individual has said and don't be reluctant to explain.

You can make statements like, "To ensure I comprehend what I hear, you state is … .. is that right?".

Likewise, saying something like, "So what I am hearing is … .. also, This offers the other individual a chance to guarantee they are letting you know all that they have to. It likewise demonstrates that you care enough to pose an inquiry to ensure you get it.

6. Utilize Some Encouragers

When somebody experiences serious difficulties traversing everything, it's alright to give some light consolation to a great extent to get them to keep talking or sharing more subtleties.

You would prefer not to race into it, yet when somebody is by all accounts highly involved with recounting to a story and stops, and you can say something short like "and afterward" or "what occurred straightaway" or "bobbed, react to that."

Nothing that will assume control over the discussion, yet little bits of consolation to a great extent as required.

7. Testing

It's splendidly fine to test for more data when required. Keep in mind that your objective isn't to assume control over the discussion; it's to tune in to the next individual effectively.

Presently when you feel there could be increasingly important data that hasn't turn out yet, it's fine to pose a couple of examining inquiries.

Asking things, for example, "how did that make you feel" or "what do you believe is an ideal approach to deal with that circumstance" are great approaches to get the other individual to share increasingly about how they feel. This encourages you to comprehend the circumstance better.

8. Insignificant Talking

I've alluded to it on various occasions during the bit by bit procedure to undivided attention; it merits its visual cue in any case.

Keep in mind, to be an attentive person, and you ought to tune in. You are looking to tune in and comprehend the other individual truly. Your job here isn't to talk much.

I can unquestionably experience considerable difficulties keeping my mouth shut when I have something to include. I need to take an internal full breath, interruption, and keep my mouth shut. I, at that point, guarantee I am centered on what the other individual is letting me know.

Being an attentive person means tuning in with insignificant talking.

9. Approve

Returning to how we try to be comprehended, it's smart to approve the other individual. Making statements, for example, "I see how that would annoy you" and "I presumably would have responded a similar way," makes the other individual feel like you are their ally.

Like you feel for them and get them. This again will help structure trust in the discussion and the relationship. Approving somebody is tremendous.

Solid relational abilities will help you in each relationship in your life. This incorporates work and individual connections. On the off chance that you can create undivided attention abilities, you will give your relational abilities a tremendous lift.

Listening is half of all correspondence. Help yourself out and chip away at your undivided attention abilities. It can dramatically affect the achievement you have at work and in your nearby close-to-home connections.

Practice Active Listening

We go through countless meetings in our work weekly. The purpose of those of these meetings is obviously to pass some message across. However, whether or whether this message reaches its target audience is the main issue. It takes active listening to capture the message just as it was intended. Thus there are no misunderstandings and no potential conflict. Here are some of the methods of engaging in active listening:

Face the speaker

You can hardly be an active listener when you are facing away. You have to look at the speaker directly so that you can take in every word and nuance. There are many nonverbal messages that a speaker sends out, and unless your eyes are on them, you will miss out. Ensure that you look at the speaker in the eyes. But be careful that you don't overdo it. Excessive eye contact can seem intimidating. Establishing eye contact makes sure that you get the whole message and also makes the speaker feel appreciated. Nothing would heartbreak a speaker faster than talking to people who were looking elsewhere but him.

Assume an erect posture

First off, your posture says a lot about you. If you have a poor posture, then it means you are low in confidence, and vice versa is true. An erect posture makes it easy for you to listen actively, for your eyes can now face forward. Avoid crossing arms over your chest or locking your legs. It is a gesture that signifies that you don't want to be disturbed, which is an unfriendly thing to do in a public place. To show the speaker that you are indeed following their every word, you might want to lean in forward slightly or tilt your head a bit as you support it with a palm. Apart from boosting your self-confidence and helping you practice active listening, an erect posture is beneficial for health purposes. It will help with back problems and also boost blood flow.

Never interrupt

Interrupting the speaker is virtually the rudest thing you can do. It shows that you have no time for what they are saying or are more important than everybody else, assuming other people are listening. Interrupting the speaker might upset their train of thought and thus ruin their message. You want to ensure that you are cooperating with the speaker and giving them respect. Some issues might be too pressing, and you feel as though you can't wait to raise them. The appropriate way of raising a concern is to note all the issues and then wait for the speaker to be done. This demonstrates your admiration for them, and you're more likely to have a good connection with them as a result.

Avoid jumping to conclusions or judging.

People frustrate their efforts of listening actively by constantly jumping to conclusions. This habit can lead to miscommunication and give rise to potential conflict. Ensure that you listen to the speaker until they are done. Jumping to conclusions indicates a lack of patience as well as immaturity on the part of the listener. Equally as bad is the habit of judging others. A speaker might decide to tell a story that touches on their lives, but the listener might decide to start weighing the story in morality scales, trying to determine the speaker's moral conscience. This habit not only takes away from an individual's capacity to practice active listening but also reduces them into quasi-morality preachers.

Avoid preparing a counter-attack.

Some people cannot listen actively because they don't listen to understand, but they listen to give a response merely. For such people, communication is like a sport whereby the winner takes it all, and they want to be the winner and revel in that glory. When you plan to launch a counter-attack as soon as the speaker is done, you didn't have sufficient concentration when the speaker was talking. Chances are you didn't get the whole facts, or you heard them in a skewed manner, thus opening up gaps for conflict. Active listening is about being attentive until the speaker is done. Then you can start to say whatever is on your mind.

Encourage the speaker

Nothing bothers a speaker more than having to talk to someone or an unreceptive group. It makes the speaker lose morale and stop putting enough effort into passing their message across. There are many things you can do to encourage the speaker. Some of these things include:

1. **Nodding**: this is a classic way of showing the speaker that you are on the same page as them. From time to time, and when you lock eyes, give them a slight nod. But you want to be sure that you are economical with the nods lest it appears as though you are trying too hard to impress the speaker.

2. **Smiling**: this is a way of showing the speaker friendliness. It makes them comfortable. Think about how you'd feel if you started speaking with someone and a group, and then they wore a hostile face? You'd feel unwelcome. But if they had a

smile, you'd feel welcome. So, learn to smile regularly at the speaker as it shows him that you are their friend, and it inspires them to keep on.

3. **Say "Yes" or "Uh-uh" and other affirming sounds**: mouthing off such sounds makes the speaker proud of himself for attracting people's attention, and more importantly, their full engagement.

4. **Don't look at the watch every thirty seconds**: we tend to frantically look at our watches when we are stuck at a place and can't seem to wait to leave. When the speaker realizes that people are looking at their watches quite frequently, they can assume that they are boring, hurting their feelings. It is enough to look at the watch just once and keep reminding yourself not to look again, for it's too soon.

5. **Avoid fidgeting**: why would you fidget? It's the speaker doing the talking, not you. Does your fidgeting stem from your nervous energy? But why is that? On the part of the speaker, such behavior is as much disturbing as it is discouraging.

Don't offer solutions unless asked to

If a colleague comes up to you and sobs about their challenges, your main function should be holding them steady and listening to them keenly. It would help if you did not attempt to say, "Oh, do this and that -" The rules of active listening demand that you only give guidance and solutions upon request. When you start giving away unsolicited advice, you ignore the wishes of the imagined victim. If you stop wasting time trying to come up with a solution for the speaker's numerous troubles, you would have sufficient time to listen to actually what's being said, understanding the message, regardless of its pain.

Be focused

Another critical facet of active listening is staying focused throughout. Both external and internal, many things might try to grab your attention, but shun them off and stick to listening. Don't expend your mental resources fighting automatic thoughts (the thoughts that seem to overpower your will) but take on the role of the observer, for eventually, these thoughts will fade away. When you are focused on what the speaker is saying, you have a decent chance of hearing the entire message as was intended. This means communication has been carried out flawlessly.

Be curious and creative.

When you practice active listening, you are bound to accurately capture the message instead of the person who's distracted or allowed himself to be distracted. But then, if you are the curious type or the creative type, you should see more than one perspective to whatever the speaker says, and thus, you should have a question. Such curious behavior goes a long way in starting and cementing ties between the two parties.

Be open-minded

This green orange – hung in space – whose name is Earth is quite large. In it, their lives all manner of people and creatures. Human beings are different. There is so much variety. For that reason, it would be unfair for any culture or distinct group to declare themselves as more worthy than any other culture or group. Thus, when you are listening to a speaker, you should have an open mind. Since you are probably unfamiliar with their background, you might not be aware of their deep convictions and philosophies, so keep an open mind and accept whatever they say as long as it is within boundaries of respect. This attitude is great for creativity. It helps you have a multifaceted conception of ideas and things.

Chapter 34:
The Benefits of Better Conversation Skills

Having top-notch conversation skills is very vital in a human being's daily lifestyle. Conversations held by an individual are supposed to be swift in the modern age. This is irrespective of which massage, feeling, or idea is passed to an intended party.

Conversation can be described as the process which entails sharing and understanding the meaning. Successful communication entails two critical things, which are to understand and be able to be understood. There is the process of successful communication is achieved through several ways, which include;

- Verbally, this is the use of a person's voice.
- Written; the written form includes the use of books and mails
- Visually, it is the use of images, maps, and graphs.
- Non-verbally, the use of body language, gestures, and eye contact is applied in this case.

Listening is a very critical component of having a successful conversation. People in society often overlook the idea. These sets of people are more focused on what they say rather than what has been told to them by other people. A great person can be distinguished in people by their ability to pause and listen to others. It always portrays the virtue of respect and willingness from the other party in listening to those around them. Active listening skills and will help a person in developing good communication skills.

There are myriad importance of having better skills of conversing which are;

- Being valued in the place of work

- In demand by business
- Helps to improve a person's career
- Helps a person to speak concisely
- Assists in building better rapport with clients
- Influences the learning process
- Helps to create a better professional image

Six Importance of Having Better Skills of Conversing

1. Being Valued at the Place of Work

A person is supposed to demonstrate a certain level of communication skills while applying for a new job or seeking a promotion. The high-class level of communication that can steer an individual to have this success includes speaking with several kinds of people from different backgrounds while maintaining good eye contact and fluency in the language used in communication. The ideas presented by a person are supposed to be appropriate when presented, even in writing. This helps a person get an advantage because they can work with a group.

An individual who can put people at ease, listen to them, and speak clearly to them is a very valuable person in an organization. This involves a demonstration of various skills such as;

I. Being able to listen and show interest in what people say

II. Having an appropriate manner in dealing with telephone conversations

III. Ability to persuade people

IV. Asking questions or expressing opinions clearly

V. Encouraging the team, a person is in In Demand by Business

Both written and oral communication proficiencies have been ranked consistently across the employment market as the top ten desirable skills by employees. Various employees worldwide are advised to take courses that offer a chance to improve communication skills. These courses can either be online trained or in-person trained. The most common skills looked at by employers are communication skills, the ability of one to be organized, team working, analytical thinking, and critical thinking.

2. Helps in Improvement of One's Career

A person will be required to seek information, discuss issues, give out orders, work in teams, and interact with people at work. A person with good communication skills can undertake these activities with ease. It is because communications prove to be a lubricant in enhancing cooperation and cooperation in organizations. The global community has been narrowed because of technology, making the issue become of global attention.

Therefore, understanding yourself and understanding others has positive effects on a person and the company they work for. This can help elevate a person to different ranks up to the international level. Employees want workers who can think about their own, find solutions to problems, and invent things with the help of people around them. It is not about doing a task well since other factors can elevate a firm.

3. Helps a Person to Speak Concisely

It is normal for people to feel nervous when they are talking to a person who is of a higher rank than them. However, a person with good communication skills has the potential of knowing how to communicate best in any situation presented to them. The skill is essential because it helps a person get the best out of a slippery position.

4. Assists in Building Better Rapport with Clients

Clients have one important desire that is always at heart. This group of people seeks to be understood by companies or firms because it helps them feel valued. This feeling is achieved when they are contented they have been heard and listened to. There are certain points employees in an organization interact with clients; successful firms are always formed by these moments since they keep client needs first after listening to them.

5. Influences Learning Process

Communication skills highly influence the processes of imparting knowledge and belief. The learning process involves public speaking and answering questions posed and airing out one's opinion. The process also involves writing; however, a person learns how to read first and is taught how to write. The presence of good communication skills helps a person to grasp information and air out their opinion is clear.

6. Helps to Create a Better Professional Image

Having good communication skills helps a person to build a good first impression. People in the current work are obsessed with conveying a positive image as their reflection when they first meet with people. This is very critical in the business world because it portrays one's company or business. A person's professionalism while handling people at the first meeting is critical for business success in deals.

Chapter 35:
Understanding Your Audience

Learning as much as you can about your audience will assist you in determining how to get your message across strategically. The more you know about them, the more wisely you can formulate your strategy.

Here is a list of questions to ask yourself or others about your audience when preparing for your next talk. Even if your answers reveal information that may seem negative, it is better to know it in advance rather than find it out as you begin speaking or after the fact.

- How many people are you expecting to attend?

- Is everyone in the audience at the same level in terms of knowledge and expertise concerning your subject? If not, what are their different levels?

- Is there any jargon you will need to explain?

- Are your attendees choosing to attend, or are they required to attend (i.e., do they want to be there)?

- What are all of the possible reasons they will attend?

- Are there any belief systems about your topic that may create resistance? If so, what are they? For example, if you are talking about healthy habits, part of your audience may believe, "I'm way too busy to add exercising to my overpacked schedule."

- If there are belief systems that may create resistance, what creative strategies could you try to help your audience reconsider their thinking?

- Are there any cultural perspectives that you need to take into account? The answers to this question may influence how you dress, what humor you choose, and how you shape your overall approach.

- What does your audience stand to gain from listening to you?

- What time of day is your talk? Are there reasons your audience may be tired (perhaps they are either just waking up or tired after a long day)? Could they be oversaturated with information (say, if you have the last slot of a weeklong conference)?

- If you anticipate they will be tired, how can you creatively address this (and not feel like you are cursed with the worst slot)?

While preparing, you may become aware of possible perceptions or misperceptions that could create resistance to your talk. It's important to directly or indirectly address these during your presentation. This will go a long way toward ensuring that your audience feels noticed and heard. This will assist you with winning their trust and opening their minds to consider your point of view.

Once you get a clearer picture of who your audience is, your strategy for reaching them will become clearer. Your "who" may also help inspire your "why." Once you get a sense of their perspectives and openness (or lack thereof), the reasons your talk is valuable may become clearer.

Does Your Audience Want to Be There?

One of the most critical questions is, "Do the participants want to be at your talk?" Determining how potentially receptive or unreceptive your audience will be to your message is a crucial step. If attendees are motivated to attend only because they are required to, you need to find a way to engage them as early as possible to be open and receptive to your message. You want them to want to be there.

Managing the Audience

Some audiences are easier than others. People may be falling asleep after a meal or too raucous after cocktails. Others might appear bored to death or do not laugh at your jokes. There might even be a heckler, someone who challenges statements and will not wait for the end of the lecture to get answers. On the other side, everything might go well during the presentation, but a badly managed question-and-answer session could sabotage a good image. Preparation can help you manage these situations.

Get the Audience to Pay Attention

If you are speaking right after lunch or dinner, members of the audience may be a little sleepy because a big meal requires a lot of the body's energy to digest. Late in an all-day seminar, you will probably experience audience fatigue: their brains are overflowing with information, and it is hard to make room for more. You cannot change your presentation, except make it a little crisper by deleting a few details and adding extra energy. To revive the group before you start, try this approach:

- Acknowledge the challenge of staying interested at that time of day.

- Have everyone stand up and do deep breathing exercises.

- Have a few witty lines ready to get them laughing.

Once they sit down, tell them you want everyone to write down, right then, the three most important things to take away.

Don't take it personally if people doze off. They may have been pulling an all-nighter at the office, may be suffering from jet lag, or had a restless night worrying about a family problem. If you wrote a brilliant presentation and practiced your delivery 100 times, a segment of your audience is not going to be paying attention anyway, even with their eyes open.

Later in the presentation, engage the audience in interactivity, such as asking them to raise their hands as you do a survey. How many of them believe customer service at their companies could be improved?

How many have plans to travel outside the United States in the next two years? But be careful not to ask them to show their feelings about a sensitive issue that could get them in trouble afterward ("How many of you think your firm has incompetent management?").

Or ask for volunteers to come up on stage to interview them about some aspect of the subject — there will always be those who love the limelight, which will help reengage the audience.

Finally, increase your vocal dynamics to decrease the hypnotic effect of your normal tone — mimic the voices of characters in your story, make sound effects, shout, use a "stage whisper," or move your voice up and down the range.

The Grumpy Audience

The crowd may only be there because they are required to attend, so acknowledge that. Tell them how what you are about to say will make a big difference in their lives if they implement your recommendations.

If you know they are waiting to hear the speaker after you, mention that you are excited to hear them, too, and offer some ideas that will support what they are about to say.

They may already have heard someone else address your topic. If you did your speech-preparation research, you would have a good idea what the other speakers will have talked about and will have aimed your remarks in a different direction (try to attend similar presentations to be sure).

If the audience is opposed to your views, try to find common ground to build rapport. You may disagree about abortion, for example, but can agree on the need to prevent unwanted pregnancies. Be sure you treat the specifics of their views respectfully, even as you explain why you disagree. Never be combative, arrogant, or triumphalist ("Now that we have the political upper hand, we'll be repealing those initiatives you rammed through the legislature").

Structuring Questions and Answers

Unless you are giving a keynote address at a dinner or are one of a rotation of brief speakers at a convention, the odds are you will be asked to answer audience questions. At a seminar, where you may be talking for twenty to ninety minutes, you will have the chance either right after you speak or at the end of the session. On the other hand, if you are talking to a small group at a business meeting, it may be expected that you take questions before moving on to each next topic. If you are teaching an all-day seminar, you will need to let the audience speak up after each segment. Whatever the format is, it needs to be agreed on in advance with your host to help you manage the audience.

There are three keys to making it likely that everyone will stick to the structure. First, have the host let everyone know what it is before you start, giving it the official stamp of approval. Second, she should tell the audience to write down their questions as they come to mind, so they do not forget and are not distracted by trying to remember and listen at the same time. This can help ensure there will be questions at the end. Third, if there are people who interrupt at an inappropriate time, the host should remind listeners of the plan. If you are on your own, you have to take care of this yourself. Smile when you lay down the rules and enforce them. Explain that you want questions saved until the end because your presentation will answer most of them. If people want to ask questions at the end of your presentation, it's great! It means they have been attentive; you have been interesting and have stimulated their thinking. If you had worn them out, they would want to run away as quickly as possible.

So the first point is to want questions, look forward to them and be pleased when they arrive.

The second point is to regard the question session as a continuation of the presentation. By that I mean give some thought beforehand to the questions you expect and how you might best answer them. Stick to the Three Golden Rules of Communication in every answer:

- Be succinct: stay focused, don't waffle. Just because someone asks for more detail or information on a topic you love, for example, doesn't mean you can launch off into a jolly, meandering ramble. Not only will the answer not be clear, but you can also significantly unpack the story you have just told and bury the key points you were so keen for your audience to walk away with.

- Be clear: make sure you are understandable, so keep it simple and in jargon-free language.

- Be relevant: only say what is relevant to the question, your presentation, and your audience. A question for more detail is not a license to say everything you can think of. Support your conclusion: what you want your audience to walk away thinking, feeling, or doing. You should have identified this at the very start of your presentation.

- Listen carefully to the question: you may very well have anticipated this question, but that doesn't mean you know exactly what the questioner needs. Listen to the whole question, don't start formulating your answer, or switch off because you have already decided exactly what shape your answer will take. There's a chance that anything towards the conclusion of the question may alter your opinion.

- Be sure to look as though you are listening: attentive facial expression, eye contact, body language. Beware of appearing fidgety, blank, or uninterested; be sure you are not frowning or looking nervous, however difficult or unexpected the question.

- When you answer, answer the whole audience, the same way you spoke to them all during the presentation; assume everyone is interested; otherwise, you will "cut off" the rest of the audience, and they will start to want to leave, which creates a serious drop in impact in the closing moments of your presentation.

- Whether or not you have anticipated the question, you aim to build on the question: agree with all or part of the content where possible; add emphasis, a new perspective, more detail. And a link to what you have presented; don't lose the focus of your presentation.

Handling a Difficult Questioner

Some people just love to quiz a presenter, but it is important not to let a dialogue develop between you and just one audience member. You will lose the rest. Using eyes and body language, reach out to the rest of the audience as you say, "Can I answer any other questions?" As the speaker, you control the session; maintain your authority using strong body language and voice. If this awkward (or shall we say "enthusiastic") questioner persists, suggest that they see you afterward to continue the discussion and look as though you'd be pleased to!

There are times when a questioner sounds hostile. There are two possibilities here. One: they may be nervous; nerves often manifest as hostility or brusqueness at least. So the first point is to make sure you never read hostility into someone's manner. Two: they may be hostile. However, your response will be the same whether the hostility is real or imagined on your part.

Handling Hostile Questions

Assume the worst: that a critic will ask you the one question you would rather not answer in public. "Isn't it true that you were convicted of stealing ten years ago?" or "Why does your company have the highest number of sexual harassment lawsuits in the state?" If there is a formal, written response available, summarize the main points and offer to email the full document. If you cannot talk about it for legal reasons, say so, but provide a reassuring statement about concern for the important matters at issue.

Never duck a tough question. Give the best answer you can think of and bridge to a related topic: your strong suit.

Never give an answer that is not honest. Someone in the audience may call you out, and your credibility and the effectiveness of your presentation will be destroyed on the spot. If you don't know the answer, tell the questioner you'll have to look into it and get back to them. Audiences will tolerate humility in ignorance, but not arrogance. Or you can ask if anyone in the audience knows the answer: this can make that person look smart without this being at your expense since no one else probably knew the answer, either.

On the other hand, if someone has an in-depth knowledge of the field and disagrees with you, you can simply state that the experts you rely on have a different consensus and note that there are usually disagreements among experts in any field.

Breathe to stay calm and manage your own emotions. You can't allow yourself to feel irritated, frustrated, angry, defensive, or aggressive.

Concentrate on how your voice sounds to make sure you in no way sound defensive or aggressive.

Never ridicule the questioner; respectfully try to show that their point of view is based on poor logic or inadequate or inaccurate information, for example.

Look for common ground in your answer; show concern, and empathize with their point of view if you can. It will make their assault less painful.

Remember that a hostile question handled well reflects well on you and poorly on the questioner.

Try not to finish your presentation on an answer, especially if the question session has been quite long and more so if it has been a bit hostile or negative. This will be the lasting memory of your presentation, and there are better memories you want the audience to have. Wrap up with a final thought or a reiteration of your conclusion or key points. It may even be worth saving your best lines for this moment.

Sometimes you may be asked a question based on a false premise: "Have you stopped beating your spouse?" Stay calm and state that you will clear up some obvious confusion about the facts in this case.

You can also get into trouble if someone asks you to rank: which are the best hockey teams in the nation? How would you rank the candidates' comparative intelligence? You can answer rating questions that are legitimate and safe to answer; otherwise, tell the audience that you do not have an answer off the top of your head.

You may also face a question based on trying to compare your product or service and another unfairly. You can deal with this one by noting that it is an apples-and-oranges comparison and then restate what is unique about yours ("We are the only union for bartenders in the state park system, so what bartenders earn in major cities is not relevant").

If a member of the audience challenges your credentials, you should be prepared to calmly take the opportunity to tell the audience something it did not already know about your background. The introduction may have mentioned your degree but did not say that you worked up from the mailroom to management in the industry and have an insider's understanding of it based on hands-on experience. Or you may have written articles for a professional journal. Or you became interested in the disease you are talking about when your mother fell ill, and you interviewed top specialists in the field to find out about cutting-edge therapies.

Do not get down and dirty in a serious argument. If your presentation did not convince the skeptic, no Q & A exchange is going to do it. Just restate the main reasons you hold to your position and move to the next question. Treat each questioner with dignity. Never attack anyone and never embarrass them, even if they try to do it to you. Stay centered, and you will impress the audience with your self-confidence.

Hecklers

Hecklers have one goal: they want to get you to overreact, make a fool of yourself, and break the rhythm of your speech. Let them spew their venom for a few moments, and then tell them that you can address their concerns when you take questions later, along with those from everyone else. That will also buy time for you to think of how you want to respond during the QandA. If the heckler stops at that point, when you come to the end of your talk, you can rephrase their question and answer it in a way that suits you. If they do not accept that answer, you can give them one follow-up question to let them get it off their chest, answer it as best you can, then tell them that others in the audience deserve to have a chance to ask questions and that you will be happy to talk with them afterward.

Be prepared with some barbed jokes in case you have hecklers. Focus on the most controversial points in your presentation and the issues where you get the most arguments. A well-developed sense of humor will make you seem cool, throw the heckler off balance, and allow you to continue your presentation.

If the heckler continues to interrupt the presentation and there is no host to intervene, ask the audience to raise their hands if they would rather have you finish your speech instead of listening to them for the rest of the period. That should do the trick. If the heckler appears to be drunk, give them one warning that they will have to behave themselves, or you will call security.

Chapter 36:
Build a Strong Relationship with an Audience

The matter what the venue or size of the group, effective communication requires establishing rapport with the audience. Even if you are giving a speech with no questions or comments possible, you still need to form a bond that allows for the smooth transition of your words to their minds.

In work environments, managers and employees or project team members have a built-in relationship already. However, this type of forced connection does little to improve how well people communicate with each other. One-time conversations or presentations do not even include this.

The idea of building a relationship like this is very similar to how companies engage consumers with meaningful and impactful marketing messages. In some ways, every conversation is a type of marketing. You share your ideas and opinions with others in hopes that they will understand and accept them.

Instead of responding with a purchase, they respond with feedback about what you had to say.

Basic audience relationship-building steps include:

- Identifying who your audience is and understanding them.
- Sharing information your audience wants or needs.
- Creating empathy and a more personal bond.
- Interact with questions, active listening, and feedback.
- Pay attention to responses and tweak your communication style to fit.

1. Why a Solid Foundation Relationship Helps?

People trust you if you establish a positive relationship with them before trying to convince them of anything. People are more likely to listen to those they know. They stay engaged with conversations for a longer period and are more likely to interact to make the communication even stronger.

It's impossible to overestimate the value of cultivating a close connection with your audience. Even in the corporate world today, people look for more personal interactions. Everyone wants to feel like they matter and that their thoughts and opinions will be taken into account. This is the type of thing that happens in a respectful relationship.

It does not happen in more traditional, standoffish hierarchies where the higher up simply expects others to listen to them without question.

Learning how to build this relationship and employing the best methods will considerably elevate your communication skills.

However, good communication is also one of the main ways to forge these bonds, to begin with. It is a continuous and interactive process.

2. Capture Audience Attention

Effectively

Every speech or important conversation must start with an effective hook. The subject of grabbing attention is often compared to fishing at a lake. You use some sort of bait to attract attention and, when the right target comes along, you set the hook and reel them in.

Communicating with impact does not involve worms or sharp bits of metal, however.

The Bait – This starts with anything from a piece of marketing material for a lecture to a simple "Hello!" The first word to say must elicit an emotional response. Every attempt at communication must attract your audience in some way. They need a reason to listen to you.

The Hook – This captures their attention and convinces them to stick around. In most cases, it includes the information that they want from the interaction. Let your viewers know right away that you're going to provide them something useful.

On the Line – Keep your audience engaged throughout the entire speech or conversation to make a true impact. This requires additional valuable information and enough entertainment to keep things interesting.

Catch Their Attention Right Away (The Bait)

Engage your audience's emotions with a surprising sentence or unexpected idea. Use dramatic emphasis effectively while conveying information that promises more. Some possibilities include sharing an unbelievable fact or statistic, asking a rhetorical question, or making a statement that seems nonsensical or purely imaginative.

"Would you take five minutes out of your day to do a simple task to increase ROI by 200%?"

"Less than 20% of people around the world wash their hands after using the bathroom."

Engage Your Audience Effectively (The Hook)

Demonstrate how important whatever you have to say is to your audience. Make it all about them. Talk about potential problems they may have, empathize effectively, and segue into solutions. At this point, keep it relatively simple. This is not the time to lecture, teach, or interact. It is the time to convince them that they want to stick around for a more in-depth discussion later on.

"Every investor has turned you down. Your only options left are personal credit cards or a home equity loan. I'll walk you through a step-by-step procedure for funding your new company endeavor without putting your family's money at risk in the next half hour.

Captivate Them and Keep Their Attention (On the Line)

Instead of simply quoting statistics or giving a step-by-step plan, make things entertaining with anecdotes and storytelling. Weave examples your audience can relate to into the more technical or idea-driven information.

Balance more complicated topics with action and anecdotes to improve comprehension for a wider variety of listeners.

"During college, I worked at the bookshop and a local gas station to pay for my classes. My friend John worked the midnight shift at the grocery store. Creative funding options for advanced education can help prevent this type of overwork and stress so your kids can focus on their studies."

Throughout the whole process of capturing and keeping your audience's attention, use your personality as a springboard for what you say and how you say it. However, if you tend toward being laid-back or laconic, you may want to inject a bit more humor or animation into your talk. After all, remember that communication is about serving your audience to make maximum impact.

Consider Multi-Media Presentations and Props

The best communication often goes beyond speaking and writing. Using multimedia presentations, printed material, and props can capture and keep attention effectively. These engage a higher percentage of your audience because people learn and remember things in different ways.

Three rules of using media and props: Relevancy – Use the right display or object at the right time during your speech for emphasis rather than a distraction.

Visibility – Make screens or printed posters large enough for everyone to see them easily.

Do not choose props that fit in your hand or need to sit on the table out of the line of sight.

Emotional Impact – While hanging a poster of your company logo can boost brand recognition, it does little to augment the power of your words. Only use extras to increase interest and put the focus on specific parts of your presentation.

Another way to incite interest is to encourage audience participation. No, you do not have to invite someone up onto the stage and make them wear a funny hat. Consider handing out printouts or physical objects that reinforce your message. Make sure they are not going to distract them from what you have to say.

This last idea works well in smaller conversations, too. Even if you are having a chat with your neighbor about vegetable gardening, sharing a packet of seeds or a piece of produce increases their investment in the communication. For large-scale corporate events, product samples or promotional items can work well.

3. Passion for the Subject Is the Best Weapon

While you can fabricate effective bait, hooks, and lectures using these tips and creativity, the best way to engage others is to let your natural passion for the subject shine through.

Giving a speech or starting a discussion about something you don't care about is pointless. Of course, you sometimes need to do this for your career and still make the communication as engaging as possible.

When your interest level is high, you have an existing stock of anecdotes to share. Your tone of voice, modulation, and emphasis will naturally empower your words. Your passion and excitement will leap from your presentation to the people listening and watching it.

Can you fake interest in a topic if you need to convey the information you do not care about? It is possible, but you do not want to risk your audience recognizing your lack of passion. Plan an effective presentation more fully before you begin because you will not have natural energy to carry you through any part. Be careful not to go overboard with volume, vocal tone, or grand gestures. If you do not have passion, you probably need more practice to make things sound natural and engaging.

4. How Voice Tone and Rhythm Accentuate the Message

Local tone and speaking rhythm contribute to how an audience receives your message. In some ways, public speaking or information exchanges with a group are similar to acting.

No, you do not have to pretend to be someone else to get your point across.

However, using techniques the professionals practice can help you convey your message that excites other people.

If you are responsible for lectures, presentations, or frequent group leadership roles, you might try a public speaking or acting class to learn these techniques. They will also help you gain confidence, allowing you to interact with the audience in a natural and anxiety-free manner.

Vocal Tone Conveys Emotion The tone of voice you use in conversation or lectures affects the emotional response of your chat partners or audience. The ability to purposefully manipulate your tone gives you a powerful tool to increase the interest and impact of whatever information you want to convey.

This is something most people have to practice, so it sounds natural yet still effective.

People have a very broad repertoire of vocal tones and wordless sounds that express emotion clearly to others. This includes everything from the "Ahh!" of fear to a "Hmm" of deep thought to the "Oh!" of happy surprise. Researchers published in the American Psychologist Journal identified different emotions conveyed by the human voice. They even mapped them.

This interesting research does not mean you should interject emotional sounds every time you communicate with other people.

Your audience may find it odd if you start shouting, "Oh!" and "Ahh!" In the middle of a lecture or group discussion. However, the tonal quality of these sounds teaches you something about modulating your voice.

Emotional Transfer Engages Audiences Any interaction between two or more people involves a transfer of emotion and thought.

Communication is all about getting your ideas and opinions into someone else's brain. Doing the same thing with emotions increases the impact of those ideas. People become more invested in things that make them feel as well as think.

How do you do this without sounding like a dramatic actor?

For the most part, it all happens naturally. If you are talking about something that excites you, your voice will get louder and higher in tone. If you switch to a subject more serious or sad, your tone drops. Unfortunately, some people have less expressive voices and need to make a conscious effort to change how their voice conveys emotion.

5. Strengthen Audience Bond with Power Words and Gestures

You may think that what you say matters more than anything else when it comes to verbal communication. While the information shared is important, making an impact depends on emphasis. As described earlier in this book, vocal modulation and tone go a long way to giving your audience hints about the most important parts of whatever you have to say.

Another way to do this is with power words.

What Are Power Words?

The term 'power words' seems self-explanatory. These specific words or phrases capture attention, convey more meaning, and create a greater emotional response than ordinary ones. They are not long, complicated, or part of any particular jargon-based vocabulary. They are words anyone can understand. After all, no one will care if they don't comprehend what you're saying.

One of the most powerful words in marketing is 'free.' When people see this word, they are more likely to notice all the written communication around it. People want free stuff. It triggers an emotional response associated with desire.

Many power words focus specifically on emotions, feelings, and sought-after qualities.

Terms like inspiring, huge, irresistible, life-changing, simple, guaranteed, and luxurious spark imagination and create positive feelings.

Power words that evoke negative feelings your audience wants to avoid also work, such as embarrassing, guilt, mistake, or unpopular.

Power verbs inspire people to take action.

Some popular ones include kick start, grow, attack, succeed, and launch.

Point of view also affects the way people respond to your communication. The first person, using 'I' and 'we,' creates a sense of camaraderie and togetherness. This can work well for group projects and shared interests.

The second person, using 'you,' focuses on individual benefits to your audience. They end up feeling like your message is just for them and that you care about their success. Third-person, using 'he,' 'she,' and 'they,' is more formal and less emotionally effective than other options.

Consider these examples for power words and point of view:

Boring and Bland – Everyone wants to make more money. These methods will help people find ways to make income go up. They will feel better when they do not have to worry as much about paying bills.

Powerful and Personal -- You dream about an exceptional lifestyle of luxury and freedom.

Learn life-changing ways to explode your income in less time than you expect. Kick start a brand-new adventure that lets you focus on fun instead of financial worry.

While these examples sound more like marketing blurbs than a conversation, they represent using powerful words in communicating effectively. You can see that the second example has more specific and expressive phrases that will get people's attention and keep it from the first sentence to the last. By contrast, the boring example feels vague and disconnected from the audience.

Nonverbal Communication and Body Language Helps

Physical gestures and body language also emphasize that many audiences need to stay connected to the conversation. Various research studies find that body positions and gestures contribute anywhere from 60% to 90% of the meaning.

This type of communication begins even before you open your mouth. Of course, it does not matter at all in written communication, so letters, emails, and text messages may need extra power words or emotional language to convey meaning with impact truly.

Three points of body language power exist:

- Body positioning, posture, and stance
- Where you put or move your hands and arms, gestures
- Movement or position of your head

Imagine you walk into a business meeting, and your manager slumps over in his chair, elbows on the desk, and head in his hands. He stares down at a folder instead of making eye contact with anyone in the room. How do his posture and positioning affect your emotional response? If you're like most people, you're definitely a little worried since his body language is obviously unfavorable.

If you walk into the same business meeting and find your manager up on his feet, smiling at each participant as they walk in the room and moving in an active yet comfortable way, you would naturally feel more positive about the meeting.

Of course, there are always extenuating circumstances. Maybe in the first example, your manager had a twisted ankle and a headache from his allergies. He may feel rundown, but it had nothing to do with the content of the meeting. Hopefully, he could convey a more positive mood and his words and tone of voice.

Managing how other people respond to your communication with positive body language effectively increases the impact and retention of what you have to say. When you converse with one person, face them with an open and welcoming stance. Use good posture for a more positive impression. Mirror body language to increase comfort levels.

Stay relaxed and gesture effectively without making people fear standing too close.

Specific tips for large-scale presentations:

- Stand up or walk about the stage to face all sections of the audience.
- Do not lean excessively on a table or podium like you are tired.
- Do not cross your arms as this looks aggressive or angry.
- A gesture toward multimedia presentations or while using props.
- Avoid excessively dramatic movements or gestures.

To clarify the last point, running and leaping across the stage excitedly or waving your arms around may make people take notice. Still, the emotional response would probably be laughter and loss of respect rather than anything positive. Even if you feel excited or passionate about the subject, grandiose gestures cross the line from effective communication to sideshow barker territory.

Facial Expressions Matter Too

Although the finer characteristics of facial expressions may not convey clearly in a large lecture hall, they contribute to the exchange of emotion present in all communication. People are more likely to take notice of and remember expressions that reveal high levels of emotion rather than the face is at rest.

The human brain is wired to make sense out of visual cues that may not mean much on their own. These include eye outline, shape and specifically width of the mouth, and symmetry when it comes to facial expressions.

Again, making extreme facial expressions while you converse with others or give a lecture is not a way to engage your audience and make an impact. Subtlety communicates just as well. However, it is important not to stand there with a blank face because other people will have difficulty figuring out how you feel and what is most important to pay attention to.

Your voice also sounds different whether you smile or frown. Telemarketers and other people who speak on the phone for business purposes frequently are trained to smile while they read their script or answer questions. It conveys a friendly tone even without any visual cues.

Chapter 37:
Fitting all the Pieces Together

It is essential to remember that your communication has many different pieces. The first of these is gestures. A mother and a daughter can often carry on a whole conversation across a crowded room using only gestures. Gestures are unique to the individual. Most gestures should be kept small unless you are on a stage making a point. Concentrating on your message should allow your gestures to come naturally. If you're having difficulty getting your message through, make sure your speech and gestures are in sync.

Eye contact is another important element of communication. According to Michigan State University, the more that you look a person in the eye, the more dominant you will appear. You will also appear more credible. Alternatively, looking away, especially down, is a sign of being submissive. If you're furious, try not to look the other person in the eyes.

It is also important to control your posture to communicate effectively. Folded arms or crossed legs make you appear very aggressive and defensive. Therefore, it is essential to avoid this position to ensure that your message is effectively received. Instead, make sure that you keep your elbows slightly away from your body and arms in a natural position with your fingers spread slightly apart. To be taken seriously, make sure that your shoulders are kept slightly back and your head held in an upright position. If you want the other person to know that you are very interested in what they have to say, lean slightly towards that individual. Alternatively, if you want to reduce the tensions while communicating, try leaning slightly backward.

If you want to lift a mood at a meeting, then dress sharply. Research shows that wearing blue jeans or baggy clothes is perceived as being depressed. Wear shoes that allow you to walk freely since they create the impression that you have a lot of energy. Believe it or not, women wearing bright red lipstick made more money than those who wore a more subtle tone. Aim to present yourself in your best possible light.

When your message seems to be falling on deaf ears, then make sure to check your facial expressions. While it may be very difficult to deliver some messages without crying, research shows that it makes your message harder to hear. Researchers are not sure why, but the left side of the face shows more emotion than the right side. In short, make sure that your facial expressions line up with your message.

There are many ways that your body needs to align with your spoken words. Make sure to use small gestures that are not perceived as hostile in any way. Look your intended audience in the eyes to ensure that your message is getting through unless you want to appear submissive, then look slightly down. Keep your body language open, and you will have a better chance of your message being heard. Dress sharply to make sure that your message presents an uplifting mood in any meeting. Finally, make sure that your facial expressions are matching your message.

Part 2:
Being a Good Speaker

Chapter 38:
Characteristics of a Good Public Speaker

Public speaking is something that you will have to deal with for the rest of your life. You will have to give presentations of some sort for your whole educational life and even for some of the sports and other activities that you might be in. When you enter the workforce, you might have to do some public speaking to get a job, talk to the client, or even announce the news on television. Many different types of public speaking are out there, and there are many different situations where you might have to give a speech. Despite all of this, many people find that it is difficult to give a public speech. They might be worried that they will look bad while they are doing it, that they will forget their lines, or they just do not like to talk in front of other people. Even if you have these fears, it is important to learn how to get over them so that you are able to perform in your role. This can help you to see if you have some of these characteristics already; if not, you will be able to develop these characteristics in order to make giving speeches easier. Some of the characteristics that are present in a good public speaker include:

- **Solid content**—even if you do not have a natural charisma about you like some speakers do, you will be able to get the audience on your side simply by having solid and valuable content to the audience. You need to make sure that all of the content you present will add value to the lives of the audience in some way. If you have a lot of fluff, just throw that out because it will make the audience bored, and they will not take you seriously.

- **Humor**—people will always remember a speaker who was able to make them laugh. The earlier that you are able to get the audience smiling and laughing with you, the more memorable your speech is going to be. This is because it will help make the audience around you more receptive to the ideas you are getting across. You don't have to be a comedian in order to add some humor to your speech. Just add in a few jokes and some irony, and you are sure to get the audience on your side.

- **Organization**—before going out for a speech, you must make sure that you are completely organized. Have all of the facts checked, the information in order, and everything in its place. No excuse allows you to ramble on through the presentation. This is just going to make the audience get lost or make you lose your credibility. If you are organized, you leave your audience with a message that they can understand and which is easy to remember.

- **Approachable**—the best speakers are the ones who seem like they are approachable. These are the ones who will meet and greet people before and after the speech and who will leave room for questions at some point. These speakers do not seem like they are in a rush to leave right away but instead would rather spend their time with the audience.

- **Authentic**—people want to know who you are; they are smart enough to know when you are trying to pull one over on them, and they will become less receptive if they feel like you are doing this. They want to hear someone who will be honest with them. If you are a shy person, it is fine to show this out a little in the speech because it lets people know that you feel that your message is important enough to share even though this is your fear.

- **Natural**—when you are up in front of an audience, you should try to act natural and calm. This will help the audience to feel like there is a connection, and they will be able to listen more closely this way. It can often spell disaster if you are sitting there acting off or being too nervous. Try to act like the audience is some of your close friends and you are sharing something with them rather than worrying about a large crowd.

- **Passion**—a good speaker is someone passionate about what they are saying. They know that their information is valuable and useful, and they want to get it out to the audience. When you are excited about the message, the audience will catch on to that excitement and be excited soon as well.

Chapter 39:
Being an Effective Speaker

The process of communication starts with the speaker or the source. The message, and even the effectiveness of the entire communication flow, can rely on the source. Without the source, of course, there will be no communication in the first place.

Here are some considerations that you should always keep in mind if you want to become a better and an effective speaker:

- **Always be considerate of your audience.** One of the first and most essential principles of communication is that you must first understand your audience. You have to consider the condition of your audience.

Do not just talk about yourself and dominate the entire conversation by talking only about yourself. As much as possible, you have to involve your audience in the conversation. Have them talk about their own lives and experiences, and that's when you start sharing ideas and messages with each other. You may also use probing questions to elicit the emotions or views of the person you're speaking with, which will help you engage them more fully in the discussion.

- **Speak clearly.** The way you talk has a big impact on whether your audience would want to listen to what you are talking about or not. If you speak so that they would not understand you, you will most likely lose your audience's interest. On the other side, if you speak in an engaging manner, your audience will be interested in what you have to say.

Also, you should not mumble or even talk in the opposite direction of your listener. Doing so will most likely imply a different meaning to your audience, such as disinterest in the conversation or, worse, the listener. You must also ensure that your listeners comprehend what you are saying. If you failed to make your audience understand what you are talking about, then in a way, you also failed as a communicator or a speaker.

- **Do not lose your focus on the conversation**. It is a rule of thumb: doing something else with nothing to do with the conversation while you are in the conversation is disrespectful to your listener. That person might think that you do not even want to talk to them since you are regarding your conversation as not worthy of your full attention. It is usually suggested that you look directly into your listener while having a conversation with them to know that you are paying attention.
- **Be as brief as possible**. Human beings naturally have a specific attention span, that when a conversation exceeds that span, we will already lose our interest and attention in the conversation. Therefore, you need to be as direct to the point as possible for you to make the most out of that limited period. Do not in any way talk over the point. This applies the most when you are doing public speeches.

Your audience will lose interest in your talk if you keep talking about things that do not even have anything to do with your topic. And as we have mentioned earlier, it is important that your message is relevant to your listener. So if you keep on talking about your life experiences up to the tiniest details, chances are your listener will feel uninterested.

- **Know how to "read" your listener**. As the speaker, you should also have an idea as to what your listener is feeling. Again, know your audience. If you can see that your listener feels a little bit uncomfortable with what you are talking about, perhaps you can change the topic or recommend talking about it some other time. The idea is that you should connect with your audience and be sensitive enough as to how your audience is feeling so that you will not (1) lose their interest and (2) hurt their feelings or say something so insensitive.

- **Learn how to level yourself with your audience.** As a leader who wants to communicate with other people effectively, you must know how to deal with other people. You need to know how to properly talk to your people so that they, in turn, will also know how to respond to and deal with you properly.

You should not be arrogant in the way you speak to other people just because you are the leader or the boss.

You should know how you level yourself so that they, too, will know their level. You should be able to gain the trust of your people so that they can share their ideas with you, but you should not be too submissive to them that they will no longer regard you as the leader and that they will already take you for granted. You must be able to impose what kind of relationship you want to establish by the way you communicate with them.

Chapter 40:
Get in Some Practice

Why wait until your event to test what you've spent hours preparing? Start with being your judge first. Get comfortable with your material and know it inside out, so you don't have to think about what you have to say next once you take the stage.

It's even better if you can have a friend sit in during your practice to let you know what they think about your presentation. This will help you get feedback and develop confidence speaking about your content to another person.

1. Practice In Front Of The Mirror

If you have the option, select a mirror that allows you to view your whole body while practicing in front of it. It's not a deal-breaker if you don't. What's good about a full-length mirror is that it can give you the chance to observe your stance or any nervous leg movements you may make.

Focus On Facial Expressions And Movements

We usually focus on what we do with our hands and our facial expressions when speaking and overlook how crucial our legs can be to our presentation. It's a good practice to move about the stage from one end to the other to engage each part of the room. That is why you want to be sure that when you do that, you don't have any awkward and involuntary leg movements that can divert your audience's attention from what you have to say.

Make Amendments

The main purpose of practicing in front of a mirror is to observe any gestures or facial expressions you don't like and change them in real-time. Did you notice an excess of quick hand movements? Stop them as you see them, and you can then add them when you see fit.

2. Make A Video Recording Of Your Practice

Think of your mobile phone's camera as your audience. Give that lens the best speech it has heard. All kidding aside, recording a video of yourself practicing is a great way to look back on what you liked (yes, it is important to highlight the positives of your work) and didn't like about your performance.

Place Your Mobile Phone At A Suitable Distance

Place your mobile phone at a distance at which you can see your facial expressions with ease, and your whole body is captured.

Observe Your Performance

You are observing every bit of your performance, including the way you walk around on your stage. Talk into your camera, and gauge how much eye contact you maintained in the playback. This will also allow you to hear any inflections in your voice that you may wish to improve.

Write Down These Points

In your notebook, make a list of the benefits and drawbacks of your speech. Write these down to remember any changes you may want to make for the final presentation.

You Will Feel The Difference

It helps at every step to be confident about yourself to keep your nerves together. That begins with being comfortable with your voice. It may seem strange, but it helps feeling positive about how you sound. Speak out loud with confidence as if your audience is in front of you. Take this chance to learn to throw your voice to not sound timid in front of your audience.

3. Present In Front Of A Friend

You can make this easier by picking a close friend or family member who you can feel comfortable practicing with.

Pick Someone Honest

Try and avoid choosing someone who you can expect to be hard on you at the get-go. Harsh negative feedback can make you feel disheartened about your presentation, and you don't want that. So, pick someone honest but understand your fear of public speaking, and practice with them.

Read Their Reactions

This form of practice is great because you get to deliver your presentation to a person before the main event. Take this opportunity to read their reactions to what you're saying.

Are they leaning back and looking bored? Are they looking at a clock nearby? Or are they nodding at the main points you're making? Don't only rely on the feedback they give you after your presentation but also access their body language during it.

Don't Only Rely On Their Feedback

People sometimes do tend to sugarcoat their feedback for you, so do some observing for yourself. You'll have a better grasp of what they're saying. This will also give you a new perspective on your work. You will learn about things you may have overlooked in your preparation and alter your presentation accordingly for the event itself.

Ask Them Specific Questions

Don't just leave it up to them to tell you what they think. Ask them specific questions on what they thought about your presentation. These questions should pertain to both your content and delivery. Make a note of what they say so that you can look out for those when you playback a recording of you presenting.

Make a note of the positives as well. It's important to feel good about what you present. You can focus on those during your main presentation to be positive that you know what you are talking about.

Chapter 41:
Use Note Cards to Avoid Relying on Memory

This point is something that should technically be taken care of during the preparation of your presentation, but it is something that pertains to your delivery. That is why we've included it here.

Don't get into the habit of writing complete speeches and memorizing them word for word. What do you think will happen if you forget one important word? Your flow will be ruined, and you will most likely get flustered trying to fix your error. This will both sacrifice the quality of your delivery and cause you to feel more anxious about another possible blunder.

Think Of Your Speech As A Two-Way Conversation

Think of each presentation like a conversation, and that it is now your turn to speak. The Q and A section after your presentation is your audience's moment to speak. If there isn't one, their feedback and reactions are their way of speaking in this case.

Speak Naturally

Think of a presentation or speech as a conversation, and it will help remind you that it is about the spoken word. That means that you speak in your natural flow. Don't try and emulate the way you write in your speech. The way you speak and write is a lot more different than you may think.

We take time and effort to construct sentences with almost all of our written work. Some of that even go through rigorous editing processes to yield the final product. You don't think about how you're going to construct a sentence when you're speaking. The words just come out as you think them, and you spend no time phrasing what you're going to say next.

Don't Learn And Recite A Written Speech Verbatim

Do not write a complete speech that you intend to learn. Because regardless of how you write it, it will still not come off as your natural speaking voice to your audience. The difference between your spoken voice and learned written speech would be more apparent if you're not a great public speaker.

It Shows Lack Of Confidence

The changes in tone when speaking naturally and reciting learned words can damage your confidence in your ability to speak. Choosing to recite pre-written words during your presentation indicates your lack of confidence in the words you come up with on the spot. Don't introduce any kind of doubt in your mind. They will allow your fear to fester, and you don't want that.

It is difficult to remember each detail of your material, yes. It does get easier if you practice before your actual presentation, but that doesn't guarantee that some important points won't go unspoken. At any point on stage, your nerves could take over and make you feel like you didn't prepare at all.

Write Down Key Points

That is a scary thought in and of itself, let alone for it actually to happen. You don't have to worry, though, because there is a very commonly-used solution for this problem: make note cards.

These should include one word or phrase for each key point you want to talk about. Use your own words to then elaborate on them. This will help you keep a consistent manner of speaking throughout your presentation. You want your audience to feel like you are talking to them. You want each word of yours to feel like that you are thinking about them when you speak.

You know more about a subject, and this is your time to educate them. That is why you mustn't get your focus drawn towards your memory on the subject. Focus instead on using your words to educate your audience.

Keep Your Note Cards Short But Effective

You should also remember that these cards are for you and not for the ears of your audience. Make them short so that you won't read them out loud. It's not an effective practice to read out a slide or note card first and then elaborate that point with more or less the same words. It's a waste of your time and your audience.

Remove All Redundancy

Remove all redundancy. Like any good piece of writing, each word you speak should matter. Get rid of every single word that doesn't serve your argument. Keep things concise and get your point across with the least amount of words you can. You have a much greater chance of holding your audience's attention that way.

Focus On Your Speaking Voice

You can walk on that stage, feeling confident when you know what to do to keep your audience attentive to what you have to say. Confidence is key in overcoming your fear of talking on stage, and one great way to do that is to focus on your speaking voice.

It is vital to recognize that your written word and spoken word are not the same. That is why you shouldn't write and learn an entire speech. It is a much better practice to use note cards to remember your material and speak in your natural flow.

Chapter 42:
How to Use Visual Aids

Visuals aides can have a powerful effect on a presentation. If you've ever watched a TED talk, you will notice the clean, straightforward visuals used. Did you know that TED has a dedicated team to help the presenters create stunning visuals and give captivating presentations? They have developed a formula that works great for the TED stage.

There are many categories of presentations that you can give: a product demo, technical presentations, team building presentations, presentations on your passion, and the list goes on. Although each presentation has different messages, the principles on how to deliver an effective presentation apply to all of them. You can apply similar principles to adding visuals to your speeches.

Rule #1: One Point Per Visual.

Each visual you decide to use should only have one main message. If you are trying to convey more than one message with one slide, then your message becomes unclear. Communication is about having a steady, logical flow of information. Having more than one message at a time is like having three people trying to tell you something different all at the same time. If you have more than one message, figure out which is the important point you are trying to make and keep it on that visual. Then, move the other important points to the next visuals. This is a great way to filter and reduce the amount of information you present. You want the message to be concise, having meaning and impact. Remove the weak points.

Rule #2: Keep It Simple.

The visual should be easily understood. Even if you are giving a technical presentation and explaining programming codes used to build the software, you have to think about what is excessive information and the most relevant information. If you have too much information, then it becomes overly complex. An overly complex presentation is not good because you are not direct about your message. As the presenter, you want the audience to understand exactly what you are trying to convey; otherwise, you lose control. Reduce the clutter and present only what is necessary.

One example is to have a large, high-quality picture take up most of the space, then include some text over the image. Here's a sample:

Remember that the visual should be a support material. What do you think it is supporting here? The speaker may be talking about the growth in real estate and housing opportunities. This visual delivers a message to the audience that this housing expansion is just beginning. The speaker can use this to talk further about the topic.

Some other books and materials talk about visual aids. Suppose you are trying to raise money for your company, and you are giving an investor presentation. In that case, there are best practices that you can find online that outline how you should deliver the presentation, especially if it is in PowerPoint.

Rule #3: Your Presentation Dictates the Visuals (the Visuals do not dictate you).

Create an outline before you put slides together. One common mistake I see among my students is that when they are notified they will be giving a presentation, their first step is to open PowerPoint and throw together some slides. They end up basing their entire presentation on the slides and are at times forced to fit points into the slides because they are there.

Instead, you should start by creating a presentation outline. As you put together the structure (the bullet points) of your presentation, that's when you start to visualize where (and which) visuals would be most helpful. The mistake is that people build the presentation around the visuals. You should build the presentation first, know what you are going to say, then have the visuals complement your presentation. In summary, think about your slides last.

If you want to see a great public presentation that effectively uses visual aides, watch a TEDTalk or watch Steve Jobs unveil the iPhone. Notice how their visuals are very clear, precise, and have one main message. They also rarely look at the visuals themselves because the speakers tell the story—using the visuals as supplements and keeping the focus on the speaker.

How To Practice:

Use this outline to put together your speech:

1. Opening
    a. Captures audience attention
    b. Leads into speech topic
2. Body
    a. Main point
        i. Subpoint
        ii. Support material
    b. Main point
        i. Subpoint
        ii. Support material
    c. Main point
        i. Subpoint
        ii. Support material
3. Conclusion
    a. Review or summary
    b. Call to action or memorable statement

Be sure you create your structure first before you start thinking about visuals. After you have designed your presentation, try to expand on the points, staying within the brief bullet point mentality. After your speech is mapped out, insert the areas where adding a visual will have a lasting impact on your presentation. You can think of your visuals as the support materials that help the audience remember and understand your important points. The most commonly used visuals are slides in a PowerPoint presentation. You can also choose other visuals such as a live computer demo, a poster, or a physical object. Avoid small visuals that are hard to see. Keep in mind that you want each visual to be viewable by the entire audience and not only the front row. A powerful visual will drive your message home.

Extra Challenge

After you finish with your bullet outline, casually throw some visuals together. They do not have to be meticulously prepared. This extra challenge is for you to see what your visuals will look like. When we form pictures of the visuals we want displayed in our head, it will turn out a bit differently. This exercise will allow you to iterate on your speech and visuals at the same time.

Chapter 43:
Using Audio and Visual Aids Effectively

Generally, it is assumed that visible information retains in mind for a longer time than the information that is heard or spoken.

When a speaker's speech or presentation is supported with visuals, then the audience can

understand the message properly.

1. **Benefits of Visual Aids**

    - Grabs the attention of the audience

    - Through words-to-visual communication, people can easily relate to what the speaker is talking about

    - Leaves a long-lasting impression on the audience

2. **Types of Audio and Video Aids**

    - Whiteboard

    - Flip charts

    - Videos

    - PowerPoint Presentation (PPT)

    - Exhibit (To showcase or explain a product by showing it)

3. **Usage of Audio and Visual Aids**

Answer the following three questions to know how and where to use the audio and visual aids:

   1. What is the most important idea you want to convey?

   2. Which areas of your speech need visual aids for better understanding?

3. What is the audience size you are addressing? (For a small audience, flip charts, whiteboards, and props are fine, but overhead projectors and big TV screens are required for a large audience.)

4. **Checklist for Audio and Visual Aids**

- Use relevant aids: Visual aids should always support the message of speech or presentation. Never distract or confuse the audience through visual aids.

- Get comfortable with visual aids: Practice getting comfortable with the visual aids before using them in front of the audience.

- Maintain eye contact with the audience: The speaker/presenter should make eye contact with the audience while utilizing visual aids.

- Check the audio and video quality beforehand: You should check the sound and clarity of the video that you want to show in the speech/presentation.

- Don't read presentation word-by-word: Add value to your audience learning's by not reading the presentation word-by-word.

5. **PowerPoint Presentations (PPT)**

To make presentations more impactful, use the following things in your PPT:

- Images
- Audio
- Videos
- Multimedia

6. **Golden Rules to Make a PowerPoint Presentation**

   1. **Less is more**: Don't overload slides with content; otherwise, the audience will get confused about reading the text/information on the slides or listening to the speaker.

   2. **6/6 rule**: A slide should have a maximum of 6 lines, and every line should have 6 words each.

   3. **Consistency is the Key**: There should be consistency in font style and size in all the presentation slides. Depending upon the importance of the point of the message you want to convey, some fonts in the slides can be made bold, larger in size, or of a different color. It needs to stand out in the slide.

   4. **Show, don't tell**: The audience can easily understand a visual message. Always use pictures and videos of high quality in your presentation.

   5. **Fact-check data**: To show any data and statistics in the slides, the data source should be genuine and checked. This helps in gaining the audience's trust.

   6. **Fonts must be clear**: Fonts used in slides must be clear and readable. The text of the slides should be in bullet points.

   7. **Choose color patterns wisely**: Some color patterns leave an impact on the audience's mind. The easy color combination is light color text on a dark background or vice-versa. The safest options are black, white, red, and blue. Never use any flashy colors as the audience may get distracted.

7. **Strategies of Content Delivery**

   1. Practice and rehearse with your PowerPoint Presentation. It is also important to time the practice to know how much time is required on a slide.

2. PowerPoint slides must have less content. Slides should have only the main points.

3. Do connect with the audience by asking the pain areas of the people who arrive early and tell them what they will learn through the presentation.

4. Change PPT slides on time and practice how to give a clue to the person operating the slides on your behalf.

5. Let the slide sometimes do the talking, i.e., do not repeat the data or figures written on the slides.

6. You should have confidence in your body language and should smile.

- ✓ Use visual aids in PowerPoint Presentation to grab the attention of the audience
- ✓ Focus on the color pattern to have clarity in the text presented on the PPT slides
- ✓ Write less and relevant content on the PPT slides
- ✓ Practice with the visual aids before using them during the speech or presentation

Chapter 44:
Be Assertive

What Is Assertiveness?

It's not always simple to determine whether someone is being forceful in the right manner. This is because there's a scarce difference between Assertiveness and hostility, and individuals can frequently confound the two. Thus, it's helpful to characterize the two practices with the goal that we can isolate them:

Assertiveness depends on parity. It requires being frank about your needs and wants while thinking about your rights and needs. When you're Assertive, you are confident and attract control from this to express what is on your mind immovably, reasonably, and with sympathy.

Aggressive behavior depends on winning. You do what is in your very own best without respect for the rights, needs, emotions, or wants of other individuals. When you're aggressive, you utilize egotistical power. You may seem to be pushy or notwithstanding tormenting. You take what you regularly need without inquiring.

Along these lines, a boss who places loads of work around your work area the evening before you take some time off, and requests that it completes straight away, is being Aggressive. The work should be done be that as it may, by dumping it on you at an improper time, the individual in question dismisses your needs and sentiments.

When you, then again, educate your manager that it will do the work yet simply after you come back from get-away, you hit the sweet spot between latency (not being Assertive enough) and hatred (being threatening, furious, or impolite). You attest your privileges while perceiving your supervisors have to take care of business.

Warning:

Assertive behavior may not be fitting in all working environments. Some hierarchical and national societies may prompt individuals to be inactive and may see Assertive behavior as inconsiderate or even hostile.

Research has likewise recommended that gender can affect how confident behavior is seen, with men bound to be compensated for being Assertive than ladies. Along these lines, it pays to consider the setting in which you work before you start changing your behavior.

Assertiveness via Body Language

Our communication through body language is entirely through our subconscious. This is how it is distinguished from sign language that is quite intentional and conscious. Although body language is accurately studied by very few people, the ability to decipher it gives a person the ability to understand the difference between a person's words and thoughts. A major portion of our communication occurs through sign language. Here are a few things that make body language an essential part of our lives.

Professional lives

From the first step of acquiring a job, our body language plays a pivotal role in our professional lives. When an interviewer is talking to a candidate, the body language depicted by the candidate determines the perception of his competence. There is a higher probability of a person with confident body language getting the job compared to a person who comes across as uncomfortable and nervous. Even when you are in a working environment, how you exhibit your body language determines how your team perceives you. People who exhibit confident body language are most likely to be leaders compared to that exhibit lazy body language.

Personal Lives

Whether you care about a person or paying attention to what they are saying is extremely important in building a good rapport and smooth communication between two people. For instance, if you lean in while conversing, it makes the other person feel important and cared for. On the other hand, leaning back signifies detachment and lack of interest. Showing that you are keen on listening is extremely important in the personal sphere.

In totality, body language is extremely important in showcasing our personality to the world. It underlies every bit of communication that takes place between the people around us and us.

It is a great idea to work on body language to understand the strengths and weaknesses that we are showcasing to the world. Working on our body language can help us come across as assertive and highly confident.

The Advantages of Being Assertive

One of the principal advantages of being Assertive is that it can assist you with becoming increasingly self-confident as you increase a superior comprehension of your identity and the worth you offer.

Assertiveness gives a few different advantages to help you both in your work environment and different parts of your life. All in all, Assertive people:

Make a great manager. They complete things by treating individuals with decency and regard and are treated by others on a similar path consequently. This implies they are regularly well-preferred and seen as pioneers that individuals need to work with.

Arrange effective "win-win" arrangements. They can perceive the estimation of their rival's position and can rapidly discover shared views with him.

Are better practitioners and issue solvers. They feel enabled to take the necessary steps to locate the best answer for their experience.

Are you less on edge and focused? They are confident and don't feel compromised or defrauded when things don't go as arranged or true to form.

How to Speak Assertively

Assertiveness has a huge impact on overall communication. When you have the right body language and choose the right words to speak, you will find yourself being more expressive, clearer, and more powerful in your communication. There are a few techniques and guidelines that can help you achieve that assertiveness:

Stating instead of just saying

There are instances when you can say something without understanding the impact that your words have on others. In such instances, you are breaking the most important rule of assertiveness that is respecting the rights of others. Sentences that convey a direct "you" message are the most damaging of them all. The idea is to highlight your feeling instead of highlighting a person's actions. This is possible with "I" statements like, "when you do not deliver on time, I feel angry."

Being non-judgmental

We are conditioned that at a very young age that it is necessary to put labels on people. Being judgmental is something that our ego teaches us to do in an attempt to keep people at a distance. In the process, good communication is destroyed. Judgmental people often make statements like "he or she is stupid." Instead, an assertive person makes an effort to analyze a situation and understand why a person makes certain mistakes.

Being Specific

Making statements that are not specific but merely sweeping statements is not the mark of assertiveness. When a person is assertive, he uses factually correct statements. It is necessary to state facts. Generalizing does not serve the purpose of ensuring clear communication.

How to Become More Assertive

It is difficult to turn out to be more Assertive; however, it is conceivable. Along these lines, if your aura will, in general, be more uninvolved or Aggressive, at that point, it's a smart thought to take a shot at the accompanying territories to assist you with getting the parity right:

1. Value Yourself and Your Rights

To be more Assertive, you have to increase a decent comprehension of yourself, just as a solid faith in your innate worth and your incentive to your association and group.

This self-conviction is simply the premise of certainty and Assertive behavior. It will assist you with recognizing that you have the right to be treated with pride and regard, give you the certainty to stand up for your privileges, secure them, and stay consistent with yourself, your needs, and your needs.

While self-confidence is a significant part of Assertiveness, you must ensure that it doesn't form into a feeling of gaudiness. Your privileges, contemplations, emotions, needs, and wants are similarly as significant as everybody else's, except not a higher priority than anybody else's.

2. Voice Your Needs and Wants Confidently

If you perform to your maximum capacity, at that point, you have to ensure that your needs – your needs and needs – are met.

Don't wait for someone else to notice what you're looking for. You may stand by until the end of time! Take a step forward and start identifying the items you need right now. At that point, set objectives with the goal that you can accomplish them.

When you've done this, you can tell your chief or your associate precisely what it is that you need from them to assist you with achieving these objectives unmistakably and surely. What's more, remember to stand firm. Regardless of whether what you need is beyond the realm of imagination at this moment, ask (cordially) whether you can return to your solicitation in a half year time.

Discover approaches to make demands that abstain from relinquishing others' needs. Keep in mind that you need individuals to support you, and requesting things in an excessively Aggressive or pushy manner will probably put them off doing this and may even harm your relationship.

3. Know That You Can't Control Other Individuals' Behavior

Try not to tragically accept duty regarding how individuals respond to your Assertiveness. If they, for instance, act furiously toward you, attempt to abstain from responding to them similarly.

Keep in mind that you can just control yourself and your very own behavior, so put forth a valiant effort to remain quiet and estimated if things get tense. For whatever length of time that you are aware and not damaging another person's needs, at that point, you reserve the privilege to state or do what you need.

4. Express Yourself in a Positive Way

It's essential to state what's at the forefront of your thoughts, notwithstanding when you have a troublesome or negative issue. In any case, you should do it productively and delicately.

Try not to be reluctant to support yourself and to face individuals who challenge you and additionally your privileges. You can even enable yourself to be furious! Be that as it may, make sure to control your feelings and to remain deferential consistently.

5. Be Available for Criticism and Compliments

Acknowledge both positive and negative feedback generous, unassumingly, and Assertive ally.

On the off chance that you don't concur with the analysis that you get, at that point, you should be set up to say as much; however, without getting guarded or furious. The Feedback Framework is an incredible apparatus that can assist you with seeing past your passionate responses to criticism and rather use it to accomplish huge, positive change.

6. Figure out how to say "No"

Saying "No" is difficult to do, particularly when you're not used to doing it; however, it's imperative if you need to turn out to be more Assertive.

Knowing your points of confinement and how much work you can take on will assist you with managing your undertakings all the more viably and pinpoint any territories of your activity that make you feel as if you're being exploited.

Keep in mind that you can't in any way, shape or form do everything or please everybody, so, significantly, you ensure your time and your remaining task at hand by saying "no" when fundamental. When you do need to state "no," attempt to discover a successful win arrangement that works for everybody.

7. Use Assertive Communication Techniques

There are various basic, however viable communication strategies that you can use to be increasingly Assertive. These are:

Use "I" statement

Use "I need," "I want," or "I feel" to pass on essential declarations and express what is on your mind immovably. For instance, "I feel unequivocal that we have to acquire an outsider to intercede this difference."

Empathy

Continuously attempt to perceive and see how the other individual perspectives the circumstance. At that point, in the wake of taking her perspective into thought, express what you need from her.

For instance, "I comprehend that you're experiencing difficulty working with Arlene, yet this venture should be finished by Friday. Allows all plunk down and concoct an arrangement together."

Escalation

If your first endeavors at standing up for yourself have been fruitless, at that point, you may need to heighten the issue further. This implies getting to be firmer (however still well-mannered and conscious) with the individual you are requesting help from and may end in you revealing to him what you will do straightaway if, regardless, you aren't fulfilled.

For instance, "John, this is the third time this week I've needed to address you about showing up later than expected. In case you're late yet again this month, I will actuate the disciplinary procedure."

Nonetheless, recall that paying little respect to the outcomes that you impart to the individual being referred to, you may even now not get what you need at last. If so, you may need to make a further move by setting up a conventional gathering to discuss the issue or escalating your worries to HR or your chief.

Request Additional Time

Some of the time, it's best not to say anything. You may be excessively passionate, or you probably won't comprehend what it is that you need yet.

If so, be straightforward and tell the individual that you need a couple of minutes to create your contemplations. For instance, you may state, "Dave, your solicitation has found me napping. I'll hit you up inside the half-hour."

Change Your Action words

Have a go at utilizing action words that are more positive and earnest when you convey. This will assist you with sending an unmistakable message and maintain a strategic distance from "glossing over" your message so much that individuals are left confounded by what it is that you need from them.

To do this, utilization action words like "will" rather than "could" or "should," "need" rather than "need," or "decide to" rather than "need to."

For example:

"I will travel one week from now, so I will require somebody to cover my remaining task at hand."

"I need to go on this instructional class since I accept that it will assist me with progressing in my job and my vocation."

"I pick this choice since I figure it will demonstrate to be more fruitful than different alternatives on the table."

Be a Broken Record

Set up the message that you need to pass on early.

In the event that, for example, you can't take on any more work, be immediate and state, "I can't take on any more activities at present." On the off chance that individuals still don't get the message, at that point, continue rehashing your message utilizing a similar language and don't yield. In the long run, they will probably understand that you truly mean what you're stating.

For example:

"I'd like you to take a shot at the Clancy venture."

"I can't take on any more undertakings at present."

"I'll pay extra for you to do it."

"I can't take on any more undertakings at present."

"Truly, this is extremely significant. My manager demands this completes."

"I can't take on any more tasks at present."

"Will you do it as an individual support?"

"I'm grieved; I esteem our relationship, yet I just can't take on any more activities at this moment."

Tip:

Be cautious with the messed-up record strategy. If you utilize it to protect yourself from mistreatment, that's fantastic. However, if you use it to menace somebody into making a move that is against their interests, it very well may be manipulative and evil.

Scripting

It can regularly be difficult to tell how to put your sentiments crosswise over plainly and unquestionably to somebody when you have to stand up for yourself. The scripting method can help here. It enables you to plan what you need to state ahead of time, utilizing a four-pronged methodology that depicts:

The occasion. Tell the other individual precisely how you see the circumstance or issue.

"Janine, the generation costs this month are 23 percent higher than normal. You didn't give me any sign of this, which implied that I was amazed by the news."

Your sentiments. Portray how you feel about the circumstance and express your feelings plainly.

"This baffles me and makes me feel like you don't comprehend or acknowledge how significant budgetary controls are in the organization."

Your needs. Tell the other individual precisely what you need from her with the goal that she doesn't need to figure.

"I need you to be honest with me, and I need you to let me know when we start spending money on anything again."

The results. Portray the constructive effect that your solicitation will have for the other individual or the organization if your needs are met effectively.

"If you accomplish this, we will be in a good position to meet our goals and may see indications of progress in our end-of-year award."

Key Points

Assertive methods find the correct harmony between detachment (not Assertive enough) and animosity (irate or unfriendly behavior). It means having a solid feeling of yourself and your worth and recognizing that you have the right to get what you need. Furthermore, it means going to bat for yourself even in the most troublesome circumstances.

Assertive doesn't mean acting to your greatest advantage without considering other individuals' privileges, sentiments, wants, or needs – that is hatred.

You can figure out how to be more Assertive after some time by recognizing your needs and needs, communicating them in a positive way, and figuring out how to state "no" when you have to. Likewise, you can utilize Assertive communication procedures to assist you with communicating your musings and sentiments solidly and straightforwardly.

It likely won't occur without any forethought in any case; by rehearsing these methods normally, you will gradually develop the certainty and self-conviction that you have to end up confident. You'll likewise likely find that you become increasingly beneficial, effective, and regarded, as well.

Characteristics of Assertive People

The assertive person presents a series of thoughts, emotions, and typical behaviors that we can summarize as follows:

He knows himself and is usually aware of what he feels and what he wants at each moment.

It is accepted unconditionally, without it depending on your achievements or the acceptance of others. Therefore, when he wins or loses, he always retains his respect and dignity when he obtains success or does not achieve his goals.

He knows how to understand and adequately manage their feelings and those of the rest. Therefore, he does not experience more anxiety than is appropriate in his interpersonal relationships and can face conflicts, failures, or successes serenely.

He doesn't demand the things he wants, but he doesn't fool himself, thinking he doesn't care.

He accepts their limitations of any kind but, at the same time, fights with all his might to realize his possibilities.

He stays true to himself in any circumstance and feels responsible for his life and his emotions. Therefore, he maintains an active attitude, striving to achieve its objectives.

As he tends to know and accept himself and express what he thinks, wants, and feels, he usually gives an image of a congruent and authentic person. He respects and values himself and others. Thus, he can express and defend his rights while respecting the rights of others.

You can communicate with people of all levels: friends, family, and strangers, and this communication tend to be open, direct, frank, and adequate. Choose, if possible, the people around you and, kindly but firmly, determine who your friends are and who are not. He usually expresses his opinions, desires, and feelings adequately instead of waiting for others to guess them.

The assertive person tends to maintain positive attitudes towards himself and others.

Positive Consequences of Assertiveness and its Importance

Assertiveness has very positive consequences, among which the following stand out:

- It facilitates communication and minimizes the possibility that others misunderstand our messages.
- It helps to maintain more satisfying relationships.

- It increases the chances of getting what we want.
- It increases satisfaction and reduces the inconvenience and conflicts caused by living together.
- It improves self-esteem.
- It favors positive emotions in oneself and others.

Those who relate to the assertive person obtain clear and non-manipulative communication, feel respected and perceive that the other feels good with them. Assertiveness is a growing interest in various areas, for example, in psychotherapy, education, or labor relations.

The interest that awakens is logical since expressing our desires and opinions, defending our rights, and taking the reins of our own lives are very desirable issues for anyone. In addition, assertiveness is an important component of what we understand by mental health, as poorly assertive individuals experience feelings of isolation, low self-esteem, depression, fear, and anxiety in interpersonal situations. They also often feel rejected or used by others and often have psychosomatic problems, such as headaches or digestive disorders.

On the other hand, various investigations show that those who have actively participated in assertiveness training programs tend to experience:

1. An increase in feelings of self-worth and self-efficacy;
2. More positive attitudes towards those around them;
3. Less anxiety in social situations;
4. Greater ability to communicate and interact effectively with others and improve their general state of health, or at least in their perception of it. To better understand what assertiveness is, let's compare it with two forms - as opposed to each other - of non-assertive behavior, which are inhibition and aggressiveness.

The 5 Parts of Assertiveness

1. Defensive skills

This area refers to the ability to manage aggression and criticism. There are specific techniques to help you defend yourself. A person with good defensive skills can avoid useless discussions and accept motivated criticism. But at the same time, he can maintain his point of view and position in front of the attacks and manipulations of others.

2. Express negative feelings and disagreement

Here we refer to the ability to assert one's rights. For example, ask others to change a behavior that causes discomfort. As in the case of a colleague who continues to interrupt you while you speak or a neighbor holds loud music.

On a more general level, it has to do with expressing one's point of view when it is negative. Take the case of some friends complaining at the restaurant while they are among them. Then the waiter arrives and asks how the dinner went, and one of them says: ' everything is fine ' - with a welcoming tone and a smile.

Some people avoid expressing their point of view if it is not the same as that of others.

3. Management of personal limits

Those who do not know how to manage their limits avoid and are embarrassed by the idea of admitting their difficulties. For example, recognize that you do not know or have not understood something. He does not accept criticism and is reluctant to discuss it. He feels uncomfortable apologizing or receiving apologies from others.

This also leads, for example, to avoid engaging in situations or tasks where it is possible to be criticized. He does not ask for help or assistance, even if he needs it.

4. Assertiveness of initiative

Who has little assertiveness of initiative is uncomfortable among people who do not know. He does not express his opinion or tell any facts about himself. Among the groups, he prefers to remain hidden or make his presence felt as little as possible. Avoid new situations and are not at ease in front of people perceived as authoritative.

The lack of initiative also manifests itself in not making decisions and behaviors of dependence on others.

5. Positive assertiveness

Positive assertiveness refers to the ability to express positive feelings, such as sympathy and affection. But also appreciations and compliments, which on the job are necessary.

A poor positive assertiveness does not like to receive compliments and does not know how to react if he receives them. Struggling to be pleased or to express approval and affection. He feels embarrassed when interacting with people he considers attractive.

Imagine for a moment that you are on a swing. One side is listening, and the other is talking. Most people have a style that is unbalanced on one side of the other.

To communicate assertively, you need to understand where you are sitting on the swing. This way, you can make a conscious effort to compensate.

If you sit too much at either end, the swing becomes unbalanced and cannot work.

The Right Way to Be Assertive

Understanding how to be sympathetic is the first step. Empathetic people may see things from the other's point of view. Empathetic assertors are perceptive to the circumstances and emotions of people around them. When learning to accomplish this, you must first realize that the other person, regardless of the circumstance, has emotions. You may then express your requirement or viewpoint after you've realized this. "I realize that you have been busy with your job, but I need that you make time for this project as well."

It may be difficult to know when to increase your aggressiveness. It isn't always a black-and-white issue. When attempting to communicate, it's important to explore all possible methods to convey your point of view before escalating. If you don't feel like you can get your point through to a polite boss, you should be firmer. "If you don't keep up your part of the bargain, I'll have to take legal action against you," for example.

Always explain what the problem is, followed by what the remedy may entail. As you learn to be more direct, you will also learn to be more forceful. The more you practice being straightforward in low-stakes situations, the more confident you will become. Whether you're unsure about the level of assertiveness you're using, ask a friend or family member if you may test your assertiveness skills on them first.

Chapter 45:
Become a Good Listener

Most people too often focus on what to say next rather than listen to the other person. Effective communication is about talking less and listening more. However, listening is not just understanding the words being said; it's also about understanding the emotions behind what's being conveyed. A good listener should understand where the speaker is coming from, empathize with them, and even anticipate the objective of the said speech and respond accordingly. Even you disagree, your first reaction is significant. Never block the dialogue.

There is a vast difference between active listening and just hearing. When we actively listen, we are engaged in what the other person is saying. Engaged listening includes hearing the changes in the other person's tone while speaking. Engaged listening is not just understanding the other person; it's also making the other person feel understood. This kind of communication helps build deeper and stronger connections.

Active listening allows us to feel what the other person is feeling. For example, we are having a conversation, and you are feeling a little stressed out. If I practice active listening, I should be able to recognize signs of you being stressed. I should be able to care enough to empathize with you and make you feel better.

How To Become An Engaged Listener?

Maintain your focus on the speaker. When you're speaking to someone, take note of his tone, as well as his body language and other non-verbal gestures.

Billy values his conversations with other people. When someone is speaking, he makes sure that his cellular phone is in his drawer or pocket and on silent mode. The same goes for his laptop. He wants the speaker to feel that he is interested because that's what he wants others to do for him.

Listen with your right ear. Did you know that the primary processing centers for speech comprehension and emotions are found on the left side of the brain? Interesting, right? The left side of the brain is connected to the right side of the body. Listening with our right ear allows us to feel the emotional nuances of the other person. Keep your posture straight; put your chin down while tilting the right ear towards the speaker. This enables you to pick up the higher frequencies of human speech, especially those carrying the emotional content of what is being spoken, with ease.

Do not interrupt when the other person is talking. Most people habitually redirect a conversation to their concerns, even when another person is speaking. Keep in mind that listening is not synonymous with waiting for your turn to speak. People in our office avoid including Cristina in any discussion because she is known for her habit of interrupting people. I don't want to be like Cristina because I don't want to be left out.

Show interest. Engaged listening is being present in the conversation. We express our interest by constantly nodding, smiling, or using verbal comments, like "uh-huh." We can also say our occasional "yes." The posture is also important. If you are slumped all the time, you come off uninterested.

Do not pass judgment. A fruitful conversation is not always smooth-sailing. It is difficult not to judge, especially if we don't like the other person. Since day one, Bo had a feeling that his coworker from another department, Ryan, didn't like him. However, Bo never let his apprehensions show whenever he was to have a conversation with Ryan. This is an example of a professional relationship. Think of some moments appropriate moment in your relationship when having a professional conversation will prevent conflict when used at the right moment.

Be generous with giving feedback. If there are some points that you need to clarify, you can simply say, "So you're saying..." or "Correct me if I heard it right..." are examples of how you can assure correct understanding. This is how you rephrase your own word, what you heard, and confirm meaning with the author. About giving feedback, always make sure to leave a reaction, good or bad. But when it comes to giving negative feedback, make sure that it sounds positive by citing an alternative solution.

Characters of a Good Listener

First, they are compassionate. Without this trait, it is hard to listen to others. Empathy and compassion are essential for a good listener. This trait makes a person less self-centered and a little bit more selfless. With these, a person has a real knack for listening and solving problems. This trait makes someone perfect for being a senior at work, school, or home. This means that these compassionate people make excellent leaders, and they excel at it. Secondly, they are open-minded. That means that they are open to new ideas and also grievances. When someone, whether low ranking to them, comes to them, they are willing to listen. They are aware that everyone has an idea, and it may be relevant. They also believe that all people should have a say in matters. These are some of the reasons why the majority of them are activists that fight for the rights of others. This trait makes them great listeners and great problem solvers.

Another characteristic is that they are curious. This hunger for information. Most of the time, this hunger is insatiable, meaning one needs more ideas. Thus, these people are always open to new and fresh ideas. They will always listen to quench their everyday thirst for knowledge. They believe listening gives them knowledge, and knowledge is power. These traits make them very considerate, which is good when one is listening to others.

They are also people who keep focus and are not easily distracted. For someone to listen to something or someone, they have to be very attentive. A great listener keeps focusing on the task of hearing people out. Keeping the focus on one thing is usually hard for many people; thus, this is a quality with few people. If one possesses this quality, then the person is a good listener and even better problem solver. Lastly, a good listener always asks questions. This helps the listener to understand and clarify the subject that they are listening to. A good listener is also an exemplary academician. Thus they will ask questions then they will get answered. This makes them very understanding and also very clear with the subject at hand. Clarity is a great way to handle things as they should be.

Being an Effective Listener

If you want to communicate effectively, you should not only be an effective speaker; you should also be an effective listener. Improving your communication skills does not mean that you only have to improve your talk to other people. It also means that you should improve the way you listen to what other people say to you.

Listening is an important aspect of our lives since it helps us build relationships with and understand other people. Listening also allows us to be entertained, show empathy, gain information, and learn. And just because you are the boss or the leader of your team or anybody in a higher position, it does not mean that you should no longer listen to what the other people are saying. That is when you should listen more. You have to hear the voice of your people to know if there is something wrong and if there is something that you need to take action on.

Here are some guidelines that you should keep in mind to become an effective listener:

- **Be attentive**. When listening to other people speaking, you need to give your full attention to him and say. If you did not understand what he said, do not be afraid or embarrassed to ask him for some clarifications. It is important that you know and understand what is being said to you to know what actions you need to take. Always remember that a minor misunderstanding can lead to more misunderstandings and major problems in the long run if left unresolved. Always remember this: you are listening because you want to understand.

- **Learn reflective listening.** Reflective listening is when you give the speaker the chance to clarify what he just said so that you both can make sure that you understand the message. You can do this by repeating what the speaker just said to make sure that you heard him right. Reflective listening only makes sure that you are on the same page as the speaker is and understand each other.

- **Focus your attention on the speaker.** Again, it is disrespectful to do something else while the other person is talking to you. That only shows him that you are not interested in what he is saying. Also, if you do not focus your attention on the speaker, you will most likely not understand a thing, leading to misunderstanding.

You should also avoid distractions, such as noise. If you find it uncomfortable because of the place or surroundings, you may want to move to another much more peaceful and comfortable place.

Chapter 46:
How to Improve Listening Skills?

Listening is a talent that is essential to the success and efficiency of the communication process. Its importance is heightened in the current context of human interaction, where technology has, over time, become a challenge in achieving effective communication. This is particularly true where technology is considered a distraction. The underlying focus on improving listening skills is to be patient and focus on becoming an active listener. Active listening is described as paying full attention to what is being said. Active listening can also be referred to as a conscious type of listening as it starts with one making a conscious choice to listen actively. With active listening, one, over time, gets to see the sustainable and predictable improvement. What makes the skill of listening essential is that it is, in essence, one giving up a resource they can never take back, i.e., the resource of time. Active listening is considered a psychological tool.

In a highly competitive world, the skill of listening can be a tool used to put one or an organization in a leadership position. Leadership that listens is considered as one that is responsive and understanding. When used correctly, listening can improve how accurate an organization or person is in providing value. When an organization adds value, it, in turn, can gain loyalty from its customers, which can mean an increase in business opportunities presented to the organization. Listening well is a tool that one can use to save time by reducing errors likely to occur due to misinterpretation.

The listening skill is applicable in varied scenarios, including at work and within the context of personal life. The advantages of listening include:

- Having the ability to make one feel heard either as a speaker or an audience. This can be useful in scenarios involving conflict or for effective selling.
- Using the skill to build strong relationships.

- Being able to build genuine connections with others.
- Being able to learn new languages.

When one feels heard, one is more likely to express their genuine viewpoint on various issues. In an environment that requires teamwork, good listening skills are critical in bringing team members into sync. This creates a work environment where solutions and creativity easily flow. Creating a positive work environment via listening skills can mean the difference between retaining good workers and losing them to the competition.

Listening skills can assist individuals in letting go of emotions that are negative. This is exemplified as utilized by counselors during counseling sessions. There are particular skills that one can use to listen effectively. These include:

Attention: Part of being a good listener is giving the speaker attention by focusing fully on the speaker. This will involve looking at the speaker and watching for non-verbal cues, also referred to as body language. Somebody's language cues are placing hands across the chest. The tone of a speaker's voice is also an example of a non-verbal cue. A speaker's tone can give a good listener a glimpse of the emotional state of the speaker. When one does not focus on the speaker, one will miss these cues. Non-verbal cues can give a listener insight into the emotional state of the one speaking. One can repeat the words a speaker uses internally in one's head to focus on a speaker. Such repetition allows one to reinforce the message that the speaker is trying to get across.

When giving the speaker attention, be sure to balance so that the speaker does not interpret the attention as staring or intimidation. Also, one should try to individualize the attention specific to the emotions of the speaker. To be a listener who gets the whole picture of the message being transmitted, one must process both the verbal and non-verbal in tandem. Depending on where communication is taking place, the listener might have to get rid of distractions, e.g., background activity mentally. Distractions can be internal or external. Internal ones include one's thought pattern moving away from what a speaker is saying.

It is also important to individualize the attention to give as what may be considered as attention in one set, e.g., eye contact may be considered rude in another culture. Giving cues to show one is attentive is more important than the type of cue.

Avoid deflection: Deflection can be defined as pushing back or away from. Developing practical listening skills is exemplified when a listener decides to move the topic of conversation from the one the speaker is currently on to one that is of interest to them. This may be due to the listener being uncomfortable or even bored with the topic at hand. It would be more subtle to use close-ended questions to shorten the speaker's message than to change the topic outrightly. The skill to be developed here is to subtly encourage the speaker to move away from the topic at hand without taking over doing so.

From the speaker's point of view, a listener who chooses to deflect comes off as one who has no respect for them or even one who is selfish.

Avoid outsmarting: To become a good listener, one must refrain from focusing on the speaker to themselves. One of the ways one does this is by choosing to share a scenario where one faced the same situation as the one that the speaker is trying to share. This portrays the listener as one who is boastful and selfish.

Avoid setting judgments: This involves holding back from being critical of the one they are listening to. This way, one gives themselves a chance to see a situation from the viewpoint of the speaker. In some scenarios, using this tool to improve listening may allow an unexpected connection to occur between the most unlikely people, even as they note the similarities between them. One should avoid voicing criticisms while listening as the speaker may decide to stop communicating. Generally, when one entertains critical thoughts as they listen, the same shows up via non-verbal cues, e.g., through frowning. The non-verbal negative cues can cause the speaker to become defensive, leading to ineffective communication.

Not judging can also help one not develop preconceived conclusions that may change the perception of what the message was intended to be. Passing judgments can also be in the form of mentally correcting one's accent or spelling. Doing so distracts one from forming the habit of effective listening.

Big picture: When listening to a speaker, one should focus on the overall message instead of the details. The latter may lead to unnecessary distractions that lead one to miss out on the focus of the message that the speaker wanted the listener to get. In a one-on-one setting, allowing distractions may force the one listening to ask a speaker to repeat themselves. This may cause the speaker to feel frustrated and may portray the listener as disinterested in the message being passed. Unnecessary repetitions due to the lack of focus on the side of the listener are also time-wasting.

When one focuses on the big picture, they may also be less critical, therefore becoming more effective at listening. When one is less critical, one focuses on the content shared in communication instead of mistakes perceived as having occurred.

Context: To be an effective listener, one must always consider the context within which a message is being transmitted. The same message can have varied meanings in different contexts.

Culture: Effective listeners are culturally aware. One being culturally aware allows for one to use tools for effective listening within a cultural context productively. Being unaware of culture may inhibit effective communication. This is because what one culture considers appropriate, another may consider insulting.

Emotions: Connecting with the emotions that a speaker displays or is feeling makes one a great listener. Doing so can allow the listener to be empathetic to the speaker. In some cases, it can lead to building a successful relationship between the speaker and the listener. This relationship can then be leveraged for other situations. The speaker will be able to tell when a listener connects to them emotionally via the mirroring of emotions that will take place via non-verbal cues on the part of the listener. For one to identify with a speaker's emotions, one has to have their full attention on the speaker, which in turn makes one a better listener as they are actively listening.

One way a good listener connects with a speaker is by amplifying the emotions that the speaker displays.

Facing: Depending on the cultural context, it is advisable to face one with whom one is in communication. This implies interest, confidence, and in some scenarios, respect. It also gives the speaker the indication or go-ahead to start or continue communicating. Looking away from the speaker may signify the opposite. When facing one speaking, be sure to get rid of distractions. One should remember when using the tool of facing to become an effective listener is to do this without portraying an aggressive posture.

Feedback: To be a good listener, one must learn the art of giving feedback. One can give feedback either verbally or non-verbally. Generally, the non-verbal aspect makes up the more extensive composition of communication. I give feedback signals to the speaker that one is attentive and interested in the message being transmitted. Giving feedback also helps a listener stay attentive. In the context of feedback, the listener should aim to mirror the feelings of the one they are listening to. Feedback can be in the form of paraphrasing, which helps in ensuring the listener and the one speaking are on the same page. Paraphrasing is also a way through which the listener demonstrates to the speaker how well they can listen.

Giving feedback can also help avoid misunderstandings, which would lead to ineffective communication if not dealt with. Feedback can also be how a listener can communicate to a speaker that they have understood the message transmitted. However, one should be aware that the feedback given should portray that one is listening yet not necessarily agree with the message being transmitted. The feedback should focus on acknowledgment instead of the agreement unless the listener agrees with the message being communicated. When giving non-verbal feedback, the listener should use one comfortable to them, yet consider the cultural context of where the communication is occurring. This ensures that they don't look or feel awkward or portray a message to the speaker that is varied from their intended communication.

Giving feedback may also reduce time wastage, as the one speaking may not feel the need to repeat their message to ensure that the one listening has understood the message that the speaker had intended to communicate. When giving feedback verbally, a good listener should not repeat what the speaker says but instead rephrase the message communicated. The focus here is to give feedback on the listener's own words. It is also essential for an excellent listener to give feedback at the appropriate time. The appropriate time is dependent on the context within which the communication is occurring. One can sometimes tell that it is an appropriate time to share feedback by studying the cues given by the speaker. Some cues here can include the speaker pausing or looking at the listener for evidence that they are being heard.

Another point to consider when giving feedback is that the response should fully be about the speaker. A good listener will not include themselves in the feedback by, e.g., using words that would be inclusive of them like the word we. When using rephrasing for feedback, it is best for the ownership of the rephrase to be the listener. The rule of thumb regarding feedback, though it should consider the context, is that it should be shorter than the message received from the speaker.

To avoid being critical in the context of feedback, one should aim not to let their value systems and biases block their ability to listen actively.

Goal: To be effective at listening, one should develop a practical goal for the same. A goal in listening effectively can be that one will only speak a quarter of the time and listen to the rest of the time that the communication process occurs. The use of this tool, though, must be applied in the context of how and where the communication process occurs. The overall goal generally would be to speak less and listen more.

Growth: A way of becoming a good listener is to consider listening as an opportunity for growth. Humans have had different experiences in life, can be a source of learning if only one truly listens. Having a growth viewpoint in the context of listening will be portrayed even in your non-verbal or body language positively. The growth viewpoint may also give one information on how to deal with issues differently. Listening can be an aid in the journey of personal growth or self-development.

Hear: To be an effective listener, one should always put themselves in a position to hear what the speaker is communicating. This may mean adjusting the volume or requesting that the speaker increase how loud they are speaking. It may also mean the listener needs to get rid of distractions or even draw closer in proximity to where the speaker is. If at all the listening part is affected by something that needs medical attention, one should aim to seek help if possible to become effective at listening.

Interrupt minimally: Interrupting an individual as they speak may lead to them getting frustrated. They end up with the feeling of not being understood nor heard and even disrespected. These feelings can lead to obstacles against effective communication occurring. Depending on the context, the speaker may decide to stop communicating. The speaker may interpret the interruption as a show of rudeness, which may destroy a relationship. Also, an interruption can be in the form of trying to predict verbally what the other party is trying to say. This has a presumption that the listener can read in advance the thoughts and feelings of the speaker.

This may result in a slew of misconceptions. It may also project to the one speaking that the listener is impatient. Interruptions give a feeling of a contest where two parties are competing for who should be heard. This does not augur well to build relationships through active listening. To avoid being a source of interruption to one speaking, one can choose to:

- Practice having one's mouth stay shut during listening. When individuals choose to focus on keeping their mouths closed, they can become better at listening.

- Take notes of what one considers to be important points raised by the speaker. Also, one can put down points that one considers important that come to mind as one listens to the other speaking. The other party may consider it a sign of respect when someone puts down what they are saying, as it means that it is important to the listener. However, it should be noted that some speakers interpret this action as evidence of the listener being distracted and may discourage it.

Change where one's attention is at. This is about placing attention on the aspect of listening as opposed to the one of speaking or responding as the case might be. One can also choose to come up to talk less than they speak at any given time.

Chapter 47:
The Importance of Listening

One of the foremost means through which we learn new information is by listening. We engage in the listening process long before we start verbal or nonverbal communication. It is not an intuitive skill—it is learned, just like speaking, reading, and writing.

Why is Listening Important?

- It allows us to understand instructions, which invariably helps us complete tasks at home, school, or work.

- It also helps us recall, evaluate, and respond to messages.

- We listen to our partners and family members as it helps us meet our relationship needs as well.

- It allows us to receive and interpret verbal and nonverbal messages.

Listening allows us to communicate our identity needs and develop an accurate self-concept. Therefore, it comes as no surprise that listening is a crucial skill to develop if we want to grow as people and professionals and enhance the effectiveness of our communication skills.

The Listening Process

Like communication, the listening process has no start or end. And it doesn't work as a pipeline—there is no step-by-step process here. Several elements are entangled in the listening process—as with communication—including behavioral, emotional, and cognitive. The listening process does have several stages, though. Let's jump straight in!

1. The Receiving Stage

This is the first stage of the listening process as we intentionally focus on and prepare ourselves to hear the speaker's message.

We listen with our ears—everyone knows that. But what most people don't realize is that we also listen with our eyes. As odd as that may be, it is true. Try walking around for a bit with your eyes closed. The world of sound would terrify you because you can't see the nonverbal cues you've come to rely on. Take, for instance, sarcasm. You can't tell if the speaker is sarcastic if they're saying something like, "No, no, go ahead. Do that again," unless you see what their facial expressions are communicating as well.

So, listening is a skill duly supported by our other senses, as it gives us a broader overview of the nonverbal cues that help us interpret messages.

Ask yourself this. Are you more likely to have a miscommunication when speaking with someone in person or through technology (like email or chat)? Since visual clues are missing in technology-enabled communication, you're more likely to agree that email, chat, and phone conversations limit your contextual clues and present you with difficulties when trying to interpret interactions.

2. The Interpreting Stage

This is the stage where we combine visual and auditory information and try to make sense of that information. Of course, several factors either help us or limit our ability to make sense of communication. Take, for instance, a conversation in the middle of the street. The blaring horn of a passing vehicle will restrict our listening, and we won't quite grasp what was said to us.

3. The Recalling Stage

Recalling is a part of the listening process. If we've heard a message and focused on it, we're more likely to remember it. If, however, we were in part distracted during the receiving stage, we're less likely to remember the message or parts of it. There is a catch, though. Even when we're paying complete attention to a form of communication, our ability to remember that message depends on its simplicity or complexity.

4. The Evaluating Stage

This is a complex stage wherein we make judgments about a message and the speaker.

- We need to decide whether the speaker is credible.
- We need to judge the completeness of the communication.
- We need to assess nonverbal cues and attach meaning to the message based on the signals.
- Equally important is the "worth" we assign to the message. Good or bad, right or wrong—these are some of the categories in which we "fit" messages.

Critical thinking skills are imperative for this stage of the listening process. Without critical thinking, not only will we be unable to evaluate messages and communications, but we'll also find ourselves limited in our participation in the communication process.

Think back to the time where you almost fell asleep during a lecture or a conference. How productive did you feel? What was your contribution to the discussion?

5. The Responding Stage

When we're passive listeners, we are unable to make sense of the communication. Equally, we're unable to retain most of what we might have heard. This affects our ability to respond. A passive listener's lack of nonverbal and verbal cues, of course, is a form of feedback to the speaker. Note-taking, head nodding, clarifying doubts, prompting questions that lead to new discussions—these are the verbal and nonverbal cues that speakers rely on to gauge their audience's reaction and decide whether to change their attitude and approach. For instance, the speaker can switch from the formal to the informal style of speech and vice versa.

What are the Types of Listening?

Discriminative

Imagine this scenario: You're sitting in a rocking chair on your porch, enjoying a hot cup of tea after a particularly heavy dinner. As you gently rock back and forth, you hear a sound. You stop rocking and strain or wait to hear if the sound repeats. Could it be the dog in the yard? A creepy-crawly on a bush nearby? Could a loose wooden plank on your porch have contributed to the sound? Or could the sound be an indication of something dangerous? Perhaps it's the cougar you heard about in the news earlier.

When we focus our hearing to isolate and process a specific kind of sound, we employ discriminative listening. In the above situation, we're listening for sounds, and in the absence of visual stimuli, we're assigning meaning to the communication. Discriminative listening tends to be physiological and occurs at the receiving stage. It is an instrumental type of listening that allows us to isolate auditory or visual stimuli and scan and monitor our surroundings. It dictates how we respond to specific communication. For example, if a co-worker were to sound 'sad' while trying to impress on you that they're all right, you might press them to be honest. You're displaying concern and being approachable, which in turn might earn the co-worker's trust and encourage them to ask you for help.

Informational

This type of listening is best exemplified with examples of everyday activities such as hearing voice messages, listening to news reports, briefings at work, instructions, directions when we're traveling, and in a classroom or university context. Here, our objective is to understand and retain the information being presented to us. This is not an evaluative form of listening. If we don't employ informational listening, then we won't perform the most basic of tasks, be it in a social, academic, personal, or professional context.

Critical

Imagine this scenario: You've just finished your holiday season binge only to realize you cannot fit into your favorite pants. Now what? You scour for quick and effective weight loss solutions. You come across one fascinating proposal. Drink this solution in the morning and at night and lose five pounds; no exercise is required. Sounds good? Perhaps too good. Wouldn't obesity be eliminated if such a miracle solution existed? And so, you move on to another suggestion.

Why? What made you decide that the first proposal wasn't worth your time?

When we stop to evaluate communication presented to us in verbal form, we're employing critical listening skills. At this stage of the listening process, we determine whether the information and speaker are credible and whether the message has faulty logic. When we're not convinced, we don't jump to speculating and conjecturing; instead, we move to the clarifying question stage of effective communication. With the tech boom, we have so many communication platforms that consumers are bombarded with messages. Critical thinking and listening are crucial skills to develop.

Empathetic

Imagine this conversation:

Supervisor: We had agreed to a deliverable for today. Why hasn't it been sent?

Employee: My apologies, but my mother-in-law passed in the early morning hours, and I have been unable to work as scheduled. Can we shift the delivery to tomorrow, please?

Supervisor: No, I want the delivery today.

Employee: But I have hospital obligations and funeral details to sort.

Supervisor: Manage it during your hours. Work must be performed within regular business hours.

Ouch, right? Who'd want to work with a supervisor like that? And what would a conversation like that do to the relationship between the supervisor and the employee? And what if other employees overheard this conversation?

Sympathy and Empathy are often used interchangeably. However, they're not the same. A sympathetic boss would say, "I'm sorry to hear about your loss, but I need that done by today."

An empathetic boss, however, would say, "I'm sorry to hear about your loss. Take the bereavement time you need. I will reassign that task to someone else."

Empathetic listening involves putting yourself in the other person's situation and relating to their experience and then determining the best response for that scenario. It requires open-mindedness and civility. Empathetic listening is crucial to forming and maintaining interpersonal relationships.

Listening skills are not taught to us, either. It is yet another communication skill that we develop as we grow. And our culture and experiences affect what kind of listeners we become. Here's a quick overview of the many kinds of listeners we may classify based on their listening habits:

- **People-oriented** - listeners who get distracted from a message or task because they focus on addressing feelings. They focus on the message to figure out what the speaker is thinking or feeling instead of considering that the message is about something that the speaker considers important.

- **Action-oriented** - listeners who get frustrated easily when communication is perceived as unorganized or inconsistent. They are interested in learning what the speaker wants. The faster the speaker makes their point, the better. They prefer compelling messages over underlying reasons.

- **Content-oriented** - listeners who enjoy complex messages and prefer as much detail as you can offer. They devote a significant amount of time and effort to determining if the message is true, the speaker is trustworthy, and the message's meaning. If the message is too brief or lacks sufficient supporting data, it will sound like an infomercial to a content-oriented listener. Solid information, plenty of explanations, and well-developed information are important to content-oriented listeners.

- **Time-oriented** - listeners who are task-oriented and prefer concisely communicated information. Lengthy messages usually earn time-oriented listener's impatience. They are prone to using nonverbal cues to express their impatience. They will tune out, fidget, or multitask when messages are too long.

Listening and Talking

A good listener contributes to the conversation. Effective listening means feeding back to others that their words and message have been understood.

It means making responses that promote further communication and understanding. Some of these responses are non-verbal, others are verbal. Listening is not a passive activity; it is a two-way process.

If we were supposed to talk more than we listen, we would have two mouths and one ear.---Mark Twain

In other words, we should listen more than we speak, but speaking and responding is important as well.

Exercise: ***What kind of listener are you?***

Think about the kind of listener you are at the moment. Answer the following questions as honestly as you can with a yes if a statement describes your listening attitudes or behavior on the whole or no if not.

1. I listen without interrupting.
2. I show that I am listening when a speaker is talking.

3. I tend to be easily distracted.
4. I ask questions.
5. I ask a variety of types of question
6. I control my mannerisms and body language.
7. When I am having a difficult conversation, I prepare my response as I am listening.
8. I sometimes finish other people's sentences to show that I understand what they are saying.
9. I check to make sure I have understood properly.
10. My concentration lapses if the speaker is hard to follow.
11. I don't let my thoughts interfere with my listening.
12. I think it is up to the speaker to make their meaning clear.
13. I find it hard to regulate eye contact with the speaker.
14. I can use a range of responses.
15. I listen for the emotion as well as the words
16. I often miss the point of what someone is saying
17. I wait for the speaker to complete speaking before assessing what they have stated.
18. I reflect and paraphrase what has been said.
19. I can put aside my personal needs while I listen.
20. I can't help responding emotionally sometimes.

For each right answer, award yourself one point. The answers are:

1. Yes
2. Yes
3. No

4. Yes

5. Yes

6. Yes

7. No

8. No

9. Yes

10. No

11. Yes

12. No

13. No

14. Yes

15. Yes

16. No

17. Yes

18. Yes

19. Yes

20. No

If you got 10 or more right answers, you have a sound basis on which to build your listening skills. Don't worry if you have fewer correct responses - you will be surprised how quickly you can develop good listening habits once you decide to do so.

If you feel your listening skills are not very good, you are not alone. One study of listening shows we use only a quarter of our listening potential and only really take in a quarter of what is said.

The other three-quarters of what we hear are forgotten, misunderstood, or not heeded, or twisted. Another study of listening effectiveness shows we tend to forget one-third to one-half of what we hear within eight hours.

Overall, it seems it is common for us to miss about half of what someone tells us. Many misconceptions are created by the fact that we believe the other person has heard what we say, although there seems to be very little assurance that communication has occurred.

The Challenge of Listening

Noise, as we know, is any unwanted stimuli or signal that affects an incoming message or communication. Noise is detrimental to effective communication as it distorts the message. For communication to be efficient, the recipient must receive the message as the sender intended.

Multitasking is a criterion for survival in our fast-paced world. Doing several things at once has become such an integral part of our lives that we no longer notice that we're doing it, and we certainly don't see its pitfalls. Anything that forces our brains to process multiple incoming communications invariably leads to lowered performance and a higher likelihood of miscommunication—whether we're willing to accept it or not.

Consider a few scenarios:

Your mom calls while you're reading an important email. You answer the phone, expecting her to talk about her day as usual. You find yourself going, "Yeah, yeah, okay, fine...wait, what did you say? Uncle Sam died? When did that happen? Why didn't you tell me before? No, I'd have remembered it had you told me that." And in the silence that follows, you can feel your mother rolling her eyes at you.

You walk into the living room and give your spouse a verbal shopping list. Your spouse looks at you, nods, and then goes back to watching television. An hour later, your spouse approaches you in the kitchen and says, "I'm heading out. Do you want anything from the store?"

And such a situation would cause you to mutter, "You never listen when I speak."

Managing several forms of media together is called media multitasking. It can positively and negatively impact our ability to listen. Why? Because media multitasking interferes with listening to its various stages. Let's see how.

- **Receiving stage** - noise can block or distort incoming communication. Remember the time you were listening to music and couldn't hear your parents call you?

- **Interpreting stage** - noise makes it difficult to understand complex or abstract information. Remember when you checked your messages during a lecture and then found it difficult to understand what the professor was teaching?

- **Recalling stage** - noise and subsequent distractions challenge our concentration and interfere with our recollection abilities. Such as when the professor asked you to read from the textbook, and you couldn't remember where he had stopped.

- **Evaluating stage** - noise in personal biases and prejudices can prompt us to interrupt the speaker or block them out completely.

- **Responding stage** - we become passive listeners when our attention is divided, owing to which, we lack comprehension of an incoming communication. This can cause misunderstandings as we don't have the subject-level knowledge to paraphrase and ask clarifying questions.

What are Some of the Barriers to Listening?

Environmental Factors

Several environmental factors, such as temperature and light affect our listening abilities. A room that's too dark makes us sleepy, while a space that's too bright makes us uncomfortable and distracts us. When a room is too cold or hot, it creates physical discomfort that diverts our attention from the speaker. If you haven't eaten enough, you might just focus on how hungry you're feeling instead of listening to the speaker. Physical injuries or ailments and our mood can also affect our listening abilities. Physical noise is another factor that interferes with listening. Construction noises, loud music, etc. Semantic noise can also cause a listener to lose focus. When you struggle to interpret the speaker's message, you get left behind on a subject level.

Cognitive and Personal Barriers

We fail to understand messages that are too complex. Since comfort with complexity levels varies from person to person, the onus to study the audience and change lies with the speaker. Media multitasking is a perfect example of how cognitive barriers affect our listening. We focus on too many things at once, or we're always thinking about all the things we need to do later (check Facebook, make that Instagram post, the online multiplayer game that we need to log into, etc.). This reduces our receptiveness toward incoming communication.

Personal barriers could include our general attitude toward listening. The 21st century is a noise-driven society. Not figuratively. People want to speak, and they want the whole world as their audience. Everyone is clamoring over everyone else for their turn to speak. When everyone is communicating all at once, who is left to listen? And what are our patience levels, and how receptive are we to others' communication when we're impatient?

Speech and Thought Rate Factor

Remember that family member or friend who rattles on like an out-of-control train, and you just can't keep up with them? Humans think and process information much faster than our speech rate—think 800 words a minute (thoughts) and 175 words a minute (speech). Is it a wonder why we find ourselves daydreaming or distracted by thoughts that don't match the speaker's communication at a subject level?

Attention Span

Attention span is another contributing factor. When we're addressing children, we tend to remember that they have short attention spans. However, adults are expected to not only have longer attention spans but also to regulate themselves and overcome superficial issues. Most speakers forget that attention is finite.

Ineffective Speakers

Remember the complexity argument? Communication senders are liable for more than just the complexity of the communication they send. They lose the listeners' attention when messages are poorly constructed, too vague, or even too simple. Barriers also crop up when their delivery fails. Verbal fillers, monotone voices, appearance, and even their nonverbal cues can distract a listener.

Openness

When we are convinced of an idea or thought, we tend to be close-minded to others' suggestions. We begin the conversation without the openness required to make us receptive to communication. We listen, but on a superficial or aggressive level where our goal or aim is to preserve our ways of thinking.

Apprehension

Most people, especially in an academic or professional context, fear their inability to understand messages or absorb information coherently. This is easily identifiable if, for instance, a student intentionally avoids a certain course or lecture.

Listening Practices that Affect Communication

The barriers mentioned above to effective listening could prove challenging to overcome as they are partially beyond our control. Despite the conscious effort we make to lessen these barriers' impact, we have to accept that limitations and biases exist within us and that we can't eliminate them.

We can change, and with greater degrees of success, we practice bad listening habits.

Eavesdropping

Intentionally listening to other people's conversations (eavesdropping) is not the same as walking into a room and overhearing someone's conversation. We're prone to eavesdrop when our curiosity overshadows our conscience. Eavesdropping is a bad listening habit—one that we must avoid regardless of how curious we are. It's better to approach the person and be honest with them.

Aggressive Listening

We employ aggressive listening habits when we want to attack the speaker even before they've spoken. This kind of listening goes hand-in-hand with conjecture. Here, we feel we know what the speaker is going to say, we are convinced that it is wrong, and we're ready with our reasons to oppose the idea and the speaker even before the first word is said. To avoid being aggressive listeners, we need to be patient and open-minded. Even if we have prejudices and biases, we must learn to communicate completely and openly before we oppose them.

Narcissistic Listening

When people often make every conversation about themselves or try to compete with the speaker at every available opportunity, it is considered selfish listening. Consider the following example.

> **Person A**: My landlord has been troubling me a lot lately. With how terrible work has been, I don't know how I'll find the time to search for another apartment.

> **Person B**: That's not so bad. You have no idea what I have to live with. My boss is nuts. My colleagues are incompetent. I'm trying to work toward my degree, but my partner keeps whining that I don't give enough attention at home.

While it may seem as though Person B is contributing to the conversation, Person B is, in essence, shifting the attention to himself.

To avoid becoming narcissistic listeners, we need to time our interruptions more carefully.

Types of Listening Responses

Listening response is how we respond to communication (keeping in mind that most communication is verbal). There are several types of listening responses, and these can vary from silent listening to evaluating to advising.

Silent Listening

A child walks up to a parent and says, "May I please play on the computer?" The parent glares at the child in silence instead of replying. The child slinks away with the understanding that they've done something wrong or undesirable.

It's acceptable to remain silent in some situations—think about lectures or briefings where we need to gather information. When used correctly, our silence can be more powerful than our words. However, when we misjudge the situation and use silence as a response, we could give the wrong impression.

Questioning

Humans are curious, and curiosity leads to questions. Questioning is a typical listening response, but only when we're listening actively. Their lack of questioning can identify passive listeners. To avoid giving the wrong impression, we need to monitor how we question (tone) and how we word our questions. We can appear insolent if our tone is too aggressive. We can also appear presumptive; for example, if someone asks, "Tell me how often you've stolen from me."

Paraphrasing

Paraphrasing is an indicator of mindful listening. It shows the speaker that we were paying attention. We typically use paraphrasing when we need to verify information before we reach conclusions. "Correct me if I misunderstood you. But did you just say that...?"

Empathizing

We use this kind of listening response to convey our understanding, be civil, and offer support. Statements usually begin with "I understand," "I'm so sorry for," etc.

When we deny someone else's feelings and pass judgment, we're not empathizing. Our response usually begins with "That's not a big deal" (or something similar) in such situations.

Analyzing

Just as we think critically and listen critically, we also analyze as a listening response. In such situations, our goal is to convey our interpretation of a speaker's message. Our interpretations often rest on the speaker's background knowledge or the message's context.

Evaluating

Evaluations are of two kinds—positive and negative. We tend to offer positive evaluations in situations where we're convinced of someone else's suggestions. Think of the times you've said, "That sounds about right" or "That makes sense."

Negative evaluations can be further divided into two categories— judgment (most often accompanied by derogatory statements) and constructive (feedback, appraisals, etc.).

Advising

Advice can be an effective and valuable listening response. However, as with any listening response, you first want to ensure that it's the correct response in a given situation. Before giving advice, ask yourself the following questions:

- Is the advice needed?
- Is the advice wanted?
- Is the advice given in the proper order?
- Are you a close friend or someone the speaker trusts?
- Will you make the speaker feel as though you're supportive?

Chapter 48:
Using Empathy in Conversation

What is the most potent factor that can bring two individuals together? Is it love, friendship, or a common goal? Maybe. Empathy, in my opinion, is the glue that keeps relationships together.

Empathy is the capacity to put yourself in someone else's shoes. You don't simply listen to anything they have to say when you exhibit empathy. You don't attempt to comprehend it only from an academic standpoint. To be empathic, you must actively attempt to put yourself in the shoes of the other person.

You don't have to worry about appearing sympathetic if you're simply talking about nothing serious. Empathy truly makes the difference between an "OK" discussion and a genuine connection when you start talking about the larger issues.

If you've ever felt heard and understood after a long discussion, it's usually because your conversation partner showed you empathy. Empathy fosters a sense of security.

It enables others to open up, even while discussing their darkest feelings or most painful experiences. This sets the tone for life-altering connections. If you want to assist someone, you must first figure out what the issue is.

The most effective approach to getting into their heads is to use your inherent empathy. It's a powerful piece of work!

Empathy

Empathy is one of the most vital characteristics of being an effective communicator. It is the foundation of all successful personal, professional, and social relationships. Identifying how others around you think and feel, and using this information to make them feel heard and understood, is one of the greatest gifts you can possess. Being empathetic allows you to reach out to people and understand how they feel by placing yourself in their shoes. You understand feelings and emotions from their perspective or experience them exactly as the person feels them. Empathy is the most important secret ingredient for those looking to boost their social skills.

Empathy is not just feeling bad for someone (like sympathy) but, in effect, feeling what they are going through as if you were going through it yourself.

I'll let you in on one of the most potent rapport-building secrets. People who demonstrate a high level of empathy listening to others, keenly tuning in to their emotions, and acknowledging their feelings can instantly build lasting bonds with others. They can communicate more effectively and understand other people's feelings and emotions. They can connect with people at a deeper level to forge more meaningful and lasting bonds. Develop higher empathy by keenly listening to others and tuning in to their verbal and non-verbal communication signals. People do not just communicate through words. They also convey a lot by leaving unspoken through non-verbal cues such as body language, expressions, and voice tone. When you plug into people's non-verbal communication patterns, you can comprehend their message at a subconscious level. This facilitates the process of rapport building and getting people to like and trust you.

Empathy is the cornerstone of emotional intelligence, and being emotionally intelligent allows you to identify other people's emotions and regulate these emotions for the overall good.

To increase your empathy factor and transform into the ultimate people magnet, place yourself in another person's position and try to understand their situation. Attempt to understand why they do what they do. What is it like to go through a problem they are experiencing? Even if you disagree with them, try to understand where they are coming from (more on pointers for increasing empathy later). Actively imagine the feelings and experiences they are encountering. What can be done to make their lives easier? How can you help them cope with their feelings and emotions without being intrusive? When someone is talking about a highly emotional experience, one tip is to question how you react in the given situation.

At times, people won't directly tell you how they are feeling. However, they'll offer plenty of non-verbal clues that allow you to understand how they feel at a subconscious level. This has been prevalent since primitive times when it didn't invent spoken language. People shared their feelings, thoughts, ideas, and emotions through gestures and sounds. Since primordial times, people have been communicating through non-verbal signals, which have withstood various phases of evolution and language creation as a form of communication. People share a lot through gestures, movements, expressions, posture, walk, voice, etc. Non-verbal communication is more effective than verbal communication, which is why people always insist that they meet 'face to face when they have something important to convey. It gives the whole statement a lot of weight.

When people do not tell you how they are feeling, and you still want to reach out and demonstrate empathy, analyzing people's body language can do the trick. Closely pay attention to read what people leave unspoken, which is evident through their non-verbal signals. Stay intuitive when it comes to latching on to the frequency of others' emotions.

Closely analyze people's facial expressions, eye movements, walk, gestures, leg movements, and posture to determine who they are feeling. Does their body language appear to match what they are speaking? For example, if a person is declaring that they aren't bothered by something but appear preoccupied or fidgety (non-verbal clues such as fluctuating eye contact, tapping fingers or toes, playing with objects, and so on), their actions or non-verbal communication is not in sync with their words or verbal communication. Non-verbal communication can be a straight giveaway when people hold back their stories. One of the most significant signs of an effective communicator is reading what people leave unsaid and matching it against what they say to identify if their verbal communication and non-verbal communication are in sync.

Empathy also involves learning to read between the lines or picking up what people often leave unsaid. Let us look at an example to understand this more effectively. Learning to read between the lines will boost your empathy factor. Say you make a reservation for your family at a posh new eatery in the city. On walking in, you are warmly welcomed and greeted by a dedicated waiter assigned to a table occupied by your family. Then comes the fancy dinner, which is nothing short of a splendid, multi-course dining experience. You are served a lavish, delicious, and impeccably presented seven-course meal with all the usual bells and whistles of an upscale dining venue. Before each course is done, the server offers everyone interesting trivia and little-known details about each dish, including its preparation method, ingredients, history, and more, with haunting tunes playing in the background.

After consuming a hearty seven-course meal, you ask for the check. The manager eagerly seeks your feedback since it is a new eatery. He inquires if your family enjoyed the entire 'wine and dine' experience. Your brusque reply is, "The dessert was nice." This disappoints the manager. He doesn't look too happy with your feedback. This seems to be a compliment on the surface. However, your selection of words reveals something that you've left unsaid. Even without saying it, you have communicated that the dessert was the only item worth mentioning on the menu or nothing other than the dessert was good. To sum it up, everything else was pretty average.

Did you say everything other than the dessert was crap? No right? Yet, it is evident that this was what you intended to imply by reading between the lines. People convey a lot, not just by what they speak but also by what they leave unspoken. If you are perceptive and have a high empathy quotient, you will understand the subtext behind what people say by tuning in to their choice of words. Notice how people tend to get disappointed or upset when someone tells them, "You are looking good today." In a sense, it implies that they don't look on most other days.

This is also one of the passive-aggressive statements often used for disarming people without sounding overtly caustic or mean. Another implication can also be that you look nice on other days but look particularly appealing on certain days.

If you want to build more significant empathy reserves, learn to listen to people carefully while also tuning in to read what is left unspoken. Several times, you'll notice people say something that isn't in tandem with their body language. This gives you more significant insights into people's feelings and emotions. Learn to stay more observant and pick up less than obvious signals used by people to communicate their innermost feelings and emotions. This will give you a clear advantage in boosting your empathy factor and understanding people's emotions.

Developing empathy doesn't imply being party to people's emotional drama. Of course, there is a flip side to it when certain people overdo it, and their woes and negative feelings completely take you over. Being empathetic and emotionally intelligent is about listening to people, offering suggestions or advice whenever required, extending understanding, and letting people know you know how they feel in a particular situation. Empathy is more about understanding things from a person's perspective and less about letting them impact your own emotions and feelings.

Extending empathy naturally comes when you begin with yourself. Start showing more compassion to yourself by understanding what you feel certain things the way you do. What makes you think, feel, or behave in a particular manner. You may not find instant answers. However, if you continue observing your feelings, you will slowly begin identifying several possibilities for why you experience a particular emotion.

Here are some tips for building greater empathy for being an effective communicator

1. Traveling and gaining exposure to multiple cultures, lifestyles, civilizations, and ethnicities is a beautiful way to start working on your empathy muscle. You'll not just develop cross-cultural skills but also be an ace when it comes to deciphering others' attitudes, ways of life, aspirations, fears, and beliefs. This will

help you appreciate and varied perspectives. You will develop greater understanding, appreciation, and acceptance of people who are different from you. Plus, you will also gather more insights into how other people think and feel and articulate these thoughts, feelings, and emotions. Get exposed to as many viewpoints and ways of life as possible to appreciate and celebrate differences for boosting your empathy.

Another critical aspect of developing higher empathy is to examine your prejudices and biases. Daily, we deal with plenty of evident and veiled tendencies. Most of these biases run so deep that we aren't even aware of them. Preferences are the most giant stumbling blocks where empathy is concerned. It poses a challenge for listening to people with an open mind, understanding where they are coming from, and empathizing with their stand or situation.

Make a thorough inventory of your prejudices to start. Try to gather as much evidence, details, and opinions that pose a challenge to your prejudices. Work with a more open mind. It helps to hold a broader worldview while communicating with people. People seldom like interacting with a firmly fixated person on their views as if theirs is the only way of looking at it. Keeping an open and flexible approach is essential from the perspective of being empathetic and an effective communicator.

Develop a natural and constructive curiosity in learning more about people and personalities. It helps to be a people analyzer, not because you want to play FBI with everyone you meet (although that doesn't hurt, either). However, this is more about learning from people without labeling or classifying them according to your own biases or preconceived notions. One of the biggest obstacles to effective communication is learning from people by keeping an open mind and lively curiosity. Look to learn from people in the most challenging situations if you want to become an effective communicator. You will find yourself changing your perception of different personalities and people by viewing them in a more positive and balanced manner. This will, in turn, boost your sense of appreciation for others, even in situations where you don't necessarily agree with them.

There is this game that I love to play when I am all by myself at the airport, doctors, café, and so on. I play this excellent little guessing game with myself to predict how someone will react or respond to a situation by putting myself in their shoes. In a way, this increases my understanding of the individual's feelings and emotions. Get into the habit of staying mindful and mentally present while people are talking. Instead of taking mental notes and constructing responses (more on listening skills later), keenly listen to people to increase your empathy and understand them more effectively.

Empathy in Communication

We've gone through a lot of scientific data regarding empathy and how it impacts our everyday lives, but we still need to look at how it aids communication specifically. The ability to manage a conflict is the most significant advantage of bringing empathy into a discussion. Nobody wants to find themselves in this position, but it does happen from time to time. People get enraged, and the discussion devolves into a screaming battle, but this does not have to be the case with empathy.

Anger is a common emotion that is intended to be utilized as a means of communication. Anger may drive others away, but what you really want is to be heard and to connect with others. The same may be said about someone who prefers passive-aggressive conduct over outright aggression. Whether it's overt or not, it's hostility. Empathy plays a crucial part in this situation. Whether or not anger rearing its ugly head in conversation, you can use these six steps to take the conversation back to neutral ground.

1. **Focus on what is happening and allow yourself to become more self-aware.**

Allow yourself some time if you are the one who is furious or irritated. Trying to communicate while you're angry isn't going to go well. Words don't always come out properly, and things are spoken that shouldn't be uttered. Emotions that are out of control take over the brain. People have a much tougher time thinking rationally when their emotional centers in the brain become hyperactive. Allow yourself to relax and cool off before seeing whether you can think more clearly and speak more effectively.

The first thing you should NOT do if the other person gets upset is telling them to calm down. This has never, in the history of the world, ever helped a person relax. Sit quietly and let the individual weep for a time if they begin to cry. Allow them to vent their emotions if necessary and resist the temptation to get defensive if they become furious. Let them know you'd want to learn more about how they're feeling. Let them know that it's OK if they're upset. Ask a lot of questions, and if necessary, tell them you'll speak later when they're ready.

2. Understand your emotions.

Whether you are the emotional one or not, you must determine why you are feeling the way you are. Sometimes we believe we're irritated, but what we're really feeling is sadness, anguish, or rejection. Once you've worked out what you're experiencing, you'll be able to express it better and assist the other person.

3. Determine whether there is any kind of erroneous blame.

It's all too simple to place blame on someone or something for how we're feeling. People may be busy, hungry, dissatisfied in their marriage, worried, or exhausted, and then blame everything on the first circumstance or person they come across. It's also probable that it's someone close to them. This is why, if someone gets upset with you, don't become defensive since it's unlikely that you're the one who's offended.

4. Become more curious.

When you concentrate on your anger, irritation, or sorrow, you are concentrating only on yourself. Negative emotions lead a person to become self-centered, according to research. Because you are locked into your viewpoint, you have no space for another person's opinion. People don't stop to think about what the other person is going through. Curiosity should be included at this point. Become interested in why someone is behaving in a particular manner. Show genuine curiosity in why the individual feels or behaves the way they do instead of becoming aggressive. Despite the fact that the majority of people do not behave intentionally, many people make mistakes that make others upset. It's likely that the individual didn't do it on purpose.

5. Have compassion.

You are enabling dialogue to take place by asking "why," and you are demonstrating respect and care for the way people behave, feel, and think. This will help to foster a more positive relationship based on empathy and compassion.

6. Communicate with skill.

When communicating with an upset person, or if you are upset, use "I" statements. This removes confrontation. But you also want to make sure that you give the other person a chance to share their perspective. Again, this should be accomplished via basic inquiries to ensure that they do not see you as an adversary. You want to be inquisitive rather than accusing.

Showing Empathy in Conversation

How can you demonstrate that you're ready to empathize with others? If you believe someone wants to open up to you, here are some steps you may take to get a better understanding of their viewpoint.

1. **Don't speak badly of others.** Maintain a nonjudgmental tone during the conversation. Conversations about other people's actions and behaviors arise in a number of circumstances. From time to time, everyone participates in some kind of gossip.

If you want someone to feel comfortable opening up to you, though, you must resist the temptation to criticize others. When you continually show your propensity to stab other people in the back, who will feel comfortable talking to you?

No one feels comfortable opening up to someone who is judgemental because they are afraid of being judged! It's also a good idea to refrain from casting judgment on what your discussion partner is saying.

You should also avoid providing advice to those who haven't asked for it. Assume they'll ask for your opinion if they want you to make one.

2. **Show that you are taking an expansive listening position.** Remember, an expansive listening position is one in which you happily and patiently follow the listener's train of thought without judgment.

The other person will shut down if you exhibit even the tiniest indication of frustration. They'll think you'd prefer to get the discussion over with as soon as possible. This isn't going to inspire people to believe in you.

3. **Directly but kindly inquire if they have something on their mind.** If your discussion partner seems preoccupied and their body language is tight, ask if they have anything they'd want to discuss. Don't be a jerk about it. Simply allow them to communicate if they so want.

Of course, if they tell you that something is bothering them, but they refuse to talk about it, you should show empathy by saying that you understand and that they are free to talk to you if their thoughts change.

4. **Give them time to "empty the tank."** When was the last time someone listened to you without interrupting or casting judgment on you? We've all had those moments when we simply want to say precisely what we're thinking and feeling to someone.

If we're fortunate, they'll understand our predicament and go out of their way to provide us with as much room as we need. Allow the other person to speak all they need to say if you find yourself in the position of the listener.

Interrupting someone sends the message that your views are more important than their right to speak. You don't want to send this message.

5. **Try to show Unconditional Positive Regard (UPR).** When dealing with his clients, humanistic therapist Carl Rogers utilized a concept called Unconditional Positive Regard. He thought that everyone had all of the resources they needed to solve their issues, but they sometimes require the proper type of atmosphere to do it.

If you're attempting to be more empathic, this is a great foundation to use. Make the same choice that Rogers made and embrace the other person for who they are, regardless of their words or behavior.

This does not imply that you must agree with their actions, nor that you should allow them to behave in a threatening or improper manner. Consider UPR as a technique for putting your prejudices aside and approaching the discussion from a receptive perspective.

When you start with the idea that the other person is a decent, reasonable person who can improve, you're more likely to exhibit genuine acceptance and respond with empathy.

The Importance of Empathy

Empathy may seem to be a unicorn in the realm of communication, yet it is critical to successful communication. Empathy is the capacity to understand and share the emotions of another. It is made up of many distinct parts, each of which has a specific purpose in the brain. Empathy may be seen in three different ways.

Affective empathy is the first. This implies that you have the capacity to share your feelings with others. People with a lot of affective empathy have strong gut responses to frightening movies and news violence. When they observe individuals who are in agony or fear, they may experience their own pain and dread.

Cognitive empathy is the second. This kind of empathy entails being able to comprehend the feelings of others. A psychologist who intellectually understands their client's emotions but does not necessarily experience those feelings viscerally is an excellent example.

Finally, there is emotional control. This refers to a person's ability to control their own emotions. To perform their work successfully, surgeons, for example, must be able to manage their emotions when operating on patients.

Let's take a closer look at empathy to see how it differs from other related concepts. Empathy, for example, requires self-awareness and the ability to preserve a difference between self and others. This is what distinguishes empathy from imitation and mimicry.

When they observe other animals suffering, many animals may exhibit symptoms of imitation or emotional contagion. However, empathy isn't always empathy if there isn't some level of self-awareness and the ability to distinguish between self and others. Empathy and sympathy are not synonymous. Sympathy is a sense of worry for someone who is suffering and a wish to assist them.

Humans aren't the only ones that have empathy, however. It has been found in nonhuman primates and rodents in experimental settings.

Many people believe that psychopaths lack empathy, although this isn't always the case. When a person has strong cognitive empathetic skills, psychopathy is more effective. When murdering or torturing a person, the psychopath must be aware of the victim's precise feelings. Sympathy is a skill that psychopaths lack. They are perfectly content to see the individual suffer and do not feel compelled to assist.

People with psychopathic characteristics are also good at controlling their emotions, according to research.

Why Is Empathy Important?

Empathy is important because it gives us the chance to understand how other people are feeling to respond appropriately. It's usually associated with social conduct, and there's lots of evidence that greater empathy may lead to more helpful behavior.

However, this isn't always the case. Empathy, on the other hand, may hinder social relationships or lead to unethical behavior. A witness to a horrific automobile accident who gets overwhelmed by the sight of the victims in excruciating agony, for example, is less inclined to assist them.

Similar to having strong sympathetic emotions from family members or individuals in your own ethnic or social groupings, having strong empathetic feelings from others seen as danger may lead to violence or hatred against others. This is why, when their kid is in danger, whether real or imagined, moms may become "mama bears."

People who can readily read other people's emotions, such as psychics, fortune tellers, or manipulators, may be able to profit from their abilities by misleading others.

What's more, individuals with greater levels of psychopathic characteristics would respond more utilitarian in moral dilemmas, such as the footbridge issue. In this experiment, participants were given the option of pushing another person over the bridge in order to save a train from killing five persons on the track.

The psychopath would force the victim over the edge of the cliff. This is consistent with the pragmatic idea that it is better to save the lives of five people by murdering one. It may be claimed that individuals with psychopathic tendencies have better morality than regular people, who are less affected by their emotions while making choices.

What to Say When You're Told Something Shocking

Empathy is one of the most valuable gifts one can offer to another person, but it should come with a caution label. When you establish a comfortable environment for someone, there's a good possibility they'll tell you their most personal secrets.

This isn't always easy to listen to. Some of these secrets may be tragic, while others will be more "regular." This category includes situations that most of us can identify with, such as feeling hopeless after losing a job or being severely sad after splitting up with a spouse.

In other instances, your discussion partner may surprise you with something they say. No matter how well prepared you believe you are or how much life experience you have, a discussion may take an unexpected turn in a matter of seconds.

It's possible that you won't be able to control your anger or sorrow. It's OK to tell the other person how you feel as long as you don't make your personal feelings the focal point of the discussion.

You are not a machine. A simple remark like "That sounds awful to me" or "I can't help but feel sorry for you" can show them that you care while also drawing a clear line between their emotions and your own.

Always strive towards truthfulness. Tell them how you feel about their disclosure if they ask. Allow the other person to feel comfortable in telling you what is going on in their heads and hearts if you are honest and upfront with your feelings.

If you can't stop yourself from reacting angrily to anything you've been told, make sure you let the other person know they're not at fault. Tell them you're grateful they decided to share their emotions with you and that you're the only one who can cope with them.

Sometimes the wisest response is to say nothing at all. People don't always open up because they want or need someone to tell them what they should do. They usually open up because they want to be heard.

In the absence of words, a single gesture may suffice. Many comforts may be provided by a gentle touch on their arm, a gradual nod of the head, or even a hug (if you already have a close connection with the individual).

Know When to Bite Your Tongue

What if you understand precisely what another person is experiencing or share a similar history? For example, when someone reveals that they lost their mother as a teenager, you might be quick to reassure them that you know what they went through if you lost your father at the age of twenty.

I do understand the urge to make a connection and to find common ground. But you need to proceed with care. Even if your experience sounds similar to theirs, even if you feel as though you can empathize on many levels, you are two distinct individuals.

You have different personalities, backgrounds, ambitions, and priorities. If you are too quick to draw a parallel between their experiences and your own, you run the risk of appearing insensitive.

Consider the situation from another angle. Have you ever poured your heart out to someone or explained how a traumatic event made you feel, only to hear, "I know exactly what you are going through! I had the same thing happen to me. Back in the day, I..." and so on.

You might have ended up just sitting there whilst they told you their own story. Even worse, you might have ended up comforting them!

Do you ever dive in with a quick "Me too!" and end up launching into a story of your own? Don't worry if the answer is a resounding, "Yes." No one is perfect. I know I've done this on occasion.

When my buddy Sam missed out on a rental flat he liked, he was drinking coffee and lamenting his misfortune. I just gave him a few minutes of airtime before explaining that I'd been turned down for my first housing option in college. As a result, I informed him, I understood his situation.

Sam was too lovely to order me to stop talking, but I afterward understood how inconsiderate I was. He's forgiving, which is fortunate for me. I've even gone close to making the same error with my clients a handful of times. When someone says they've had poor self-esteem since they were teenagers, I'm tempted to respond, "Me, too!" and tell them about my adolescent struggles.

I'll never be entirely free of the need, but I've learned to manage it. I remind myself that this isn't a discussion about me. If a session brings up some painful memories, I debrief with a buddy afterward or take some time to relax and absorb what happened.

Of course, if someone asks, "Do you know what I'm talking about?" or "I'm not sure if you've ever encountered anything like this?" feel free to offer your own experience.

Don't be shocked if you're exhausted after a lengthy discussion. Empathy may sometimes be as easy as commiserating with a coworker over the bad traffic on the way to work.

It takes little effort to sympathize with someone in this position, and they are unlikely to sit with you once the discussion is over. Listening to someone speak about a loss, a severe illness, or a divorce, on the other hand, takes a lot of emotional energy.

You don't have to be a human sponge to help others. If you know, you'll be having a long conversation with someone when you next meet up, set aside some time for yourself for a couple of hours afterward.

I deal with people who have a history of complicated psychological and emotional issues from time to time. Traumatic experiences are often the cause of them. They tell me tales that make my hair stand on end. I'm glad to be sympathetic and assist them in resolving their issues, but I've learned that I need some time alone after our meetings for my well-being.

Compassion fatigue may creep in for those of us who deal with individuals going through difficult periods in their life. Never forget that your well-being is just as important as that of anyone else.

Chapter 49:
Owning Your Content

I've probably seen thousands of presentations over the years given by industry colleagues and my students. One thing I would immediately notice is whether the presenters truly owned their content.

When I say owning content, I don't mean memorization. In almost all cases, memorization is the opposite of ownership.

Ownership has to do with being comfortable with the content to the extent that you understand it.

That doesn't mean you need to be an expert on the entire subject. But it does mean that you need to be an "expert" as far as the presentation's content is concerned.

However, while this may seem contradictory, if you genuinely don't understand all aspects of your content, sometimes the perception of owning your content can be just as excellent or good enough. I'm not encouraging you not to learn your content, but I'm realistic. I'm sure you've heard this before – perception is reality.

When you own your content, you speak to it with confidence. People command the room when they own their content, and this directly correlates with your confidence.

I've seen introverts turn into extroverts when they deliver an excellent speech and own their content. I once had an introverted student who needed some improvement. He did an exceptional job on the final presentation of the semester. It came alive. He gave a presentation on day trading and shared that he was a day trader. He owned his content. He had a command of the ideas and words coming out of his mouth. He had a great time presenting, and his confidence was at an all-time high.

One of my best friends, whom I've known since elementary school, is one of the most confident people I've ever met. He was a high school and college track star who is now an actor and a high school teacher. Will he ever become the next Al Pacino or Matt Damon? Likely, that will never happen. But no matter what he does, acts, or teaches, his confidence is his greatest asset. It's not BS; it lives within the core of his chest and pours out in whatever he does.

Everyone sees it.

Own A Piece, Instead Of The Whole Thing

As I mentioned above, you don't have to be an expert on all facets of your topic. Either the perception of expertise or having expertise or high-level knowledge of a piece of it also works.

Anytime you're doing a presentation, you wouldn't be presenting on an entire topic, anyway, right?

Package your presentation in a way that keeps your topic as tightly wound to the objective instead of trying to be too ambitious. That "naturally" helps you not only stay focused but offers you a better chance of being knowledgeable only on certain aspects.

For example, if you're presenting contemporary trade issues between the United States and China, focus on what's going on and the surrounding issues/implications. And weave in the general knowledge that one would need about the trade for your presentation to make sense. (Again, keep in mind what type of audience you have). But there's no need to get too far into basic international trade theory.

First, there's genuinely no need for it since your objective would probably begin to break apart, and your presentation would likely suffer. And second, what if someone were to call you out on an element of trade that you may not be aware of? What would you do then? I mean, after all, who are you, Henry Kissinger?!

Ownership vs. Memorization

Ownership doesn't mean memorization. If you genuinely feel the need to memorize, and you can do it without coming across as robotic, go for it. Steve Jobs did this, for the most part, when he delivered his famed Apple Keynotes throughout the years. But I can tell you, as a marketing and innovation guy, Jobs was the exception in many ways. Most of us are not like him.

There's one other exception—actors and performers.

However, they are trained on how to come across as natural. It's part of their craft and is expected of them. That's why they call it acting.

But most of us, including myself, are mere mortals. If you try to memorize, you'll most likely come across as robotic. You can trust me when I say that your audience will be able to tell. Your eyes will have a strange or even blank look to them. And you'll have an unnatural look on your face as if you're processing data and trying too hard. Why? Well, because you are.

It's exciting because when someone is trying to memorize their presentation, you can always genuinely see it in their eyes. You'd see a sheet of paper scrolling down the inside of their brain, line by line if you could see inside their head.

The other problem with memorization is that if you miss a word, that may completely ruin your presentation. One missed word can generally throw everything out of sequence. So don't work so hard if you don't have to. Or work hard towards other aspects of your presentation. Actors need to memorize their scripts. You and I do not.

Environment

Granted, while you may not always be able to control your environment, if you have the chance to get familiar with it beforehand, that could help with your overall confidence, which has a lot to do with owning your content.

When I do a presentation, if and when possible, I try my best to go to the venue beforehand. Again, if and when possible. I'm not suggesting you drive out of your way, waste gas, etc., just to get a feel for the environment. However, if you're giving a presentation at work, arrive the day before to familiarize yourself with the conference room, auditorium, or other venues. If you're a student, try to get about 10 minutes alone in the classroom you're going to teach in. If the door's locked, etc., maybe you can ask your instructor for help accessing the room.

If it's not feasible to physically go to the venue beforehand if there's someone you can ask to email you a picture of the room in a few angles, etc., that could help. I understand that it may seem a bit much to go as far as asking for photos. But you'd be surprised, "little" things like this can make a BIG difference.

Chapter 50:
Managing Your Stage

Movement for the Stage Novice

You may not be inclined to agree that your presence has more to do with performance than anything else, but this is just one of those facts you will have to accept. There is already a connection between you and your target audience. The audience may play dormant as the observer. Still, an unspoken dialogue that ensues and mastering your movement on stage can help you take charge of that conversation and lead it in the direction you want it to go. Earlier on, we talked about confidence and body language. These are essential attributes that will help you make better use of your stage. Knowing how to move on that stage is the next step to maneuvering the stage to your advantage. I will start you off on the basics. Over time, the rest of it will come naturally to you.

1. Be deliberate in your actions

Every movement you make on stage should appear deliberate. Pacing the floors of your stage aimlessly would give negative feedback on your competency; random movements with no visual purpose would highlight your nervousness. Shuffling your feet among other unnecessary hand or foot movements is out of the question. I like to use a trick to imagine that I have a small invisible cage around me restricting my range of movement. So, where my arms would extend out in a very wide gesture, I consciously narrow my movements. This makes it appear less random and more deliberate.

2. Let your movement portray your message

If the speech you are giving has a motivational tone, the way you move on stage should reflect this. Now, what do I mean by this? A motivational message is meant to inspire the listener to take action, right? Well, your movement should convey a sense of urgency to your audience that demands action. Hand gestures should also be used to provide a lot of positive reinforcement. Let me give you a tiny but significant gesture that has a lot of impact on space and communication. When you point your index finger, you automatically create a focal point. Point it downwards, and you convey time (now, present, this moment), point it forward, and your message takes a tone of responsibility (you are assigning responsibility). Point that same finger upwards, and it can be interpreted as denoting authority.

3. Know where everything is

This has a much more practical function. You need to know where everything is to enhance your performance. This means that you have to arrive at the venue on time...perhaps while the organizers are still setting up to know where the equipment you might be using will be located. You don't want to get on stage and start fumbling around with the projector or trying to figure out where to put down any of the props you might need during your presentation.

Speaking and Being Heard

These days, there are many fancy tools that make public speaking a much more impactful experience for both the audience and the speaker. But no tool is more powerful than your voice. Learn to control it, and half your battle is won already. During a regular conversation, your voice takes on a regular tone. This way, you can be heard by the peers you are having a conversation with, and you don't need to increase your voice and make any extra effort to enunciate your words. On stage, the game is a little different. Not only do you need to project your voice, but you also need to enunciate your words carefully. To make matters worse, there is a very strong possibility that fear might make your voice sound a little coarser and hoarser than it naturally is. This is why you would find some people suddenly battling a coughing fit when they get on stage in an attempt to clear their throats.

To prevent this, here are some things you can do:

1. Take things slower

Trying to rush your words can seem like you are trying to talk past the hot potato in your mouth. Your words are not clear, and your pitch tends to be a little higher. Take a deep breath, exhale and then pace yourself while speaking. This will keep you within audible range and give your listeners an impression that you are knowledgeable on the subject. Speak slow, be loud (but not high pitched) and speak clearly.

2. Eat something before your presentation

Given the tension you feel in the pit of your stomach before you go on stage, some people worry about eating. The general fear is that they might throw up on stage. Except in very extreme cases, there is a slim to none chance of that happening. And contrary to how you feel, a light meal can go a long way to improving your performance on stage. At least two hours before I go on stage, I try to have a high-protein lunch. Not only does it make me feel energetic, I feel more alert.

3. Avoid cold things

A nervous sweat brought on by a nasty case of stage fright might have you reaching for iced water, but this can only make your voice coarse and thus make your stage experience worse. Warm water, lemon drops, and honey are excellent if you are already battling a sore throat but used on the regular; you can expect that your voice would be crisp and clear, which is perfect for public speaking.

Turn Up the Drama

I did say earlier that being on stage as a public speaker is somewhat like being a stage performer. You may not be theatrical, but there are theatrical techniques you can employ to enhance your performance and engage your audience. Even if you will be reading your speech directly off a piece of paper, you still need to know when to look up at the people you are reading it. We already talked about being too monotonous in the delivery of your speech. The dramatics I am referring to here doesn't mean that you suddenly have to include pantomimes in your routines. It is about improving your sense of timing. A dramatic pause can create tension in a room so thick that, as they say, you can cut through it with a knife.

To turn up the drama, you just need to do the following:

1. Talk confidently

Injecting confidence into your voice even though you don't feel that way can bring a massive dose of drama to your presentation so that even though you are talking about quantum physics to a group of high school students, they would want to listen. It can take a lot of practice, but it will eventually come to you effortlessly if you keep at it.

2. Keep it short and sweet

People have a very short attention span. Waiting until the last minute to reveal your card might not work. Stir the drama by doing a quick introduction and then launching straight into the subject matter. This keeps your audience interested in what you have to pitch and sustains them to the end. Prolong things for longer than five minutes into your presentation, and your big reveal may not even matter.

3. Don't complicate things

If you find yourself trying to explain your point five minutes after you made it, you probably have not done a good job explaining it. Being dramatic in public speaking has little to do with complications. If you are speaking to people about makeup, there is no need to use terms specific to the aviation industry. You just end up confusing them. Use relevant colloquial terms to connect with your audience, convey your message and command their attention. After all, that is what the drama is all about at the end of the day.

Using the Stage for One

An actor must consider the presence of other people on stage while performing and do their best to ensure that everyone gets a time to shine. For a public speaker, you only share the stage with the idea you are hoping to get across. Other than that, the stage is really about you. Whether it is a big platform or a small podium, do your best to own it. Before you get on stage, you will be given a time limit. Do everything you can to ensure that you stay within this time limit and try not to think of it as a limit. For me, I like to think of it as a slice of time given to me to digest however I want to. Since most of my public speaking has had to do with training, I focus on driving my point home in that timeframe. To do this, I like to give bullet point presentations. This makes it easier to assimilate. I rarely use up my entire time, as I am more interested in interacting with my message than having them react to my message. I feel that if they interact with my message better, my point is driven home faster.

Set your schedule for the time slot allocated to you and work that to your advantage. Above all, remember to enjoy yourself during the process. There is no rule that says you can't.

- Your movement on stage sets the tone for the communication success you will achieve with your audience.

- Eating an hour or two before your presentation can keep you energetic and help you sustain an even tone of voice throughout. Starving yourself has the opposite effect.

- You need to employ the use of theatrical techniques to sustain the interest of your audience.

- The stage is designed for you to use as you will. Decide on your objectives and plan towards achieving them within the timeframe that you are given.

Your tasks:

1. Besides making a name for yourself as a prominent public speaker, what are your objectives? Specifically, what do you expect to happen to your audience every time you get on stage? This will help you plan effectively.

2. Record yourself speaking. Listen to it, assess your performance and point out areas for improvement.

3. Practice your regular speech and a compressed version of this speech. This frees you up to be flexible if your time is suddenly cut short. This way, you can still have an impactful session with your audience.

4. Think of three possible questions that your audience might ask that will throw you off your game. Draft fresh and inspiring responses and then practice those responses.

5. Draft a response to a question that you may not have an answer to. Let the response be as fresh and inspiring as possible, and then rehearse this also.

Tips to Overcome Stage Fear

So today, I've chosen to discuss a common fear called "Glossophobia," which affects most individuals. Do you understand what it means? The most feared fear of public speaking is known as public speaking phobia. Not just you, but many others, including myself, have had stage fright or, at the at least, have been very anxious before performing in front of an audience. What do you think? Are you aware that you are not alone in this situation? Famous actresses like Nicole Kidman, politicians like Abraham Lincoln, and even national leaders like Gandhiji have expressed a fear of speaking in front of an audience. Isn't this to say that you're not alone? So, in essence, this is proof that even renowned or successful individuals have Glossophobia. So, based on my experience, there are a few tried-and-true methods that may assist you in overcoming your fear of public speaking.

So today, let's take a few steps together to overcome Glossophobia.

Calm the adrenaline rush

You should focus on your breathing for this since it can calm you down. So, when you're anxious and have a lot of adrenaline coursing through your veins, you start breathing quickly, which creates anxiety, which causes your performance to suffer. As a result, the approach is to begin concentrating on your breathing to remain calm before your performance. I recommend that you breathe in and out at least 10 times before beginning your speech. This will help you decrease your heart rate, anxiety and calm down, and I believe this method is very feasible; it's simple, and you don't need any special equipment; all you have to do is breathe in, breathe out, and relax your thoughts. Apart from breathing in and out, there's another thing you can do to relax: start visualizing a good result for your speech. By doing so, you'll put yourself in the proper and confident frame of mind for the speech you're about to give. So, the first step is to decrease worry and boost confidence.

The power of pausing

I'm going to share with you a golden strategy to overcome Glossophobia. I'm sure that many experts would vouch for this strategy, and that is the most powerful tool for good speeches, "pausing," that's right. This will not only help you make an impression, but it will also help you control the nervousness that arises throughout the speech.

Because speaking at a graduate speed, when you talk slowly and gradually, you have more time to consider, right? This is a secret I've been using for years, and as you can see, when a leader speaks, they often pause. To affect, they want to give you time to digest the information they're providing you; otherwise, it'll be an information overload, and you'll lose touch with the leader. And, of course, stopping allows me to gather my thoughts. Pausing is thus beneficial in every aspect; it is a win-win scenario for you and your audience. This is an art that may be learned through practice.

Mockup your speech

One method proven to be extremely effective for me is 'giving my words to another person.' You may deliver your speech to various individuals around you, including your spouse or wife, a buddy, parents, a sister, or a brother, right? You can give your speech to them, and the best part is that speaking in front of an audience will help you relax and gain experience because if the people listening to you have any questions about your speech, there's a good chance the audience will have similar questions to ask you. You'll be better prepared for the final presentation. As a result, you will be more prepared for any expected queries or difficulties that may arise during your speech delivery. Also, if you're practicing your speech with someone else, tell them to rate your performance on a scale of one to ten, indicating the excellent and the areas where you can improve, so you may get constructive feedback and work on it. As a consequence, you'll be able to improve your overall performance, and this is a tip that has worked well for me. So remember to practice in front of a mirror.

Own yourself in the mirror

I'm going to offer you another checklist, this time for practicing in front of the mirror, but wait, I'm assuming you already know that rehearsing in front of the mirror or recording yourself on your smartphone to enhance your delivery is a good idea. To make an impression with your speech, this is a must-do phase. Pay attention to a few things when practicing in front of the mirror. The first is your facial emotions; if they don't match your words, it seems that you've memorized your speech. That's all there is to it; you've memorized it and are now reading it. So make sure you're expressive with your face as well as your words, and when it comes to facial emotions, a grin is a must, and it should be present throughout your speech. Not just to provide the impression of confidence but also to soothe your anxieties. Smiling has been scientifically shown to decrease anxiety, so be aware of your facial expressions and remember to smile. When practicing in front of the mirror, pay attention to your gestures, which include your body motions and the way you use your hands. Are you throwing your hands about aimlessly? Do you slouch when you speak? Is it possible that your shoulders are too tight and unnatural? Well, you should attempt to avoid such body language since it has a bad impact on your performance. Apart from your facial emotions, pay attention to your body language.

Choose topics wisely

Don't just pick up any topic to talk about; yes, that's very, very crucial, don't just pick up any topic. So I recall the day when I froze on stage because I had to talk about politics, which was not a subject near to my heart since I don't follow politics on a daily basis, and I had to speak about the political impact on people's lives via social media, and so on. I was out of ideas, searching for words, and there was a large audience waiting for me to continue; I'm sure you'll understand. That was a really tense situation for me. So, based on my own experience, I would recommend that you choose a subject that you are passionate about. Well, I've prepared a checklist for you that will assist you in deciding whether or not you wish to talk about the subject. So, when you choose a topic, ask yourself three questions. The first is, "does this issue affect me?" The second question should be, "Do I want to talk about this with other people?" "Will others truly profit from my understanding of this topic?" is the third question. So, before you decide to air your opinions on a subject, you should answer these three questions. So now you have a checklist to follow when deciding what subject to talk about since this choice will have a significant effect on the outcome of your speech. It's simple: if you're passionate about a subject, you'll be in your element, so pick your subject wisely.

So, before we go through the five methods for overcoming Glossophobia, you should realize that you are not alone, okay? Others have suffered from, or are now suffering from, stage fright. Second, before you begin speaking, learn to relax, breathe in and out ten times, envision a good result, then pick your subject carefully. Finally, rehearse in front of the mirror, paying close attention to your facial expressions and body language. Finally, practice your speech in front of an audience, and don't forget to include the magical pauses that will elevate your performance.

Chapter 51:
Ways to Connect with a Large Audience

The audience wants to laugh

Using comedy to connect with an audience is one of the greatest and easiest methods to do it. Remember that your audience does not want to be serious and wants to laugh now and then. You can bring on a lot of energy by making jokes and rewarding your audience with funny one-liners. Your audience will respond to your speech more enthusiastically and give you the confidence to keep going the same way.

Go slow

Apart from the number of words, you should also focus on the tempo and ensure that you go slowly so that every member of your audience gets the chance to hear what you are saying. Because it will take some time for your words to reach everyone in the room, you should slow down a little and ask your audience whether they can hear what you're saying.

Energy levels

Make sure you have a filling meal before addressing a large audience, as you have to keep your energy levels up. A large audience will give off and require high levels of energy to keep the show going. You have to make sure that you become louder as you go and come across as a strong speaker. Keep your energy levels high throughout the speech and crank it up a few notches after every subsequent pause. You should be able to feed off your audience's energy so that you can keep them motivated and interested in listening to what you have to say.

Simplicity is key

When you address a large crowd, you have to bear in mind that there will be people from all walks of life. Some might not be able to grasp high concepts and end up misinterpreting your jokes. You should, therefore, keep it simple so that everybody understands what you are saying and can respond to your speech positively.

Interactive

When addressing a large audience, you must make the session as interactive as possible. It is the only way in which you can keep everybody interested and keep going. Your speech should make you sound enthusiastic and full of energy and ask your audience to participate as much as they can. You should feed off their questions and answers and keep addressing them throughout the speech. If you make it all about yourself, you will end up sending across the wrong message and make it sound like you are boasting about yourself.

Be assertive

You should be as assertive as possible when it comes to speaking to a large audience. Many people make the error of asking too many questions in an effort to gain the audience's favor. This will make you appear nervous and make your audience think that you are not well prepared. So be assertive in whatever you say and avoid asking our audience if they agree with you. You have to make them agree with you without pushing it. So instead of asking, "What do you think?" you should tell them, "This is what I want you to think."

Don't be overwhelmed

It is obvious that the higher the number of people in the audience, the more the difference there will be in opinions. It's very important not to get caught up in it and to keep your cool while speaking with them. It would be best if you got your audience to come to you rather than you going to them. You can easily do this by being assertive and telling your audience that you are decided on your stand, and they will have to accept it.

Get into character

Think of getting into your character when addressing your audience. Have an idea of what you wish to appear like to your audience, and then get into full character mode for them. That way, you will know the parameters to stick with and can modify your approach to suit the needs of your audience. You can look up a few videos to help you out. Remember to enjoy yourself and not be too stringent trying to play a character on stage.

Clarify from time to time

If your audience ever had any questions or concerns, ask them straight away and address them. This will give you the confidence to continue ahead without worrying about whether or not your audience comprehends what you were saying. Once everything is clear, you can proceed to the next concept with confidence.

Chapter 52:
Public Speaking

How does Public Speaking serve you?

This sounds like a simple question, but by simply asking yourself this, you could find several reasons why it is good to practice public speaking. For one thing, it certainly reduces your fear and increases your confidence to a large extent. Have you ever shown up at a public event socialized, then given a presentation, and then gone back to socializing? If so, did you feel a difference between the social interactions before the presentation and then the ones afterward? The probable answer is most certainly yes. If you are new to presenting, then trepidation concerning your upcoming speech is what you quite likely would have felt beforehand. But on the second encounter, you'll more than likely feel a rush of relief or confidence overwhelming you, and those social interactions the second time around will be more enjoyable for you. Not to mention you'll probably feel like you're more proactive in the conversation. Competently and fluently holding a conversation with less social anxiety is an indirect benefit public speaking can give you. Some of the more direct benefits are better ability at public speaking, the ability to hold a crowds' attention and improve your confidence speaking to an audience.

Public Speaking is required in most if not all leadership situations. To become an effective leader, you must communicate effectively what you want your team to do. The benefit from this is higher productivity from your team and a more peaceful working environment. If employees or team members are clear on what they need to do, then less chaos in the form of continued questioning, emailing, stress and worry will crop up.

Team projects, as a result, will be more fluid, and operations will smoothly be completed if there is one thing public speaking can do to help you in the work environment, networking. You can guarantee that if you make a speech to your industry colleagues, they will remember you. If the time comes that you need a new job, your new employers may very well have been at the conference or event that you gave a speech at, your resume will be the one that stands out from the crowd, and you'll be going into that interview with an edge. One comforting fact to note is that if you can do a good job presenting something to an audience, an interview will feel more like a step down for you.

How to get better at Public Speaking?

This is similar to improving your social skills; increased frequency of presentation practice will gradually bring you the result you are looking for. If you listen to any public figure or speaker who's mastered public speaking, they often refer to practice as a fundamental core or reason for their success. The next best thing to do is to join a public speaking club or club that practices or involves communication. Toastmasters is one example of a public speaking club you could join to improve your public speaking skills. I have tried this club out and suggest it is worth the membership fee to join. What you'll get is a competent communicator booklet filled with ten speeches you can practice while at the club. On top of that, toastmasters also allow you to take on leadership responsibilities requiring you to communicate effectively using these roles. Anyway, the main point of toastmasters or any form of social club is that it can effectively improve your communication skills while at the same time serving as an enjoyable social event to attend.

Practicing in front of a video or camera is, in my opinion, the best way. Today living in the information age, it is straightforward to film a video of yourself, upload it to YouTube and have it available for the whole world to see. That's how easy it is. Just a few clicks of a button. If you're not interested in doing this, then just recording yourself can serve as a good measure of feedback on your progress. But I would suggest uploading videos to YouTube as this can serve as a suitable method of accountability if your videos obtain any traction online. It will help you create that habit of creating more and more videos. If you haven't guessed already, the more practice, time, energy, and focus you put into this, the more you will get out of it. If you are not so into recording videos, why not try practicing in front of a friend or a mirror. Phones these days hold recorders so you can create audio of your voice to listen to without having to see yourself talk. Try it out. What have you got to lose?

How to Practice Public Speaking?

Practice is one of the most effective ways to overcome any anxiety and prepare for your public speaking. This might seem like something that you should not have to do; you have all of the information right in front of you, and you have been spending a lot of time on the project, so you feel like you are an expert on anything that has to do with this topic. While this may be true, getting up and really talking about the topic may be a totally other experience. You might find that your notes are not enough, that you are not sure how to do transitions, that you freeze up, or that your flow is not as smooth, or you need to add something else in. It is much better to find out about these things before you get up in front of a lot of people and make mistakes. Practice at least a few times before you have to go up in front of the audience and talk to them, but if you have time to do it many times, then you should do that as well.

Write out your speech

Writing out your speech is one of the things you may want to attempt. If you believe it will be simpler, get out some paper and a pen, or use a computer. The writing tools do not matter as much as getting something that will be able to capture everything that you plan on saying during the speech. Practice is one of the greatest ways to overcome any fear of public speaking and prepare for it. Of course, when you get up and talk in front of people, you are going to change around some of the wording or say something that is a little bit different, but at least now you will have something that is written down that you will be able to practice from. You should also read through what you have written in order to find out if there are any spots that are really awkward or if there seems to be any information that is missing.

Memorize Your Speech

This one might seem like it is a little bit out there, but you should use the speech that you just wrote out and learn it all by heart. You should read off the sheet a few times to start so that you can get the pacing and the tone of voice down without having to remember all of the words. After a few times, you will feel a little more confident about what is going on, and you will eventually not need to have the paper anymore. When you are practicing, find somewhere in your home or in your office that is secluded and where you will be able to be alone. This is a fantastic method to get the confidence you'll need to deliver your speech and sound fantastic while doing so.

When doing this step, you need to learn how to be natural when talking. Even though you have memorized the speech, you do not want to sound like you are just reading off the screen. Instead, pretend that you are an actor and this is your script. You need to add in some passion, something extra to get the audience's attention and make them feel like you really know what you are talking about. If you just read what you memorized, the audience is going to notice, and they are going to get bored really easily. The point of memorizing your speech is to give you the confidence that is needed to keep going and not to falter. You will then be able to go off the script a little bit if you need and then go back if you begin to fumble. This is a great way to give yourself a little bit of freedom during the whole process.

Practice Speech Out Loud

It is important that you take the time to practice your speech out loud once you have it memorized. You should start from the beginning and work all the way through the body of the speech before ending with the conclusion. It is best to try and do it the same way that you would in front of the audience; if you are skipping around or just practicing one part and not the other, you might find that you are not as prepared as you would like when it comes time to talk to the audience. Also, while you are talking out loud, pretend that there are others in the room with you, even though there is not going to be anyone there. You should not only practice the words that you are going to say but practice the inflections that will go with the words, the hand gestures, your movements, and any comedy that you plan to throw into the mix.

The more that you practice all of this and put thought into it, the better it is going to come out when you are all done.

The important part about this step is that you practice as closely as you can tell how you would like the speech to come out when you actually meet the audience. Everything that you practice is going to seem much more natural if you do it at least a few times before. When it comes time to deliver the speech, if you spend all of your effort memorizing the words and nothing else, you will sound stiff and difficult to understand.

Practice without the Notes

It is important to start the presentation practice with the notes on hand. This will allow you to go through everything while just looking down if you forget something rather than going through things later and finding out that you were completely wrong. It's time to put your notes away and practice without them once you've had some time to practice with them. Ideally, you are going to have enough time before the presentation that you can learn the material and not have to keep notecards or other papers around with you. Of course, if you are only given a few days to put the whole thing together, you might not have time to do this, but if you have a month or more to prepare, it is going to look more natural on stage if you are able to give your speech without any of the notes at all.

You can start this part off slowly; perhaps do each section of your speech without the notes a few times so you can get it down. After a couple of runs, you will realize that you already know the material, and you do not need to have it on you in order to be successful.

Record Yourself

It's a good idea to record yourself after you've become comfortable with your speech and whatever you're saying. First, get out a little radio recorder and have it turned on while you are saying the speech. Go through the whole speech without pausing or second-guessing yourself. When you are done with the speech, sit down with a pen and paper and then listen to the audio recording from the beginning to the end. Do not worry too much about how the speech sounds and instead use this as a learning experience. Take down notes of what you have done wrong, spending more time on the delivery of the speech rather than if you missed some information or not. If you have a lot of 'umms' in your speech, figure out how you can get rid of these so that the whole thing flows together better. You will also be able to catch on to things that you thought were good to have in the speech, but now that you are hearing them played back, they sound really bad or really forced. Make adjustments to your speech, and then do it again with the recorder. You will find that each time you do this process, you are going to get more comfortable with the recorder, and things will begin to fall into place. Continue doing this process until you think that everything sounds perfect.

After you have gotten everything to sound good on the audio recording, it is time to bring out a camcorder and do it over again. Take a video of yourself giving the speech, following the same steps as before. The point of this process is that you will now be able to see how you look to the audience. Are you twitching a lot or wringing your hands in nervousness? Do you look like you are about to fall over? You should also make sure you're dressed in the clothing you'll be wearing during the speech so you can see how you'll look in it and with your speech. Do this a couple of times until you get everything down.

These steps should be able to prepare you to give your speech in a natural way to the audience. You will have had plenty of practice with your speech and can almost recite it in your dreams. This can help you to continue on during the process without the hindrance of your notes or having to worry about forgetting important information. It can also help you to get the confidence that you need to keep on going, even if you make a mistake, and that confidence is going to radiate out to the audience and make them like you and your ideas.

Fear of Public Speaking

Almost everybody you come across will have dealt with the fear of public speaking; it's a challenge everybody faces from time to time.

But what does fear mean? Of course, it will depend on the circumstances, fear in most cases, to protect you from danger; it's a sign of a threat nearby. But in terms of public speaking, fear is not overly practical; the acronym I like to stand by is FALSE EVIDENCE APPEARING REAL, that's it. The best thing we can do is go through the fear; in this case, if you feel fear when public speaking, then there is nothing you can do to get rid of it at the moment. Of course, you can avoid it by not going up onto the stage, but you let the fear control you and dictate your actions by doing this. It doesn't serve your best interests to do it. If you practice in front of an audience long enough, the dread will fade or vanish, or you will get used to the sensation of being on stage; either way, it will have little impact on you. If you have read my other book on public speaking, you'll have learned that there is never a permanent solution for fear. It will always come back after a while if you stop practicing your public speaking, the fear will gradually come back. If you challenge yourself by presenting to larger crowds, then you'll undoubtedly feel uncomfortable. Fear can be used as an indicator when you feel uncomfortable doing something within reason, then means you are growing as a person. So ignore the fear, don't let it control you, instead be proactive in social situations you find yourself in. Volunteer to speak up on stage or approach that person on the street, ultimately your feel better for it. If you don't, you'll only regret it later, and regret is something nobody ever wants or need to experience.

The Importance of Public Speaking

If you are asking most people, they would possibly say that they don't want to talk publicly. They can also admit that they are afraid because public fear is a very common fear. Or they may just be timid or introverted. For these purposes, if they can, many people avoid talking to the media. If you are one of those people who don't talk to the press, you lose out.

Over the years, education, government, and industry have played a significant role in the public sphere. Words have the ability to inform, convince, educate, and even entertain themselves. And the spoken word in possession of the right speaker may be much better than the written word.

If you are a small business owner, a student, or a passionate citizen, you will benefit if you develop your personal and professional skills as a public speaker. Such advantages for the public include:

- Improves confidence
- Better research skills
- Stronger deductive skills
- Ability to advocate for causes and more

Public speakers are particularly important for corporations because they have to get their message to potential consumers and promote their business. Salespersons and managers alike are also forced to speak well in public.

Effective Public Speaking

Powerful Public Speaking is a significant skill in imparting learning and communicating thoughts to gatherings of individuals. It is an essential mechanism for introducing and selling your items and thoughts. Having the option to impart adequately to different people or to gatherings verbally is fundamental in school, business, just as your own life.

There is a requirement for individuals who can viably make introductions and address others. Your insight and aptitudes around there can help advance your profession or improve your business. Also, if you are good at or like public speaking, you may choose to pursue it as a career.

A gifted Public Speaker will get the thing going notwithstanding during the hour of emergency. Numerous speakers have achieved extraordinary changes by the sheer impact of their successful talks. You also can be one of those rare sorts of people who have deserted a trail of history that will keep them in the recollections of the ages to come.

You can figure out how to turn into an increasingly viable speaker by utilizing the correct methods and rehearsing your public speaking aptitudes. Here are a few systems to pursue:

1. **Care About Your Theme**

Enthusiasm goes far with regards to being a successful speaker. The group of spectators can tell in case you're emotionless. They won't mind if you don't give a damn if you don't care. Much more dreadful, you can appear to be a phony.

Then again, in the event that you earnestly care about your theme, the group of spectators will get on that as well. They'll see you as being progressively true and trustworthy. They'll listen all the more near find why your subject is so critical to you. Furthermore, they're bound to pardon any minor errors you may make.

2. **Keep in mind Your Speaking Objective**

We've all likely tuned in to, at any rate, one speaker who appeared to continue endlessly always about nothing specifically. One motivation behind why this happens is on the grounds that the discourse isn't centered enough. The speaker is attempting to cover excessively and winds up exhausting their audience members.

Right off the bat, during the time spent building up your discourse, distinguish the motivation behind why you're speaking. Make it a point to adhere to this objective during your introduction. Try not to get derailed off-subject.

3. **Bolster Your Central matters**

Each point you make in your discourse should be bolstered with either a model, a representation, or certainties. When you're supporting a point, it's ideal to be as explicit as you can be.

For instance, in a discourse about the significance of clean water, this announcement is excessively ambiguous:

"Numerous individuals don't have clean water."

Expressing this measurement from the U.S. Community for Sickness Control is an increasingly successful approach to help your point:

"Around the world, 780 million individuals don't approach an improved water source."

4. Recount to a Story

Individuals love a decent story. As a result, if you want to improve your public speaking skills, tell a tale.

Narrating is an incredible method to make your material additionally captivating and to identify with your crowd. Ensure your story is relatable and important.

In case you're speaking is about your business, here are a few instances of stories you might most likely tell:

- A client story. The account of how your item or administrations addressed an issue for a particular client or tackled an issue. Fulfilled clients are regularly glad to share this.

- Your organization story. The narrative of how your organization became. This can be particularly compelling if it's client situated.

- An item advancement story. The account of how you came to offer another item.

Obviously, there are numerous different sorts of stories you could tell contingent upon the kind of speaking you are doing.

5. Use Introduction Instruments Shrewdly

Slide introductions regularly get a notoriety for being dull; however, that is on the grounds that numerous speakers are uninformed of what their introduction devices can do and don't utilize every one of the highlights. To more readily draw in your group of spectators, figure out how to utilize the further developed highlights of your device.

For instance, here are only a couple of ways you can utilize PowerPoint and Google Slides (with connections to related instructional exercises):

- Add movements (PowerPoint, Google Slides)
- Add video (PowerPoint, Google Slides)
- Add sound (PowerPoint, Google Slides)
- Construct a timetable (PowerPoint, Google Slides)

Furthermore, these highlights are only a hint of something larger. To truly lift your public speaking procedures, you'll need to get the hang of everything your introduction programming instrument can do.

6. Utilize an Expert Layout

While we're discussing introduction devices, we should likewise discuss the introduction plan. Your introduction configuration influences how your group of spectators sees you. Regardless of whether you've retained your discourse, give it flawlessly, and have the most astounding theme - your group of spectators may even now pass judgment on you contrarily if your introduction configuration is messy and amateurish.

Obviously, you could utilize a standard layout (similar to those that everybody uses) or structure your own format (exorbitant and tedious). In any case, a superior arrangement is to utilize an expertly planned introduction format that you can without much of a stretch tweak. The introduction formats from Envato Components and GraphicRiver, for instance, are demonstrated, simple to utilize, and proficient. Also, there are hundreds to browse - so you will undoubtedly discover one that addresses your issues.

7. Pace Yourself

With regards to public speaking, a typical novice mistake is to talk too rapidly. This is generally brought about by a mix of nerves and not understanding how quick you're really speaking. Be that as it may, talking too quickly makes it harder for your audience members to comprehend what you're stating.

Compelling public speakers know to pace themselves. They talk at a characteristic pace and work short, normal delays into their discourse.

It likewise encourages on the off chance that you make sure to inhale during your discourse. An astonishing number of individuals hold their breath without acknowledging it when they're anxious (I'm one of them). In any case, holding your breath will just build your tension. Thus, make sure to inhale profoundly during the breaks in your discourse. On the off chance that your discourse is a long one, taking a taste of water throughout a break can likewise help.

8. Include Visual Guides

Visual guides can fill in as an incredible representation of your discourse. People utilize their sight more than some other sense. In this way, on the off chance that you can come to your meaningful conclusion by indicating it to your audience members as opposed to portraying it, they are bound to recall it.

Be cautious, however. To be powerful, your visual guide must be of high caliber and effectively unmistakable to all individuals from your group of spectators. Abstain from fusing messy designs into a slide introduction. In like manner, don't hold up a visual guide that is physically unreasonably little for those tuning in to see.

9. Dress Easily, Yet Expertly

What's the correct outfit to wear in the event that you need to be a successful public speaker?

All things considered, there's nobody answer. How you dress relies upon who your audience members will be. Yet, the general guideline is that you need to dress expertly to establish a decent connection. Try to watch great prepping and cleanliness leads as well.

Numerous specialists feel you should dress, as indicated by how your group of spectators dresses. In the event that the crowd is dressed officially, you would prefer not to appear in shorts and a tee-shirt. Similarly, if the group of spectators is wearing shorts and a tee-shirt, don't dress officially.

10. Maintain a Strategic Distance from Unbalanced Fillers

"Um," "uh," "like." We as a whole slip these filler words into our discussions without acknowledging it. In any case, abuse of these words during an expert discourse can make you sound not exactly sure. In the event that you can, get out from under the propensity for utilizing these words to improve as a public speaker.

Practice can enable you to kill these words from your discourse designs; however, you might be so used to utilizing them that it's difficult to see when you're doing it. This is the place a discourse mentor, instructor, or companion would prove to be useful. They could tune in for these words and help you get out from under the propensity for utilizing them.

11. Use Motions (Yet Don't Exaggerate)

Characteristic development during a discourse is an indication of a successful public speaker. Hand motions and notwithstanding making a couple of strides over the stage can be great public speaking strategies insofar as they're regular, intentional, and not exaggerated.

Development can cause you to show up increasingly agreeable and help your group of spectators identify with you. You've presumably observed the hardened speaker who conveys their discourse while standing stock still, hands hanging flaccidly close by. Which would you rather tune in to? That firm speaker, or a speaker who intersperses their discourse every once in a while with important hand signals?

12. Permit Questions and Answers

Question and answer sessions (question and answer) are one of the most underused public speaking strategies. Numerous speakers simply state what they're going to state and, after that, plunk down. What a waste!

The excellence of question and answer is that you get the opportunity to hear your audience members' worries straightforwardly and address them publicly, further fortifying your case.

You can get ready for a question and answer session by making your very own rundown of inquiries and potential complaints that crowd individuals may have (with answers). Concentrate the rundown cautiously, so you're comfortable with it. Don't freeze if someone brings up something you hadn't considered. They don't anticipate that you should know it all. It's splendidly worth it to take their contact data and reveal to them that you'll hit them up once you have the appropriate response.

Chapter 53:
The Art of Public Speaking

Qualities of a Good Public Speaker

A public speaker is best suited for a particular circumstance, but there are some characteristics that put you on par with the big boys. It is not by the number of Instagram followers that you have or the number of events you can book annually, or even by the amount people spend to book you for an event. Those are the perks that come with building a solid brand for yourself and require the right combination of publicity, hard work, consistency, and possession of certain qualities that I will be discussing very soon. These distinguishing qualities are sometimes innate talent that is built on over time with training and practice. However, you can move from where you are right now to become good in your craft by honing in on the following skills:

1. **Connecting with your audience**

All of your tasks and training right up to this point would not serve you well if you cannot connect with your audience. They are the reason you are on that stage in the first place. To connect with your audience, you first understand that being there is not about you even though they have come to hear you speak. It is about them. You are the speaker, but rather than segueing into a long, drawn-out monologue, you are responsible for making it seem like a dialogue without the other parties doing it. It may not immediately turn you into a crowd whisperer, as the charm switch that you need to turn on is unique to each crowd. Still, we will cover the basics to help you do more than just get by.

2. **Being a master storyteller**

This is not because I am a person who just loves to share stories about myself. This is a deliberate attempt to:

    a. Stop you from being bored

b. Make the concept more relatable to you

   c. Prove that this is not something that was lifted off some other person's page but an experience

Storytelling humanizes your idea and paints a picture that your listener or audience might find more conceivable. You may have the best theories and the greatest solution for a problem in this century, but it will always remain a theory if you cannot get people to understand it. A good public speaker must master this. So, when you share, create, or look for a story that best illustrates your ideas.

3. Voice modulations

Before you continue reading, take a minute to read a few sentences of this book out loud in a slow voice without any inflections. Disregard the commas and any other punctuation marks. If possible, record this on your phone. You will observe that you sound uninteresting, and if you keep at this for at least twenty minutes, your voice would have a snooze-inducing effect on you. In a crowd, this effect is multiplied, and you don't want that. Voice modulations help you build on the two points listed above. You can give your speech a semblance of a conversation that is essential to keeping your audience engaged. Master this, and your storytelling will take on a new dimension. Think of the narrators in a movie. The emotional inflections in their voices help you connect with the story even though you don't see them.

Charming Your Audience

A public speaker shares their ideas with an audience. A good public speaker shares their ideas with an audience and holds them in their sway. In today's world, there are many distractions. The advent of the mobile phone makes it that much more difficult to compete against them for the attention of your audience. You can employ simple strategies to get and sustain the attention of the crowd, whether it is a small presentation with a handful of people or a stage delivery with a large crowd.

1. Come with a message that would surprise your audience

The Internet provides a wealth of information, and there is a very strong possibility that a significant number of the people in your audience may have more than an average idea of the topic you want to discuss. If you stick to the general information, you might end up feeding them with the same boring stuff, and that kind of recycled information can earn you a few minutes of their time. After that, you may have a tough time regaining their attention.

2. Use a language that they understand

You want to impress your audience, and I get it. But don't use bogus words that sound impressive without the ability to convey the true meaning of the words or the message you want to get across. For instance, the word I want to use in describing the true state of your audience if you choose to use big words in your speech is discombobulated. But don't you think it sounds a lot better and keeps you on track with this article if I replaced that word with confused instead? Stringing a few sentences together using big words could make it difficult for people to follow your train of thought, and even if they manage to scale through the first few minutes of your speech, there is no guarantee that they would keep this up throughout. Stick to simple and easy-to-understand words.

3. Get off the stage

Just because you have been set up on a podium shouldn't mean that your movement is restricted to that space. The entire room is your stage, and as long as the movement does not interfere with the audio, there is no reason you can't do your thing from where the crowd is. This makes you seem accessible, and when people feel this way about you, they become more open to your ideas. And when people are more open to whatever it is that you have to tell them, they pay more attention. It is really that simple.

4. Be flexible

For a novice public speaker, I can understand why you would want to create a script for your performance and stick to it. But if you observe several yawns a few minutes into your speech, it may not be working for your crowd. In this case, you may have to flip the script. If you were too upbeat, you might have to tone it down a little bit. If you are taking it slow, you may have to increase the tempo. And in some cases, you may have to veer completely off course (we talk about this in the next segment) and get the crowd buzzing in excitement before you bring them to the topic in focus.

Showing Your Witty Side

To make your audience laugh, you don't have to be a stand-up comedian. And while it would be great to hear that glorious sound, the objective for public speakers is to inject some excitement into the room and, in so doing, keep your audience engaged. For someone who is just overcoming their natural tendencies to be shy, it is a very daunting prospect to get on stage and amuse a crowd. From my personal experience, you can get the crowd moving by doing nothing more than being yourself. You have different options on using your wit to create a humorous moment. I am going to list a few ways you can do this. Go with what comes naturally to you. In fact, with practice, you may even discover a technique that I did not include on this list, and this is one of the things that makes the remarkable journey you have embarked on that much more interesting.

1. Tell a story

We all have that embarrassing tale that we have lived through. Narrating that experience with a few exaggerated details can turn out hilarious. Sample this story with a small crowd and observe their reaction. If it is what you hoped for, embellish it a little and tell your audience. Be sure to include every funny detail you can recall into the narrative. However, it is important that you pay attention to the kind of crowd you are sharing this story with. An audience from your workplace who are there to witness a presentation where you pitch your ideas to them might not appreciate a joke about your escapades at the club. To avoid a situation where you might offend a race, gender, or religious belief, it is safer to stick with narratives that are self-deprecating.

2. Give an activity that your audience can carry out

This may not immediately cause anyone to go into a laughing fit, but at least it would get your audience moving. However, only do this if the crowd is not much and if you feel that the energy levels are dropping. From my personal experience, this works very well during training. I split my crowd into teams and come up with group bonding activities that pit them against each other. The competition gets them fired up. For a small crowd of people who are just meeting each other for the first time, at the start of the session, I ask everyone to fill out a card and drop it in a box. The instructions on the card ask them to tell two truths and a lie about themselves. About twenty minutes into a one-hour session, I pick three random cards, call out the names, read the contents of the card and then ask the audience to guess the truths and the lie. This takes about five minutes, and then we get back to the session. It creates an atmosphere of familiarity and eases the tension in the room.

3. Tell a joke

Now, this right here requires timing, gesticulating, and timing (again) to get the desired results from your audience. You might hear the same joke from three different people and have three different reactions to the joke, and this is because of how the joke is told. Sure, when the same joke is told over and over again by the same person, it loses its humor. But when some other person does it and with flair too, you find yourself laughing even if you know exactly how the story ends. The key is the technique. You have to know when to smile, when to wriggle the eyebrows, where to screech, and where to throw in the punch line. You'll need to rehearse your joke in order to pull this off effectively. This part may be tough for those of us who have trouble getting through our own jokes without laughing our heads off first. However, if you have a knack for this sort of thing, this might be the best weapon in your arsenal.

Elocution

I think that this builds on the point I made earlier about using a language that your audience would understand. The emphasis, in this case, is on more than just the use of big words. The objective is to ensure that you are able to communicate concisely and clearly to your audience. So, matters like the clear enunciation of your words, the variance of your voice pitch, and the use of body language are thoroughly examined.

Enunciation: This is your ability to speak clearly and pronounce words in a manner that is understood by your audience. For people with speech defects like having a lisp or stuttering, there are speech therapies designed to help you navigate the difficulties associated with your condition. I, for one, am of the opinion that there is nothing that can stand in the way of you attaining your dreams. With hard work, commitment and consistency, you can turn your biggest disadvantages into a platform that sets you up for the future that you desire. If English is not your native language and you are speaking to an audience that is comprised mainly of English speakers, a speech training class might help you with the enunciation. Make friends with your dictionary. Learn new words every day and practice the proper tenses where those words apply.

Pitch variation: To maintain a certain mood in your crowd, your voice decibel must not rise or fall below a certain level. If you go above, you start to appear as though you are screaming the words at your audience. That may work if you use it on a particular word to create emphasis about something you want to illustrate. Use it sparingly, and even then, you have to time its use properly. If your voice note dips too low, you become inaudible to your audience. Maintain this note for too long, and you might as well pick up a violin and play a slow accompanying tune that would lull your audience into a deep sleep. At the same time, keeping the same pitch throughout your speech can quickly become monotonous. This could instigate the same sleep-inducing phenomenon as keeping your voice too low.

Body language: The movement of your body parts, as well as your facial expressions, may provide others clues about your mental state. Without saying a word, your facial features and body language can tell anyone if you are frightened, excited, or just plain bored. If the words that come out of your mouth say one thing and your facial expression says another, anyone listening to you may have a hard time connecting with the words that you say. The gestures that you make on stage help add character to the words that you say. You would seem ridiculous if you were delivering a presentation and remained absolutely still with no movement or facial emotion. The same thing will happen if you use wild gesticulations. There has to be a balance between both extremes to keep the audience engaged and to communicate with your audience effectively.

A public speaker is a performer of sorts. They are not expected to use theatrics in the delivery of their role, but there are techniques employed by stage performers that would prove very useful for a public speaker. Master these techniques; you will dominate the stage and keep your audience in your thrall. Remember, consistency in practice can make a difference.

To become a good public speaker, you must work on developing and mastering certain qualities. You should connect with your crowd, craft your stories masterfully and learn to control the rise and fall of your voice pitch.

To win over your crowd, you need to keep your content fresh. Use words that your audience would understand and be ready to change things at a moment's notice to accommodate the atmosphere of the crowd.

To showcase your wittiness, you only need to be yourself. Find out the unique aspect of you that people connect with the most and use that to your advantage

Finally, communication is everything. Your clothes, your confidence, and your platform mean nothing if you are unable to get the right message across. Learn the technicalities of speech and practice daily.

Your tasks:

1. Every day, learn at least three new words. Your learning of these words should include the meaning, the correct use in sentences as well as the correct pronunciation of the words. The richer your vocabulary, the more articulate you become.

2. Practice four to five jokes before your next speech. Choose jokes that are appropriate for the event where you will be speaking.

3. This one is more of a suggestion than a task; consider taking a class in elocution or speech training. There are several online options.

4. Watch and take notes of the techniques of other public speakers. This is not so that you copy the way they do things exactly. This is to inspire you to do things a little differently from the usual.

5. Do exercises on facial expressions. The more exaggerated, the better. Your audience should be your mirror. Start with anger, curiosity and then keep going. The more expressions you master, the better your stage performance becomes.

Chapter 54:
The Golden Rules of Public Speaking

There are three golden rules to public speaking, which, if followed, will immediately improve both your gravitas and effectiveness when communicating. Classic orators used these same methods and continue to be remembered for their masterful command over both their voice and their ability to mesmerize their audiences. Great speakers were even seen as some of the pinnacles of human intelligence and pillars of society.

Given this knowledge, where would you wish to be on this spectrum?

Now, this is not to say being able to speak well would instantly make you seem intelligent to all! Nor do you need to be one of the aforementioned pillars of society to be seen as a great speaker. To really make use of one of your biggest advantages and maximize the virtue your voice may bring your way, you need to grasp a few basic principles and ideas. But rather than dedicate several pages to the esoteric thoughts behind them, these rules can instead be summarized as:

1. Energize your main point by adding a strong emotion or inflecting a change in volume. People tend to listen when you drop to a whisper.

2. Pause for emphasis before announcing key points to captivate your audience.

3. Go down in pitch at the end of a sentence to make a statement unless asking a question.

If you follow these rules, your public speaking technique will improve overnight. This is one of the very rare instances which do not require hours of methodical practice to see improvement. However, there is potentially a fourth, often secret, rule which is overlooked by many as it is not such a simple matter as descending in pitch at the end of a sentence.

To learn this, you must first identify some common public speaking problems.

Common public speaking problems:

When most people are put in front of a microphone or a crowd, their individual personality vanishes, and a social mask takes its place. This is unfortunate, as people are often chosen to be public speakers due to the appealing nature of their personalities!

In the world of audio recording, voice actors and audiobook narrators often struggle with what I refer to as 'Shatnerism' after the great ham himself. They see a microphone or script before them and affect a jarring personality which is not their own, often overemphasizing or placing stress upon unimportant words such as 'and,' 'is,' and 'the.' It is imperative when you are either placed before a microphone or an audience you communicate with your own emotions and speak as naturally as you would as if talking to a close friend. If you are passionate and educated on your topic, your audience will no doubt be spellbound by what you have to say if you deliver it in a natural manner. However, if you attempt to aggrandize your voice by affecting a tone or style which is stereotypically stentorian in an effort to impress your audience, it shall not be convincing.

Similarly, by imagining you are having a conversation with your audience, you will also eliminate the possibility of affecting a Shatneresque delivery.

One point of note is resonance. When attempting to make their voice resonate, inexperienced speakers often raise the pitch and volume of their voice in an effort to speak over their listeners rather than directly to them. Not only does this sound amateurish, but it frequently results in injury and inflammation of the vocal cords, along with other symptoms of exhaustion. To use a metaphor: when a steam train's whistle is blown prior to moving into a tunnel, it can sound weak. Yet despite putting out no-less air, the whistle increases in volume tremendously when inside a tunnel. This is due to resonance, which in vocal terms, would be the ability to match the natural echo of your voice and the room you are speaking in.

Of course, the latter part is not always possible, but creating vocal resonance is often merely a matter of ensuring that when talking, your teeth are not touching. It may take some practice, but the natural cavity of your mouth is a purpose-made resonance chamber. If you are unsure how to produce a resonating sound: yawn. You will notice how your voice suddenly becomes deeper and more 'rounded' in sound due to the extra space available for the soundwaves to resonate within. Practicing creating this resonance in the echo chamber of a shower is ideal, as it allows for your voice to sound louder than it actually is.

Another common trait adopted by some public speakers is 'pulpit tone.' This common affliction is heard amongst even the most experienced newscasters, journalists, or audiobook narrators who deliver words with a predictable sing-song cadence, as they tend to focus too much on the sound of their voice rather than what they are saying. Actors, narrators, and similar professionals can struggle for years to remove this predictability due to often spending years building the habit in an attempt to sound similar to an old-fashioned newscaster. Much like ' Shatnerism,' pulpit tone seems only to arise when the individual is put before a microphone or a script. One of the best cures for this is a form of vocally detached practice. Practice by breaking the speech down into its key points and summarising them with your own words to aid familiarity with understanding. Only then should you practice by taking the script one part at a time and eventually reciting the speech in its entirety until you gain a natural fluency.

Yet why do so many become afflicted with 'Shatnerism' and 'pulpit tone'? One potential explanation may be anxiety. A change of mentality may help. I personally have the mindset that fear is simply your own mind believing it can expect what will happen in the future. However, if this were true, you would be playing the lottery with the numbers your mind expects to arise rather than worrying!

Of course, anxiety can be justified; just as you would feel fear if you stepped into the ring with Muhammed Ali, so too would you feel fear speaking in public for the first time. Consider that if you were to watch two mechanics take apart a car, one a master and the other an apprentice, the master would act in a way that allowed him to deconstruct the vehicle without secondary concern confidently. The apprentice, on the other hand, would be hesitant due to a lack of experience. Public speaking is exactly the same. With confidence comes competence, and you should attempt to speak in public or read aloud as often as you can if you truly wish to free yourself from anxieties over public speaking. Anxiety can often cause some speakers to subconsciously wish to deliver all the information as quickly as possible, leading to a rapid delivery of words in a jumbled mess. To prevent this, you must first be well versed with your topic. Anecdotally, I am sure you all know of someone who has once delivered a speech on something they clearly had not prepared, leading to a disastrous performance. You should therefore ensure you can competently answer questions regarding your topic to help free yourself from any worries. Of course, knowledge of your topic doesn't automatically free you from fear! One tip would be to count '1, 2, 3' slowly in your mind, or keep time by tapping your fingers together as you talk.

This will help set a mental pace for you to follow when speaking.

However, there are those who are exceptionally well-versed in their chosen topic and yet still feel frightened when speaking in public. If this is the case, I suggest reading some of the great books on dealing with public speaking fear.

Chapter 55:
Tips for Public Speaking

Here are some tips that you can take into account when you are getting ready to speak in front of an audience.

Getting Ready

- **Breathe**—there is nothing wrong with slowing down and taking a breath during the speech. A pause that seems really long to you is usually only a few seconds, so just breathe, collect yourself and keep going when needed. It is easy to forget to breathe during the speech, which can make you go through the information too fast and makes you feel really nervous. No one is going to mind if you take just a few seconds as a segue to the next point in your speech, and it can help to keep the pacing.

- **Make an outline**—this outline can be a lifesaver if you do not have much time to prepare and are worried about getting all of the information right. Make the font a little bit bigger so that you are able to read it with a glance rather than having to concentrate too hard and lose your space.

- **Own your speech**—you are the expert on this topic so let others know that. They have come to you for advice; do not let your anxiety get to you. You are the expert and know what you are talking about, so let that get out to the audience when you are talking to them.

While Speaking

- **Eye contact**—it is a good idea to maintain eye contact with the audience while you are talking. You should be able to get your energy from the audience, and they are going to be able to help you a lot more if you are able to give back to them. Look your audience in the eyes while speaking to keep them interested and create the appearance that you are in charge.

- **Practice to avoid nervousness**—one of the best things that you will be able to do if you are nervous is to go over your speech ahead of time. You will learn the material better, have something to fall back on if you forget, and gain the confidence that you need to keep going on.
- **Save questions for the end**—some speakers will feel like they should have questions open at any time. They feel this will make them more approachable to the audience. This is generally a poor idea since it will muddle your thoughts and lead you to forget your place. Kindly tell the audience that you will be happy to answer their questions at the end of the speech so you can effortlessly get through the material.

Avoiding Bumps

- **Do not panic about the timing**—when you are presenting at home, you may find that you are calmer and collected. This could result in a conflict of timing if you get nervous at the presentation and talk faster. A good way to keep track of your timing so you are not trying to rush through everything is to place your watch on the podium in front of you. Then you can see exactly how much time is left and plan accordingly.
- **Watch for nervous habits**—this can include things like playing with your necklace or twirling your hair. The audience will pay more attention to this than to your speech, so learn how to prevent it or refrain from wearing any clothes or jewelry that may entice them.
- **Bring supplies**—if you are worried about getting thirsty during the speech, bring along a bottle of water. This can help avoid issues with dry mouth and help you if you get stuck-no one will notice a long pause if you are taking a drink from your water. Also, some tissues in your pocket are nice if you have to sneeze or have a runny nose. Bring along a few little things that you will be able to stuff in your pockets and use if the need arises.

Chapter 56:
One Technique That is Sure to Engage Your Audience

Everyone has experienced a conversation where the other person seemed to speak a foreign language because the conversation wasn't anything they could relate to. People don't enjoy listening to someone speak about topics that aren't relatable, and it makes answering questions and engaging in conversation boring. Luckily there's a simple technique to make sure that the person you're talking to understands the points you are trying to convey.

When you communicate with people, make sure that you tell compelling stories. When you become a storyteller, people can connect with what you're saying and become intrigued enough to continue the conversation. Everyone loves a good story because it's relatable and entertaining. As a storyteller, everything you say can be used to get your point across and engage the person you're communicating with to take action.

While you're communicating with someone new, you can discuss examples of what you're saying by adding a story. Say, "For example," or "For instance," to lead into a story that the other person can relate to. As the other person hears what you have to say, they'll relate to the story and connect what you're saying with a similar experience that they've had before. It's an incredibly effective way to engage people, build rapport, and fit in a lot of additional information during your conversation with someone else.

Telling stories makes you an effective communicator with one person and when you're speaking in a group. If you've ever worried about what you should say in a group presentation or to a single person, if you find a story related to what you're going through, you can effectively communicate without stumbling over your words. Since you are just retelling something that has happened to you, your speech will feel natural and easy to communicate with others.

When you use the power of storytelling to communicate with others, they get a feel for who you are and the experiences that you've had. People will feel like they understand who you are and the values you hold when you effectively tell stories. The beauty is that you can share a story with someone about any point in your life, and it will create new topics of discussion for everyone involved who has shared a similar experience naturally.

Another Great Technique For Effective Communication

In addition to matching perspective, another effective technique for building rapport is using similar language to the person you're speaking with. As they speak, listen to their particular wording and match it back to them. For example, you may overhear someone say, "Oh boy, I'm just exhausted!" The perfect reply would be to match them by saying, "Why are you exhausted?" because it connects directly with what they said.

If I had selected, "Why are you tired?" as a response, rapport would have been delayed. That's because everyone uses language differently, so they might not associate being tired with being exhausted. Instead of continuing their conversation with you, the other person's mind would have to stop and think, "But I just said that I'm exhausted, not tired... so what do you mean by that?"

The more minor delays you receive in communication, the better! That's why it's important to mirror the language of the person you're speaking with.

Have you ever conversed with someone bilingual? Perhaps they even speak the same language but use different vocabulary. Sometimes hearing words used differently stops rapport from being made because the other person has to consider exactly what you mean based on the context before moving on. The same goes for overly complicated words that aren't used in regular speech. Your language is more simple the easier it is for someone to connect with you and build rapport with you.

The next time you begin a conversation with someone, make sure you notice how they use language and the language you use. Here are some simple questions you can ask yourself:

- Does someone use language differently from me?
- How did I respond when someone said something out of the ordinary?
- Am I using language that is complicated to understand that breaks communication?

When you learn how other people speak and pay attention to their choice of words, it becomes easier to mirror them. Mirroring someone's language and making sure that you speak in a manner that's easy to understand will make you an excellent communicator.

How to Show Others that You Are Engaged in the Conversation

It's easy to tell when someone is disengaged with the conversation that you're having. To make sure that you continue building rapport with another person, you need to make sure you stay engaged. These four simple best practices will ensure that the conversation keeps rolling without one of you losing interest in what the other has to say.

Use the other person's name.

Everyone likes to hear their name. When you are introduced to someone, use their name casually every once in a while during the interaction to make sure that they are focused on your conversation. It's a great way to make the other person feel valued and important since you took the time to learn and use their name.

Make great eye contact.

Maintaining eye contact shows the other person that you're interested in what they have to say. Of course, naturally breaking eye contact is normal, so make sure that you don't stare at the person you're conversing with. However, if you do break eye contact, make sure that you regain it a few seconds afterward to show people that you're engaged in the conversation.

Connect your response with the end of another person's statement.

One of the best ways to show people that you're listening and engaged in the conversation that you're having is by starting your response to what the other person says the same way that the other person finished their statement. Here's an example of an interaction where you use this technique.

Them: "I can't believe that it was such a horrible experience."

You: "I'm sorry that you had a horrible experience. At least you know what to expect the next time you go to work...."

When you connect your response to what another person has said, you form a stronger rapport with the person simply because you're showing that listening to what the other person has to say.

Non-verbally show that you are paying attention.

Nodding, smiling, and generally reacting to what the other person says shows that you are engaged in the conversation. People can tell when you are actually paying attention and not just respond or nod your head. They know this because your non-verbal actions will usually be in unity with what they say. Make sure that you incorporate all of these techniques when you're conversing and building rapport.

Chapter 57:
How to Use Metaphors to Communicate Better?

This amazing language pattern is abundant in our everyday interactions. We employ as many as six metaphors on average within one minute of spoken language. Magical things begin to happen as you learn to recognize metaphors in other people's speech.

The ability to use metaphors in everyday speech opens up a world of possibilities, from altering other people's minds or addressing their issues to eliciting laughter or inspiration.

Metaphors vs. Logical Mind

Imagine your buddy saying, "My business isn't doing well!" This individual is referring to a particular incident or circumstance in their life, as long as they are neither a pilot or an airline owner. Perhaps you might disregard the metaphor and just ask, "What do you mean?" Obtaining obvious knowledge about how this issue is represented in their minds and then connecting to this particular metaphor, on the other hand, has a much more powerful impact. Why? Because their rational thinking isn't engaged, all of your efforts are squandered.

In such a scenario, fighting with their rational mind would be a near-impossible task. When your buddy explains to you what they meant when they said their company isn't taking off, they'll probably come up with a lot of good reasons to back up their metaphor, making you feel even worse. "… Oh, how desperate I am! I can't even manage my own affairs!" Even if you were a master of rhetoric and dismissed each of these self-deprecating reasons one by one, they'd most likely come up with new ones. More or less correct, yet perfectly accurate for their rational thinking.

You bypass your interlocutor's conscious thinking and speak to their subconscious by referring to a metaphor. Metaphors are formed unconsciously and, in most cases, have no direct relationship to the actual problem they are addressing. This almost eliminates the possibility that the so-called "inner critic" (internal voice) would start wreaking havoc in this person's mind, making them feel even worse. It's difficult to talk about anything using a metaphor!

Move Inside the Metaphor

What does it mean to "move over the metaphor"? This is the process of interpreting a metaphor literally and referring to it as if it were a regular, logical statement rather than a metaphor.

Let's use the example of a friend's company that isn't taking off. "Are you sure you accelerated your aircraft to maximum speed before trying to take off?" you could ask instead of asking for specific reasons for not taking off or "How long is the airstrip?" "What can you do in such a scenario to bring the engines up to full speed and ultimately take off?" or "Have you read the proper handbook on how to fly this specific plane?"

There are many choices available. You might go even farther and suggest, "Perhaps you could try taking off with a better, newer model plane?" "Are you sure you're sitting inside a plane?" or, more jokingly, "Are you sure you're seated inside a plane?" Is it possible that it's simply a weird car?" Each metaphor offers a new solution or encourages the other person to go further into a specific problem. "Next time, refuel your aircraft before attempting to take off, or you'll end up driving all over the runway and making ground control laugh!"

The most unique aspect of metaphors is that the subconscious mind will always discover the analogy's relevant and essential meaning. It's not uncommon for two individuals to discover solutions to two separate issues (that have nothing in common) in a single metaphor. This whimsical linguistic structure's high flexibility makes it helpful in a variety of circumstances. Perhaps this is why it appears in so many religious texts and folklore tales. It is very beneficial to our minds, and our forefathers were aware of it.

"I feel like I've had my hands bound with a heavy rope for a very long time..." a friend and colleague once told me. "Do you want to go about begging people to cut these ropes and liberate your hands, or do you want to gather yourself together, locate a sharp hook, and rip them to shreds?" I said. "I prefer to discover the inner power and chance to rip these cords up," he simply stated, nodding his head meaningfully. This short exchange of ideas helped me immediately recognize who I'm working with and how to approach him in order to encourage him to solve his issues.

Remember that it's important to have a strong connection with your discussion partner before you start using metaphors.

The technique for referring to metaphors in daily speech is fairly straightforward, and it consists of two stages:

1. Specification of a metaphor.
2. Searching for solutions.

In all phases, you stay on the surface of the metaphor without delving into the specifics of what the comparison means to the person with whom you're conversing.

To help you understand what I'm talking about, I'll use an example from Sue Knight's book, NLP at Work. She worked for a business where the CEOs often used the following phrases in their conversations:

- "I was under heavy fire…"
- "To go after the competition…"
- "Aim for the ideal place…"

In this case, this method of thinking about their company was not a good cognitive strategy. Instead of concentrating on how to enhance their business, these CEOs were preoccupied with their "adversaries" and the "war" they thought they were leading. Instead of concentrating on finding fresh, innovative methods to make their company stand out, they were spending their energy on continuous preparation for the "battle."

I'd ask them things like, "Who's fighting who here?" and "What are you fighting for?" and "How will you know you've won the war?" Taking into account the two stages of dealing with metaphors, and so on.

Knowing the answers, I'd suggest looking for answers using analogies from war or combat to help you find them. "Wouldn't it be better if you buried the hatchet or, at the very least, unified your troops?", "You will never build a large empire based only on fighting." Perhaps it would be preferable to concentrate all growth efforts inside the team?"

If you refer to an issue in that manner, it's virtually likely that the individual who views the world in that way will understand you. To provide an effective metaphoric answer, you need not need considerable knowledge or specialized abilities since metaphors are generally straightforward.

Below is a list of several additional metaphors that are often used in talks.

- I feel like I'm carrying a tremendous weight on my shoulders, and there's a large, thick wall in front of me.
- Someone hacked off my wings.
- I'm at a loss for words.
- I'm still stuck in the same spot, unable to go ahead.
- We don't use the same wavelengths for transmission.
- He's like a time bomb on the verge of exploding.

Where Can You Use This Knowledge?

- In any conversation, with any person, to play with the language and improve your linguistic skills. Catch metaphors, change them, seek solutions and make others laugh.

- When you want to help someone - people very often describe their problems with the help of metaphors. Expand on the metaphors they use and try to find better solutions for them on the level of these analogies.

- To influence and inspire others - when someone verbalizes some of their obstacles/blocks in the form of a metaphor (e.g., "it's out of my league"), refer to it without getting into logical arguments and introduce that person to new possibilities.

- When you want to teach someone or open their eyes to something important - a good metaphor can be the key to understand even the most difficult issues. It's sometimes enough if you start a sentence with: "It's just as if..." to make someone's mind "click."

These are just a few ideas on how to apply operations on the level of metaphors. Across the vast ocean of possibilities, you will surely find out what is the most useful for you.

The world of metaphors is truly fascinating, and I encourage you to start discovering it—mastery of this particular linguistic structure in conversations takes communication to a new level.

The Power of Metaphor

Language is one of the most reliable tools for communicating. Language is particularly vital for literal communication, whereby what is said is what is meant. However, there are additional features of language that seek to make it more interesting, with one such feature being metaphors. A metaphor is essentially a figure of speech in which the words infer indirect connotations with something else. The metaphor thus renders deeper meaning to language and serves to make it quite beautiful.

One of the reasons why metaphors are highly preferred is that they create empathy and harmony. For instance, standing in someone else's shoes is a metaphor that seeks to create harmony in society. The literal meaning is to try to relate to someone else's situation. When it comes to metaphors and language use, some are pretty common in terms of usage. Similarly, other metaphors are also not very popular, and it is generally best to avoid them. This article will analyze the role of metaphors in everyday language use and highlight the most commonly used metaphors and those that they should avoid.

Metaphors in communication and empathy creation

Clear communication is vital for your capacity to empathize and understand the situation that another person is going through. Metaphors make it possible to use linguistic tools to enhance the overall clarity of communication. Using these tools can demonstrate some of the challenges that a person can be going through because of their status or position in society. For instance, 'a black sheep' is a metaphor that can be sued to denote a person who is alone in terms of their difference from the rest. The metaphor is quite strong and can elicit empathy since one can relate to this scenario in which you are in a group of people but are singled out for being different.

Foster understanding

Metaphors can also be used to foster understanding and harmony. There might be various situations that, at first glance, might seem confusing. However, a good metaphor might render deeper meaning to them, thus enhancing understanding. For instance, someone might face a seemingly harsh destiny, a death row inmate or life sentence convict. At first glance, it seems quite harsh when one is faced with the prospect of imminent death or having to spend the rest of their life in a confined room. However, an appropriate metaphor such as one who lives by the sword must die by it. This very strong metaphor simply means choices have consequences that are related to them.

Metaphors in an expression of emotion

Metaphors can also be used in the expression of human emotion. Human emotion refers to strong feelings that are times difficult to capture using mere words. For instance, you can say someone is annoyed, but this might leave one hanging. One might be left asking themselves questions such as how much annoyed was he? Therefore, a simple word might fail to fully capture the range or extent of the human emotion in question.

For this reason, metaphors can also come in handy in explaining the extent of human emotion, thus making one appreciate the nature of the situation. For instance, a good example would be to say someone is on cloud nine. In essence, this is not a practical expression since putting someone in a cloud and specifying the cloud's number is impossible. Nonetheless, this metaphor does a lot to capture and convey exactly how the person must have felt. To be in cloud number nine refers to someone being extremely happy, and therefore, the level of happiness could be quite high. This is why they are being compared to someone who is up there in the highest cloud possible.

Popular Metaphors and Their Usage

- **Inspirational metaphors**

These are metaphors that seek to inspire others. Inspirational metaphors make one yearn for more in terms of pursuing opportunities and overcoming challenges in life. A person is considered an inspiration to others if they can do something extraordinary. This is because; people will only look up to other people who have risen above society's expectations.

He is a shining star

This metaphor refers to someone who has performed exceedingly well in a certain area. A star is considered one of the most attractive heavenly bodies capable of standing out from the rest. This is considered a very popular metaphor in everyday language use. It is an expression that denotes excellence and is also used to encourage people to work extra hard in whatever they do in life. Therefore, a person described as a shining star is considered someone to be admired by others and looked up to as a good example to the rest.

The world is a stage, and all people are nothing but players

Sometimes, metaphors can be used to enhance understanding of a phenomenon. These are ordinarily beyond human understanding, but they can be explained away using these unique language tools. For instance, 'the world is a stage, and all people are merely players' is a metaphor by renowned writer William Shakespeare. As we know it today, the world or global society is perhaps one of the most complex eco-systems ever to exist. No words can effectively define the world, which comprises millions of living organisms, physical features, and synthetic artifacts. To this end, the author used a simple but effective metaphor to describe the world as a stage which is a description that adequately covers the world and everything that is in it. In this context, the metaphor uses a very simple definition to describe a very complex subject. It thus makes it easy for just anyone to understand what is being described.

To be a high flyer

A high flyer is a metaphor that describes a high potential individual. This is someone likely to enjoy an elevated status in society because of their academic or corporate achievements. For this reason, a high flyer is usually seen as someone who can go beyond the skies and realize goals and objectives that might be out of reach for an otherwise normal person in society.

Empathy – To be in another person's shoe

Various metaphors can also be used to relate to how another person might be feeling. As earlier stated, metaphors can also elicit feelings of empathy and compassion towards others. Anyone needs to understand some of the issues that affect other people to arrive at a common ground. To be in another person's shoes is a metaphor that enhances empathy and seeks to encourage people to have an open mind and see things from the perspective of others.

- **Lifestyle metaphors**

People are unique, and this uniqueness extends to the lifestyles they choose to lead. Lifestyle metaphors honor the individuality of others while also emphasizing some of the difficulties they may be experiencing.

You are nothing but a hound dog, crying all the time

Some of the most popular metaphors owe their status to the popularity of the people who first came up with these figures of speech. Popular culture is a term that refers to a system of organizing society around icons that act as trendsetters. Popular culture also lends itself to metaphors whereby some of the metaphors in use today are considered part and parcel of popular culture. One such metaphor is 'nothing the hound dog, crying all the time.' This metaphor is the title of a song by Elvis Presley, considered one of the most successful musicians of all time. The metaphor describes a person who comes out as needy and a handful to deal with. Therefore, such a person needs a lot of attention, which might take a toll on anyone associated with them.

He is a couch potato

A couch potato is also another metaphor that has a negative connotation. Generally, this metaphor refers to a person who is regarded as lazy. A couch is a comfortable set of cushioned chairs that is used for resting. Being a couch potato is thus someone who spends a lot of time sitting down and not doing anything particularly useful. Laziness is considered a negative attribute, and when you refer to someone as a couch potato, then you might take it as an insult. However, such a metaphor can only be used if you want to evoke a strong reaction on the part of the individual in question and encourage them to appropriate adjustments to their lifestyles.

Chaos is a friend of mine

People lead different lifestyles according to their situation. Some people might lead peaceful lives, while others lead lives that are considered more conventional. 'Chaos is a friend of mine' is a metaphor first used by English Rock Star artist Bob Dylan. Like a Rock Star, he leads a lifestyle that entailed many activities, and this metaphor sought to highlight this lifestyle. 'Chaos is a Friend of Mine' is a metaphor that refers to a person leading such a lifestyle those others might see as confusing and not in line with the lives of ordinary folks.

- **Love metaphors**

Love is considered a special kind of emotion that can evoke strong emotions in many people. Some of these emotions might be positive emotions such as happiness, joy, and contentment. On the other hand, love can also result in negative emotions on the lovebirds, with some of the negative emotions being sorrow, sadness, and heartbreak. For these reasons, thousands and thousands of metaphors are specifically meant to address the issue of love and how it affects many people's lives. Love metaphors serve to bring out the different perspectives associated with this emotion.

When it comes to love metaphors, most of these metaphors relate to the romantic kind of love. Romantic love is considered a key area of interest because it is the kind of love that elicits the strongest response and emotions on the parties involved. Furthermore, romantic love is considered a mixed bag in terms of experiences. This is because many people have had an experience that is deemed positive concerning romantic love. Equally, many people have experienced negative emotions occasioned by this kind of love.

Love is fire

'Love is a fire' is a good example of a love metaphor that seeks to describe the emotion associated with being in love adequately. A deeply in love person is likely to experience intense feelings and emotions, and it is this intensity that has seen love being compared with fire.

Love is journey

'Love is a journey' is also another love metaphor whose usage seeks to enhance an understanding of the overall experience associated with love. A journey is an event that takes a considerable amount of time to accomplish. Furthermore, a journey might involve different stages from the start to the end. In comparison, true love is seen as something that does not develop spontaneously; instead, it involves different stages at different points in the lives of those involved. Being in love also entails going through a myriad of experiences, and it is such experiences that make up the entire journey that is love.

Love is a garden

'Love is a garden' is another love metaphor that seeks to capture the essence of strong emotion. In a practical sense, issues to do with love are complicated and accorded the attention they deserve. This is the reason why love is compared to a garden. A garden must be tended to for the flowers in it to flourish. Equally, a relationship between two people in love should entail; both parties taking their time and attending to the needs of the other person for their relationship to succeed. This is indeed the reason why love is compared to a garden since, for it to flourish, it must be attended to.

Love is a flower

Love is a flower is deemed to be a pessimistic outlook concerning the strong emotion that is love. This is because a flower is often considered a very delicate plant that flourishes and becomes beautiful over a short period but then dies off soon afterward. Equally, they are those people who think that love and romantic love, for that matter, is an emotion that is strongly experienced during the initial stages of a relationship but fades soon afterward.

Love is a battlefield

The final love metaphor of love is 'love is a battlefield.' 'Love is a battlefield' is an equally pessimistic metaphor for its perspective on love's strong emotion. In this context, love is being compared to a place, scenario, or situation inherently uncomfortable. A battlefield is where people are fighting or engaging in one form of conflict or the other. The metaphor, therefore, sees love as something that can bring many conflicts in the lives of those involved. The role of the parties to the relationship is to address such conflicts hence the comparison to a battlefield constantly.

- **Unpopular metaphors**

Some metaphors are considered unpopular concerning their usage. Such metaphors are unpopular because they might offend someone of a specific category of people. For instance, some of these linguistic tools might have racist connotations, while others are designed to offend the specific individual they refer to. The usage of unpopular metaphors might be very controversial, and for this reason, they are not generally preferred.

Black or grey metaphors versus white or light metaphors

Racism is one of today's most contentious issues. Racism refers to the practice of undermining other people based on their racial heritage. Most often, their light-skinned counterparts have discriminated against dark skin people. For instance, African Americans were brought into the United States as slaves to work in white-owned farms and estates. Furthermore, colored-skinned people such as Mexicans continue to be discriminated against in predominantly white societies, which is a good example of present-day racism. A racist mindset advocates that their race is somehow superior compared to other people's races.

The issue of racism is also quite evident when it comes to metaphors and their usage. This is especially true when it comes to black metaphors vs. white metaphors. In general, black metaphors are used to depict something bad and negative in society. On the contrary, while metaphors are meant to depict something good or accepted in society.

The black sheep of the family

The black sheep of the family is another metaphor with negative connotations. Ideally, this metaphor refers to someone or who is uniquely different from the rest. In the real-life scenario, being different can relate to both the positive and negative sense. However, referring to someone as the 'black sheep of the family' is mainly meant to portray them negatively. This, therefore, implies that a person who is referred to in such a manner is not good in terms of their character.

Similarly, such a person might have deficiencies that make them naturally unattractive to others hence the connotation 'black sheep'. Therefore, the 'black sheep of the family' is a metaphor that should not be regularly used unless in unique situations that call for such reference.

Black market

A 'black market' is also another metaphor that might have racist connotations. This metaphor refers to a marketplace that is unsanctioned. In many cases, the black market is described as a market where illegal and contraband goods are traded. Sometimes, the 'black market' is where people go for hard drugs such as cocaine and heroin. The racist association can be underscored by the fact that 'blacks' is also a term that is generally used to refer to African American people.

Gray area

'Gray area' refers to an area that presents an element of confusion regarding ordinary usage. A gray area is not meant to be a good thing since people like to understand the issue they are addressing. As a color, gray is the darker shade that is quite close to black. Some might perceive the metaphor gray area as a metaphor that uses color to depict an unwanted and unfavorable situation that one might find themselves in.

Light at the end of the tunnel

On the contrary, white or bright metaphors most often than are used to depict something positive. One such metaphor is 'light at the end of the tunnel.' This metaphor represents some degree of hope when it comes to its normal usage. When someone says that there is 'light at the end of the tunnel,' they expect that something positive will happen, notwithstanding the difficult situation they might be facing.

White elephant

A white elephant is also another color-related metaphor that might be interpreted as racist. However, this metaphor is quite different from the examples mentioned above since it uses white instead of black. This implies that 'white' people might also have some sensitivities regarding metaphor usage since a 'white elephant' depicts an undertaking that is negative and has no benefit to the society.

- **Dead metaphors**

Dead metaphors also generally fall under the category of unpopular metaphors. Precisely, these are metaphors that might not have a semantic rendition within the context of the present-day world since their usage is considered outdated.

Raining cats and dogs

When it comes to metaphors, one can also refer to a special category of metaphors referred to as dead metaphors. As the name suggests, this is a group of metaphors that are no longer effective in their capacity to relate to a context that they were originally meant to relate to. The existence of dead metaphors implies that metaphors relate to everyday life and experiences as a figure of speech. They can only be effective if they are relatable within the context of the people using them. Some examples considered dead metaphors include 'raining cats and dogs' and 'a heart of gold.' Furthermore, when metaphors have not been in use for so long, they might end up falling under the category of dead metaphors.

To kick the bucket

To kick the bucket is another dead metaphor that means to die. Several other metaphors are generally preferred when it comes to death, such as 'pass on' to 'meet one's demise.' Such a metaphor is not preferred because many people might not understand the connection between kicking a bucket and death, thus rendering the expression unpopular.

Conclusion

To sum it all up, metaphors can be described as figures of speech or linguistic tools that entail one object used to refer to another one or an activity. There are various reasons why metaphors are considered essential linguistic tools. They serve to create empathy on the part of the listener. A metaphor can make you relate to the situation that is being described. These linguistic tools also play a key role in enhancing understanding of the issue that is being described. Metaphors also make it easy to capture human emotion since it might be very difficult to so suing ordinary words, but unique expressions such as 'being on cloud nine' can help you get the job done.

Several metaphors are used in various expressions and communication. Some of the metaphors can be described as popular metaphors since they are mostly preferred over others. Popular metaphors are easily relatable since they can easily be applied in contemporary life scenarios. Some popular metaphors include: To be a shining star, be a high flyer, and be in another person's shoe. Some popular metaphors have been used for hundreds of years but are still considered relevant in the present-day scenario.

Furthermore, love metaphors such as 'love is a fire' are also quite popular.

Similarly, some metaphors are considered unpopular such as the black sheep of the family, black market, and white elephant. Such metaphors can be deemed to have racist connotations hence their unpopularity. Finally, dead metaphors that have lost their semantic connotation also fall under the category of unpopular metaphors. A good example of a dead metaphor is the expression of raining cats and dogs.

Part 3:
Enriching Your Vocabulary Effectively

Chapter 58:
Verbal Dexterity

A language is a robust tool that provides us with a plethora of incredible possibilities. When utilized correctly, it may take your discussion anywhere you want it to go, make a lasting impact, and influence the choices of your interlocutors.

I want to tell you about Robert Diltsa's invention, dubbed "sleight of mouth." He chose to look at Richard Bandler's (the founder of NLP – Neuro-Linguistic Programming) most common communication patterns. He took the ones he thought were the most successful and tweaked them to create his method. Now, therapists and trainers all around the globe utilize "The Sleight of Mouth" mainly as an effective tool for altering beliefs in a discussion.

To cut a long tale short, it's a collection of fourteen linguistic patterns that may be used in almost every discussion. These patterns are distinct from one another, and it is up to you to determine which one would work best in a given scenario.

Each pattern, in its way, aids in broadening a person's viewpoint and horizons and assisting them in seeing additional possibilities. With a bit of experience, you can quickly alter your interlocutors' minds.

It allows you to assist those who are stuck in their narrow view of the world. You'll be able to convince others that, in addition to their restricted viewpoint, there are other, superior choices after you've learned to utilize these patterns.

I've included all of the patterns as I understand with some alterations, with the example of three beliefs, to make it easier for you to comprehend. You'll be able to sympathize with the situations when these methods are most effective.

Here are three harmful ideas that will be debunked by using the patterns:

a. It is difficult to learn languages.

   b. NLP is not appropriate for our company.

   c. It is hard to make new friends.

1. **Hierarchy of Values**

Connect a belief with some greater value.

   a. Consider the independence and variety of new opportunities that learning a second language may provide!

   b. Let's look at how NLP can help you thrive in business and in your specialty.

   c. A little effort put into meeting new people will give you a lot of happiness and joy.

2. **Intention**

Change your belief's motive to one of positivity.

   a. That may also mean that learning new languages is very important and it is worthwhile to gain it.

   b. As a consequence, it is an excellent moment for our company to explore new growth opportunities.

   c. It seems like this is a fantastic chance to push yourself while meeting some fascinating and entertaining individuals.

3. **Redefinition of Meaning**

Using new words change the meaning of the belief, resulting in a different response.

   a. The fact that someone studied Spanish for a long period and got poor results does not imply that everyone needs the same amount of time and effort.

    b. It's not that NLP doesn't agree with our company's style or direction. It's simply that NLP has to be applied properly and intelligently in order to provide substantial results.

    c. It's not about how difficult or simple it is to meet new individuals. It is simply worthwhile to invest a little time and effort in order for the connections we form to be both satisfying and long-lasting.

4. **Consequences**

Demonstrate a negative outcome that will debunk a belief.

    a. Will it be simpler for you never to leave your country or to go about with a dictionary in your hand, continuously mispronouncing words, butchering the language, and strengthening foreign prejudices about our country?

    b. This strategy will prevent workers from achieving fast and effective growth… and, as a result, improved productivity and innovation are reduced.

    c. The more difficult it is, the more valuable it is to acquire this skill… Otherwise, you may spend the rest of your life alone.

5. **Chunk Down**

The ascent to a higher degree of detail. Find one aspect of your belief that you can use to disprove it.

    a. The fact that someone else has difficulty with different pronunciations does not imply you will as well.

    b. I am convinced that the techniques of establishing good contact with clients can be very useful and profitable for us.

    c. Which aspect of meeting new people is the most difficult for you?

6. **Chunk Up**

Getting on a more general level. Generalize a belief so that you can see it from a different perspective.

   a. Learning a new language takes time, but once you've mastered it, you'll be able to communicate in it indefinitely.

   b. Do you mean to imply that efficient customer communication isn't suitable for our company?

   c. Remember that our lives have real significance and depth when we have meaningful connections with others.

7. **Counterexample**

Find a specific case that will disprove a notion.

   a. Learning Spanish was very simple and enjoyable for me.

   b. I'm familiar with this business, which has a comparable profile to ours. They've been utilizing NLP for years and have had a lot of success with it.

   c. Do you remember how you met John? It was natural for you, and you understood each other very well from the very beginning!

8. **Analogy**

To disprove a belief, use an analogy or metaphor.

   a. Everything is tough, according to a buddy of mine. He has yet to do anything in his life.

   b. I used to believe that running my own company was unsuitable for me. Now I'm the CEO of a thriving business.

   c. Building an anthill, like ants, takes a lot of effort. Nonetheless, it is the purpose of their existence, and it is how this species has endured for hundreds of millions of years on our planet!

9. A Reference to Oneself

Refer to the most significant aspect of a belief and place blame on the individual who holds it.

    a. ...and it's difficult for me to accept another explanation like the one you're offering.

    b. I use NLP daily... does it mean that I'm inadequate for our company?

    c. It's me who it's hard for when I have to beat that nonsense out of your head for another time.

10. A Different Result

Find another result of having that belief.

    a. If you rely on others all of the time or behave like a traditional stupid tourist when traveling, your life will be difficult.

    b. It is unacceptable to put our business in jeopardy by using antiquated methods that seldom succeed.

    c. When you have no one to turn to, your life will be difficult.

11. Change of Frame

Place a belief in a new setting to evaluate it.

    a. There wouldn't be many individuals who could speak five or six languages fluently if language acquisition was so difficult. All language schools would go out of business, and individuals would be less likely to travel alone.

    b. From a five-year perspective, we should consider how utilizing NLP methods in our business may alter our path and increase our sales.

    c. Everyone would be lonely if what you stated was true, and humanity would have died out long ago.

12. Meta Frame

Formulate a belief about a belief.

> a. So you must be quite knowledgeable about the learning process of many various languages across the world?
>
> b. Could it be that NLP isn't right for you since no one has shown you how to utilize it effectively?
>
> c. So I'm assuming you've previously attempted to meet everyone on the planet?

13. Model of the World

Consider a belief from a new viewpoint, as if it were a distinct model of the universe.

> a. You're probably just saying this to explain why you haven't attempted to study a foreign language.
>
> b. NLP is said to be one of the greatest things that has ever occurred to many renowned and successful individuals.
>
> c. The fact that this is such a large task adds to the excitement and allure.

14. Strategies of Reality

Make your interlocutor aware that a single belief may mean many various things, depending on the point of view.

> a. What exactly do you mean by "hard"?
>
> b. What precisely were you trying to convey when you said: "NLP is not appropriate"?
>
> c. What does "hard" mean to you?

When you've mastered each pattern, you may start using it whenever you speak with someone. The essential thing is to listen carefully to what the other person has to say. Listen attentively to what they have to say, and employ suitable language patterns based on the circumstances. In some instances, some of these patterns and examples may be too arrogant, while others may be too weak to penetrate through someone's mind-shell. To alter someone's mind, you'd have to be delicate at times (for example, while speaking with a teacher or professor), and at other times you'd have to unleash the heaviest artillery (I sometimes had to use several patterns to succeed in explaining something to someone finally). Because each scenario is different and needs consideration of numerous variables, it's up to you to decide which of these patterns to use. You should pay particular attention to concealed beliefs in verbal signals that suggest someone is incapable of doing anything, that something is challenging or too difficult, that something is impossible, and so on.

To be able to utilize these patterns more effortlessly, it would be ideal if you practiced a lot. As a result, it's recommended to choose just two designs each day to practice. It would be best if you had significantly increased your ability to detect the context after some time. That's when it'll become second nature to fit a pattern into a circumstance. Your intuition will provide you with appropriate topics to discuss. These patterns may be utilized in various situations, including negotiations, discussions with clients, conversations with partners, dispelling concerns in others, inspiring loved ones, and assisting others in solving issues. There are as many applications as there are subjects to discuss.

Choose one or two patterns to practice each day. Take note of what occurs when you apply each of these patterns to a specific situation.

Another four beliefs are shown below, each of which may be broken down using linguistic dexterity. Attempt to solve these on your own:

- I can't start my own company because it's too dangerous.
- Relationships usually end in suffering.
- Long walks are boring.
- Only lucky people succeed in life.

Start now!

Chapter 59:
Stop Counting Vocabulary Words

To become proficient in a language, how many words do you need to know? Some experts would argue that this isn't the proper question to ask, but it's one worth considering.

Many language learners think that after they have learned a large number of words, they may consider themselves proficient. This was a concept that I was fascinated with when I first started studying languages. If only I had a list of the 500 most often used terms... the top 2,500 most often used terms.... the top 5,000... Isn't it true that I'd be fluent?

If only it were that simple. Counting words is not an effective way to evaluate fluency. There are several reasons for this.

- Language specialists differ on how to assess vocabulary size; therefore, it's difficult to come up with a precise quantity of words that shows fluency.

- Not all words are created equal when it comes to learning a language. Some words are more essential than others to learn, and the order in which we learn them matters.

We'll look at the best method to learn a new language and track our progress in this part. We'll also look at various ways to assess the competence and connection between learning specific words and learning a new language as a whole.

So, how many words do you need to know in order to converse in a language properly? Not only do experts differ, but they also argue on what defines a term and what it means to know a word.

We need to unpack this question and scrutinize its parts to understand it better.

What is a word?

You may think that when people speak about a term, they all mean the same thing, but this isn't the case.

Experts in the field of language have different predictions on the number of words individuals have in their vocabulary. According to one expert, a natural English-speaking high school graduate should know at least 35,000 words. According to another expert, the typical native English speaker has a vocabulary of 10,000 words.

It isn't logical that individuals with higher levels of education have fewer vocabularies than those with lower levels of education. What is the source of this discrepancy?

The differences in the statistics are due to how specialists assess what they're assessing. They're each measuring something different. They don't agree on the definitions of "word" and "know," so it's not surprising that their responses are so disparate.

Some scholars consider each variation of a word to be a distinct word. They count each version of the verb "to see" individually, for example. Under this measure, "to see," "see," "sees," "seeing," "saw," and "seen" would all be considered six distinct words. The same reasoning is used to nouns, with "cat" and "cats" being counted as two distinct words by these experts.

Other experts count the core term, not the many variants. As a consequence, they arrive at considerably smaller figures. Because they are all versions of "to see," these experts consider "to see," "see," "sees," "seeing," "saw," and "seen" as a single word. They also regard "cat" and "cats" to be the same word since they are both forms of the same root noun.

People learning a root word, such as "to see" or "cat," they believe, are learning a new word for the first time. When the same individuals acquire various versions of the root word, such as "sight" or "cats," it should be regarded as an increase in their grammatical knowledge rather than a vocabulary expansion.

After all, this is how humans learn languages, according to these experts. We begin by learning one form of a word. Then, when we get a better understanding of the language structure, we extend the word's usage to new contexts by using its many forms.

Experts who count all forms of a word will come up with a significantly larger word count than experts who count the root forms when assessing the number of words in people's vocabularies. Even though both sets of specialists are studying the same language and the same groups of individuals, this is the case.

What does it mean to "know" a word?

Experts also differ on when a person is able to recognize a word.

There is a difference between active and passive vocabulary for those who learn languages. Some individuals feel that they only know a word if it is in their active vocabulary, while others believe they know all the terms in their active and passive vocabularies together.

If you can recall a term quickly and use it without hesitation in your thoughts, speech, or writing, it is in your active vocabulary. When you hear or see a passive vocabulary term, you may identify it and comprehend it to a degree. Even yet, you have trouble remembering the term and are hesitant to use it in conversation. The amount of words in native and non-native speakers' passive vocabularies is typically many times more than the number of words in their active vocabularies.

After seeing or hearing a new word a few times, most people integrate it into their passive vocabulary. The term becomes part of their active vocabulary when they encounter it more often and have a greater understanding of its context and many meanings. (Moving terms from your passive to active vocabulary is one of the most effective methods to increase your language understanding.)

So you see the problem: in assessing how many words a native speaker knows, do you count their active or passive vocabulary?

Using vocabulary ranges instead of word counts

We can return to our initial question about how many words you need to know to be deemed proficient now that we understand why language specialists produce such disparities in word counts. For the sake of this debate, we'll consider just root words (not their many variants) and only the terms in people's active vocabularies.

This is the method used by the Common European Framework of Reference for Languages (CEFR). The CEFR is the current standard for describing language learners' achievements in Europe and, increasingly, other countries. The Council of Europe put it together between 1989 and 1996 as the cornerstone of a "Language Learning for European Citizenship" program. Its primary goal is to offer a learning, teaching, and assessment technique to all European languages. The six reference levels (see below) quickly become the de facto norm for assessing a person's linguistic ability.

We may divide individuals into six categories or levels depending on their language competence using this assessment technique.

You may think to yourself, "Well, I'd want to strive for level A2 before my vacation to Spain next year," after looking at these ranges. That's fantastic; you've defined your objective. But what's next?

Expanding Your Vocabulary

Another part of inclusive communication is to expand your vocabulary. This gives you a favorable stand in different social settings and situations as you have an arsenal of vocabulary at your disposal. It is a societal belief that those with a high vocabulary arsenal have more intelligence and can use them more correctly in different communication variants.

Your understanding and appreciation of complex words and phrases place you at a high personal and professional advantage.

How to Study Vocabulary

How do you decide which method is the most effective for learning the vocabulary terms you'll need to accomplish your objectives? Here's what I'd suggest.

Step 1: Decide what kind of vocabulary you want to learn

If you lived in an ideal world where you could wave a magic wand and have whatever learning materials you wanted were given to you immediately, you'd begin by choosing what sort of language you wanted to acquire. This may seem to be a little issue, but it is really very complicated.

- Are you going to a trade fair for industrials in Germany? You might want to pick up very highly specialized, technical vocabulary to understand the gist of what people are discussing.

- Maybe you work at a hospital with a large Russian-speaking community in Brooklyn, New York. For major medical issues, it may be beneficial to have a rudimentary understanding of anatomy and terminology.

- Or maybe you're an accountant who works in a large Spanish-speaking community in Los Angeles. Your focus might be on vocabulary that deals with math, numbers, and tax issues.

These are, of course, specific use situations. It's more usual for language learners to desire to acquire general-use vocabulary, so suppose you're a general-interest language student in the examples above.

Step 2: Get a vocabulary list

Even if you're a language student with a broad range of interests, there are a variety of vocabulary lists from which to select.

Lists of sight words. You might begin with something called sight words, for example. These are simple phrases that are often directed towards toddlers. The majority of these terms are exclusive to a certain subject. Words like mother, father, dog, cat, tall, short, eat, cry, play, and sleep are common sight words.

These are pretty simple terms, as you can see, but they are just as important to an adult language student as they are to a native-speaking kid. Sight-word vocabulary lists may vary from 50 to 250 terms, depending on the type and source. While sight-word lists for English are extremely popular, they are not necessarily simple to come by for other languages. With a little Internet searching, you can usually discover free word lists.

Lists of travel words. Alternatively, you might learn some popular travel terms. These lists are readily available in a variety of travel publications and include a considerably wider range of terminology. More abstract words, such as "justice" or "political system," get more attention. These are words that are difficult to express visually. Travel-word lists are usually considerably broader in scope, even if it means they include terms that aren't very common.

A travel-word list could contain terms like lobster, muscles, clam, and tartar sauce in the cuisine area. While I'm sure you recognize these terms in English, none of them are likely to be used as often as the word "breakfast." Most of these terms may be replaced with "seafood."

Many trip books include travel-word lists, but phrasebooks are less likely to include them all in a list format. The majority of the time, they are dispersed throughout the text, making it difficult to locate them.

Lists of words that occur often. Finally, you can use word-frequency lists to your benefit. Lists like this are rather simple to come by for languages with a large number of native speakers but virtually non-existent for languages with fewer native speakers. The reason for this is simple: compiling such a list is complex and time-consuming.

Researchers, for example, compile English word-frequency lists every few decades. They collect a huge sample of text from different topics in print, film, and audio, then data-mine the words and rank them in frequency.

Other languages go through the same process, but it takes a lot of material from various sources and a lot of people to mine it. As a result, listings like this are less frequent for lesser-known languages. Simply said, there is less material and less personnel available to complete the job.

Numerous publishers sell word-frequency lists in book form, and several open-source lists are freely accessible on the internet. If you take this path, I recommend making use of a free list.

Many languages include at least 5,000 of the most frequent terms, with most lists ranging from 1,000 to 10,000 words. The reason I recommend using a free list is simple: if you're an academic statistician, you may need to know if "mom" or "dad" is used more often. You may also ask whether the less formal "mom" is more or less prevalent than the more formal "mother."

If you're learning a language, though, none of this matters as long as you have these terms on your list. Furthermore, those phrases are so frequently used that I can almost guarantee they will appear on whatever list you create.

The list I'm looking for doesn't exist. I've always been amazed by how little work is put into creating a useful-word list. Let me give you an example. "The" is at the top of every English word-frequency list I've ever seen, at position #1 or #2. The next item is "a," which, depending on the list, alternates with "the" for the top position.

While the terms "a" and "the" are often used, they are not very useful. Except for definite and indefinite articles, you could learn anything in English and be completely understood by native speakers. (You'll understand what I mean if you've ever talked to native speakers of Slavic languages like Russian, which lack articles.) Consider a scene from a famous espionage film: "I explode the explosives immediately, Mr. Bond!" Is Mr. Bond perplexed by the absence of a "the" before "bomb"? (Not.)

But I digress. Let's get back to how to learn your vocabulary.

Step 3: Begin to study – with some caveats

It's time to dive in — with some cautions – after you've chosen your word list.

Variety is the spice of life. You'll want to make sure your word list covers various parts of speech, including nouns, pronouns, adjectives, verbs, adverbs, and the like. This is important so you can start to build basic sentences as you expand your vocabulary.

If you spend the first few hours, days, weeks, or months trying to memorize the body parts, how would you tell someone that a part of the body was in pain? If you focused exclusively on foods, how would you tell someone you were hungry or that a particular food was tasty or bland?

Similarity may also be sour. While you're about it, try if you can find out whether the language you're studying has any cognates in English. What exactly are cognates? These are terms that are shared by two languages. They're sometimes spelled the same way. They're sometimes pronounced the same way. It's uncommon, however, for them to be spelled and spoken the same way. Words like "Internet," "coffee," and "metro" are cognates that may be found in many contemporary languages.

Simultaneously, you should be wary of "false friends." These are words that have similar spellings or pronunciations in various languages but have completely distinct meanings.

A few examples of false friends include the following:

- Spanish: actual -> "current" in English
- French: bras -> "arm" in English
- Italian: morbido -> "soft" in English
- German: winken -> "to wave" in English

It's all about the technique. You may be tempted to study vocabulary by reading words aloud, writing them down, labeling a lot of objects in your house with Post-it notes, or creating flashcard decks, either physically or digitally. None of these methods are inherently harmful, but do you understand the distinction between learning and studying? While both are valuable, studying is not the same as learning. This is all too familiar to anybody who has ever prepared for a test, only to flunk the final exam.

So, although some of these techniques may and should be tried, you should also strive to better your vocabulary by studying the terms in context. This necessitates the use of simple words and sentences.

How to learn words in context

One of the most common ways effective language learners employ to develop large vocabularies rapidly is learning words in phrases and sentences.

Sentence mining, often known as the "10,000-sentence technique," is another real-world use of this method. Followers of this technique simply expose themselves to 10,000 phrases in their target language that have been translated from English. There is no intentional effort to remember; rather, understanding is the goal. The notion is that if a language learner is exposed to a big enough number of sentences, they will acquire a substantial vocabulary and intuitive understanding of the syntax of the language.

Guided Immersion

Each of these methods, in my opinion, is great and just a variation on the others. This concept is continued in my technique, Guided Immersion, which I discuss in a later part. I'll skip the specifics for now, but here's a quick rundown of how my approach works.

Compared to 10,000 sentences, Guided Immersion utilizes a considerably smaller data set. And based on my language learning results and those of my students, Guided Immersion can "do more with less."

Language learners exposed to a smaller volume of content end up with greater command of their target language in less time.

How do I do this?

1. Teaching 1,500 of the most useful phrases and high-frequency words, presented in a low-stress environment, with spaced repetitions and built-in reviews.
2. By making every phrase short, easy to remember, and interchangeable with every other phrase.
3. By embedding more than 1,000 of the most common words (which account for over 80 percent of spoken language) into these phrases. This approach is at the core of my method.

I don't want to come out as though my approach is "the greatest." I think it's really cool, but like I've stated before, what works for one person may not work for someone else. Every language student, in my opinion, should have access to a variety of resources.

To return to the original subject, you may study your vocabulary using any technique that you choose. For many language learners, there is a time and place for active, intentional study. However, any version of Krashen's Input Hypothesis will work if you wish to acquire new language to use in daily conversation, as long as:

- You have a fairly decent collection of words, statements, phrases, or even short tales that are accessible in your target language and that you can comprehend in English (or your native language).
- You have a fair number of materials and devote a reasonable amount of time to examining them.

Take a broad approach... and have fun

One last thing to mention. Many (struggling) language learners, in my experience, concentrate almost entirely on language studies.

I don't think this is a very effective approach. It's not enjoyable – which means you'll eventually burn out – and it's not very effective since this just isn't how human beings learn languages. It's OK to use a textbook. I'd argue it might be better to read short stories. It's absolutely fine to play video games, listen to the radio, work with a tutor, or watch YouTube videos. You'll just remember that you'll be far more successful by exposing yourself to a broad range of inputs and enjoying them than you'll be by focusing intensely on a narrower range of content and trying to memorize it.

Don't focus on memorizing definitions

Many individuals start learning a language by memorizing high-frequency terms and their meanings. Adherents typically concentrate on the first 500–1,000 vocabulary terms in their chosen language.

There's nothing wrong with it; I've used it with a few of the languages I've self-taught. However, if this is a method you're contemplating, think about where you obtain your vocabulary lists and how they were produced before proceeding. Return to our discussion of "what is a word" and think about how you learn definitions.

You don't have to remember all of the definitions of the terms you're learning. Because some popular terms have many different meanings, this would take a long time.

(The term "murder" in English, for example, usually implies "to kill.") It's a term that often appears in news reports. "A swarm of crows" is another definition. This alternative term is unfamiliar even to native speakers, much alone language learners.)

Instead, learning just a handful of the most frequent definitions — the ones you're likely to use in everyday discussions – is much more effective. Then, as you get more experienced, you'll automatically pick up more when you hear the phrases in various situations. As a result of repeated exposure to the language, you will absorb the language and learn it naturally.

You'll be able to pick up the language much more quickly if you concentrate on studying the most frequently used terms (and their most commonly used meanings) rather than trying to learn everything at once.

How to Build Up Your Vocabulary?

Here are tested and trusted tips to help you build up your vocabulary.

1. **Learn and use a new word each day** – Grab a dictionary in the morning, look up a new word, learn it, learn how it is used, and use it for that day. Find a context in which you can use it and try to fit it into a conversation. If it seems to be a wrong fit for conversations, try telling someone about the word you have just learned and tell them all about it.

2. **Expand your vocabulary through online games and gaming apps** – Different apps and games online can help you expand your vocabulary. Find one that you are comfortable with and start playing. Not only will you improve your vocabulary, but you will also be helping someone in need, especially if it is an app that donates to those in need every time you get an answer correctly.

3. **Be enthusiastic with words** – Enthusiasm is a great build-up for passion. When you become enthusiastic about learning, your passion swells and builds as well. Learn a word, break it down, get a deeper meaning of the word, formulate new words with it, and construct it into sentences. Think of words as a Rubik's cube that brings about different unique combinations when turned in different ways. Learn the structure and the roots and attach different stems to it to form new combinations of words.

4. **Read extensively** – Restricting yourself to just one genre or topic will narrow your thinking. Your mind is meant for the world, don't limit it. Explore new topics, read complex magazines or articles, read high-level subjects and topics, read challenging topics and challenge your brain. It improves your vocabulary and aids you on the journey to become a well-rounded individual and an effective communicator— one that is capable of having and handling a conversation with anyone.

5. **Learn to ask** – If there's no one you can ask of the meaning of a word, then pick up your dictionary and look it up. When in a conversation with someone and you feel like you don't understand the word the person just said, feel free to ask the person for the meaning or mark the word down and check the dictionary if you are too shy to ask.

How to Expand Your Vocabulary?

If you can show a wide vocabulary in social settings, you will be regarded more positively. When a person understands the meaning of many words and can use them properly in regular speech, most people presume greater levels of education and intellect.

Those who can decipher and appreciate complicated words and phrases have a distinct edge in their personal and professional lives. Today, you'll discover why having a large vocabulary is beneficial, as well as how to expand your dictionary.

Why does your vocabulary make a difference?

There is a connection between vocabulary and job performance. According to a study conducted by linguistics and education expert Johnson O'Conner, individuals who score well on vocabulary exams are more likely to acquire high-level jobs in the workplace.

When gender, age, and degree of education are taken into account, the conclusion remains the same. Even more intriguing, proficiency on a vocabulary exam predicts success – and this isn't simply a result of working in high positions or interacting with educated people.

So, what exactly is going on? In a word, having a large vocabulary is the greatest basis for communication, and communication is the first step toward success. You'll be in a better position to convey precisely the correct message if you have more words at your disposal.

The more vocabulary you have, the better you will express complex concepts and comprehend new lines of thinking and reasoning.

Someone with a large vocabulary may adapt their oral and written communication to various audiences, allowing them to cultivate fruitful connections with others.

A large vocabulary also lets you absorb knowledge from various sources, giving you the tools you need to enhance your personal and professional abilities. Suppose you can read and understand high-level textbooks, for example. In that case, you are more likely to profit from advanced education and training than someone who can just identify ordinary daily terms.

Because you won't have to stop to clarify a term if you're acquainted with complicated words, your reading speed will increase. Isn't it self-evident?

Here are a few tactics that can assist you:

1. **Use a new word every day**: There are hundreds of free apps and games available to help users learn new words. It's a simple multiple-choice game in which you'll have to put your vocabulary to the test. The more questions you answer correctly, the more difficult they get!

2. **Extend your vocabulary by using apps and online games**: Hundreds of free applications and games exist to assist users in learning new words. It's a straightforward multiple-choice game that puts your vocabulary to the test. The more questions you correctly answer, the tougher they get!

3. **Become a word enthusiast**: Learning words in isolation may help you increase your vocabulary, but understanding a word's structure and roots can help you understand new concepts in the future.

Break a term down into its component pieces when you first learn it.

Anything "associated to or caused by an upright posture" is referred to as "orthostatic." If you dissect the term, you'll see that it's a combination of the words "ortho" (which means "straight") and "static," which means "concern with bodies at rest." Prefixes and suffixes have meanings that may help you understand new words.

4. **Read widely**: This is a tried-and-true piece of advice for anybody who wishes to come off as knowledgeable and well-informed. Don't just read the same books and periodicals you always do. Explore new subjects and read denser, more difficult material to keep oneself challenged.

Every day, set aside at least 15 minutes for reading. There is, in my view, no reason not to read – it will not only help you expand your vocabulary, but it will also help you become a well-rounded person capable of interacting with almost anybody.

5. **If you don't know what a term means, ask someone who does.** When someone uses a term you don't know, it's natural to feel ashamed, but it's also a great chance to learn something new.

If someone attempts to make you feel bad about yourself because you don't know what a term means, that's their issue. If you can't inquire right away, at the very least, write down the term and check it up later in your dictionary.

Wrapping up

You don't need to know a specific number of words to become competent in a new language. When counting words, linguists employ a variety of methods, and when evaluating what it means to know a word, they use a variety of criteria.

It is more useful to group people by their language proficiency according to a rough estimate of the number of words they know, such as the CERF ranges.

In my opinion:

- Beginners are those who know between 250 and 500 words.
- Those who know 1,000 to 3,000 words can have a conversation in daily situations.

- People who know 4,000 to 10,000 words are considered advanced language users.
- Knowing over 10,000 words qualifies them as fluent or native speakers.

When it comes to learning a language, not all words are created equal. Learning some kinds of words can help you advance more rapidly than learning others. Focus on the most frequent terms before studying more specialized vocabularies to be most successful in learning a language. Also, instead of memorizing every term, study the most frequent ones first.

You'll have the most success if you start by studying what you can put to use straight away. Instead, attempting to study a dictionary from cover to cover, understanding every term and meaning in the language, would be inefficient at best and wasteful at worst. (I know this because I attempted – and failed – to utilize this technique.) It's tedious and ineffective.)

You may begin naturally absorbing the language by learning the most frequent terms and meanings. You'll be able to infer new words and meanings from context and other pertinent signals as you hear and read more words in the language. This is comparable to how you acquired your first language when you were younger. You will become more proficient in your new language the more you expose yourself to it.

To become proficient, you don't need to keep track of how many words you learn. Instead, spend your time and energy where they will have the most impact. Focus on the most frequently used terms to speed up your language learning and allow your natural language-learning abilities to take control.

Combining targeted studying and assimilating language by experience is the most powerful and efficient way to master a new language.

Chapter 60:
How to Master Grammar?

Do you dread studying grammar as you learn a new language? If that's the case, I've got some good news for you: it's not critical. It has the potential to slow you down or perhaps throw you off track.

Here's the truth: You don't need to study grammar to learn to speak a foreign language.

Language teachers (and students) all over the globe are baffled by this phenomenon.

Grammar is just a fancy term for the rules that govern a language. While this is the most basic definition, it is not entirely true.

In fact, grammar is a collection of observations made by academics while documenting a language. Native speakers of the language create such patterns, and their brains, like all human minds, seldom follow established patterns.

Resistance To Nature's Way

Many people are unwilling to accept this and fight vehemently against it. Among teachers, some don't believe anyone can learn a language without studying grammar first.

Reality disagrees. Education departments worldwide focus on grammar instruction, but students still fail to learn to speak languages fluently. In many cases, so many students struggle to speak languages at the most basic levels because they believe that learning grammar is the foundation to speaking a language proficiently.

You did not learn your native language via grammar study. While native speakers of a language usually communicate "according to grammatical norms," few of them are aware of such rules. And since there are so many exceptions, the rules don't always matter.

The French language is a good example. It is essential to study the numerous exceptions to each rule you learn in French. This implies that while learning a new language, you can't simply think about the rules; you also have to consider any exceptions.

Imagine that you are considering the rules and exceptions while discussing with a friend. Your buddy will be playing his third or fourth game on his phone by the time you examine all the ways you may build a statement.

After all, you didn't learn to speak your native language by studying grammar. You didn't learn grammar until you started school, and by then, you were already fluent in your mother tongue. You had no idea what a verb was or how to conjugate it, but you had a good understanding of verbs and how they were conjugated. By the time you were two or three years old, you were speaking full, grammatically perfect phrases.

How Children Learn Language

Many parents have personal experience with language learning. Their youngsters begin to talk incoherently at first. Second, they start saying just one word at a time, often repeating a word that has been spoken to them. They then construct two or three-word phrases. Then they create long, grammatically incorrect sentences. Finally, they improve their capacity to communicate in proper phrases.

Even if the kid has never read a grammar book, the procedure outlined above happens. It occurs as a result of her listening to the native speakers in the area. She also receives assistance from adults who correct her language when she makes errors - and youngsters make a lot of errors while learning a language.

Here's an example.

"Gimme dat one," the kid says.

"Do you want that one?" the parent asks.

"Yeah, that one," the kid replies.

Children learn languages by repeating sound patterns that they hear throughout the day. It begins with a single word, followed by identifying things in their environment and short, basic phrases. Children repeat the words they hear as they get older and how they sound to them. They ultimately master speech pronunciation after hearing the words hundreds of times.

To mimic the method that infants utilize to acquire their first languages, it is helpful to watch how they do it. After all, they seem to have no trouble learning languages. Adults should be able to acquire languages in the same way that children can.

I must admit that learning a second language is not the same as learning a first language, and some people think the two should not be compared. Adults may find it more challenging to learn a second language since their original language may interfere, but they also have many benefits.

For example, an adult who understands how to study already has an advantage during language training. However, studying has a role in every adult's language learning activities. However, studying grammatical rules first is not the best strategy.

Learn Grammar By Listening First

Acquiring a language is similar to learning any other skill in that it requires a combination of practice and study.

Take, for example, learning to play a musical instrument. If you learned to play an instrument the way educators taught grammatical concepts to children, you would study music theory without ever touching your instrument. That, however, would be absurd. Because you can only develop a skill via practice, theory and hands-on application go hand in hand while studying a musical instrument.

Unfortunately, this is seldom the case in most academic classrooms when it comes to language acquisition. Before diving into the fundamental phrases needed to participate in a language and benefit from native speakers, students are often taught formal grammar.

Language instruction can be done differently, and it requires us to apply a new technique. It will be essential for you to notice the grammatical expressions and the specific ways native speakers speak. Then it'll be up to you to take such phrases and integrate them into your language usage and writing. Although many individuals use it spontaneously and intuitively, few formal language programs encourage or promote it. This is why so many language learners struggle to acquire a new language.

Grammar only has a minor part in language learning. Completing lessons is a standard part of grammar education, although this does not always imply that the learner can speak or write the language correctly and clearly.

If you practice copying the words and phrases you hear from native speakers, you'll be able to speak and write a language fluently. It is not essential to learn grammar to do this. Grammar simply serves to clarify the rules that you are learning via listening.

For someone learning a new language, phrasebooks are very helpful. These books are a wonderful investment since they include instances of real-life conversation. Any resource that provides the reader or listener examples of spoken language is more superior to a grammar book for learning.

When I'm studying a language, I usually don't give grammar any thought. I pay attention to how native speakers construct their sentences and attempt to do the same with my own. You'll learn the grammar (and new vocabulary terms) in a far more pleasant way if you spend your time concentrating on one phrase at a time.

Chapter 61:
How to Practice Pronunciation?

When most people set out to learn a language, they intend to speak it- eventually. It astounds me that so few language schools devote so little time to real speaking. Their focus is on the written word, and I believe they do a disservice to those learning to speak their new language.

In this section, I'll lay out a few approaches you can take to improve your pronunciation and develop a greater comfort level in speaking your new language.

1. Separate writing and speaking

First of all, think about each foreign word in two ways: its spoken form and its written form. Keep them distinct. It's helpful to hear a new word and say it a few times before seeing it in print. Memorize spelling after pronunciation.

Imagine you're learning French. The French word for "fish" is *poisson*. Now, if you were to think about the lettering of this word just before you spoke it, you might get tripped up and say something that sounds like "poison." Then, having gotten confused once, you could form a mental block that causes you to keep messing it up. Thus, you may get a little flustered and tongue-tied each time you request seafood at a Parisian café.

On the other hand, if you learn how to spell "poisson" after you hear its two syllables, you'll be in better shape.

In addition, before speaking this word, you might try to hear the "pwa" and "ss" sounds in your head. If it helps, when you're a beginner, you could even picture the shapes your lips will form when you say the word. You'll pucker up for the first syllable and round your lips for the nasal vowel at the end.

2. Take one step at a time

Every language has some long words, and they can present challenges even to native speakers. But don't let those lingual behemoths scare you off.

To use a French example once more, the word compétitivité means "competitiveness." Naturally, what makes this word daunting is its six rapid-fire syllables, including two accented vowels.

However, on its own, each syllable is straightforward. Therefore, as you say this word, you'll want to play each syllable, one at a time, in your mind. And, as soon as you hear each syllable, you can repeat it out loud. Don't rush, but don't linger over any part of the word. With care and confidence, you'll get through the whole thing, and with practice, you'll be fine.

3. Immerse yourself

This is important.

When you frequently listen to people speaking another language, you can pick up all kinds of pronunciation tricks, sometimes on a subliminal level. Thus, as often as you can, rent movies or watch television shows in the language you're learning. With the Internet, you can view a variety of foreign programming right on your mobile device.

Indeed, your smartphone can be an incredible language teacher. Whenever you're driving, walking, waiting for a bus, waiting for your dentist, or doing countless other chores, you can be listening – with or without headphones – to a foreign language. Listen to books on tape. Subscribe to a podcast. Follow radio shows in a different tongue. The options are endless.

Through it all, pay close attention to the accents, the pauses, the syllables that are emphasized, and the rise and fall of the voice. There are all kinds of minute yet critical lessons you can discern on your own, and they all contribute to the uniqueness, musicality, and conversational nature of a given language.

Most worthwhile of all, talk to native speakers as much as you can. Maybe the folks who live next door speak German. If you're studying German, why not have them over for dinner? If you're working on your French, how about a long weekend in Montreal? You get the idea. At first, you may feel self-conscious, but many individuals are pleased that you'd want their help. Plus, most of those same people love to speak a second language they're fluent in.

Having an actual conversation forces you to think through your phrasing and helps you grasp colloquialisms, idioms, and snippets of body language that don't always translate well.

When it comes to languages, it's all too easy to get rusty. For that reason, try not to let a single day go by without some exposure to the new language you want to speak. Don't make excuses, and don't let up!

4. Be a stickler

Imagine you're working on a long algebra problem. You complete each step accurately, except that you forget to "carry the one" at some point. You get the answer wrong.

So it often is with languages. Mispronouncing one sound can throw off an entire sentence's meaning. Worst of all, you might even say something offensive without meaning to.

With that in mind, concentrate on every vowel and each consonant cluster. Once again, don't merely memorize the spelling and meanings of words. Strive to learn stressed and unstressed syllables and every other nuance of sound. Listen to your tapes and apps with your full attention. If it helps, close your eyes, relax your muscles, and soak in each sentence.

If you're taking a course, you might ask your teacher or professor for permission to record your lectures on your phone. That way, you can revisit them later on. As you repeatedly listen to the vocabulary words and sample sentences, you'll drive each detail into your memory banks. And, if you're having a little trouble, you might ask your teacher for extra help sessions or a tutor. With one-on-one instruction, you'll be able to address any pronunciation inaccuracies.

5. Learn in context

Here's a simple rule: saying entire words aloud is more productive than repeating a certain sound on its own.

Maybe the "é" in French throws you off. Instead of making that sound over and over again, try speaking different words that contain an é. After all, the é can have a slightly different ring depending on the word it's in. What's more, isolating a particular sound can cause you to distort or over-emphasize it. Repeating that one vowel excessively could result in you over-thinking every é you encounter, making your delivery a little stilted.

As a result, speaking an entire phrase or sentence is more useful than reciting a single word or a list of words. That's because every sentence has its rhythm and cadence, a distinct ebb and flow. Also, in some languages, certain words are said faster when they're together than they are separate.

6. Don't be afraid of your shadow

Shadowing is a valuable technique for practicing pronunciation. It goes a step or two beyond merely listening to instructions or programs in a foreign language.

First, find an audio sample of a person reading a short piece in a foreign language. It could be a news article, a story, or something else. Or you might settle on a page of text from a language learning app. This material shouldn't be too easy or too advanced for you. You should be able to understand nearly all of the words of the text. At the same time, comprehending the whole thing ought to be a bit of a challenge.

Once you've found the right material, begin the exercise in earnest. Listen to the text thoroughly a few times. Make sure you understand the gist of it, if not all of the specifics. Once you have an overall sense of what it's about, you can take it in more slowly, pausing here and there to search the Internet for the words or phrases you don't know.

Now that you're very familiar with the reading, it's time to speak. Starting from the top, play as much of the recording as you'll be able to remember verbatim. That might be one sentence; it might be a few sentences. Press stop and repeat what you just heard. Articulate your words as clearly and accurately as you can. Do your best to reproduce the audio you just played.

As you're speaking, record your voice on your smartphone or another device, and then play back your words a few times. Listen carefully to your pronunciation. How close to the speaker do you sound? What do you need to work on?

Keep reciting the passage until you've got it down cold. You don't have to record every repetition if you don't want to. Continue this process until you've made it to the end of the piece.

When you're finished with this assignment, you'll know, or almost know, the text by heart. That's good. Later on, you can repeat this activity with a wide range of written materials, everything from love poems to travel brochures. All you need is an expert's voice on a tape to guide you. It's great to practice shadowing as often as you can.

Why is shadowing so beneficial? When you merely listen to your voice as you speak, you can get a warped sense of how you sound. It's easy to imagine we sound better than we do. But when you're forced to hear your voice on a recording, you can perceive what you're doing right and wrong with much greater accuracy. Then, when you immediately compare your pronunciation to a fluent speaker, you get an even more precise sense of your current proficiency level and what you need to do to improve.

On top of that, when you listen and repeat the same sentences over and over, you can fine-tune the speed of your words, your breathing, and your pauses. As a bonus, you pick up new expressions to use in future conversations. Because you've said and heard them so many times, they'll stick in your head, and you'll recall them as soon as you have a use for them.

7. Get good, not perfect

Wait a minute. Doesn't this rule contradict the "be a stickler" rule? Well, in actuality, these two directives go hand in hand. Yes, you should always do your best to reproduce every foreign language sound that you hear precisely. Work hard. Focus. And always take your time.

Even so, there may be a diphthong or a rolling consonant that gives you trouble every time. Try as you might; your throat or tongue won't get it out correctly. In that case, feel free to take a break and attempt a different exercise.

You're allowed to have an accent! Many people in countries all over the world function extremely well with pronounced foreign accents. Don't let anyone's pronunciation hold back your studies or steal your momentum. Keep moving forward; keep learning new words and sayings.

Have fun and build bridges

In the end, learning a new language should be fun. Sure, it's a lot of work, and it demands a deep respect for other ways of life. But it's exciting to watch a foreign movie and know what the performers are saying without the subtitles.

It's even more thrilling to speak to someone else, at home or abroad, in their native tongue. By doing so, you're not only enriching your life and broadening your wellspring of experiences, you're building a bridge across two cultures. With your newfound pronunciation skills, you're making the world a little smaller and a little more peaceful.

Chapter 62:
Acing the Language and Speech Game

Here we'll discuss speech, language, and voice skills to grow your charisma, increase your confidence in social situations and leave a positive impression. Are you expressing your views in a positive, persuasive, and self-assured manner? Are you a compelling communicator? Are you articulate when it comes to addressing a group of listeners/audience? A good conversation/speech has several attributes. Intonation, inflection, tone, words, and more pack more meaning into your overall message to help you put across your point articulately.

Here are some ways to boost your speech and language skills to sweep people off their feet.

1. Build an impressive vocabulary

An articulate communicator with a solid vocabulary is much sought after. People who can express themselves with the most appropriate words, phrases, and expressions are irresistible. Work on your vocabulary to enhance your confidence in social situations. Every day, commit to learning three to four new words. People with a large vocabulary have less difficulty expressing their ideas and seem more confident while conversing with others.

The gap between a functional and broad vocabulary may be likened to the difference between a black-and-white and a vibrant, colorful image. To make the discussion more engaging and captivating, use your words to paint a picture.

Avoid using unnecessary words and phrases. Use conversation fillers sparingly. Keep your phrases brief, succinct, and to the point. To show off your vocabulary, avoid using the most esoteric terms. Instead, be a good communicator by choosing words that accurately express your thoughts and emotions. In a discussion, less is always more. Make an effort to communicate more with fewer but more effective words and phrases.

Consider more effective and eloquent methods to express your feelings and thoughts. For example, instead of saying "extremely hungry," you might say "famished" or "livid" instead of "quite furious" or "disturbed." Make an effort to communicate your thoughts using more effective language. In your everyday interactions, replace unnecessary words and phrases. Instead of stating, "They said xyz about my appearance," use, "They remarked on my appearance." By replacing ineffective words/ones with more significant expressions, you may improve your speech to a crisper, more articulate, and tighter one. Words and phrases like "big" can be replaced with "gigantic," "massive," or "colossal." In the same way, frightened people may become "petrified" and "spooked," hungry people can become "famished," and so on. Think of more efficient methods to communicate the same message consciously.

This practice will make you come across as a more engaging, interesting, and vibrant conversationalist. A richer and more power-packed vocabulary lends more character, feelings, and sensory experiences to the conversation.

Use a journal or notepad to keep track of new words and phrases you come across daily. You may also choose three new words from the dictionary at random each day to study and attempt to utilize in your speech or conversation. Install word-a-day apps on your phones to keep your vocabulary growing. It's still in the works. You'll never be able to know all there is to know. Breathe easily, even if you think you have a restricted vocabulary or can't conduct a conversation because you don't know how to express yourself. If you take the initiative, there are many methods to develop a strong vocabulary.

2. Use inflection for more meaning

There are multiple ways to make your conversation more punchy and effective. One of them is to use the power of inflection. Inflection or intonation adds more value and meaning to the communication.

Avoid speaking in a singsong manner if you want people to take you seriously.

Try to vary your tone frequently to avoid sounding like a staccato sound like a newsreader. Don't talk in a monotone if you want to come across as an excellent communicator. Intonation will instill more feeling in your speech. It helps the listener comprehend whether you are asking, requesting, commanding, pronouncing a statement, or suggesting something. This reduces miscommunication.

At times, ineffective inflection leads to miscommunication. Let's suppose you want to ask someone to do something or if they're interested in doing it. Instead of raising the tone at the end, if you keep it flat, it will sound more like a statement. It appears as if you are pronouncing a statement or ordering them to do something instead of checking if they can do something. The difference between the two is that you aren't giving them an option to say no to the former, while they can refuse in the latter.

Make an effort to bring more variety and character to your tone if you want to come across as a compelling communicator. Intonation packs more punch in your words and phrases to communicate the perfect ideas and emotions. At times, even a little inflection can change the entire meaning from a harmless suggestion to condescending. At times, the tone makes all the difference. Our tone and inflection are pretty much the cause of most communication misunderstandings.

Be mindful of the pitch you employ while speaking. Three fundamental pitches are widely used in regular speech - high, mid, and low speech. As an effective communicator, use different pitches to play around your voice to convey feelings, emotions, and intentions as desired.

I always suggest recording your voice or standing in front of the mirror while speaking when you are working on improving your speech delivery. Narrate a story or talk about any topic extempore for a minute or two. You'll realize exactly how you sound and recognize areas of development.

3. Make your sounds and pronunciations more articulate

Actively work on your articulations and sounds if you want to come across as an effective communicator. Master phonetics to sound good and eliminate the scope for misunderstandings. You'll put across the right appropriation and sounds.

Don't mumble, mutter, or speak under your breath. Few things are as unimpressive as someone whose words are barely audible. You will keep repeating yourself multiple times, leading to greater misunderstanding and confusion. Open your mouth loud and clear while talking, so your speech has more clarity. The aspiration of sounds is also important when it comes to increasing your speech clarity. Understand where to stretch and condense sounds. A single letter or similar letters can be used to create several sounds, which you should be aware of while speaking.

For example, "bit" and "beat." While the former has a shorter "I" sound, the latter has a more elongated or stretched "ee" sound. Also, "pool" and "pull" are aspirated and pronounced differently, even when "u" and "oo" convey similar sounds. Pronouncing a word differently is crucial if you want to communicate the perfect meaning. When in doubt, go through the pronunciations of words online or using a handy smartphone app while using it.

The same letters can be aspirated differently using different phrases and words. For instance, "the" in "thick" is more aspirated or puffed than the "the" sound in "they" or "the." Like "they" and "day" are pronounced differently even when they sound the same. If pronouncing and articulating specific sounds is challenging, try mouth exercises to make your jaws more flexible. Say tongue twisters loudly to master different sounds and articulations.

4. Emphasize the correct word

Emphasizing the correct word is important since it can completely alter the meaning of what you are trying to express or communicate. For example, let us consider a sentence along the lines of, "Did you hit him?" If you emphasize "you," it implies that you are asking the listener, was it you who hit him, or was it someone else. Similarly, if you emphasize "hit," it implies that you are asking the listener if they hit the person or did something else to them. Again emphasizing "him" means you are questioning the other person if they hit the person you both are referring to or did something else. The meaning and implication of the sentence change when you emphasize different words! Emphasize the right word to make all the difference when it comes to being an effective communicator.

5. Be mindful of the speed at which you make your speech

Notice how some people speak so fast; you can barely understand what they are trying to say. At times, they speak so slowly that you just can't wait for them to finish. The big rule for communicating your point effectively is to keep a steady, uniform, and consistent rate of speech. If you speak too quickly, you may come across as anxious, dramatic, nervous, or dominating. The listener may not understand what you are trying to communicate. The message is unfortunately lost.

On the contrary, speaking slowly may make you come across as a boring, uninspiring, and drab person. The listener may comprehend what you are trying to convey but may run out of patience, waiting endlessly for you to finish. The conversation becomes uninteresting and long-winded. The midway is to speak neither too fast nor too slow. Keen an even rate of speech at around 140-160 words/minute, which is perfect. Anything more than 160 words will be tough for your listener or group of listeners to process!

When you make an important point that should stay with your listeners for long after you've finished saying it, pause to create the right effect maintain silence for a few seconds before heading to the next point. Allow the feeling of what you've just said to sink in.

Chapter 63:
Phrases to Purge from Your Dictionary

There are certain "very ineffective communication" words in our verbal arsenal that need to be totally removed and replaced with other, smarter, and harmless language in both work and home settings. Many of them are so widely used in our society that you may be shocked to discover that you use them on a regular basis. Let me now tell you about the most harmful and ineffective things you might say in informal and professional settings, as well as what to say instead.

Casual Situations/At Home/Relationships

1. This is a huge one. I'm certain that nearly everyone has heard it at some time in their life. Yes, I'm referring to the notorious, corny, and clichéd statement, "We need to speak." First and foremost, it generates a great deal of needless stress even before the discussion begins. Second, it has a very serious meaning in our society, so instead of having a more casual discussion, you will create a more tense and uptight environment. Third, it sounds ridiculous, like a poor C-class TV soap opera from the 1980s that my grandmother watched. "Romeo Alejandro Maria Antonio Rodriguez, how could you cheat on me for the fiftieth time this season with Esmeralda Rosalia Julia Desgaldo!? We've got to talk!" But that's just my view. To put it another way, you must eliminate this word from your lexicon! Instead, what should you say? "I need your assistance." People like assisting others. Did you know that we like individuals we've helped in the past more than those we haven't? One of the social psychology methods is to ask someone to assist you with a little job if you want them to like you more. You are activating good emotions in them when you communicate these sentiments, and they feel wanted. They'll pay greater attention to what you're trying to convey as well. It's a good start for a "serious discussion," which doesn't have

to be taken seriously and may instead be more casual and fruitful.

2. Another phrase we often use when someone gets us off track, says something unexpected, or acts out of character is, "What's wrong with you?!" It's a great way to make someone feel terrible, but if you want to solve an issue or deal with a tough circumstance rather than irritate or upset others, you should delete it. Nobody wants to acknowledge that they have a problem, so don't inquire, "Are you harmed in any way?" Rather, inquire, "What is troubling you?" By asking this, you are not only demonstrating your concern for that individual, but you are also avoiding creating an even more tense and neurotic environment. You're rephrasing the scenario by focusing on a specific issue this individual may be experiencing rather than on what may be wrong with them as a person. If the individual continues to be rude or withdrawn, saying things like "Nothing..." while rolling their eyes, you might say something kind like "Well, alright." Keep in mind that my door is always open for you to speak with me about anything." You may certainly use other words, but you must demonstrate that you are always there to listen to them. You may get a favorable response, such as "Right... I'm simply tired and irritable; I apologize for my grumpiness," or a response pointing to a specific issue, "Yeah, always open for me, correct! I simply wanted to speak to you the last time..." In any case, you'll be closer to the actual issue and its solution.

3. Another important item in our "Hall of Infamy" is a word that elicits a negative emotional reaction on a subconscious, physiological level. It's something like, "You said *something*," or "But you just stated..." Any time you say anything like this, your interlocutor becomes frustrated, upset, and furious. When was the last time someone attempted to persuade you to do or say something you didn't? How did it make you feel? Right away, you were probably angry off or maybe violent, right? Your brain's natural

reaction is resistance: "NOPE!" THAT IS NOT SOMETHING I HAVE EVER SAID!" Even if you're certain that someone said anything, saying, "I heard/I understood *something*" is always wiser, classier, and more effective. Before I reply, let me explain what I just heard, okay?" Phrases like this have the power to alter the outcome completely.

4. Now, let's move on to another overused cliché and bad phrase that is all too common in our society. "It is what it is," says the narrator. What exactly does that imply? Nothing. It's meaningless, difficult to comprehend (particularly for youngsters), and an irritating thing to say. "Buttons, hair combs, dumplings, scissors," you might just as well say. "I adore grapes," or "My jammies are perfectly starched!" If you don't want your interlocutors to feel irritated, puzzled, or ignored, say something like, "I think it's this way because it has to be this way at this point where we are right now," or "I believe everything is the way it should be at the time to make us stronger and..." Make every effort to eliminate the useless phrase "It is what it is" from your discussions, particularly when tension or stress is present. It's good to read in ancient Stoic philosophy scriptures but not suitable for effective everyday communication.

5. Finally, I'll tell you about the final one in this book. When you remark, "That doesn't make sense," your speakers are likely to think, "You don't make any sense." You want to be more accurate while avoiding potentially unpleasant circumstances. Instead, say, "I don't understand..." as in, "I don't comprehend precisely what you mean by stating that..."

Professional Situations

Let me tell you about certain socially acceptable words inappropriate for polished, knowledgeable, and successful communicators. You must also remove them from your repertoire if you want to be regarded as a professional and accomplish your objectives more easily and quickly. Let's begin with the first:

1. "No problem!" How often do we hear it when someone does us a favor? In a shop, in the office, during a business meeting, etc.? While you might be surprised, as the phrase is extremely common in everyday life in English-speaking countries (and not only), it implies a problem attached to the thing they did (or we did). Since our brains don't understand and can't perceive negations at the subconscious level and because you don't want to subconsciously communicate that there was or could be a problem with you doing someone a favor, it's much better to simply say, "You're welcome!" instead.

2. We often hear, "Do you want/do you need..." (e.g., "Do you want a bag?") while being served in stores. "I don't understand," you may be thinking right now. What's wrong with saying it?" you must first understand that depending on the tone of voice and way of speaking, "Do you need..." may be seen as condescending by certain consumers, particularly if the seller is repeating it for the fifty-first time that day or is just weary. Also, the phrase "Do you need" or "Do you want" may occasionally imply concealed regret (implying that there is an issue with someone desiring something again). Second, with the assistance of these questions, consumers are often questioned just about their preferences, not extra services—for example, whether they want sugar in their tea or coffee—they have paid for it, so it just comes down to their choice. Instead, say, "Would you like...?" It's more general and professional. It is not only more attractive, but it also works in almost every situation.

3. Let's have a look at another one. The term is "unfair," and it should never be used in the workplace. The harsh reality is that "fair" has little to do with working conditions (and never has). The same may be said of life in general. When you go to your boss and say, "I don't feel I was treated properly," or "I believe I was handled unjustly," they're probably thinking, "Yeah, life isn't fair indeed sweetie pie." It's the most effective method to come off as a weak and unprofessional person.

Instead, say something like, "I don't think I was handled fairly in this circumstance." No one ever guaranteed that work or life would be fair, yet most people are sensitive to equal rights and opportunities. That's far more polished, appropriate, and helpful in professional settings, and it's less likely to fail.

4. When we want our message to have a greater impact, we often use words like "very" because we believe they will emphasize and bold our message, making it stronger or more persuasive. It's frequently the opposite way around—removing adjectives like "extremely" or "very" makes our messages stronger and more polished. Many women have this issue since they tend to utilize these phrases more often in their vocal communications. Men do it as well, although not as often. Stop using these phrases to boost what you're saying (they wind up sounding ambiguous or bad instead) and instead write basic, uncomplicated communications if you want to communicate your thoughts more professionally in the office or in a business setting. Is it more serious to say, "It's hazardous!" or just, "It's dangerous"?

5. "I can't handle..." Never say something like that in front of a group of people! It makes you seem like a weak, neurotic, or even poisonous "victim type" person who acts more like a grumpy adolescent than an adult. It's 10 times better to say, "I'm having trouble dealing with..." You could also provide a question for others to contribute to this issue. Let's suppose you're talking to your boss about a nagging coworker and how your team works: "Listen, Bob, I'm having trouble dealing with Mark's frequent and unexpected behavior." Do you have any suggestions or recommendations for what I could do?" Not only does it demonstrate that you are a problem solver, but instead of just dumping your problems on others, you invite them to help, making them feel wanted and valued. It's a professional and efficient approach.

6. Whenever someone is not behaving normally in a professional situation, you should avoid saying that they act "strange,"

"weird," or "funny." It can be perceived as a mean thing to say, even insulting (that's for sure), but moreover, that doesn't sound professional and can make that person start acting even more extreme. Additionally, it's just your opinion you're giving, which is not always wanted, needed, or positively perceived in many different work situations. Anytime you see that someone's behavior is unusual and they are not acting "normally," it's much better to say, "I'm noticing a change from the regular pattern of so-and-so's behavior..." or something much more objective and diplomatic. This way, you sound like a professional, not expressing your subjective opinion but simply stating a fact.

7. Another thing on our list is "normal." The problem with this adjective is that it's very difficult to define and relate to. What does it mean nowadays? What type of business or what job is normal? What family model is normal? What appearance, what car, what type of relationship, or what kind of career is normal? In most situations, we can't objectively say that.

8. Moreover, it's polarizing. When you say someone is normal, the other side of the coin is "not normal," which could be offensive to some people. Instead, it's much safer and smarter to say "average" or "usual." It's almost impossible to receive it wrong and misinterpret it, and it's much more specific, defined, and easier to relate to.

9. Now, the last one, and a little talk about the right attitude on top of that. In your utterances, you should change "Because..." to "Because I...." Let's say that you lost your job and it's hard to make a living now. You could say, "Because my boss fired me, I lost my job, and now I am struggling to make a living and..." or, "Because of the bad economy, I lost my job, and now I'm...." Instead, you should say, "Because I used to spend too much and failed to save enough money to make a living before I'm able to find a new job or start a business..." or,

"My employer was able to locate individuals with better credentials than mine who would work for the same amount of money since I stopped improving myself and learning new things..." Apart from the fact that you may despise your employer and your current position due to the poor economy, doing so teaches your brain not to blame other people or situations and instead to learn from your errors, flaws, and faults. Remember that altering your linguistic patterns alters your thinking patterns as well. Change "Because my vehicle engine stopped..." to "Because I neglected to take care of my car before..." next time someone asks why you're late. Simple, but not without difficulty. But a powerful thing to start doing today!

Chapter 64:
Effective Communication in Personal Relationships

You've read this in every advice column, and it isn't a secret—communication is the key to any successful, rewarding relationship. I know it sounds similar to "just be yourself." But how does one do that? It sounds amazing in theory and social media posters. However, how can it be applied in our practical, everyday life? Here are some practical and highly actionable tips and insights to increase your communication skills regarding personal relationships.

1. Avoid Communicating When Under High Stress

In high-stress situations, we often say or do things we later regret. Happens all the time, right? There is also a tendency to take everything that a person says personally. Our judgment becomes skewed, and we lose our sense of logic. Instead, focus on returning to a calm state of mind before addressing the issue or concern. You'll think more and speak more coherently.

You won't end up saying things you'll regret or that will further aggravate the problem. You'll know whether to react to the situation or stay quiet when you're in a peaceful and comfortable frame of mind. Use stalling techniques. Offer yourself some time to think and go over the issue. Pause for a while and collect your thoughts. Pausing is better than rushing into a response only to say the wrong things. The golden rule of communication within personal relationships is to avoid saying anything under stress and duress. Wait to calm down, and then make your points coherently and logically.

Of course, it is easier said than done because strong emotions are involved. However, each time you find yourself getting stressed or angry, just keep a technique ready to gain more calm. For example, when things get heated up and stressed, some people just like going out and walking for a few minutes before getting back to the discussion. They come back calmer and less stressed.

Even in the middle of a heated argument or discussion, don't lose your balance. Speak coherently, keep an even tone and make eye contact with the person you are addressing. Your body language should be relaxed, calm, and open. Don't reveal any signs of nervousness, anxiety, or stress through your body language. When you notice that things are getting emotionally intense, swing into action to bring down the level of emotional intensity! Bring down stress, manage your feelings and act appropriately.

Our body automatically gives out signals when we feel stressed and anxious. Your muscles will feel tighter. The hands will slowly clench. Your breathing becomes shallower. These are all physical symptoms of stress. Take a deep breath and calm down. If you are not up for it, postpone the conversation or take a short break before getting back to it.

Sensory experiences are one of the best ways to kill momentary stress. You can beat stress through sensory experiences, including sound, smell, sight, taste, and movement. For instance, pop a candy in your mouth and notice how it tastes. How about taking a few deep breaths? Or visualizing a happy memory! These are sensory-rich experiences that can help reduce your stress. Every person has a different response to sensory inputs. Identify things that relax and soothe you.

2. Be Assertive

Being assertive doesn't mean you fight with your loved ones on every issue that comes up. It simply means standing up for yourself and not letting people walk all over you. Being assertive in personal relationships helps you set boundaries and prevents people from taking you for granted. It also paves the way for clear communication, decision-making, and increasing your self-esteem.

Assertive people express their thoughts in an honest, confident, and open manner. They stand up for themselves and respect others around them. Being assertive should not be mistaken for being hostile, demanding, dogmatic or aggressive. It is about understanding the other person and being understood without focusing on winning the argument. An assertive communicator will always attempt to suggest a middle way rather than being obsessed with winning an argument or forcing their opinion on the other person.

How does one develop greater assertiveness to communicate effectively in personal relationships? Value yourself and your views/opinions. Understand that they are as important as the other person's. Identify your needs and wants and learn to express them without trampling on other people's rights. Learn to express even negative thoughts positively. Stay respectful even when you are involved in an ugly feud with a person. This gets people to listen to you and take your words seriously. Being disrespectful takes away from your credibility while also making people switch off after a while!

One of the most important things for being an assertive communicator is knowing your limits and saying no when you mean no. Don't let people take advantage of you. When you aren't up for something, politely, firmly, and respectfully say no. Look for solutions where everyone will feel happy with the outcome.

Demonstrate an empathetic assertion in personal relationships, where you acknowledge the other person's feelings and express yours freely and clearly. For example, "I understand that you've been working very hard, but I also want you to make .... for us." Then there's the escalating assertion, which can be used when your initial attempts to be assertive are not successfully met. For instance, "If you don't stick to what we've mutually agreed about your addiction and abusive ways, I will be forced to consider separation/divorce." This is different from threatening a person. You are merely stating the consequences if your rights or needs are overlooked.

I know some people aren't naturally assertive or don't have a confident personality. It can be developed with practice. Start by practicing in lower-risk scenarios to build up the confidence and skills for high-risk situations. Practice assertiveness techniques on people whom you trust and who are capable of giving you honest feedback.

3. Focus on Collaborative Communication

One of the most significant communication problems in personal relationships during modern times is a misconception where the objective of communication is concerned. Most view it as a battle or debate between two parties, when in fact, the idea is to cooperate and collaborate and not compete. Suppose either partner goes into the conversation without an accurate reality perception. Both parties don't have access to identifying what the reality is.

The purpose of communication is, therefore, determining what the real situation is. Communication involves collaborating as both parties share their feelings, perception, ideas, and thoughts to arrive at a correct understanding of what happened.

While approaching a conversation with your partner, disarm. This simply means give up your obsession to be right or to win the argument. This isn't a war that has to be won. If any damage is done, you both lose. Again, on the other side, this doesn't mean you have to compromise or give in to everything they say. You have the right to feel the emotions you feel. However, all the same, think that your partner may have something to say worth hearing or considering. Stop treating every conversation as a battleground where you have to prove you are right all the time. There is no real victory in these situations.

4. Identify the Other Person's Communication Style and Your Own

Recognizing your and the other person's communication style is one of the best ways to communicate more effectively with them while also eliminating instances of misunderstanding and conflict. Here are some primary communication styles that can be identified and built upon to accomplish more harmonious and fulfilling interactions.

Assertive communicators. These are people who possess a high sense of self-esteem, self-assuredness, and self-confidence. This is the healthiest communication style that seeks to work out a middle way between being too passive or aggressive while also staying away from manipulation games.

Assertive people realize their limits and don't want to be pushed around by people who want to use them to get things done. All the same, they won't violate other people's emotions or rights to fulfill their purpose. The assertive communicator style is win-win because confident communicators come up with solutions that are beneficial for everyone involved, compared to merely thinking about their own needs.

Typical characteristics of an assertive communicator—they accomplish goals without hurting others; they protect their rights while also respecting other people's rights. They are more socially and emotionally expressive. Assertive communicators make their own choices and accept responsibility for these choices.

Their typical nonverbal behavior includes medium pitch, volume, and speed of speech. Their posture is open, relaxed, and symmetrical. They stand tall, and there are barely any signs of fidgeting or nervousness. Their gestures are open, expansive, and rounded. Assertive people typically make good eye contact and maintain a spatial position that conveys they are respectful of others and in control.

Typical things they say include, "Please would you reduce the volume? I am finding it difficult to focus on my work" or "I am sorry I won't be able to help with your homework because I have an appointment scheduled with my physician." Try and be an assertive communicator if you want to be effective.

Aggressive communicators. This style is all about winning—unfortunately, at other people's expense. Aggressive communicators act like their needs are supreme, and nothing or no one else matters. They behave like they are born with greater rights and have a bigger say in things than others. Predictably, this isn't an effective communication style. Since aggressive communicators focus excessively on the delivery of their message, the content is invariably lost.

Their nonverbal behavior includes loud volume, bigger and more expansive posture than other people, fast and jerky facial expressions, and a spatial position that invades other people's space or tries to stand upon other people. The typical language used by them includes "you are insane" or "this has to be done in my way," or "you make me mad." Blaming, taunting, name-calling, insulting, sarcasm, and threatening are all characteristics of an aggressive communicator.

Passive-aggressive communicators— These communicators appear passive on the outside but are playing out their anger 'behind the scenes.' These people generally feel powerless and are mostly resentful. They subtly undermine targets of their resentment, often even at the cost of sabotaging themselves. A passive-aggressive communicator will typically say things like, "why don't you move ahead and do this. My ideas aren't of any value anyway", or "you always know more than others anyway." There is a hint of sarcasm in what they say.

Their body language involves speaking in a sweet, sugary voice, maintaining an asymmetrical posture, jerky and quick gestures, and facial expressions that appear sweet and innocent. The passive-aggressive spatial position involves standing too close. At times, even touching other people while pretending to be friendly, warm, and generous!

Submissive communicators— Submissive communicators are about pleasing people and avoiding confrontation at any cost. They will bend backward to please other people, often at the cost of their wants and needs. Typically, submissive communicators place other people's needs before theirs. They believe their needs aren't as crucial as the people around them. This leads to disillusionment and frustration. The typical language used by them includes, "Oh! It's nothing, don't worry" or "Oh! it is fine, I don't want it any longer" or "You pick, anything is alright with me."

Typical submissive communicator body language includes a soft volume, diminutive, head down posture, fidgeting gestures, and a spatial position that makes them appear lower in stature than others. An evident victim mentality marks it, and refusal to try initiatives for improving things.

Manipulative communicator. Manipulative communicators are shrewd, scheming, and calculating. They prey upon other people's feelings and emotions to serve their purpose. Manipulative communicators possess the ability to influence and control people for their benefit. The words they speak almost always have underlying or hidden messages, which their victims are unaware of.

Their typical vocabulary includes, "you are so fortunate to enjoy these delicious chocolates. I wish I were lucky enough to have them too. I can't afford such pricey chocolates" or "I didn't have time to purchase anything, so I had no option but to wear this attire. I'm crossing my fingers that it doesn't make me seem too bad." Their voice is patronizing, often bordering on envious, high-pitched, and ingratiating, while facial expressions are typically "hangdog."

5. Use "I" Statements

Of course, you want to express your feelings, desires, and needs. It is an important part of being an assertive communicator. You can express your needs, desires, and feelings without attributing blame to the other person. This is one of the biggest secrets of communicating effectively in personal relationships. You can communicate what you want to say without offending the other person using "I" statements instead of "You" statements.

Using "I" instead of "You," you take responsibility for your actions rather than passing on the blame to another person. It is direct, non-accusatory, and honest. It emphasizes the person's behavior and its after-effects. "I" statements comprise talk about the other person's behavior, your feelings, and consequences. Typically, it is like "I feel……. when……. because……… " Or "even I feel……. when you……….and would prefer………."

Be specific when referring to another person's behavior; refer to a current or recent incident instead of generalizing it. Ensure you own your feelings and that you accept responsibility for your feelings rather than accusing others. No one can make you feel something. Keep your body language and tone calm, relaxed, and open. Avoid making these statements in a more passive-aggressive or sarcastic manner. It won't come across as genuine.

Some examples of accusatory "you" statements and "I" statements are as follows. While blaming "you statements," state something like, "you are working late again, just like always." The same statement can be converted into an "I" statement by saying something like, "I feel frustrated when you work late because it doesn't allow me to spend more time with you." Similarly, instead of saying, "you don't love me anymore," try saying something like, "I feel lonely when you stop calling me for long periods. Can we work something out so I don't feel like this anymore?"

See what we are doing here? We are accepting responsibility for our feelings instead of blaming or accusing the other person. You tell the other person that you are experiencing a particular feeling rather than being responsible for it. You are expressing your desire without pointing the finger at the other person, which works wonders.

6. Make Small Talk

Yes, I know it's your partner of 20 years, a family member, or a close person we are talking about here and not a stranger you've just met at a party. However, if experts are to be trusted, small talk about seemingly insignificant things has a more substantial impact on your emotional ties than so-called profound emotional conversations. Psychoanalyst Harry Stack Sullivan created an approach that he referred to as "detailed inquiry." He recommended therapists accumulate as much information about a client's life as possible to find clues about their personality.

Research conducted by John Gottman and Janice Driver researched this suggestion with a group of married folks and discovered that boring or mundane details or the seemingly trivial moments which are a part of a couple's everyday life have a greater bearing on a relationship's health than emotionally serious and so-called meaningful conversations. This makes making small talk with your partner an excellent idea!

Similarly, research published in Psychological Science reveals that we connect better with others when talking about everyday experiences. Say, for instance, you attempt to repair a ruptured relationship or marriage, start with the children. Speak about positive memories and amusing/cute incidents related to your children. Avoid referring to moments of conflict or discord. Find shared memories and moments—this can be one of the most effective solutions when it is about a child you both adore.

7. Listen, Listen, Listen

This is all the more critical when it comes to our relationships. Since we are so used to having the person around us, we often take what they are saying for granted and don't practice active listening. Knowing that what you are saying is being keenly heard is one of the best feelings in the world. It creates a feeling of community amongst individuals.

One way to sharpen your listening skills is to practice active listening. You are not just nodding your head and offering verbal acknowledgments, but you also comprehend what is being said. Understanding can be conveyed through everything from your smile to a word or a phrase to whatever unique nonverbal cues you use to communicate you are listening to the other person. Interrupting the other person while they are speaking or asking for explanations are examples of active listening (which reveal you have been listening to the other person).

Disagreements also signify active listening. But how can you disagree with a person if you haven't heard what they are speaking about? If you are interrupting the person to seek permission, say something like, "sorry for interrupting you, but can I ask you something?" This is a reasonable request if you want to ask something when the person hasn't finished speaking yet. If you disagree with the person, wait until they've made all their points or finished speaking.

They might say something that you may agree with at the end of their talk, so hold on until the end to disagree. If you feel that they haven't described something accurately, seek more clarification rather than downright accusing them of manipulation, lies, or deceit. You may gain greater clarity by asking them more questions.

Part 4:
Being a Good Thinker as a Speaker

Chapter 65:
Preparing Your Voice, Body, and Energy Level

Public speaking differs from all other everyday situations. Therefore, you can't engage it in the same way as other things.

Some speakers fail to understand that voice is just a byproduct of your whole body language. Before speaking on a stage, they only do some simple voice exercises as preparation. I think this is a grave mistake.

Sure, your voice is your number one tool in public speaking. You should be able to use it effectively.

But to get to this, you can't just do voice preparation but prepare your whole body and, on a deeper level, hike up your energy level, so you are ready to perform.

This, also, is a great way to crush any fears. Having a high energy level stomps on the fears.

Having Rockstar Energy

Like a rockstar, you need to be ready to give your best. The audience is not waiting to see and hear the average you, but the "best you." Give them just that.

In a sense, as a speaker, you need to be hyperactive or hyper-energetic. You need to make sure you are full of energy and able to express that.

When you are giving a speech, what may seem "over the top" or "exaggeration" in ordinary life, is in fact, very good.

To you, it may feel like you are going overboard with your energy. With time, you get used to that.

For many public speakers, just being in front of a live audience or cameras gives a spurt of energy. They step into a different mode.

But you can't rely on the audience or the cameras to be your only source of energy. Make sure you have prepared yourself in other ways.

Here are some ways I've found helpful to prepare before going on the stage.

Simple Exercises To Build Up Your Energy Level

Tony Robbins is an excellent example of a high-energy speaker. Everything he performs on stage seems natural to him.

Before going on stage, Tony jumps on a trampoline. For him, this is a great simple way to activate his whole body.

On the trampoline, all of your body is going up and down and getting a gentle exercise without breaking a sweat.

For me personally, I like walking around. I either walk behind the stage or go outside. That boosts my energy nicely before going on stage.

Other speakers I know do some whole-body exercises and stretches.

What for you would be the best way to raise your energy level and prepare your whole body for performance?

Find a way to prepare yourself in a way that works for you. You need to have your whole body prepared before going on stage.

Now that you know this, we can finally take a look at how to prepare your voice.

Why We Need To Prepare Our Voice

In our normal daily life, we all tend to have our voice more monotonous and not articulate words that clearly. But when you are on stage, you can't be monotonous or inarticulate.

How does one use one's voice effectively? Well, for example, by changing the volume. This means that you can speak loudly and then again softly, even whispering at times.

Also, to fight monotony, you should be able to change your pitch to higher and lower. Just think about how people vary their voice in Spanish-speaking countries, and you will get the idea.

For example, when you share a story, you should change your voice to emphasize different parts and different moods of the story.

But how, then, should you prepare your voice?

Let me be clear here: You should not worry if you have a speech impediment or if you are speaking a second language with a funny accent.

These are just part of you. They add to your character.

Just think about Arnold Schwarzenegger: his Austrian accent hasn't done him any harm, but rather it is his trademark. In the same way, embrace those parts of you and let them be part of who you are.

Then again: Not opening up your voice with proper vocal warmup exercises just isn't professional.

My Number One Voice Preparation Exercise

Many people think that to prepare or warm up your voice, you should focus on your throat or your tongue. Sure, these are important, but they are not the most important.

To pronounce well and articulate clearly, you need to prepare first and foremost your lips and your jaw. You have to wake up your jaw and lips to have clear articulation.

There are many voice preparation exercises. I've tried many of them, but there is one that stands out from the rest.

For many of my students and me, this exercise does more than all the rest combined.

Here is the formula:

1. Find a place you can be by yourself.

Usually, preparation is something you favor doing alone. You don't want to have any distractions, engage in conversations, or anything like that.

With this exercise, I'm giving a heads-up that you might look goofy doing it, so having privacy gives you an extra benefit.

   2. Extend your tongue as far as possible.

You don't need to overdo it to feel a gag reflex but stick it out as far as you reasonably can.

   3. With your tongue sticking out, count out loud numbers from one to twenty, actively using your jaw and lips

This sounds like "waw – too – tee" and so on, all the way to "tweety."

Now, this is the part where you might sound and look funny, but that is not a problem.

And what is the benefit of this?

Well, you can test it for yourself. Do the exercise and pay attention afterward. Do you hear the difference? You should notice especially how your S's sound. They should be much clearer now.

Finally, if you don't have time to prepare quietly (and don't want to seem foolish in front of others), you may complete this exercise secretly.

Chapter 66:
Be Mentally Prepared

Needless to say, the most important thing that you can do before any public speech or presentation is to become mentally prepared. While much of the anxiety of public speaking can be attributed to physiological causes and general shyness, the truth is that it is also directly linked to how prepared a person is. In general, the more prepared you are, the less worried you will be. There are several ways in which you can prepare for an event, including practice, organization, and increasing your familiarity with the subject at hand.

Organize Your Material

Much research has been conducted to identify the most successful business and professional practices methods. One of the most widely accepted findings is that a chaotic environment is more likely to fail. This affects not only groups of people but individuals as well. When a person is disorganized, they fail to fulfill their full potential no matter what the given situation might be. However, when a person takes extra time and effort to organize such things as their schedule, tasks they need to perform, and other such elements they increase their chances of success exponentially. Furthermore, increased organization has been shown to significantly decrease stress and anxiety, thereby making both individuals and groups of people more effective as a result. Subsequently, in order to reduce the anxiety and stress of a public presentation, it is vital that you organize your material.

One way to organize material is to reduce the actual amount of material you have to deal with. People often believe that the more material they have, the more prepared they are. Unfortunately, this can lead to clutter, confusion, and a general sense of chaos that only serves to undermine the individual's performance. Too much stuff is never a good thing, so get rid of anything you don't need right away.

Transferring information from different sources into a single reference sheet is a smart method to accomplish this, reducing your workload to a more reasonable level. Furthermore, you can organize the material you are covering by reducing it to bullet points, thereby condensing large blocks of information into smaller 'bites' of information that you can expand upon with your own personal experience and knowledge.

Focus On What You Know

Another significant reason why many people struggle with public speaking is that they often feel out of their element when it comes to the topic. This can be a real problem in the event that you are giving a speech to a group of people who are well versed in the subject of your presentation. Any time you feel like you're competing with the people you're conversing with, it'll just add to your tension and worry. Therefore, only ever give a presentation when the subject is something that you already know a whole lot about. You will feel more at ease speaking in front of people if you are more educated.

This proves especially true in the event that members of the group you are speaking to ask questions about the topic of your presentation. If you are speaking about something you don't know much about, you will probably be caught off guard by questions you don't have the answers to. Although you won't necessarily be expected to have all the answers, you should at least have most of them. Therefore, make sure you only give presentations on things you have a deep understanding of. This will prevent awkward moments where you appear unprepared and out of your depth. It can also serve to make the experience more fun as most people enjoy talking about what they understand or are passionate about.

Keep It Simple

Keep it simple is maybe the most important piece of advice offered by great public speakers. Simplicity avoids chaos and the tension and worry that comes with it; thus, it goes hand in hand with always being prepared. However, rather than referring to the physical material, keeping it simple refers to the presentation itself. Most people feel that a successful presentation has to cover a wide range of information. This can result in a person trying to discuss too much material in the time given, moving from point to point without taking a breath in-between. Not only does this add to the stress of the presenter, but it also leaves the audience feeling overwhelmed as they are bombarded with countless facts and information, proving more than they can make sense of.

The fact is that a simple presentation is better for everyone involved. Not only is it easier for the speaker to talk about six or seven points instead of twenty or thirty, but it is also more beneficial for those listening to the presentation as well. After all, if you were introduced to four or five people, the chances of you remembering their names would be better than if you were introduced to fifteen or twenty people at once. The same holds true for any introduction of information. It's simpler to remain focused and on track, if you keep things simple, and it makes the presentation more informative and memorable for the audience.

Practice Makes Perfect

Anyone who makes a living as an actor or stage performer will tell you that the key to being successful is practice, practice, practice. This philosophy holds for any form of presentation, whether it's reciting lines in a play, acting in a movie, or simply giving a public speech. As the axiom states, "Practice makes perfect." Therefore, if you want to reduce public speaking stress and anxiety, make sure that you practice your presentation repeatedly until it becomes second nature. The more familiar you are with the material, the less afraid you will get it wrong.

While some people content themselves with practicing their speech in their minds, the truth is that practicing it out loud is far more effective. There are several reasons for this. First, you will become more comfortable hearing yourself as you practice your speech out loud. Many people feel self-conscious when they hear themselves speaking, and this can cause increased stress and anxiety at the time of the presentation. However, if you become familiar with the sound of your own voice, you can avoid that stress, making the experience easier as a result. Second, by practicing the speech out loud, you can discover any parts that might be tricky, either because of word choice or just because of how things are arranged. By practicing your presentation aloud, you can discover these pitfalls in advance, thereby eliminating them from your public performance.

Get Emotions Out of the Way

Train yourself to go beyond emotions when you want to solve problems of any sort. Think about what you have to do and dwell on that, and the emotions will subside. Do not be dramatic. Do not yell at colleagues or get overly animated, gesturing at them. Control your emotions and let your body language respond similarly. This will help you to remain objective through the resolution process.

Have a strong will, and use that to keep yourself composed as you handle the issues at hand. You are needed to show concern and care so that all hope for the goals is not lost under the prevailing situations.

Take Control of Your Thoughts and Emotions

A commonly accepted definition of stress is when someone believes the demands of something exceed the social and personal resources they have access to. When people are stressed, they make two judgments. They feel threatened by the situation. And they feel they must judge whether or not their resources and capabilities are sufficient in order to meet that threat.

How stressed a person feels depends on how much damage they believe the situation will cause them. Perception is the key to making a situation not stressful anymore. It's your interpretation of the situation driving the stress levels you're feeling. Sometimes you are right in what you feel because some situations can be dangerous or threaten you physically, emotionally, or mentally. Stress is the early warning system that alerts you to a situation that threatens you.

However, sometimes you're harsh and unjust to yourself in ways you wouldn't be with a team member or a family member. Negative thinking coupled with this unfair judgment of yourself can cause stress to become severe and undermine your self-confidence.

Here are some techniques for overcoming nervousness before delivering a speech.

Thought Awareness

When you think negatively about the future and put yourself down, you damage your confidence and put your performance in jeopardy. A major problem with negative thoughts is they will flit into your consciousness, do their damage, and disappear in a second. Their significance has barely been noticed, and since you don't challenge them or correct them, you don't pay attention to them. That doesn't get rid of their harmful effects, though.

Thought awareness is the ability to observe your thought and become aware of everything that pops into your mind. One method to accomplish this is to stream your awareness while you're thinking about a difficult scenario to become more aware of your thoughts. Don't suppress the thoughts, but let them run their course as you watch them and write them down as they happen.

Another general approach is to log stress in a diary. One of the benefits of doing this is, for one or two weeks, you will log all the unpleasant things that cause you stress in your life. This includes negative thoughts and anxieties and can include memories or situations you perceive as being negative.

When you log these, you are able to find patterns in negative thinking. When you analyze the diary, you can see the most common and damaging thoughts you have. Tackle those as your first priority. Thought awareness is the first step to managing your negative thoughts. Without being aware of them, you have no idea how to control them.

Rational Thinking

The next step to deal with your negative thoughts is to challenge them with rational thinking. Look at every thought you wrote in that diary and challenge them by asking yourself whether they're reasonable and do they stand up to fair scrutiny.

Let's say you've had some of the following negative thoughts.

- You feel inadequate.
- You worry your performance will not be good enough.
- Anxiety that everything is out of your control undermines your efforts.
- You're concerned about how others will respond to your work.

Now let's look at how you can challenge these thoughts.

- **Feeling inadequate**: Are you educated, and have you trained for your speech? Do you have the resources you need to perform it well? Have you prepared, and have you done all of this and still feel inadequate? Then maybe you're setting yourself too high of standards for this speech. Analyze and see if it's true.

- **Worries about your performance**: Do you have the training reasonable for this task? Have you planned? Have you prepared for this speech? If you haven't, then do those things. If you have, then know you are well-positioned to give the best speech you can.

- **Problems with issues outside of your control**: Have you made a contingency plan for things that might go wrong? Did you think about the risks and challenges appropriately? If you can say yes, then you are well prepared to handle problems that may arise. If not, then write down your fears and go over what you can do to prevent them.

- **Worry about other's reactions**: If you put in the effort to prepare and you are doing the best you can, then that's all you need to know. If you perform as well as you possibly can and you stay focused on your audience, then fair people are going to respond well. If people are not fair, it's not something you can control.

Positive Thinking and Opportunity Seeking

Where you use rational thinking to challenge those incorrect negative thinking, it's also useful to use positive, rational thoughts and affirmations that will counter them. It's also good to look at a situation and notice if there are opportunities offered by it.

Affirmations will help you build self-esteem and self-confidence. When you base your affirmations on clear, rational assessments of truths you made using the rational thinking section, you are able to undo the damage done by negative thinking.

Affirmations have to be strong and specific. They should be expressed in the current moment and have very strong emotional content.

In addition to using affirmations, part of positive thinking is to look at opportunities the situation can offer you. If you successfully overcome the aforementioned obstacles in the last section, then the situation may offer you a positive opportunity. You might gain new skills, be seen as someone who handles difficult tasks, and open up new career opportunities.

When you think positively, be sure to recognize those possibilities and concentrate on them.

Let's look at how you may truly capture the audience for an outstanding public address now that you know how to move beyond emotionally negative ideas and take control of your thinking process!

Do Not Go Personal

Things do not always play out logically. For instance, company politics and many other dynamics can influence the ongoing processes and pose challenges. It's a collective responsibility, and everybody is involved. You do not need to justify your thoughts and actions of how this could have been avoided. Focus on staying committed to solving the problem and returning systems to normalcy. That is all that is needed for you.

Take control and show that you are doing it well so that you have the support of everyone. Do not get every issue too close to the heart. Do not allow external noise and politics to rule over your thinking and decision-making capability.

Be Optimistic

Keep a positive attitude. You can afford a narrative that gives inspiration and hope. Have the resolve to get things together and better, and stay reminded of your leadership expertise, experience, and role. Show strength, smile, and show your sense of compassion.

Set the right pace and tone. Positive-mindedness gets to work by itself to begin neutralizing chaos, so you follow on to set the right course of correction and advancement. As you do this, focus on harnessing everyone's positive values and setting the correct momentum for everyone's good.

Chapter 67:
Awareness of Self and Others

Self-awareness is inner work, but it is well worth embracing if you want to succeed in the workplace. In 2019, the American Management Association (AMA) reported a study conducted by Green Peak Partners' organizational consulting firm. The study, titled "What Predicts Executive Success," found that a high self-awareness score was the strongest predictor of overall success for executives.

The research continues by stating that "A self-aware CEO who is excellent with people will be better at dealing with customers and business partners, understanding and executing strategy, and achieving bottom-line outcomes. These largely low-ego, trust-inspiring leaders nonetheless set the bar high and expect exceptional results, but they do it in a way that emphasizes excellent interpersonal skills and respect."

The words lower-ego and trust-inspiring are the cornerstones for using awareness to build meaningful connections with colleagues, coworkers, and staff. Even if you're not an executive today, there is no doubt that you are engaging in interpersonal relationships at work if you are reading this book. If you hope to advance in your career, increasing your self-awareness by managing your ego and building trust will be critical.

Awareness allows us to tune in to what is happening in our inner worlds and what is happening in our environment. This provides us with a higher level of social awareness and emotional literacy whereby we can identify and process our emotional states and empathize with others' emotional states. Crucial to effective communication in and out of the workplace, awareness of self and others is a core leadership quality.

Self-aware people have developed a sophisticated sense of their emotional range, take responsibility for their actions and impact, are clear about boundaries, and can self-manage under challenging situations. This helps us tolerate workplace frustrations, navigate conflict, reduce stress, and make us less impulsive and argumentative. As our awareness expands, we can put aside self-centeredness and see and understand others' perspectives. We become more naturally curious and open-minded. This leads to empathy, allowing us to see past differences and find common ground—which is more important than ever given the diverse, global nature of most workplaces.

Being Aware of Yourself

Sir John Whitmore, a founder of the contemporary executive coaching movement and author of Coaching for Performance, defines awareness as knowing what is happening around you and self-awareness as knowing what you are experiencing.

By heightening personal awareness, we can connect with sometimes hidden or unconscious aspects of ourselves that may be driving communication or decision-making processes without our conscious knowledge. We can discern the difference between reacting and responding. In a way, self-awareness is like simultaneously appearing in a movie and watching it. Our minds and bodies are engaged, our senses are taking in and interpreting our environment, and we react and respond. At the same time, there is a somewhat detached observer self-monitoring our behavior, a part that is "watching" the movie. A mentor of mine described this aspect of self as the part of us that knows we are sleeping when we are asleep. You can engage this observer self to heighten your awareness in interactions.

Many of us respond to situations, including crucial decision-making moments at work, based on our social or family conditioning. We come into our careers armed with a set of preconceived ideas and expectations. Our responses, particularly to stress, confrontation, or conflict, are often automatic and reactive. The communication tools that may have been effective at home or school may not serve as well in a professional setting. When we lack awareness, we lack choice.

Here are some tips to increase your level of self-awareness:

- **Shift the focus to within yourself.** Mindfulness is key to developing awareness. Take time each day to focus on your internal process. Slow your breathing and be aware of your physical sensations. What information are you getting proprioceptively (physically, from the outside environment) and processing internally? Acknowledge and name your thoughts and feelings.

- **Manage distractions.** When engaging with someone in person, mute, put away your phone, and step away from your screens. Allow yourself to focus fully on conscious, intentional interaction. Be aware of who and what you bring into your energy and emotional field. Managing distractions is also important to your mindfulness practice. Set aside time away from screens and devices to connect with yourself.

- **Be aware of your personas.** Social media and the digital world have enabled us to develop personas or versions of ourselves that we use online. The persona you use in texting may not be the same as the persona you portray in a professional exchange or one that you use on a social media channel. Be aware of your personas and the different ways you interact. Having different personas can be fun, but it can also create dissonance. Can you align these personas to reflect who you truly are?

- **Consider your impact.** Unless you are working entirely remotely, your workplace is a shared environment. Be aware of the impact you make on the people around you. Mute pings and notifications, keep your voice at a reasonable level when speaking out loud, and use earbuds or headphones if you are someone who needs to listen to music, podcasts, or the radio while working. In interpersonal interactions, notice how people respond to you. Are they drawn to you? Do they run from you? Watch for verbal and nonverbal cues that reveal the impact you are having. A daily journal is a great tool to use to record what you notice.

Being Aware of Others

I started working with a bright and highly motivated young manager I'll call Javeed shortly after being promoted to lead a small team of four. He struggled with the change in rank from coworker to manager regarding directing his former peers. Javeed also felt his boss rejected his ideas and perceived his boss as generally negative, leading to frustration and anger. He was having trouble controlling his emotions. He was stressed and irritated much of the time, and although he was not aware of it, he was taking out his frustration with short-temperateness and overly criticizing his team.

We established that Javeed needed to develop a greater awareness of his impact on others and his emotional states and responses through the coaching process. Javeed was open to learning more about himself, willing to explore blind spots, and genuinely curious about how his emotions affected his ability to communicate and make decisions.

As part of the process, Javeed agreed to begin a daily journal. At the end of each workday, he took notes on his wins and challenges. He reflected on his observations about himself and others, particularly concerning interpersonal communication and emotional reactions. This practice enabled Javeed to look at himself and his workplace situations objectively. Over time he began to identify both positive and negative behavior patterns and their impact on others. He was also able to chart his growth and increasing capacity to deal with conflict. His openness to change and commitment to professional and personal growth helped him learn to identify his feelings, thoughts, and assumptions and overcome blind spots. You can do this, too.

- **Step outside yourself.** Focus your attention outside yourself. Every day, take a few minutes to notice the people around you. Pay attention to what you see and hear. What do you feel or sense in the environment? Be mindful of your coworkers. What is their body language, tone, or stress level? Practicing daily mindfulness will help you attune to what is around you and increase your awareness of others. Use a journal to track your observations.

- **Practice listening first.** The next time you step into a meeting or the lunchroom, rather than launching right into the discussion, practice attentive listening. What is the emotional tone of the casual conversation? Who is being heard? What nuances are you aware of? How might these cues and nuances inform the way you communicate in this setting? Use your awareness of others to assess the best communications approach.

- **Practice awareness online.** It is more difficult to do, but you can demonstrate your awareness (or expose your lack of it) online as well. I recently texted a coworker, expressing my dissatisfaction and concern over a major project. She texted back: "I hear you. Let's schedule a call." A similar e-mail to another colleague received this response: "At least you've got a large project to work on!" I'm sure it is easy for you to discern which colleague is more aware.

- **Bonus Tip:** A great way to develop awareness is to watch a video of people interacting with the audio turned off. Take notes of your interpretation of the feelings indicated by the cues and signals you see. Then watch it again with sound. See how accurately you interpreted the interaction.

Best Practices for Better Awareness

- **Adopt a mindfulness practice.** Consider meditation training or classes or use one of the many mindfulness or meditation apps available for smartphones. Take time each day to simply be present to yourself and your surroundings and attune to your senses.

- **Become an observer.** Practice noticing the way you react in different situations. Consciously take the observer seat and see if you can identify your thoughts, feelings, strengths, and weaknesses in different interactions. Track your insights by keeping a daily journal either online or in a notebook.

- **Seek feedback from others.** We all have blind spots. Ask a handful of trusted friends or colleagues to list what they perceive as your strengths and weaknesses and provide constructive feedback to you in areas where you may not yet be self-aware.

- **Manage screens and devices.** When with others, focus. Mute devices, step away from screens, and seek opportunities to engage face-to-face, either in person or via video chat. Engage in co-present conversations.

- **Consider your impact.** Every workplace has a beautiful diversity of personalities, styles, and approaches. Consider your impact on others in your workplace, including those of different cultural or social backgrounds. Be sensitive and practice empathy.

Chapter 68:
Know Your Audience, Understand Their Needs

Another important aspect of your preparation is ensuring that you know your audience so that when you compile your speech, you do so with that specific audience in mind.

If possible, what you need to establish are the demographics of your audience, for example:

1. Age group;
2. Predominant Gender;
3. Occupation or profession;
4. Knowledge of your subject
5. Perhaps social class as well.

If you're delivering a presentation to a group you already know, you may use your current expertise to answer these questions. This might be the situation if you are, for example, making a presentation in your company or group.

However, even in this scenario, your audience will be made up of individuals with their own specific needs.

If you're giving a presentation on creating a handbook for a new computer operating system, for example, you should concentrate on the technical aspects if you're speaking to the individuals who will be compiling the manual.

Suppose, however, you are presenting to the senior management and marketing people. In such a scenario, the advantages of creating this handbook are likely to pique their attention much more than the technical specifics, which they are unlikely to care about.

Outside your work environment, you may be expected to speak to an audience of strangers, in which case, it is necessary to do some more research to get to know your potential audience more thoroughly.

If feasible, the most effective method to accomplish this is to attend a comparable meeting to get a sense of the situation.

For example, if you have been invited along to talk to a group that meets regularly, go to one or two earlier meetings before the time you are scheduled to speak to get an idea of the 'dynamics' of the group. Although the individual members in the audience may be slightly different when you present your speech, the dynamics or the way the group reacts is unlikely to change a great deal.

Similarly, if you are expected to make a presentation at work, and there are similar talks scheduled that will take place before you have to present, go along to see how it works.

Once again, whether you are in a position to undertake in-the-field research of this nature or not, you can look for additional help and guidance on the net.

For example, if you are scheduled to give your Boxer dog talk to the local Dog Owners Club, going to a couple of their meetings would be great, and looking at the breeders websites would also be a help as you can get a good 'flavor' of what to expect about the type of people that may make up your audience.

You need to know and understand your audience before even beginning to prepare your speech because you have to know what they want and expect from you.

For example, suppose you made a presentation for one hour about quantum physics to highly qualified physicists. In that case, you need to include a great deal of detail and data in your presentation because it is fairly safe to assume that these people are not listening to you. You can, after all, tell a nice joke!

Your presentation needs to be 'pitched' to suit your listeners. Getting the right level of information and interest is essential, get it wrong, and your presentation will either 'go over the heads of your audience or bore them to tears with stuff they already know. Either way, they will feel that their attendance has been a waste of their valuable time.

If, however, you are the person talking to the Dog Club about keeping boxer dogs, then your talk should probably be far less technical and possibly somewhat less serious as well.

Of course, it cannot be 10 or 15 minutes of complete waffle because your audience is there. After all, they want to learn more about keeping this particular type of dog, so you have to give them some facts and useful information. Nevertheless, there is more scope for a degree of humor and lightheartedness in this particular example than there would probably be in your quantum mechanics presentation, provided, of course, that you do not detract from the importance of your advice.

When thinking about your audience, these are the essential questions that you need to be able to answer:

1. Why am I making this presentation in the first place?
2. Who am I making this presentation or speech to?
3. What format will I use to display the data?
4. Perhaps the most important question of all is: what do you want your audience members to do after they have finished listening to you?

For instance, you may want your audience members to buy a product or service that you are promoting, or you might want them to take another action such as using a keep-fit regime, adopting a healthy diet or philosophy accept teaching or doctrine, or changing the way they care for their Boxer dog.

In other words, what is it that you are trying to teach, explain or persuade people to do? You must be very clear about the answer to this because knowing your objective allows you to make certain that your speech or presentation is 100% focused on the goal that you have in mind before ever standing up.

You also need to consider why the audience is there in the first place. You need to know what they want and expect as well as what you are trying to achieve. Use visualization; think of the empty room, hall, or venue and try to visualize the type of people who will make up your audience.

Who Will Occupy These Seats?

Put yourself in the position of your listener, imagine yourself as part of the audience; what are you expecting to hear, learn, and benefit from? For example, are you part of a group of people who volunteered or even paid to attend on a social basis, or with a need to further your knowledge about the advertised subject because the topic is interesting on a general or personal level (e.g., dog care)?

Alternatively, are you there because your job requires you to attend as part of your in-house learning? Or is the information presented something that you must know or have to help you carry out your work?

In effect, you need to establish the audiences' reason for being there first because armed with this information, and you can then make sure that your talk or presentation is targeted at or matches their requirements.

The more you know about the people to whom you will be talking, the more effective your message will be. Before starting to prepare your speech, conduct as much research as you can about your prospective audience and the dynamics of the group.

Chapter 69:
Knowing What's at Stake for Your Audience

Consider 'what is at risk for your audience' as one method of putting a public speaking engagement into perspective. What do they stand to gain or lose if they listen to you? As a public speaker, it is your responsibility to be extremely clear about why what you are saying is essential. Investing completely in the stakes of your goal can help you capture the audience's attention and respect. It'll be a subtle reminder that this isn't about you.

Are There Always Stakes?

You may be asking whether there are any situations when there are no stakes for the audience, such as a wedding speech. No, there's always something on the line. If you're delivering a maid-of-honor speech, your main audience, the couple, will either hear about your love and support for them, or they won't. That's what's on the line.

Declan Donnellan, a film and stage director, explains why it's critical for a production to have greater stakes for the role than for the actor portraying the part in his book The Actor and the Target. (In a word, the performance will be fantastic if the actress portraying Juliet focuses only on her connection with Romeo and not on what the famous agency in the fourth row is thinking about her.) The same may be said about giving a good presentation. The stakes for the objective or message must be greater than they are for the presenter.

When the Stakes Are Personal

There are many things on the line at times. "My employer warned me that unless my next presentation on our new cybersecurity system goes very well, I won't get promoted," a customer said. This is critical information, and it may be what prompted the individual to seek counseling from me. But it doesn't alter the fact that your primary emphasis should be on the audience.

Consider what it would be like if you were this person. Your stakes are as follows: you may win or lose a promotion. You may earn or lose your boss's regard. You may or might not receive a raise. The stakes are very high. They're also very nerve-wracking. This viewpoint can draw your full attention to yourself. This will make you feel awful and divert your attention away from the beneficial and necessary stakes for success.

Instead, concentrate on what's at risk for your audience, and you'll have a far greater chance of delivering a successful performance. What will they gain if they take action? What will be lost if nothing is done? You may create a crystal-clear image of what the prospective customer stands to lose if they do not invest in a cutting-edge security system in the cybersecurity presentation. Then you may tell them about all the benefits they'll get from using your company's services. You are assisting them in understanding what is at stake—for them. You'll feel uncomfortable, worried, and self-conscious if you become mired down by your own stakes of fretting about a promotion. And no one in the room will benefit from this situation.

Knowing the Stakes Can Help You Ignite Passion

Assume you work for a social service organization and your neighborhood is bracing for a rare heatwave. It is your responsibility to warn your community about the risks of leaving children and pets in the vehicle in such severe heat during tomorrow's town hall meeting. Checking up on older relatives and neighbors is also essential. What's on the line? Children, the elderly, and animals' lives. Lives may be lost if people do not listen and act. Lives can be saved if the audience pays attention. In this situation, if you get emotionally involved in the audience's stakes, your passion will be sparked, and you will want to be seen and heard by everyone in the room.

Chapter 70:
Putting Yourself in the Shoes of Others

The truth is being a good citizen is not the only motivation you'll need to put yourself in other people's shoes. If you are on the path to influencing, you will find that this tip comes in handy too. And I'm going to dive right deep into what it means to put yourself into the shoes of others. As you must already know, the phrase has nothing to do with Louboutin or Nike footwear. However, it all boils down to empathy and mutual understanding.

Influencing is a game of numbers. Numbers, in their plural form. You start to consider yourself an influencer when you can consciously name two disciples who see you as a source of inspiration. Take a moment to consider the world's greatest footballers in this age: Cristiano Ronaldo and Lionel Messi. They are revered by millions of people, even though only a very tiny fraction of the people who consider them as influences play professional football. How do these stars achieve this level of influence?

Quite simple. When they are on stage or television, they put themselves in the shoes of the millions of people that tune in.

Every football fan screams for a win, goals, dribbles, and attractive football. These stars understand this feeling far too well. They've been spectators themselves before they became stars, so they know what the average fan expects. This way, it becomes easy for them to deliver and gain the crowd's confidence. They put themselves in your shoes as a spectator. They ask themselves what you would expect from them, and they go all out to put up a pleasing display. That's simple logic and arithmetic.

However, it can get more demanding in some areas. I can quickly tell the reason you are on this page is that you want to learn empathy. But I can't say the same when I walk into a conference room filled with Fortune 500 chief executives, entrepreneurs, and Silicon Valley leaders. They all have different perceptions of business, profit, technology, and leadership. How do I put myself in the shoes of people with diverse backgrounds and attitudes?

The answer is not too far off. There is an everyday shoe we all wear. There is a common denominator in every human gathering, an ideology that levels every individual within that space and time. At a protest ground, it is the sense of justice and fairness. It is the desire for a feasible, profitable, and sustainable business model at a business gathering. At a religious gathering, it is faith. Regardless of prior intention, the common denominator makes it easy for everyone to agree on several basics. The common denominator is your key to influence any group of individuals on the earth's surface.

At every given time in your life, find the common denominator amidst a group of people and exploit it as you've only got one chance at it. Well, maybe because you do. But you shouldn't miss the point.

If you must achieve the goal of influencing, your first entry into a room full of people should not be marred by pleasantries. Consider the different factions in the room. What brings them together? What have they been through? What are their expectations? Once you find answers, leave room for no further questions.

What You Want to Say vs. What The Audience Wants To Hear

It would be unrealistic to pretend that there are no times when ideologies clash, and you do not believe in a jot of what the people you seek to influence believe in. Surely, there are times when the common denominator is a concept you hate with all your innermost.

If you are caught on this web, you have two options. You can either say and do what's on your mind and lose your audience irredeemably. On the other hand, you can do what a maestro will do.

What will a maestro do?

Good question. A maestro will find the balance. Influencing is people-centered. You revolve around your audience, so your audience can revolve around you. That is the process influencing follows, and this doesn't bend for anyone.

Finding the balance involves you making your audience know that two truths can coexist. Imagine you were made to convince people that trees grow on rocks, even though they believed something entirely different (you know this by being in their shoes). You have to persuade them that not all pebbles are created equal! Some boulders contain soil detritus that may help trees develop, while others might harm seeds. Then you leave them to try it out. Whatever outcome they get, it is a win-win for you. You did not mislead them, yet you did not go back on what you aimed to say.

You must be ready to balance what the audience wants to hear and what you intend to say.

There is a caveat, though. Going back on life truths is not worth the blind loyalty of a couple of followers. There is a greater common denominator you must never sacrifice – humanity!

Chapter 71:
Build Your Speech on a Solid Foundation

Do you know the number one enemy of a great speech?

Boredom.

There's nothing more disheartening to a speaker than to look out into the audience and see people looking at their watches, yawning, or reading a book.

When your speech is boring, your audience will tune you out completely. It's as if your voice was a radio broadcast, and the listener tells himself, "That's enough!" — and changes the channel. And once you've lost them, it's almost impossible to get them back.

If that's happened to you in the past, I'm sorry. But take hope. You'll be able to create a speech or presentation that will keep your audience interested from beginning to finish using what you'll learn today.

Sound good?

Now let's lay that foundation.

Capture Their Attention Right From the Start

The first words that come out of your mouth should be so good they're impossible to ignore.

The first few minutes are vital. At this time, your audience is most likely to want you to succeed. Add to that the fact that we all size up someone in as little as 17 microseconds. Some studies say that you have up to two minutes.

With all this in mind, why wait to thrill your audience? You're much better advised to assume that people will only give you a few seconds to win them over.

So how do you grab someone's attention?

Throw out an alarming fact or statistic. Here are 3 about road traffic accidents.

- The total annual global cost of road traffic accidents is almost 230 billion dollars.
- An accident victim occupies every tenth hospital bed.
- Road traffic accidents cause injury to about 50 million people in the world each year.

You can also grab attention with a story.

What do we watch on TV? Movies based on stories. And when you curl up with a good book, chances are it's telling you a story.

Stories offer a great way to illustrate your main idea as it works in the real world.

Have the Main Point and Give it Full Support

"Repetition is the mother of learning," you've undoubtedly heard.

Then your English teacher tells you that you shouldn't be repetitive when you speak.

When you need to remember something, what do you do? You repeat it to yourself. Then you do it over and over until you can recite it from memory.

Also, if you want to remember something, you can't dwell on a thousand unrelated thoughts. The only way to absorb something is to give it your full attention as you master it.

Here's how this applies to your amazing speech.

First, have one main point.

No more. No less.

One point gives you focus. It's like staring down the barrel of a rifle. When the cross-hairs line up on your target, you have the best chance of hitting your mark, don't you?

So make sure your speech has a single target, one mark to hit. When you do this, you'll have a lot more clarity and precision.

Second, have three supports that reinforce your point.

You may back up your assertions in a variety of ways. You can use stories, metaphors, facts, statistics, testimonials, or current events. Think of them as arrows that are aimed at a single target — your main point.

However, be sure to change it up a little. Don't make all three support the same thing. Use facts for one, a story for another, and a personal application for the third. Or find another way to mix it up. When you do this, you'll fight the number one enemy of every successful speech — boredom.

So why use three? Does the number matter?

You bet it does.

One or two isn't quite enough. Five or more supports are too many to absorb. Three is perfect. That's the basis of the rule of three for writers. Three is the perfect number to establish credibility. And it's not so many that people get tired of listening to you.

So stick to three, okay?

End Strong

When you've grabbed their attention from the beginning, kept it with one main point and three strong and varied supports, be sure to leave them with something they can use.

Restate your main idea.

Don't assume they remember it. Go ahead and restate it.

Summarize your supports and show briefly how they prove your main point.

You've given them the meat in the body of your talk. Now let the last bite be something they can take home and digest later. Challenge them to take action on the ideas you've presented. You might even encourage them to let you know how it goes when they try it.

Now Make Your Next Speech Amazing

They say knowledge is power.

The truth is that only applied knowledge is power.

Now you know how to give a speech that will be persuasive and entertaining. You'll do this by grabbing attention from the start, keeping it with one main idea and three different supports, and closing by giving them something valuable to take away.

Build your next speech on this solid foundation, and you'll have all the preparation you need to be amazing every time you speak.

Chapter 72:
Organize Your Thoughts

Next, it's time for you to organize your thoughts! Sure, it sounds like a cliché, but it's true: An unorganized mind won't be able to produce viable results simply because it in itself is already confused. Your audience doesn't know what's on your mind—that's true. But, that does not mean that you can just allow them to see that you do not know what you are talking about, have not practiced well, and are not confident enough to be on stage.

Make an Outline

Here's the thing: Whether in writing or speaking, outlines matter. People often forget to organize their thoughts logically, and thus, when they present their ideas to an audience, the audience feels that it's all cluttered. It's so hard to make a point when your ideas are cluttered!

You know you can make use of cue cards even in impromptu speeches. This is because it's always better to present your thoughts clearly and coherently instead of jumping from one topic to another.

Get some cue cards (i.e., index cards, notebook/notepad pages, etc.) and outline the topic you've been given.

Here's an example:

Main Topic: Today's Music and How Much it has changed

Outline:

1. Brief History of Music
2. Artists who are on top of their careers today

3. The biggest difference between yesterday and today's music
4. Is today's music entertaining?
5. Pros and Cons of today's music
6. How music could still evolve

After outlining, you could just look at the cue card and focus on one item at a time, instead of say talking about how music has evolved, talking about its history, and jumping to differences between yesterday's and today's music. You have to start from the beginning and then just let your ideas branch out. Having an outline will also prevent you from using fillers and having dead air, making anyone feel bored.

Think of a Diamond

Wait, what?

Okay, in case you're confused right now, let me clarify this for you. A Diamond starts with a point that could then expand to another point and end close. A diamond is perfectly shaped—it's not like a circle that just goes on and on. In short, when you begin to form your thoughts as a diamond, you get to start with a strong point, make valid arguments, and you'd then get to close your speech strongly and plausibly.

In short, make sure that you get your audience's attention right away. One good way of doing this is by asking a question.

For example:

> Quick: Have you heard about the recent growth in the number of mass shootings in America? Crazy, isn't it?

See, with that kind of question, you already get to create a sense of urgency, plus you also get the audience to think because you have just asked about an important matter—something that concerns everyone. Thus, it becomes easier to expound—it becomes easier to evoke people's emotions and make sure that they're listening to you.

Make use of examples and arguments

The thing about public speaking is that it doesn't have to be verbatim. You can make use of examples related to what you have in your outline. You can use arguments, and of course, you could also ask your audience some questions.

It's all about making sure that everyone is involved. For example, say that One Direction may be today's The Beatles. See how your audience reacts—and then expound on what you said. It's also important to be well-read to use a lot of examples and help your audience understand what you are talking about.

Know What You're Talking About

Just like what I have just said, you need to know what you're talking about instead of making your audience feel like you're as clueless as them. Also, make sure that you still get to narrow your thoughts down to a coherent conclusion after expounding on the topic. This way, people won't get confused and would understand what your point is. Make sure you leave them with either a question or a call to action. This way, you'd also feel good about your speech—and will not be scared the next time.

Organize Your Brainstormed Ideas

This will allow you to brainstorm informed ideas that you may not have thought of before reading up on the topic.

1. Cross Out

Now, cross out all those ideas which you do not want to include in your final work. Yes, out of sight, out of mind, holds for this case as well.

2. Use Numbering Method

Number each point that you want to use according to the order in which they will appear in your presentation. Use another blank page to create a working outline with each point listed in the order you want to present. Only then begin to elaborate on each idea in detail.

3. No Fluffy Content

Including content that is both well researched and organized can alter your perception of your work. And this is an important part of building confidence in your ability to speak publicly about any given topic.

4. Use Credible Sources

The fewer doubts you have on the credibility of your material, the better. Valuable information can also convince your audience that you know what you are talking about. You feel less nervous, and speech delivery becomes better.

Good material that is organized well is doubly beneficial to your confidence. You won't have to fret over which idea to discuss next during your delivery because you will have neatly planned what you discuss. You can also walk on stage, believing that what you have to say is of value and can bring some difference in someone's life. Keeping positive ideas like those in your head does wonders for your confidence.

Chapter 73:
Identify Your Purpose

One of the fastest ways to attain your goals and be at peace with yourself is by learning how to find your passion and purpose in life. Without having a sense of purpose to guide you in the right direction, you might end up feeling unfulfilled even after achieving your goals. Every one of us is born with a distinct life purpose (no two people have the same). Identifying and honoring this objective in our lives is perhaps the most critical action successful individuals take. It's essential to take out time from our busy lives to understand why we're here on earth and then pursue it with enthusiasm and passion.

For some people, it's already clear what their purpose in life is, right from when they're born. All of us were created with a set of talents, and while some of us quickly discover what they are on time and utilize these skills, a few others need to develop them through constant practice and determination. Individuals born with natural talents end up honing them over time and ultimately turn the skills into something they're passionate about and use to achieve their dreams. For some, it takes hard work even to figure out if we're good at anything, so we end up giving up and doing what others are doing so we wouldn't feel left out. When you choose to do what you're not passionate about, you'll eventually start to notice how your life lacks a deeper meaning.

Explore the Things that Come Naturally to You

We're all born with a purpose that we have to discover during the process of our lives. It's not something you have to fake since it's already there; all that's required for you is to discover it. You need to uncover what your purpose is to build the life you want.

One of the easiest ways to figuring it out is to think about what you love doing or what comes effortlessly to you. Whatever your purpose is, it should feel natural – not forced. Work might be required to hone your skills after discovering them, but suffering isn't always necessary. If you're struggling and suffering to keep up with something you assumed was your purpose in life, then the chances are you're probably in the wrong field.

Sometimes the process is as simple as following what your heart tells you. Many people fail to realize that we all have an inner guidance system inside us that helps us get to various points in our lives. You could think of it as an internal GPS of sorts that guides us through multiple aspects of our lives.

With every image you visualize while trying to realize your dreams, you're "Inputting" the particular destination you need to reach at a specific time. And each time you express your preference of something over the other, you're unconsciously stating an intention.

In most cases, the things that bring you the most amounts of joy and pleasure are aligned with your life's purpose even without knowing it.

Doing what you love increases your productivity levels

You'll notice that when you're doing what you enjoy and love, you're more engaged and devoted to the exercise. You'll be motivated and excited to complete various tasks assigned to you by your boss or other people; this translates to increased productivity.

Individuals that genuinely love their jobs never feel tired doing it. They remain motivated because their job doesn't feel like a chore to them. Focus on doing the things that drive you positively to avoid getting bored with your life. Passion differentiates good work from great ones.

Just by looking at your work, any sane person with a keen eye can tell if it was something you were passionate about or not. It all lies in your attention to details or not. Not only will the work you're excited about have premium quality, but it'll also have an emotional value attached to it.

Steps to Identify your Purpose

- **First of all, understand what the term means**

While there are many definitions of "Life Purpose," the main thing to note is that identifying it is to make an in-depth review of everything you've ever done in your life that brought meaning and fulfillment to it. Whatever you come to terms with needs to be straightforward; it shouldn't be overcomplicated.

Your life's purpose could be to bring order and chaos to the lives of those around you, help others achieve their goals, or use your talents to bring change to the world. To begin identifying what it is, try connecting the dots from your childhood up to the point you are now and discover who you've always been and the impact you've made on people's lives.

- **Honor what you love doing and slowly start separating yourself from the things that drain and exhausts you**

The chances are that you won't be able to feel or honor your purpose in life if you're always tied down with activities that you dislike or people you don't admire or respect. You'll find out that when you separate yourself from demoralizing situations and focus on things that motivate you to do better, that your sense of self-worth would begin to improve. Finding our life's purpose is only possible when we take action and honor our needs and values. The key here is to start behaving like you're worthy of having one in the first place and begin saying no to work and activities that you despise.

- **Identify new ways you'd like to be of help to others**

It could be through your hobbies, work, or volunteering for a cause that means a lot to you and others. Most individuals who focus on being of service to the people around them all agree that helping out makes them feel alive and useful. It makes them feel like they're part of something greater than themselves.

You are your life's purpose because it shows how you live, interact with others, support growth and positivity around you, and use your natural talents to add to the lives of others.

If you're still unsure of what your purpose is or how to discover it, just start with recognizing a new way to do something that not only gives you a sense of achievement but also fills you with joy as you're doing it.

What is the Purpose of Your Speech?

There has to be a reason you are delivering your speech – that goes without saying – but you would be surprised to know that many people don't highlight the purpose behind their speech when they deliver it. What do you aim to achieve? - An audience who is left scratching their heads, wondering why they just listened to a speech that didn't seem to have any point.

As a result, you must ensure that you have a critical goal or aim and that it can readily comprehend your purpose or target. When trying to ensure that you highlight your objective or purpose, ask yourself: "Why am I delivering this speech? What message do I want to convey? What do I hope people will learn from and walk away with after listening to my speech?" With these questions in mind, you can then start to develop a speech that will set out to answer these questions.

You should always make sure that your key points are easy to understand and that your audience will gain something from them. Share your knowledge with your audience by being genuine and allowing yourself to be in the present. Don't try to alter what you know or the experiences you want to share simply because you think your audience will like your presentation better. Doing this can be a big mistake at the end of the day because it can make your speech difficult to understand and relate to, thus making you speechless successful than you intended.

Think of your message as extremely important and valuable to your audience. With this in mind, you will deliver a speech that will get your point across and relate to your audience, which means that your speech will succeed.

Chapter 74: Understand People's Emotions

The definition of motivation involves three concepts: Willingness, effort, and goals. Willingness is when a person is agreeable towards engaging in a goal-motivated behavior. Effort is the amount of work a person invests towards a goal. Goal is the end, or the result, of someone's striving. Understanding these components and their role in motivation is essential towards understanding how our goals in life become aligned based on our feelings and emotions. Understand that there is one common characteristic, though—that all behavior is motivated by something.

Let's start by quickly going through the different theories of motivation and seeing where feelings and emotions come into play.

Instinct Theories of Motivation

These theories have a common denominator: All people engage in goal-directed behavior because they are programmed with evolution. These theories were widely accepted until the 1920s, before other motivational theories were proposed.

A notable proponent of instinct theories was William James. He came up with a list of human instincts that included play, attachment, anger, fear, modesty, love, and shyness. At this point, note that anger and fear are emotions while love is a feeling.

Incentive Theory of Motivation

Rewards are at play under this theory as it proposes that people's behavior is motivated by incentives.

Drive Theory of Motivation

More on the biological aspect, this theory proposes that people get their motivations from unsatisfied needs. This can be illustrated by behavior that seeks to get water because of thirst. However, a certain degree of criticality is involved in this theory. Some people can still eat even when they are not hungry.

Arousal Theory of Motivation

This theory says that we strive to maintain a subjective level of arousal. This subjective level can be referred to as a sense of equilibrium. When we perceive an imbalance in our arousal levels, we seek to make it optimal. Hence, if we have a high level of arousal, we seek to do activities that will lower it, and when our arousal level is low, we tend to engage in behavior that brings it up.

Humanistic Theory of Motivation

Directly related to Abraham Maslow's Hierarchy of Needs, the humanistic theory of motivation states that people have cognitive reasons for performing their actions. This explains why we move from one specific goal to another, such that we fulfill our biological needs first before moving on to greater goals like self-actualization.

Bringing it All Together

In our lives, we are made to choose over two or more goals. Our choice, plus the order in which we approach things to achieve the goal, are summed up based on our needs and what we want. This concept falls under prioritization. When we prioritize or make our choices, there is a perceived conflict that happens within us. This is accurately captured under the concept of conflict. This concept proposes one idea that determines our emotions and feelings: We approach an attractive goal (Approach Process) and stay away from an undesirable goal (Avoidance Process). But where do emotions and feelings come in?

The Approach Process

When we approach a goal, we generally perceive it as something beneficial or beautiful. Anything that helps us improve or live better is something considered "approachable." However, the timeline between our initial goal-directed behavior and the goal itself is marred by challenges. Hence, we change our behavior, and this change can lead to three results:

If we do poorly, we experience sadness and depression.

If we do well, we experience eagerness and delight.

If we do it just right, we are in a neutral state.

The positive and the negative results above are where our emotions and feelings are found. Depending on our response, the goal may be achieved, or it may be unreachable.

The Avoidance Process

When we avoid a goal, we perceive it to be harmful. Anything that we perceive as negative is considered "non-approachable." So, the Avoidance Process involves two opposing sides that can lead to the following results:

If we do poorly, we experience fear and anxiety.

If we do well, we experience relief and calmness.

If we do it just right, we are in a neutral state.

In the same way, our emotions and feelings result from successfully avoiding something or not.

The relationships presented above lead us to understand where our emotions and feelings are functional, as seen below:

The closer we are to the goal we intend to approach, the more joyous our emotions become and the happier we feel.

The farther we are from a goal we intend to approach, the more depressed our emotions become and the sadder we feel.

If we encounter an obstacle as we begin to approach our goal, the more attentive we become and the more motivated we feel about pursuing it.

If we encounter an obstacle when we are nearing our goal, our emotions will become angrier, and we feel frustrated.

If we are farther from the goal we do not wish to pursue, the more relaxed our emotions will become and the more relieved we feel.

If we are closer to the goal we do not wish to pursue, our emotions are more fearful and more anxious.

If we are closer to the goal we do not wish to pursue, and something happens to get us out of it, the more surprised our emotions will be and the more relief we feel.

If we are far from the goal we do not wish to pursue and manage to get out of it even without doing anything, our emotions might cause us disgust and guilt.

If you follow the patterns above, each item's first set of behavior is an emotion while the latter is a feeling. The same applies to what we do every day. This is to say that our feelings result from our emotions because our emotions are reactions to our environment. So, how can we put this information to work to achieve our life's objectives?

How to Develop Emotional Awareness and Reach Your Goals

Understand the concept of emotional intelligence. Emotional intelligence is not the same as the concept of I.Q., but the same principle applies when people say that you have a high level of E.Q. That simply means you're better at relating to other people, you're better at managing your emotions, and you're better at using your emotions to achieve your goals. So it pays to understand four concepts:

>**Self-awareness.** You will never be able to understand others if you fail to understand yourself. Self-awareness in this context means understanding the triggers of certain emotions. Why do you experience such emotions? What cues do you get from the environment? How do you recognize them?

Self-management. Recognizing and understanding your emotions is not enough if you don't know how to manage them. Managing your own emotions requires a certain degree of sacrifice and compromise that does not lead to feelings of frustration and dissatisfaction.

Social awareness. You can become aware of other people's emotions if you're good at recognizing your own. Social awareness entails a degree of understanding of your current environment and understanding the reason for other people's emotions. Without this level of understanding, you will never be able to find reason in other people's emotions.

Relationship management. This is the part where you relate to other people effectively in any social context and regardless of other people's behavior, social status, race, etc.

Developing emotional awareness is important in propelling you to the achievement of your goals. Take the following steps to bring you closer to touch with your emotions.

Learn how to manage negative emotions. Positive emotions are pretty good to entertain because these make us feel better, but negative emotions come off as a challenge. Seeking self-destructive ways to manage negative emotions leads to negative feelings, so learn about proactive ways to manage negative emotions so you can keep yourself in check.

Be agreeable and open-minded. If you are the type of person who does not yield, this is the right time for you to start recognizing that each individual possesses a different idea. Conflict is certain to occur in every situation. Learn to be agreeable while keeping an eye on your goal. It is fine to be expressive but remember that your goal is there waiting.

Be empathetic. Empathy is a skill. Unfortunately, it's a skill that many do not have. To empathize means walking in someone else's shoes while recognizing that the pair of shoes is not yours. Empathy can lead you closer to your goal if you learn to relate to other people and understand how they are instrumental in goal achievement. If you make enemies out of spite, your goal will stay as it is forever.

Be critical. Be critically positive. Keeping your emotions in a positive light might be difficult nowadays because we have many things to think about. But you can start by analyzing a given situation and acting on it rationally. Notice how rational decisions cause minor impacts when it comes to negative emotions. In most cases, they yield positive feelings all because you decided based on what is best.

Be optimistic. Maintaining a positive attitude is necessary if you are to maintain positive emotions. A positive attitude rarely leads to negative emotions. If you stay positive about reaching your goal, you are apt to survive the obstacles that may come. The same is true for those goals that you are trying to get away from.

Never avoid your emotions. People sometimes deny what they feel. They even lie about it. Beware; lying leads to feelings of guilt, so it compounds the amount of negative emotion you feel. Instead, recognize your current emotional state and acknowledge the feeling that goes with it. Plus, avoiding your emotions causes you to lose what you invested in your goal; it damages your relationships and is exhausting.

We always have a choice in our life. Our choices won't always be right, but they do not necessarily take us away from our goals. We always have a chance to start over. By keeping our emotions in check, we avoid experiencing undesirable feelings.

Is Emotional Intelligence Innate or Acquired?

Innate human characteristics are those born with and from which instinctual responses are derived. A debate exists as to whether emotional intelligence is inborn and is part of a person's personality or whether it can be acquired in adulthood.

The term personality is used in psychology to refer to an individual's thoughts, emotions, behaviors, and attitudes that are unique to that person. Emotions especially are a core aspect of the subject of this book. For example, some people are happy, talkative, and full of energy, while others can be described as having a steady, calm, and reliable disposition. This is to mean that personality influences introversion and extroversion tendencies in people.

The reason why the subject of personality is of importance here is that it is in-born or innate. Although we can improve our personalities, the changes made will be very slight and tend not to vary much from whom we innately. Emotional intelligence, on the other hand, may involve the application of already present natural abilities into practical everyday situations, such as in exercising sound judgment based on clear thinking patterns.

Whereas two people may share common tendencies about their personalities, how they apply themselves to real-life situations will be very different. For example, of two individuals with a melancholic personality, one may possess very high levels of personal motivation and ambition while others may not.

If, as a manager, you are seeking to employ someone as a salesperson, conducting a personality test will not be sufficient. However, it may show that the person is talkative and friendly enough to make contacts and sales. There would be a need to know how a person would come under the pressure that comes with deadlines and that they will persist in the face of insurmountable challenges and work-related disappointments. A test of their emotional intelligence would equip them with that kind of information.

An employee may have a very pleasant and 'fun' personality, but that does not necessarily equate to success. To achieve professional success, employees with high degrees of emotional intelligence will regulate and manage negative impulses arising from their personalities.

Some studies claim that human beings are to a certain degree born with a measure of emotional intelligence, which they term as 'innate emotional intelligence.' They point to an infant's ability for emotional sensitivity and the potential to retain and later recall all the emotional information they are taking in from their environments during infancy. This information later forms the core of an individual's emotional intelligence.

An infant emotionally learns to sense when its mother is angry because they associate some of her repetitive reactions to anger. As they grow, this stored information forms the basis from which they can sense other people's feelings. This so-called 'innate intelligence' can be continually developed or damaged through life experiences.

An infant can start life with some degree of emotional intelligence and then unlearn it by imitating unhealthy emotional tendencies from his caregivers. Unhealthy environments of abuse and neglect can also contribute to this unlearning process. Similarly, some infants may show low levels of emotional sensitivity but, with the right emotional nurturing, end up scoring very high as emotionally intelligent adults.

Chapter 75:
The Art of Persuasion

By definition, persuasion is the act of making an effort to convince someone to do something or change their beliefs in favor of some that you think are worthwhile. Empathy cannot lead you to persuasion because it causes you to see that the other person is right in his own right. However, if you fully understand where a person is coming from, you can strategize and develop a way to persuade them to change their minds. This is why persuasion is said to be an art.

You see, art is any activity that a person uses to express the emotions buried inside. It conveys complex messages that words wouldn't carry. It, however, can be intellectually challenging, complex, and coherent. That said, the product of your art must be an original piece. It, therefore, demands a great deal of skill and patience.

The art of persuasion does not check all boxes in the definition of art because people take various approaches to persuasion. Some will persuade without even showing an ounce of emotion, while others are all about the emotional appeal. In addition, you cannot talk of persuasion as an art in the sense that other art forms like music and paintings are. It is also easy to persuade without intending to be unique in any way. However, persuasion does indeed contain other qualities that qualify it to be an art: it is complex, intellectually challenging, it conveys a complex message, it can be quite original, and it highlights your point of view.

You may wonder what the point of persuading is. Why should you waste your precious time and energy persuading others? Isn't it also a form of manipulation? The truth is that you need to learn how to persuade others to achieve any success in life. Every seller has had to persuade a customer to buy their products. Every teacher has had to persuade parents that he can do a good job. Every married person has had to persuade their partner to marry them. Every employee has had to persuade the employer to hire him. Every successful politician has had to persuade voters to vote for him.

As you can see, almost every success in life demands that you convince others that you can fit and fulfill the mandates of the position you intend to fill. Persuasion seems to run in the bedrock of every human endeavor.

The Basics of Persuasion

The following are the principles of persuasion that govern the ability to convince people to share your ideologies and points of view:

1. Scarcity

People are more drawn to people, products, or opportunities that are exclusive or limited in edition. When people perceive an impending shortage, they tend to demand scarce resources, and if they can be bought, they buy them in excess.

Companies take advantage of this tendency and suggest shortages in their supply (only five pieces remaining), limiting the time an offer is available (available for three days only), or suggesting scarcity in the frequency with which an offer is made (annual sale). Customers, driven by the fear of missing out, respond by making purchases, most of which are unplanned and impulsive.

In life, everything is measured by its relative value. If someone thinks something is valuable, I will be driven to accord the same value to the item. We often want to own things because others have them. As such, if you want something to be considered valuable, you must make it scarce, and that includes yourself too. In communication, if you want people to value your words, talk less.

2. Reciprocity

Whenever you do good to someone, there is a natural nagging and drive to reciprocate the gesture. This behavior is ingrained in human DNA so that we can help each other survive. Interestingly, you also could tip the reciprocity scale to favor you disproportionately by giving some small gestures that show your consideration to others. When you ask for some help or a favor, others will happily offer it.

3. Authority

It is impossible to persuade anyone to do something when you do not appear to have expertise or knowledge in that field. No one wants to be led to the shaky ground of trial and error. A persuader must radiate special skills and expertise. Experts are more likely to be trusted. They radiate authority in their fields. Therefore, when you intend to persuade a person to take a particular stand, ensure that your knowledge and familiarity with that subject or area is beyond reproach. When you do this, you will build your reputation as an expert or personality in that particular field.

4. Liking

One of the impossible tasks is to convince an enemy to do anything. It is an exercise in futility. No one trusts or likes dealing with someone they consider unpleasant. What if you are dealing with strangers? How do you get them to like you? It's very simple. You only need to appear open, kind, attentive, sympathetic, and empathetic. Also, let people know that they are highly regarded and appreciated. Appreciation is demonstrated through giving presents, inviting the people to special events, offering 'inside' information, and making regular phone calls. People also appreciate feeling that you understand them and their interests. If you have the chance, give valuable ideas or suggestions, and you will have them eating from the palm of your hand.

5. Consistency and Commitment

Consistency assures a person that they will get the results they expect or got in a previous similar engagement. Before people commit themselves to you, they want to see signs that you are committed too, and consistent in your giving results. The best thing is to give these signs of commitment and consistency step by step, and the other party will slowly buy into your ideas.

For example, when dealing with a customer that wants to buy a dress, create the consistency that convinces the customer that you are best suited to sell the dress. You could say, "Yes, we have the dress in red, yes we have a changing room where you can try on your dress, yes, we can also deliver the dress to you, yes, we have an in-house seamstress who will make your preferred alterations for free, yes, you can carry your dress home today." Ensure that all the customer's concerns can be addressed, and when you are done, the customer will have no choice but to stick with you.

Suppose a friend or coworker calls asking if they can come over to share some personal information, show that you are committed to listening to what the friend has to say, and to doing all you can to help. Say, "Yes, I am available to speak to you now (or in a little while), I promise that our conversation will be confidential, you are free to speak to me about anything, I will help you as much as I can, you have my complete attention." When you say this, the individual will likely feel safe and will want to speak about the issue of concern. After the conversation, assure the individual that you will be available to talk when called upon to do so.

6. Social Proof and Consensus

People are the ultimate advertising tools; when someone considers you or the items you are selling to be good, they will make that known to other people the person comes into contact with. What's more, human beings tend to be more convincing than other ad methods. For example, a customer is more likely to read customer reviews and believe them, over and above ads on various media platforms. Therefore, as you market yourself and your products or services, always refer to those who have something positive to say, such as references in your resume or happy customer reviews. Their opinions will be more convincing than anything you would say to market yourself.

Learn How to Persuade People

Having understood what persuasion is and the principles that govern it, let's now see how to go about it. The first thing you ought to keep in mind is that you can persuade anyone, naturally, without even trying much. The following steps and techniques will teach you how to influence, from a marketing and a personal perspective, but these techniques are viable in any interpersonal engagement you are involved in, from making new friends, convincing an employer to hire you, networking, and relating with friends. They include:

1. Take Up Mirroring To Help Create A Subconscious Agreement With The Other Party

Mirroring is presumed to be one of the easiest and quickest ways to create accord between two parties. It refers to the acts of copying someone's volume, speed of speech, tone, and body language in a bid to reflect that person's behavior to them, just like a mirror would reflect.

Research shows that mirroring a person's behavior produces more considerable social influence over the person being mimicked. The study found that individuals who mirrored had more success persuading the other party and were regarded with more positivity than those who did not mirror.

Mirroring works so well because behaving like the other person tends to put the individual at ease, which increases the possibility of building a rapport with them. It breaks through any form of subconscious resistance the person may have and encourages them to trust you.

Typically, people subconsciously mirror others, but when you are learning how to do it for persuasion, you must do it consciously until it comes to you on autopilot. It is now a natural part of your interactions. The easiest way to start is to try to match the other party's conversation tempo and stance. However, you do not just jump into it immediately. One cardinal rule of thumb is to wait it out for about 5 to 10 seconds before you start mirroring the other party's stance so that your attempts are not too noticeable. Remember that your mission here is to gain trust, not to arouse suspicion.

Be careful that mirroring sometimes backfires, especially when you mirror negativity, such as raising your voice when another raises his or taking up negative postures like crossing your legs or your arms. Turning your body away from the individual also communicates negativity. Be careful not to do any of those

2. Be Surrounded by Other Influential Persons

The law of averages states that the result of any particular situation is the average of all possible outcomes. Jim Rohn brought a new perspective to this law, saying that a person is the average of five people they hand out with most of the time. He said this because while we interact with hundreds or thousands of people in daily life, only a few of those impact us. Their influence is very significant, to the point that they influence how we speak, how we think, how we talk, and how we react to situations, among others.

Whenever you keep the company of people you aspire to be like, you will naturally begin to emulate them and will eventually have risen to their level. Therefore, when you want to learn how to persuade and influence other people, you have to keep the company of some influential people so that you be in a position to absorb their mannerisms, reasoning, general outlook on life, and knowledge because these are the factors that have contributed towards their success.

We all have the option of selecting our friends and the people with whom we spend our time, and it is preferable to choose individuals who will help you become a better person and make it easier for you to accomplish your life objectives, one of which is to become influential.

3. Encourage the Other Party To Talk About Himself

People like speaking their minds. Science confirms that about 30 to 40 percent of the words we speak are solely about ourselves. We love expressing our viewpoints, talking about our experiences, achievements, and others. Some are even comfortable talking about the struggles they are going through because it gives them some form of relief and eases the stress in their minds. When scientists studied the brain as people spoke about themselves, scans showed some activity in parts of the brain that are primarily linked to value and motivation. This same brain area is linked with a person talking about himself and other thrills such as drug use, sex, and money.

Therefore, whenever you meet someone new, one of the ways to establish rapport is to encourage them to do an activity that will make them feel good about themselves, such as talking about themselves. Start with some small talk, then proceed with some meaningful questions. As the person speaks, keenly listen to the answer given, and where possible, turn the answer around into a follow-up question to let the speaker know that you are enjoying their talk. This encouragement causes the other party to go deeper and reveal information they did not intend to give.

As the individual continues speaking, you will have a broader look into who they are, what they believe. You will also figure out the areas of common ground so that it becomes easier to make a personal connection with them. The more you listen, the higher chance you stand to influence the person.

4. Take Advantage of the Pauses and Moments of Silence

As we mentioned before, silence is uncomfortable for many people. It makes them feel prompted to speak to fill it. An influential person must be fully aware of the effect that silence has on people and use it to their advantage. Use silence to make the other party disclose some more information, give clues, or even make a mistake that could be to your advantage.

On the other hand, when you indicate that you are not afraid of silence so that you are unhurried and more deliberate in your speech and actions, you elicit a feeling of confidence and control. Therefore, even in uncomfortable situations, be patient in your discourse, and you will appear confident.

Another advantage of the silence and the pauses is that they allow you to process the information you get better. You also get the time to consider the best approach for communicating some thoughts so that you present your ideas in a humane, empathetic way that will help deepen the connection you have with others.

How Persuasion Works?

Persuasion is an inherent attribute of others, but it is also an ability that can be mastered and enhanced. Using the following steps to develop your organizational persuasion skills.

Assess the Needs of Your Target Audience

You may already know what your audience wants in some cases. In other situations, some research may be required. Before proposing a solution in sales, you can start by asking customers about their needs or requirements. Here are a few more examples from different audiences:

- Evaluate work and change your cover letter to the position.
- Ask the team what they'd want for a package of rewards.
- Speak to registered voters about a political candidate's campaign slogan.
- Tailoring promotional copy to a target audience group's tastes.

Build Rapport With Your Audience

To be credible, the audience needs to believe that you have their best interests in mind. It takes courage, and courage takes time to develop. To write, ask questions, and listen actively to the responses. Ask for the needs of the family and others and discuss who you are.

Creating relationships is an ongoing operation. For example, even after you have obtained a team buy-in for a project, you can keep developing relationships for future work with team members and thank them for a successful job. Take the following examples:

- Ask a customer about their children if they have any.
- Congratulations to an employee on the completion of a mission.
- Escort a customer out for coffee without any clear motive.
- Prepare breakfast for community service initiative leaders.

Focus on the Benefits

Display the advantages of your plan. Specify how the action or the shift in perspective can benefit the audience. Examples:

- Express the benefits of working for an employer in the sense of a knowledge recruitment event on campuses
- Appeal for a trial or preliminary hearing to a judge for a motion
- Request that the management recruit additional workers for your department
- Receiving and writing a testimonial for a corporation as part of a product or service advertisement

Listen to and Counter the Concerns of Stakeholders

Prepare yourself for potential complaints and listen to the ones on the spot. Objections are easier to resolve if you have explicitly sought to heed and acknowledge other people's concerns regarding a new idea or undertaking. Examples of the workplace include:

- Meeting with employees to evaluate their response to a proposed company restructuring
- Illustrating the need for quality control and extended time limits in building projects

- Chair a recruiting committee to review a single vacancy by multiple potential applicants
- To educate a consumer more deeply about the advantages of a commodity
- Presenting a justification to the management to extend a departmental budget
- Responding to the opponent during legal proceedings.

Recognize the Limitations of Your Proposal

Generally, if you demonstrate transparency and recognize valid objections to your plan, people are more persuasive. Such instances are as follows:

- Recognize that someone gave you constructive information that you didn't know when you first proposed a project
- Realize that your salary offer needs to be increased to secure a top employee

Find Common Ground With Stakeholders

Most of the plans need to be compromised. It is good to know in advance which elements of a proposal can be flexible. For Examples:

- Merger talks for higher wages or improved benefits
- To convince opposing parties to consider a fair compromise in the divorce mediation
- Propose a proposal to employ a lead sales assistant who has suggested that they quit due to their workload issues.
- Reduction of the set price of a product or service

Clarify the Final Terms

Nobody wants to go back and start over when a stakeholder has not explicitly grasped the definitive terms of an arrangement or contract. Confirm that everyone is on the same page, and take the time to address any lingering questions or concerns. Here are a couple of examples:

- Contracts for studying with students in the classroom
- Before and after signing a consumer contract
- Design, distribution, and analysis of customer feedback surveys
- Call a patient to confirm their health status after a medical or dental operation.

Ethical Persuasion

If you're going to use persuasion, you'll have to consider certain ethical issues. There are a few individuals out there who use persuasion to exploit or harm others. Consider how your persuasion will affect them if you are successful before you begin.

Undue influence is a phrase used in the legal field. This implies that you're encouraging someone to behave against their will. When a person is handicapped in any manner and unable to make their own choices, this becomes a problem.

When a caretaker attempts to persuade an older person to alter their will and leave everything to them, this may happen. It's great if you want to be persuasive, but it's better to avoid exerting excessive influence.

If you're not cautious, you may wind up fabricating evidence in the name of persuasion. This is another legal issue. You want to be a moral persuader, making sure everything you say or show people is true.

Persuasion is neither good nor bad in and of itself. It is your purpose behind your persuasion that determines whether it is good or harmful. It is your responsibility to ensure that you utilize it honestly and ethically. Being unable to persuade others may be a significant disadvantage in life. Buying a house, getting a promotion, getting a job, or taking the next step in your relationship may be difficult. Fortunately, it is very easy to understand, and as long as you think rationally and clearly, you should have no problems.

Tips and Tricks to be Persuasive

- **The Best Should Come First**

In other spheres, the best is saved for last. However, when it comes to persuasion, what you say first sticks. Therefore, start with the best characteristics, then move lower.

- **Use The Extremes**

When you speak about stuff, go to the extremes, talk about good or bad, right or wrong, left or right, and other similar extremes. Once this is done, get to the 'just right' sweet spot, and ensure that it appears better than any of the extremes you described earlier.

- **Practice Brevity Of Speech**

Your words should be quick, easy to understand, and easy to evaluate. Let your words sound like short tweets rather than long passages. Long speeches tend to have run-on sentences that bore the listener; keep your sentences short and meaningful.

- **Adjectives Spice Up Your Speech**

After all that school learning, you finally get to use your knowledge of adjectives! Adjectives are the 'bold,' 'italics,' and 'underline' of your speech. Therefore, use them to emphasize and add weight to your words. Use adjectives such as gorgeous, smart, brilliant, adorable, beautiful, meaningless, faithful, eager, worst, and delightful. Sprinkle these into your short sentences, and you will see the impact they will have.

- **Take On The Present Tense**

Nothing makes people sit and listen better than information about what is happening. They want to know what they might have missed or your thoughts concerning what is going on. For this reason, ensure that you always present a uniquely intelligent and uncommon perspective; you will get their attention and admiration. If you talk about the past, you will be surprised that most of your listeners will have stopped listening before you are done.

- **Rely On Science And Statistics**

Of course, not all scientific information and statistical data available will be accurate. However, use it anyway. People will think that you are smart, resourceful, and trustworthy, perhaps.

- **Take A General Perspective**

Be inclusive and general when referring to people. For example, say, "Everyone says..." or "Everyone knows...." People become more attentive because they want to be categorized among those who 'say' or 'know,' provided you speak about something positive. Make what you are saying 'obvious' and 'the only way,' and everyone in your audience will want to be part of the winning tribe.

- **Butter Them Up**

It is said that flattery will get you anywhere. However, this flattery should be in the right amount: too much, and you appear treacherous, too little, and you appear disinterested and unknowledgeable. Know how to strike a balance, and for heaven's sake, mean what you say. Don't try to oversell something you do not believe in.

- **Use Anger Cleverly**

Most people work to avoid conflict at all costs. Conflict is uncomfortable, but if you are tenacious enough, you could use it to your advantage by creating a conflict situation and allowing the tension to escalate to a particular level, enough to let the other party back down. When this happens, enforce your idea, which must have been the better option to adopt. Be careful to use this conflict method sparingly, and don't do it due to a loss of self-control, driven by your emotions.

- **Remain Calm And Detach From The Conflict**

Another approach to a heated situation is to remain calm, unemotional, and detached from the conflict. When each party's voice is high, and everyone wants to be heard, stay calm. People tend to turn to the ones that are calm and seem to be in control of their emotions. They trust them to provide a lead in the issues at hand.

- **Talk About What The Person Will Lose**

Nobody likes loss. When you bring it up, be sure that you have caught your listener's attention as he tries to understand the circumstances that will drive failure into his life. People are convinced that they know how to gain something, but the reality that loss can come from any direction makes them lie awake in the night. For example, if you are selling a shirt, start by letting your customer know that he stands to miss the sale of a lifetime. This will work better than telling him that he is about to get a good shirt if he purchases it now, during the sale.

Chapter 76:
Look at Things from a New Angle

Whether it is conflict or decision-making, understanding how things appear from a different angle is beneficial. It helps to be interactive and inclusive. Differences may exist between people and partners in a social, family, or working relationship. When this occurs, it is necessary to do less political strategizing and think of different angles for solutions. Looking at things from a new angle requires three skills: perspective-taking, perspective-seeking, and perspective-coordinating.

1. Perspective-taking

Perspective-taking is a critical component of communication. Depending on where we stand, the way we perceive facts and their meaning can be very different. The perspective we adopt influences what we consider obvious or obscure, central or peripheral, and present or absent. Like the way we perceive the physical world, perspective influences the human experience in the social world. If we can see things from a different angle, we can have more constructive responses from another person's perspective rather than several strong disagreements. At the least, we can be careful in what we do or say in challenging times to avoid escalating negative outcomes.

2. Mistaking perspective-taking

When we try to look at things from a different angle, we should avoid two pitfalls: overconfidence and uncritically considering another person's view as valid. More often, we get overconfident that we are succeeding in viewing things from a different perspective. Remember when your friend was displeased with the birthday gift you bought her or doubly upset for not understanding her troubles. The fact is that you may have tried to take their perspective but ended up with a mistaken one.

Studies have revealed that people are often inaccurate when they infer the thoughts and feelings of another person by observing the behaviors and facial expressions of that person. More important, people become overconfident that they finally managed to get a different perspective right.

Another common pitfall is the idea that most people treat another person's perspective as valid, thereby using it to solve a problem. When our perspectives are based on wrong assumptions, the effect is missing the real issues or misleading conclusions. An example is a leader making judgments on an incident to assume that they had access to the critical information for decision-making. However, if the assumption is wrong and not questioned, the judgment could solve an integrity issue when the real one could be information quality.

3. Perspective-seeking

To successfully view things from a new angle, you also need to have the skill of perspective-seeking. Once one can listen to other people's perspectives, one should judge whether it is right or wrong. This skill involves understanding another person's point of view on a particular point or circumstance. It is about being curious to hear and learn more about other perspectives.

The greatest trap on this skill is reaching out to people with a similar point of view that you have to validate a hard decision you plan to make. It is important to listen to people who may have a different opinion from yours and discover new things and potential blind spots.

4. Perspective-coordinating

Once you can take different perspectives and seek them out, you need the perspective-coordinating skill to utilize the information you received. Perspective-coordinating entails observing what lessons are available from the other perspectives. This skill helps us to understand other people we speak to and the impact of our final decisions on them. Also, perspective-coordinating enables one to understand the contributions of different viewpoints in every situation and how they help in decision-making.

How to Radically Look at Things from a New Angle?

Perspective-taking not only brings empathy in our social relationships, but it also brings in compassion and mindfulness of the people we connect with. Below are how you can successfully view things from a new angle by considering other people's views.

1. Think of others

When we are in the presence of other people, we naturally begin to think about what they are thinking. We observe their behaviors, such as where they are looking, what they are doing, and their body language. This observation helps us determine whether we can be comfortable around them or further associate with them. If you think about other people and feel comfortable around them, you begin to think of connecting with them. The information you get by observing others will prompt you to speak up in a conversation and learn their perspective.

2. Regulate your emotions and empathy

Taking perspective depends on our ability to share emotions as well as the capacity to regulate our emotions. To be effective with other people, we must understand the things that trigger us to refocus ourselves on what is happening to others. We should understand what other people would do in a particular situation rather than what we would do concerning empathy.

With stronger empathic accuracy and emotional regulation skills, you can be successful in considering different perspectives. The skills can help you predict others' expectations, intentions, and attitudes, which may differ from your own.

3. Reading others correctly

Our perspective-taking guides are the emotions, which help us to read and study people. Our eyes and brains help us to track the behaviors of others and determine what they are feeling or thinking, then determining their intentions and motives. By being sensitive to other people, you will sense their possible emotional changes, which can help gauge how to show up in the interaction successfully.

4. Interpret words

Most people do not speak directly, which often requires that we infer the mean of what they are trying to say. However, this always creates a lot of room for misinterpreting the message, particularly those sent via email or text. By accurately interpreting what the other person is saying, you will be able to make the right decision on what to say and avoid conflict.

5. Respect the existing differences

To take the perspectives of other people, we need to have the maturity to respect the personal beliefs of others and respect their knowledge. If we disrespect others, they will separate themselves from us and avoid sharing their constructive ideas. It is important to be highly attuned that people hold different beliefs and world views and remain open-minded and respectful as we interact with them.

6. Be interactive

We must interact with people to develop empathy and learn from their ideas. Interactions are made possible by asking questions and listening to find out the concerns and experiences of other people. When individuals engage in naturalistic connections, they can tell each other what they truly think rather than what the other person wants to hear. As a result, this opens up doors to learning new perspectives.

Quality interactions build social cohesion, promote mutual trust and reciprocity norms. Over time, these traits motivate people to see things from others' perspectives, promote collaboration, and facilitate conflict resolution.

7. Strike a balance between subjectivity and objectivity

To empathize with another person's perspective, you need to adopt that perspective with subjectivity and emotions actively. But note that empathy should be accompanied by a certain level of detachment to maintain objectivity for effect perspective evaluation. Detachment refers to the ability of an individual to step back from an idea to see the bigger picture. This way, we can learn other people's perspectives and apply them adequately.

Chapter 77:
Broaden Your Horizons

Broadening your horizons always means experiencing or learning something you have never known before and opening yourself up for new ideas. There are several ways to expand our horizons, but the most common metaphor is usually through traveling. Although traveling is a big part of life accompanied by many experiences, the metaphor means more. Expanding horizons require courage. You must leave your comfort zone to learn or try something new, which may be difficult in a society where people are okay with following the status quo.

Fantastic Ways to Broaden Your Horizons

Stop limiting yourself. Often, we get held back from exploring because we believe in false barriers. Whether you believe something because someone told you it's the "truth" or from your own experience, notions that limit you can prevent you from living a complete, fulfilling life. Self-limiting factors are those things we can never challenge; we consider them truthful even if they are not. For example, if you believe that you cannot possibly swim, then you may probably never swim. In this case, you limit your ability with the belief that you are unable to.

Keep constantly pushing yourself. Broadening one's horizon is never an easy task. We do things in a particular manner when they are predictable, and the outcomes are not scary. You must put in additional effort, work harder, and be able to spend more time and go the extra mile if you want to expand your horizons. If you do this, the rewards will be much better than a simple part on the back for a job done well.

Move away from your comfort zone. Most of the time, we don't do things in life because they are not "comfortable." This means that they make us uneasy and feel out of control. You must be willing to keep going even when you don't feel secure or know how things will end out if you want to broaden your horizons. However, this does not mean that you put yourself in harm's way, but it means putting yourself in an awkward, weird, and persevering position. Since everyone can adapt to feeling uncomfortable, you should not be scared of the risks.

Be quiet and listen. We are always busy telling others about ourselves or how things are going that we forget to stop and listen. To broaden your horizons, you need to listen to others and challenge your own beliefs. If you spend all your time trying to convince people that you are always right, you will never stop to consider their ideas and perspectives. Broadening horizons require that you keep quiet and let someone else talk.

Ask yourself why. The older you get, the more you will realize that the things you thought you knew might not be the case. I have gone through being a Republican to a Democrat and back again many times. If you believe in a particular political system, you might have asked yourself several times why you accept that without having any reason behind it. The moment you stop asking yourself questions, you will have stopped growing. To broaden your horizons, you have to stop believing everything as facts and ask questions about them.

Do the opposite. Doing the exact opposite of the things you always do is another way of expanding your horizons. When you see two people having an exchange, consider the devil's advocate position and go with it. When you usually go left, take a right this time. If you always swim on weekends, consider going to a dancing lesson or hiking. The change with impact all your life experiences and further enhance your thoughts.

Develop empathy. It is critical to put yourself in someone else's shoes if you wish to widen your views. Look around and see what you have that others do not have. Often, we make a lot of effort to convince people that we deserve what we have and forget to see that others are deserving. This limits the way we carry ourselves and the life we live.

The 5 Types of People You Need in Life to Broaden your Horizons

If you choose to only surround yourself with people who have the same background as you, same age group, and same circumstance, you will be leading a boring, homogenous life without new things or ideas to explore. Your perspectives will be limited to the group of people you associate with. Variety is the spice of life, and having versatile people can expose you to different lifestyles that you may not have considered before. Thus, if you need to broaden your horizons, consider associating yourself with the following people:

The wise guru: Many young people immerse themselves in the belief that they cannot have friends with older people. They believe that older people cannot relate to anything they are going through. But this is not the case; they were your once, too! It is important to have wise friends who are older than you share their perspectives, life experiences, and wisdom. Always smile with your elderly neighbors, take some cookies to your grandparents, and have regular kickback sessions with some of your elderly church members. These people can impact your life by sharing their stories and wisdom.

The "Phoebe": These are people with free spirits always willing to go an extra mile in pushing you to further your limits. They are friends that convince you to take a last-minute trip to another country and who will remind you never to take life too seriously. It is in their nature to seek adventure, live in the moment, and view life through rose-colored glasses. Such people will make you enjoy life as they challenge you to engage in challenging tasks.

The over-achiever: These are the types of friends who made it to the varsity and graduated with honors. They work very hard and earn a lot of money while still getting enough time to volunteer for charity organizations on the weekend. They are so disciplined and incredibly collected. Instead of being jealous of them, it is essential to embrace such people to encourage you to become a champion in life. Learn their habits and behaviors, and ask them to teach you the ways to succeed.

The mentee: Mentoring, a younger person, will give you the happiness and joy you need to grow in life. Mentoring someone gives you the chance to be a much-needed positive influence on someone and reminds you of how to strive towards success. Become a mentor at your former school, volunteer at a community home, or help your cousin or daughter with homework. Mentees help you to expand your horizon to get even more influential.

The person in the mirror: Nothing can broaden your perspective than actually getting to know yourself. While growing, we tend to care about making new friends and wondering about what the world thinks of us. However, we always end up neglecting ourselves in the process. You cannot fulfill your potential if you fail to discover yourself. Spend time alone, treat yourself solo to a vacation, journal, or treat yourself by going for a hangout at the coffee shop. These gestures not only expand your mind but also lift your spirits for future adventures.

Chapter 78:
Plan the Landing

This is akin to a plane landing at the chosen destination. Just like a plane knows the destination before taking flight, you need to know where you want to arrive before you begin going there. Don't stand up on stage with a great introduction and incredible content without knowing how you want to land.

Once you have a rough draft of the body of the speech, begin to plan how you want to bring your content to completion.

To write your speech's conclusion, keep in mind these three steps:

1. Understand the Landing
2. Choose the Paradigm "Thing"
3. Structure the Conclusion

One: Understand The Landing

Near the back of the aircraft, my sister and I sat close to each other. The pilot announced that we would be landing soon. As frequent flyers, we did the regular rituals to prepare for the customary landing and hoped against the type of landing that makes your stomach lurch.

We often played a game where we tried to do a ten-second countdown to when the tires would touch the ground. 10-9-8-7… still in the air… 6-5-4-3 would we guess it… 2-1-0-0-0 … 0?

"Wait a minute!" we thought. When had we landed? The plane was on the ground, yet we never felt the landing. Every passenger on the plane looked around with perplexed looks. This type of landing rarely occurs. Suddenly the entire plane burst into the type of spontaneous applause reserved for Avengers: Endgame!

Every single time I board a plane, I remember that perfect landing. My wife grows tired of my repetitive nostalgia, yet I keep retelling it. The pilot landed flawlessly. What an incredible way to end a flight!

That is how your speeches and presentations should end: smooth, purposefully, and memorable.

Common Communication Crashes

Instead of landing like the perfect pilot, many speakers terminate their speech similar to these following scenarios:

The Crash Landing

At one conference, the speaker walked his audience through a well-rehearsed and meaningful outline (I still have the notes). As he finished his content, it seemed like he didn't know what to do next. "Alright. Well…" The moment was awkward and surprising. He had just instructed a room full of educated leaders, and that is not an easy task. "Alright, have a good day." Then he walked off the stage.

Have you seen anything like this? It doesn't matter if the content was bad, good, or even great, but when it was time for the presentation to end, it's as if the pilot just aimed the plane downward to get it done as soon as possible; CRASH! BAM! DONE! OVER!

This kind of closing kills the positive effect of great content and jars the listeners, leaving everyone wondering more about the end than remembering the points of the speech.

The Circle-Circle-Quick Landing

In the movie Die Hard 2, a terrorist had taken over the airport. As a result, planes were not allowed to land. Instead, the planes circled and circled and circled and circled and circled until eventually one of them had to land as quickly as possible.

Sometimes speakers don't know how to transition from their final point to where they engage the landing gear and bring the audience in for a landing. As a result, the presenter stands up there, rambling, over-explaining, or repeating. "So, you see, the initiative I mentioned before is crucial. Let's walk through these points..." "So now that you see how this initiative will help us achieve our goals..." "This initiative has been proven by..." "This initiative is vital to organizational health..." "There are so many benefits to this initiative..." In these circle-circle situations, often the speaker has three concerns: she didn't think of how to transition to the closing, she doesn't know what she wants in the closing, or she feels that saying more will add more, even though she has already said everything she needed to say.

After endless circling, it becomes apparent to the speaker that she has spoken too long, so she just finishes up quick (almost like the crash landing) and often apologizes for going too long.

I've seen this many times (and I'm sure I've done it many, many times). One funny situation was at a fundraising banquet. Each person was supposed to give a ninety-second story of how the organization had impacted them. Several dozen people were in the hotel conference room, so ample time had been reserved for this planned storytelling event. The media team had a ninety-second countdown on large screens to help people make their small speeches. In addition, the organizers had asked key people to go first to demonstrate how to maximize the ninety seconds.

Even after preparing the audience, many made the circle-circle-circle-land approach. A man stood up and started his story and then added more to the story. The addition made him retrace back to the beginning. The time had already run out, but he just kept going on the goodwill of the people. His first story finally ended, and we prepared to applaud, but he wasn't done. He restarted and added more elements to it. Oblivious to his ever-increasing period, the organizers finally came over and kindly prompted him to end. Suddenly, this man realized he was way over. He said something like, "well, and that is why this is meaningful to me. I mean, sorry about that. Haha. I guess I can just keep going sometimes and just had so much to say. Yeah. Sorry." Then he sat down, and his wife spent some time whispering in his ear.

The 'Tricked You' Landing

My four-year-old kid is a huge fan of superheroes. We sat down to watch the Teen Titans GO movie together. We laughed, wrestled during the fights, and ate popcorn. Then my communication observation kicked in at the very end.

The movie ends with Robin giving a very inspiring speech to the whole superhero community, including Batman, Superman, and Wonder Woman. He discusses what it means to be a genuine hero and what it takes to be a hero. The screenplay writers did a great job! He ends. Batman starts applauding slowly at first but then more enthusiastically. Then the entire group of heroes starts applauding. Robin delivered a compelling speech.

Robin, noticing that he had done a great job and had their attention, begins a second speech. The crowd confusingly pauses their applause. Luckily, Robin's team makes him stop, and the movie ends. Many speakers do what Robin did. Unluckily for us, no one tells them to stop while their ahead, so they start up a new topic.

This landing is like a plane that touches the ground flawlessly, and then instead of slowing down, the pilot says, "That was fun, let's do it again!" and up the plane goes for a short flight, a landing, a short flight, a landing and so on until finally, the pilot deems himself ready to be done.

This type of landing devalues the speech. Instead of contemplating the points presented, the listener is caught off-balance. Different modes of listening are employed during the introduction, body of the speech, and conclusion, just like your body adjusts differently to take-offs, main flight, and landing. Imagine if a pilot truly did this; it would make you sick. Likewise, it sickens our receptors by being taken up, settling into the flight, and preparing for another landing.

Politicians, preachers, and keynote speakers are some of the most guilty when it comes to this landing. There is a common joke about this when it comes to preachers: "What does it mean when the preacher says 'in closing'? —That he has another twenty minutes to go." I've seen politicians do this when they are ending their speeches. The people are engaged with the message, so the speaker ramps up, declaring, "And one more thing!" I've heard keynote speakers do this as they land that final one-liner, the crowd getting ready to applause, just as the speaker realizes that he is not ready to give up the microphone: "I don't usually do this... but I've just got to give you one more nugget of wisdom."

Land the Plane

Your speech should be your speech. Plan what you want to say to be in the body of the speech. If you can't say it in the speech, then don't say it. Keep it for a different speech, or print it as a supplement. Don't try to add on to the existing speech.

It's not about you.

That four-word sentence is one of my favorite speaking strategies. Remember that no matter how great it feels to have the audience listening to you, it's not about you. You are speaking to give them action, direction, clarity, insight, education, or motivation. Yes, it feels great when you know you did great. It feels great to see people connect with you and your content. But the flight can't go on forever. Nobody gets on a plane to just fly and fly and fly and fly. Flights are designed to take people to a destination. Once you masterfully take them to this destination, land the plane, and let them enjoy the experience.

Two: Choose The Paradigm "Thing"

Go back to your big 'WHAT.' Consider these focus questions:

- 'WHAT' are you trying to accomplish?
- 'WHAT' do you want your group to walk away with?
- Does your 'WHAT' concisely summarize your points?
- 'WHAT' stands out to you?
- Do you have one point that stands out among the others?

These questions help you know which "thing" you end with. Yes, "thing" is what I call the closing paradigm in the conclusion. There are three "things" used to conclude a speech:

1. The One Thing
2. The BIG Thing
3. The Next Thing

Before crafting your conclusion, choose which "thing" answers the focus questions above.

1. The One Thing: Not all points are created equal.

'The One Thing' paradigm is best when you realize that one point is far more important than the others. This one point epitomizes your 'WHAT.'

When you select 'The One Thing,' you choose to end by highlighting, revisiting, or emphasizing this one point.

You may even say something like, "Among all the points we covered today, this One Thing stands out."

2. The BIG Thing: The sum of the parts.

'The Big Thing' paradigm is best when your 'WHAT' has been broken into small parts. This is 'the big idea' or the 'speech in a sentence' or your thesis statement.

When choosing 'The BIG Thing,' you aim to pull together all the points into this big 'WHAT' statement. Therefore, it becomes very important to work on a memorable one-liner, which encompasses your other points.

You may say something similar to my politician client, who summarized her points into her big 'WHAT.' She said something like, "When we focus on these three goals (her points), we will be one step closer to TURNING OUR OBSTACLES INTO OPPORTUNITIES."

3. **The Next Thing: Just tell them how to respond.**

'The Next Thing' paradigm is best when your speech is so big that you need to give them one thing they need to do, know, or feel.

When choosing 'The Next Thing,' you explicitly tell your audience that you realize they just processed a lot of content. Although the audience needs to be aware of the entirety of your speech, they need to respond by doing, knowing, or feeling this specific thing.

You may say something like Rachel did when she spoke at a University, "You may be feeling a bit overwhelmed as you process today's talk. Don't be too overwhelmed. I'll tell you what to do next...." Rachel laid out something for them to do that day. She gave them the next action to get them closer to her big 'WHAT.'

Three: Structure The Conclusion

Now you understand the importance of a smooth landing. And you have chosen the "thing" you want in your conclusion. Now it's time to structure the conclusion. Here are the three elements needed in your conclusion:

1. Transition.
2. Outcome.
3. Closing.

One: Transition

After pilots follow their flight plan and near their destination, they announce the beginning of the end. Coincidently, I'm on a plane even as I write this. Even now, I anticipate the pilot's voice announcing our initial descent in the next hour.

This transition to the conclusion subtly but clearly announces that the 'WHAT' has been communicated and the end is approaching.

To transition:

1. **End your last point.**

Sometimes, speakers start the conclusion during their final point. This creates confusion, as the audience wasn't mentally prepared for the awkward fusion of content and conclusion.

Ensure that you complete the train of thought for your final point.

2. **Repeat what you told them.**

This is classic speech advice and holds in most cases. It includes a very simple restatement of your points. Don't add additional commentary; just say the point. If you feel that you didn't fully explain the point earlier, take notes and adjust for your next speech.

Don't use the recap to reopen the points.

To build on an example used earlier, you may repeat what you told your audience, saying something like:

We want the company to thrive. That only happens when all of us thrive (the 'WHAT'.)

That is why we explored how to use the Pareto principle in our work and personal life rhythms. What do we do?

- Spend 80% on your work
- Invest 20% in creativity
- Take time to replenish

3. **Tell them the "thing".**

Once your points have been fully communicated, you may choose to repeat the points as a way to signal you are done with the body of your content. Or you may skip the repetition and move straight into your closing paradigm: the One, BIG, or Next "thing".

Continuing with the example above, I will illustrate each closing paradigm. These samples are simply for illustration. Therefore, they are shorter and less precise than the typical work I do with clients.

The One Thing:

"Each of these rhythms is vital. However, I know YOU! I know you, and I watch myself. We have developed a culture of overworking. Effective immediately, I am asking you to take time to replenish. We have had a busy season and now are going to focus on this one thing."

The BIG Thing:

"When you add these three together, you see that we have a choice: adopt these rhythms to thrive, or continue with our current culture, which has led to stress and lowered our quality of life. Let's face it; we've just been surviving. No more. If it is between survive and thrive, I vote for embracing these rhythms together to thrive!"

The Next Thing:

"This will be a significant adjustment for all of us. What are our options now? Here's what I want you to know: you are permitted to conduct experiments and work on personal projects during working hours. You need to know that you have my permission to explore, create, and design other areas of interest."

Choose the "thing" that best helps you communicate your 'WHAT'. Then craft your transition sentences in a way that takes you from the body of your speech to its conclusion.

To go from the body of the discourse to the conclusion

1. End your last point.
2. Repeat what you told them.
3. Tell them the "thing".

Two: Outcome

With your transition in place, it's time for you to do the actual body of the conclusion. Yes, the conclusion itself is a three-part speech. The transition into the conclusion is the introduction of the conclusion. The outcome is the body of the conclusion. And the closing is the conclusion of the conclusion.

The outcome is your final desire from your speech. It's how you want them to respond to your 'WHAT'. What is your desired outcome from your audience? After you speak, should they:

- Know something (educational presentations, process, information, lessons)
- Do something (motivational speeches, action-oriented sermons, instruction)
- Feel Something (toasts, ceremonies, inspirational speeches)

When you transitioned to the speech, you used the closing paradigm (the "thing"). Now, it's time to choose an outcome to follow that transition.

Suppose you desire for them to know something. In that case, you may extend the "thing" into a very carefully crafted paragraph tying lots of ideas together or sharing a final statistic that illuminates the information in a new way.

Include some brief actions at the end of your presentation if you want your audience to take action. This will give them clear and quick instructions. For example, if you taught on the need for increased cyber security with a do outcome, then you may want to provide three quick steps for greater security. Don't do another speech, but just give them two to three minutes of very simple and actionable items directly related to your presented content.

If you want your audience to feel something, you will probably craft a two to three-minute story, which ties into the closing paradigm and evokes the appropriate emotions.

Each speech needs a clearly defined primary outcome. What do you want them to know, do, or feel after you present your content? Don't assume they will come to their conclusion. Do the work for them. Choose the outcome and lead them down that path. Returning to our pilot and plane analogy, no pilot has ever asked me to choose my destination while in the air. The pilot leads me safely to my destination, and I feel grateful for their leadership. Lead people to your desired outcome based on what you know about them due to your work with the starting questions.

Typically, conclusions should be two to five minutes long. Often, a speaker will desire a secondary outcome along with the first. The emphasis should be on the primary outcome, but secondary and even tertiary outcomes may be present. Ultimately, the length of your conclusion will depend on the complexity of your desired outcome or outcomes.

Three: Closing

Remember what I wrote about concerning the different types of landings. Choose to finish your speech with purpose. Don't stumble to the final destination; choose your final one to three lines. Here are some simple samples:

"And that is why we are in the people business."

"Revenue is up, expenses are down, and we will keep this up."

"When we protect the integrity of the alienated party, then we become a part of healing their hearts and their future family."

"You don't have to do all of this; you just need to do what you need to do."

"When you say yes to our company's goal, you are saying yes to your future."

Be purposeful in your presentation. Finish explaining your desired outcome. Then pause. Finally, speak your last few lines with clarity, slow, measured pace, and confidence.

Don't Say 'In Closing'

Saying "in closing" is like announcing, "I'm nice." If you are nice, you don't have to tell people; you just have to be nice.

If you structure your transition, direct the outcome, and close with purpose, people will know you are near completion. You don't have to tell people you are closing because you are doing it subtly yet clearly.

People often say "in closing" as a filler because they don't have their closing prepared. They announce "in closing" as a way to try to force themselves to close. Instead, they often open up new points, which directly contradicts their declaration.

Put It Together

It's time to put all of these elements together so that you can conclude your speech with confidence.

1. **Understand the Landing**
2. **Choose the Paradigm "Thing"**
   - The One Thing
   - The BIG Thing
   - The Next Thing
3. **Structure the Conclusion**
    a. **Transition:** Start landing your speech with the transition from the body to the conclusion.
       1. End your last point.
       2. Repeat what you told them.
       3. Tell them the "thing".
    b. **Outcome:** Spend the bulk of the conclusion by directing the audience to your desired outcome.
       - Know

- Feel
- Do

    c. **Closing:** Craft a powerful closing in one or two sentences.

Say these sentences purposefully, slowly, and confidently. Finish the sentence. Pause. Smile.

Follow this formula, and the audience will know you have landed the plane. Perhaps they too, like my sister and I, will applaud your perfect landing.

Chapter 79:
Deliver and Evaluate Your Message

At this point, you already have listened to the other side. It's always a good idea to understand what that other person is saying and what their pauses mean. This way, you have a clearer understanding of the context. If you're like most people, this is precisely when you just deliver the message you have planned all along. You think you have a good idea of the big picture of the conversation and the outcome that you're looking for. These are reflections of your values and your character, so what's the big deal?

I would say that you should stop and listen to some more. Experienced conversationalists and effective communicators have a simple rule, "When in doubt, stay out." In other words, you remain engaged with the person you're communicating with. You're occupying the same physical, as well as mental and emotional space. Your goal is to produce a mutual level of comfort. Stay within that space, but when it comes to relaying the message you want to deliver all along, you might want to stay out a little bit longer.

Delivery Must Always Be In The Context

Whenever you're talking to somebody, you are given a tremendous opportunity to learn more about that person. With a little bit of curiosity (which, unfortunately, is in such short supply recently, thanks to social media), you will be able to understand that person in context. You will be able to get a working appreciation of what this person wants to hear, what they're prepared to hear, and what could throw them off.

Here's the secret to effective communication: do not settle for telling people what they want to hear. When you do that, you're in their comfort zone and let's face it, from time to time, this works. Many people would like to be reassured, welcomed, and feel like they belong. But they can get that through coping mechanisms. You're not breaking through. You have to dance around the edges a little bit, which means reading the outer limits of what they're prepared to handle.

When you do this, you challenge them. They're more likely to remember you. How many times have you gone to a meeting and casually discussed something you already knew with someone? They made you feel like how you usually feel or how you make yourself feel. Let me ask you, do you remember their names?

Most people probably don't because they didn't move the needle. They didn't have much of an impact. The majority might remember those who you felt uncomfortable around. Even then, those annoying people like somebody who cuts you off, who keeps interrupting you, or just an obnoxious person have very short durations.

I'm sure if you can't wait to go home and tell your girlfriend, wife, boyfriend, husband, or partner what went on. The nerve of that person. How annoying and ridiculous the situation was. Eventually, the heat fizzles out, and things settle down, and you forget about that person. But you're more likely to remember those people than individuals who come across who made you feel normal.

Establishing Mutual Comfort Is A Starting Point

It's essential to understand that if you want to impact when you're communicating face-to-face, establishing mutual comfort is just a starting point. You may utilize a variety of techniques, such as mirroring. For example, they make certain gestures, or they have terms that they throw out habitually. Mimic some of them, but don't make it too apparent that it would come off like you're mocking them. You'd be surprised by the results.

This is a simple trick that works all the time. Why? People like to feel good about those who appear to be similar to them. This creates mutual comfort. However, if you want the conversation to be remembered and to have an impact, you have to do more than establish comfort through mirroring and other forms of conversation positioning. Those tricks can only take you so far. You provide comfort at the end of the day for one reason alone: to push things to the next level. This is how you stand out.

I remember chatting with random alumni at a college reunion of a friend of mine. She was in a tight circle of friends, so I pretty much knew everybody in the room. It was a blur. It felt good, and I was comfortable, but this one woman who shared with me a story of being held against her will in a tropical jungle in South America blew my mind. She stuck out. Why? She forced me to go outside of my comfort zone.

I didn't know what to say. Instead, I was gripped by the story and the details that she shared. I could see myself in the jungle with steam rising from the rain forest. The slow-moving swamps of mosquitoes as well as the silent dangers and stagnant pools of water. It was a gripping story, and I wasn't surprised at all that I remembered a lot from her story, and it all traced back to that very haunting vignette for all practical purposes, being kidnapped in the middle of nowhere.

I share that extreme example with you because it's too easy for people to talk in ways to seek comfort for the sake of comfort. There's nothing wrong with this if you see that person again, if you are friends or family members, or you already have a relationship with them. However, if you're communicating with somebody that you just met or you're not sure if you're going to meet again and you want to have an impact, you have to build on that comfort zone. You have to push against its walls, and that's precisely sadly what this woman did with her story. You have to deliver your message from this context. How do I make an impact so that the larger message of what I'm saying is remembered or has an effect?

Evaluate in Real-Time

Effective communicators don't operate using formulas. Effective communication means you are constantly recalibrating and changing up your message in light of your receiving signals. You start receiving feedback after you've reached a comfort level and start pushing yourself by telling startling tales and providing unexpected information.

Keep in mind that most of this feedback is not obvious. It's not like somebody will cut you off and say, "That's weird. That's strange," or "Shut up." No, you're going to get feedback usually in the form of nonverbal signals. You will also get feedback in the form of questions. You're going to have to account for these. They need to have an impact on the things you say after you receive them. This is how you organically craft your message in real-time.

It involves a dynamic evaluation of your message. You're not lying. You're not cutting stuff out just for convenience's sake. You're not going along to get along. Instead, you are positioning what you have to say to increase its impact. Does this sound hard? of course, it does. It requires practice. It also requires a tremendous amount of curiosity on your part. You have to be genuinely interested in the other party to keep this up, and this takes energy.

The good news is, it can easily become a habit. Before you know it, you don't even have to think about it. It just comes naturally to you. The key is to start. That way, you expose yourself to situations where you recalibrate what you're saying so you can get confirmation that what you said resonated. This is the secret to effective communication. You must be completely engaged in the discussion. Again, you have to be there physically, mentally, and emotionally. None of this is possible without genuine interest and curiosity on your part.

Understand The Big Picture and Live By It

Since you already have a plan or a set of outcomes that you're looking for, live by them. I don't know about you, but I'm not planning on participating in arguments that aren't necessary. I'm not out there to prove that I'm right and other people are wrong. I'm not out there putting other people down to make myself seem nice. I would rather allow my curiosity to help me get to the outcome that I'm looking for. I want to increase the mutual levels of comfort while accurately figuring out what the other side is prepared to take and then working within that space.

I'm not saying that you should follow in my footsteps, but bear in mind that if you view conversations as either a soapbox to make yourself look good and create new fans or debate arenas, you're confusing the forest for the trees. Effective communication is not about trying to boost your image. It all comes down to how eager you are to learn more about individuals and to occupy the space necessary to understand them.

This does not imply that you must agree. This doesn't mean that you have to compromise your core beliefs. This doesn't mean that you're weak by trying to pander to them or come off as something you're not. Instead, you let your natural curiosity and interest in the moment guide you through these steps of increasing mutual comfort. You have to remember that people are not dumb. A lot of us act dumb from time to time but deep down inside, we're not stupid.

We can figure out if somebody's blowing smoke up our backsides or if they are sincere. You must go deep inside yourself and connect with genuine interest. You must truly desire to know what's going on behind those eyes. That's how people feel that they matter. When you work from that space to push against their comfort zone, you resonate. It triggers something in them that triggers something in you, and it's a positive challenge. It is not a pissing contest, nor is it a debate. Instead, it is what it is: a distinct and human connection.

Effective Delivery

To deliver your speech effectively, you need to look natural in front of your audience. Avoid being too stiff or being too shaky. For you to be more natural and confident, you must:

1. Act Normal

It would help if you kept in mind that your speech is like any other normal conversation you can have with any other normal person.

A speech is only a little different because many people are listening to you all simultaneously.

You do not, however, need to be concerned. Just think of everyone as your friend. Smile and be confident. There is nothing to be concerned about if you are properly prepared.

You can just imagine everyone in their underwear. If this old trick works for you, then go for it. Don't try to act it out. As much as possible, maintain a feeling of normalcy.

2. Be Enthusiastic

Even if you are the one speaking, you need to show some enthusiasm over your topic.

If your listeners see that you are excited about speaking, then they might be excited too.

This will spark some interest in your audience and help you keep their attention for a longer time.

3. Be Confident

As much as possible, maintain a feeling of normalcy.

Don't be too conscious of yourself in front of your audience. It will only increase your nervousness.

If you are not confident yourself, how will your audience have confidence in you and what you say?

4. Maintain Proper Contact

When speaking, do not avoid the audience. What you should do is engage with them. Remember to maintain eye contact with everyone.

Shift your focus from one person to another to see if everybody is listening. Maintaining your focus on only one person may cause them to be uncomfortable.

However, if you stare into blank space, your audience may not find your speech exciting or interesting. Also, try to use a friendly tone of voice. Don't talk too loud or shout.

You just need your voice to be heard clearly. You may raise your voice when pointing out a fact or an important idea.

But throughout your speech, you should try to talk in a calm and friendly manner. Also, don't forget to smile.

Remember to smile when you can and smile at the audience. If possible, position yourself near your audience. This will create familiarity and comfortable air around you.

Methods of Delivery

You can deliver your speech in many ways. As a speaker, you need to be familiar with the different methods of speaking.

But soon enough, you can try to develop your style and approach to speaking. Here are the most common types of delivering a speech.

1. Manuscript

Speaking with a manuscript is the easiest way to do a public speech. You just need to read a prepared speech and hope that everything goes well. Most people do this type of delivery.

However, this restricts you from maintaining eye contact with your audience, which is a must.

You can still try to have brief eye contact as you read, but much of your focus is on the paper you are reading.

This also restricts you from moving your body to show a point or portray conviction.

As much of your attention is on the paper, you are reading, and you don't have much freedom to move and express yourself.

This type of delivery, although easy, may be boring for the audience. Soon enough, their attention will drift away from you, and you will have a hard time getting it back.

There are, however, methods to give an excellent speech while reading a document.

With enough experience and practice, you can speak in front of an audience without them getting bored, even while reading from a manuscript.

If you are about to read your speech, here are a few things you need to do:

- Use presentation aids to keep the attention of your audience.
- Take some time to read the whole speech and be familiar with it. This will help you avoid stuttering and making mistakes.
- You may also keep eye contact with your audience.
- Use a font style that you are familiar with, and try to put large spaces between your manuscript lines. This will allow you to read it with ease and avoid misunderstanding words or phrases.

2. Memory

Delivering your speech from memory is a hard thing to do. First of all, if your speech is long, it would be hard to memorize it all.

Second, sometimes, you may forget something important during the actual speech, and you end up confusing your audience.

However, delivering a speech from your memory may make you appear more professional.

If you can do it properly, you took the time to make your speech and know the important details you need to discuss.

Sometimes, you really can't help but forget something, so it is important to make an outline.

If you have memorized your speech, you can bring this outline with you while you talk. Sure, it does not contain your whole speech, but it has the key points and ideas you want to talk about.

But if you are still a bit unsure, you can bring your manuscript with you. Just take glances when you forget something.

There are still instances when memorized speeches are used. Speeches like this are common in toasts and introductions, where you only need to say a few short sentences.

Delivering a speech from memory has a few advantages:

- You can maintain eye contact with your audience if you deliver your speech from memory and analyze how they think or react to your speech.
- Maintaining eye contact is important for you to keep a certain bond or connection with your audience.
- You can move around freely. Without a piece of paper consuming your focus, you now move around and interact with your audience. You can go around the stage and move your limbs freely. This will help you convey information more effectively.
- You can express yourself more and vary the tone of your voice. You can smile, frown, or laugh when you have the most of your focus on your audience. Like having the freedom of movement, this will also allow you to express your message more effectively.

3. **Impromptu**

Impromptu speaking is when you are not prepared to give a speech, which means you need to improvise.

This can happen in many places, especially at celebrations, where you will be asked to do a little speech for someone.

This can also happen in school when your professor asks you to summarize a lesson from your book.

When speaking impromptu, you can be unprepared, but do not panic. There are things that you can do to ensure a good outcome for your speech.

Take a deep breath and focus on the situation. If you can, try to do a little bit of research first, but if you can't, focus on what you know about the topic and what you want to say to your audience.

Write down the key idea, phrases, or topics you would want to discuss on a piece of paper. If you can, arrange them into a neat order and use a simple outline.

Stay focused on your topic. Do not wander off; try to talk about other things, get straight to the point, and avoid too many words.

Don't speak too fast because your audience may not understand you. Instead, try to appear calm and speak slowly. This will allow you to gather your ideas while speaking.

Developing Your Message

You package your information by developing your message. Every presentation should be message-driven. We'll learn how to craft an engaging message in this stage. Developing your message is a critical step in making a great speech. The message is the theme of your presentation. It should wind through your presentation like threads in a fabric. The message is the central idea and focus of your presentation. The message is what you are seeking to impart to the minds of your listeners. It is the mental take-away from your presentation.

Developing a clear message might seem like a simple step. However, this is the most underappreciated part of the whole speaking process, almost an afterthought. Most speakers are so wrapped up in writing and delivering the presentation that they fail to consider how to formulate the message.

Goal-Driven Messages

Before we can craft the message, we have to understand the goal. Every presentation needs a goal. A goal is a desired action, what you want the audience to perform with the information. The first step in crafting the message is to understand that the message is goal-driven. The goal sets the target you wish to reach.

To establish your goal, begin with the end of the speech. After your presentation, you expect a response. The expected response is the goal you wish to achieve. The expected response should be clear in your mind. It is essential to understand the response you wish to receive from the audience. After all, you would not leave the house to go on a trip if you did not know the destination. To present effectively, you have to know your goal. The following questions will help you to define your goal.

Do you want to influence them to think about something in a different way? What is the new thought or idea you wish to implant into their minds?

Take your time to think about your answers. They represent a crucial aspect of defining your goal: what you expect from the audience.

Examine what you've written carefully. Underline the answers that appeal to you. If some of them sound the same, then combine them. Look for keywords and phrases. Try to distill the goal into a single sentence that focuses on one or two main ideas generated by the exercise. That single sentence is your goal.

In the workplace, our bosses exercise influence mainly through authoritative power (their official positions). Their positions grant them a particular privilege of power. Authentic power is defined as the power to persuade and influence others within an organization, regardless of one's title or position. It cannot identify those with authentic power on any organizational chart. Authentic power is derived from the demonstrated ability to apply critical thinking skills in the real world. Authenticity instantly flows from the person who can communicate ideas. Authentic power gives you, the well-prepared and articulate speaker, a unique advantage. By developing and honing your message, you gain authenticity, allowing you to tap into the wellspring of human emotions to persuade and influence your audience to accomplish your goal.

If possible, try to narrow your goal down to one or two desired outcomes. You might be able to combine multiple goals into a single goal. Remember, it is your job as a speaker to ensure that you deliver a clear and coherent message. You may muddle your message and confuse your audience if you try to accomplish too many goals. To help your audience retain as much information as possible, keep the goal simple. Try to narrow the goal to one sentence. In a presentation, complexity is the last thing you want. Anything more than one sentence may be too complex for you to express and for your audience to process and retain.

Now that you have a goal, you can work on your message. Perhaps you think that the message and the goal can be the same thing. No, your goal is to alter behavior, change minds, influence, and persuade. You are trying to influence people to do the right thing when it comes to recycling. But your message is to illustrate the importance of recycling. Your message will show how recycling saves the environment and saves money. You must craft the message in a way that achieves the goal of altering the behavior. If you state that recycling is good, then you may or may not alter the behavior. You would be leaving the result of your presentation up to chance. Instead, in the course of the speech, you want to convince your audience that recycling is good, we must do our share to save the planet, and so forth. Do you see the difference?

Must a presentation have a message? The short answer: Yes! Otherwise, why bother to put it together? In essence, a presentation is about gathering and organizing information and presenting it to your audience. The audience should quickly grasp what you are trying to tell them. The audience should also understand clearly what action(s) you wish them to take. Take a cue from a television advertisement. By the end of the 30-60 second commercial, you know exactly what the advertiser wants you to do. Their objective is to persuade you to make a purchase. The message may be that your life will be enhanced, improved, or made easier by using this product or service. It is your job to accomplish the same thing with your audience. Your message conveys how their lives are made better by achieving your goal.

Can there be multiple messages? Yes, but I would recommend against transmitting too many messages to your audience. If you make too many points, then your audience may not be able to recall them. A good message should fit into what many people call the "elevator speech." The elevator presentation is one you use when you get on the elevator with your boss, and she asks your opinion about a matter. Of course, you have less than a minute to speak your mind. That means you have to zero in on the main point and forget about everything else. That's how one should reveal the message in your speech. It is the one thing you want to stick out in their minds, the one unique element in the entire presentation.

Connecting with Your Audience: Emotions

When framing your message, think about emotions. That's a strange concept for the buttoned-up, corporate world. Do you mean we have to deal with feelings? Yes, emotions are the most critical leverage that a speaker has with an audience. You want to appeal to your audience's emotions. Emotions, or feelings, are deeply connected to what people think. By tapping into emotions, you as a speaker are tapping into the deep level thinking of your audience. It would be best if you reached down into their consciousness. What are their experiences, hopes, and dreams? Does your message connect with your audience at that level? By tapping into that spring of emotions, you open them up to your message. Emotions are the key to being able to influence and persuade your audience.

In framing your message in the emotional realm, keep in mind the behavior you wish to influence. The message is designed to influence a behavior change.

As a speaker, your message needs to appeal to what your audience fears or loves.

Playing on fears might seem manipulative, but the results of even fear can be positive. You might persuade your boss to purchase a particular computer system because the competition may be using the same system. You appeal to your boss's fear of losing a competitive advantage if the purchase is not made. Your goal is not to scare him. Your objective is to boost your company's competitiveness.

Look at it from the point of positive or negative reinforcement or affirmation. You can appeal to the audience, affirming the benefits they will receive when taking the recommended action. Or you can speak of negative consequences, of what might occur if your recommended course of action is not followed. Positive and negative affirmation achieves the very purpose of connecting with the emotions of your listeners. Everyone wants to feel good about a choice they've made.

Connecting with Your Audience: Who Are They and What Do They Know?

Depending on the audience, your message will vary. The message to an older, retired audience might stress the safety of mutual funds, how the investments can guarantee a good steady stream of income, and so on. The older group is more interested in security than growth. If you presented this material to those who have just graduated from college, your goal is the same, but the message will differ. With a younger group, you want to stress the importance of saving for the future. You want to show that mutual fund money invested in more speculative markets will garner the younger person a more secure retirement in the future. The common goal of getting the client to purchase the product is emphasized, yet with a different twist to appeal to different needs.

I've put up a set of questions that can help you fine-tune your message for your intended audience. Jot down the answers to these questions:

Who's my audience? Is the audience made up of clients? Is it your superiors, peers, or subordinates? What is the background of this audience concerning your subject? What issues or concerns will they have concerning this topic?

What do they know about me? For an audience—any audience—to be open to your message, you must establish credibility, trust, and rapport. What does the audience know about you? Is it positive? Great! You have something to build upon. Use that positive energy to motivate the audience. Do they have negative images of you, perhaps some negativity involving not you but also the organization you represent? Then you will have to work hard to build up credibility. You have to understand that you are starting with a deficit and must work your way up the trust ladder. There are many ways to build up credibility, and it's often easier if the audience does not know you.

What do they know about the subject? Does your audience know anything at all about your topic? This is important to know in part because it determines the depth of detail you cover with information and explanations. If the audience is well-versed in the subject, jargon, and terminology may not need to be explained. But be careful. Once while attending a technical briefing, a technical presenter went through his whole presentation using specific terms and jargon unfamiliar to his audience. They were lost because he hadn't answered the question: What do they know about the subject?

On the other hand, I have seen a technical presenter turn and ask the audience if it was okay to delve into some of the finer details. With audience acquiescence, the presenter was able to dive down into the minutiae without worry. But all along the way, he checked to ensure that he had not lost his audience.

If the audience lacks a high degree of knowledge on the subject, it is your job to present the material to be easily understood. It would be best if you gave them a coherent overview of the subject, a basic outline of the lay of the land. Usually, it's not necessary to go into great detail. However, you should be prepared to zoom down and talk about the road signs and billboards. This often surfaces later on in the presentation or during the question and answer time.

Conclusion

Finally, knowing how to communicate clearly and effectively so that others can comprehend what you're trying to say is an important aspect of communication. Normally, when you speak, you will say the first thing that comes to your mind. This is not often the best way for you to communicate. Rather, it would be best if you started paying attention to what you are saying and how you are saying it so that you can communicate effectively.

Understanding what you want to convey is the first step in achieving this. When you are speaking, your aim should be to elevate the understanding of the person receiving the message by thinking about your message can be received. When you do this, you can be sure that the words you use will help prevent being misunderstood or creating friction with other people.

Then it would be best if you made every effort to communicate clearly. What this means is that you pay attention to the words you are saying and how you are saying them. You should pronounce your letters clearly, making sure that as you do so, you sound intelligent. This gives the impression that you are mature and capable of good communication.

Non-verbal communication also has a role to play with the spoken word, as it is used to reinforce or support the message that you are sharing. To ensure that you are communicating every time you speak, you should do the following: -

- **Watch your Posture**. It is amazing how much your posture can affect your ability to speak clearly and effectively. It is likely that when you are speaking, you will either be standing or sitting. It would be best to get yourself into a position where you can manage your breathing with ease. When your breath is under control, whether standing or sitting, make sure that your back is up straight. When sitting, make sure that you hold your stomach in as though you are pushing it out towards your spine.

- **Could you keep it simple?** Many times people try to sound more knowledgeable by using large words and complex jargon. It would help if you were also careful about the message you are sending out, particularly when you consider rage and gender. The words that you speak should not cause anyone to feel offended. It is also important that you pay attention to the words you are saying and articulate each syllable clearly. For proper English pronunciation, you need to be able to differentiate between different vowels.

- **Keep it light**. When speaking with other people and taking on a serious tone, you may lose their attention after a while. In this instance, you could be speaking, but your spoken word is not effective. To turn the situation around, you should make use of humor. Ensure that it is well-timed and fits well with the situation at hand. This will help break the ice, make it easier for you to communicate with others, and drawback attention to what you are talking about.

- **Take your Time**. Your words are likely to be jumbled up or unclear when you rush your conversation. If you want to communicate well, you should speak slowly and clearly. This means that you take some time before you open your mouth. Take a deep breath. This will prevent your lungs from running on empty when you are in the middle of a sentence. When you take your time, you prevent yourself from sounding hurried and become more mindful of your speech.

- **Watch your Grammar**. If your grammar is not good, your speech will not be good. This is the words you speak are a result of what is inside our mind. It would be beneficial if you spent some time improving your grammar by producing written word documents. Within these, make a note of the tone you are using and the precision you are writing. You will note when you are rambling on or where your thoughts have stopped being comprehensible.

- **Take Stock**. When you are speaking, tape yourself with a tape recorder. Then, after you've found a quiet place, listen back to make sure you understand what you said and how you expressed it. Hearing yourself in this way will make it easier for you to discover where your conversation is not up to par. Making immediate improvements will be a breeze.

- **Have a Little Fun**. Teaching yourself how to speak can be boring at times, and you may find yourself slipping back into old ways and unlearning everything you have learned. It is possible to learn how to speak well and have a little fun while doing so. This can be done by using tongue twisters. These are normally quite challenging to pronounce, and as you struggle to get each word perfect and have a few laughs when you do not, these have a great effect on language. A great place to start is 'He sells seashells on the seashore.' Take note of the syllables that are causing you problems, and then practice the syllables.

Although it may sound strange, you will need to put in some practice if you want to speak more clearly. You can do this by taking time to speak to yourself when you are on your own. You can do this while looking at a mirror to see how you sound the words. The more you practice your words, the easier and more natural it will become to speak clearly. During the process of practice, sound out your syllables as slowly as possible.

www.ingramcontent.com/pod-product-compliance
Lightning Source LLC
Chambersburg PA
CBHW070451120526
44590CB00013B/641